M000277984

The Complete Trading Course

Founded in 1807, John Wiley & Sons is the oldest independent publishing company in the United States. With offices in North America, Europe, Australia and Asia, Wiley is globally committed to developing and marketing print and electronic products and services for our customers' professional and personal knowledge and understanding.

The Wiley Trading series features books by traders who have survived the market's ever changing temperament and have prospered—some by reinventing systems, others by getting back to basics. Whether a novice trader, professional or somewhere in-between, these books will provide the advice and strategies needed to prosper today and well into the future.

For a list of available titles, please visit our Web site at www.WileyFinance.com.

The Complete Trading Course

Price Patterns, Strategies, Setups, and Execution Tactics

COREY ROSENBLOOM, CMT

John Wiley & Sons, Inc.

Published by John Wiley & Sons, Inc., Hoboken, New Jersey.
Published simultaneously in Canada.

Library of Congress Cataloging-in-Publication Data:

Rosenbloom, Corey.
The complete trading course : price patterns, strategies, set-ups, and execution / Corey Rosenbloom.
p. cm. – (Wiley trading series)
Includes bibliographical references and index.
ISBN 978-0-470-59459-9 (cloth); ISBN 978-0-470-94729-6 (ebk); ISBN 978-0-470-94728-9 (ebk);
ISBN 978-0-470-94727-2 (ebk)
1. Technical analysis (Investment analysis) 2. Investment analysis. 3. Stocks. 4. Speculation. I. Title.
HG4529.R67 2011
332.63′2042–dc22

2010032311

10 9 8 7 6 5 4 3 2 1

To my parents, George and Debby, for without the life-long support, encouragement, and life-lessons you both taught me, none of this would be remotely possible.

Contents

Preface

When you first look at a stock chart as an opportunity to make money, where do you start? How do you classify all the conflicting signals , cut through the noise, and get straight to the point of what matters most? How do you structure your analysis? And when you find what you think could be a trading opportunity, how do you enter, manage, and exit the trade most efficiently?

The Complete Trading Course answers these common questions of traders from all experience levels and provides you a specific pathway for analyzing your chart to find specific trading opportunities. These opportunities are built on time-tested price principles that winning traders have used for many years, but have been buried under the information overload of today's high-speed, indicator-driven markets. Building from a foundation of price principles that guide your analysis, the book then overlays specific strategies onto the developing structure from insights in candlestick charts (showing not just the pattern, but how the pattern forms and its importance in assessing turns in price), price patterns, and Fibonacci retracements, all of which fit into the specific context of the life cycle of a price move on any timeframe. Knowing where the chart exists in the life cycle of a price move reveals what strategies are most effective and what indicators reveal the best setups, which guide your specific decisions on where to enter, place stops, play for a specific price target, or hold for a larger gain as you monitor open positions as new data emerges on the chart in real time.

Knowing how to identify trades based on price trend, momentum, and volatility are all foundation concepts which are covered in detail in the first part of the book. The section on edge reveals specifics of trade execution tactics geared to your unique personality, which is not covered in most trading books that reveal "buy here, sell there" strategies that do not take into account the unique experiences and personality of the trader putting on the position. If you do not understand why you are entering a trade, you will almost certainly not be successful in that trade, as you will lack the confidence and edge necessary to recognize a proper opportunity, manage it in real time, and exit the position properly without emotion negatively affecting your decision. This book specifically addresses the importance of combining objective chart information with your understanding and experience; as such, the confidence you have in your strategies and methods will combat the natural tendency to enter when you feel most confident and exit when you feel the most pain, both of which allow emotions to erode your accuracy and monetary trading edge.

I wrote this book from my combined experience and education as a Chartered Market Technician and trader of many markets and strategies; I wish this book had existed when I began my journey as a trader, as it would have saved me countless hours of wasted time and effort. What separates today's traders from those 50 years ago is the sheer amount of information, webinars, seminars, books, courses, blogs, web sites, ebooks, and so on that inundate the new trader with too much information, and too many voices saying their methods are the best. Lured by the promise of instant riches, a new trader buys a new indicator or attends a single expensive seminar, only to find the information too complicated to apply, or worse, absolutely ineffective in a real-time, fast-paced trading environment.

No one book, indicator, or seminar can teach you all you need to know to be a successful trader. Instead, your goal should be to learn foundation price principles, effective strategies, how to assess your edge, and then incorporate your unique personality, experiences, stage in life, risk-tolerance, and individual psychological make-up into a lifetime of learning, starting with the basics and building a unique creation from there as you progress month to month and then year to year as a developing trader. Trading is a performance discipline, not unlike the training and commitment required to become a professional athlete, physician, scientist, or musician. All professionals must start with the basic, time-tested principles of their respective disciplines, and then carve out their own specialty with the information they have learned and the methods that appeal to them—or "speak to them" as it has been said. Some methods will speak to you while others will not; learn more about trading methods that call to you and interest you as you develop as a trader. This book lays the basic foundation upon which to build a life-long trading career.

While each chapter could probably be a whole book in itself, and there are in fact several books written on the specific material I cover in this book, what I do for the reader in *The Complete Trading Course* is cut through the theoretical aspects and esoteric information, such as candle patterns not even professional technical analysts use, and combine only the most important information from a variety of disciplines such as Fibonacci retracements, Elliott wave, popular price patterns (such as the head and shoulders and bull flags), and effective candle signals. Unlike other books, I focus on the logic behind the pattern, how it fits into the broader context on a price chart, and how to assess the integrated whole of the chart, within the context of guiding price principles that underscore all trading decisions. In fact, the strategies and setups all derive from the specific principles you will learn, and in so doing, you will increase your confidence and learn how to manage open positions effectively, using the objective chart evidence rather than your emotions.

I show examples on multiple timeframes because the principles and strategies apply to all timeframes, from the one-minute intraday charts in a hyper-fast day-trading environment to the more deliberative, longer-term positions you can identify and manage on the weekly or even monthly charts. This is another way *The Complete Trading Course* appeals to all traders, as the strategies cut to the heart of what moves price—the supply and demand relationship of buyers and sellers.

Individuals who are new to trading and cannot commit full-time to a professional trading career will benefit from learning these principles and incorporating them into a swing-trading strategy that can be implemented with evening research and placing orders before going to work to manage positions that span weeks or perhaps months at a time. The tactics also apply to those who are part-time traders with part-time jobs which provide steady income as you develop your track record as a trader before making the leap to full-time trading. The book also benefits those who are currently full time and are struggling to achieve profitability, or who feel they are being blown around by different exciting strategies while being grounded in none. This book provides a foundation to make objective, clear decisions based on trend structure, momentum, and volatility as principles to guide your specific decisions, no matter what timeframe you analyze and trade.

Day traders will benefit from understanding multi-timeframe analysis and how to set trades up intraday that take advantage of the higher timeframe structure and levels to watch, particularly on the daily chart. Day traders will be able to use leverage and more aggressive strategies that swing traders cannot, though day traders tend to hold less open positions at a time than a swing trader.

Examples in the book include stocks, ETFs, futures contracts, and inter-markets, all of which highlight the application of these principles, strategies, and setups on all markets and all timeframes. All that is required is a liquid market driven by supply and demand, with the ability to plot prices on charts, and these principles will apply, though as you develop, you will begin to specialize in the specific nuances of your chosen market, vehicle, and timeframe.

HOW THE BOOK IS ORGANIZED

The Complete Trading Course progresses from a solid foundation of time-tested price principles through modern charting strategies into specific setups, and I recommend progressing through the book in the order I have arranged the material. I sought to answer the question "where do I begin in my analysis?" and have arranged the book with the answers unfolding in a journey through the material.

We begin our journey in Chapter 1 which outlines the foremost price principle on the importance of price trends, how to define these trends, what constitutes a true reversal, and how to frame the remainder of your analysis within the context of the trend structure. After learning how to recognize trends, Chapter 2 seeks to assess the health of a trend in motion by defining momentum and how it confirms a new trend and then disconfirms a mature trend. By learning how to identify momentum divergences, you can anticipate the end of a trend prior to the official reversal signal. Being a foundation principle, momentum's leading edge also explains why we take certain specific trade setups that we do, and how momentum factors into price patterns. The last of the price principles, Chapter 3 details the Price Alternation Principle, which explains why some indicators work well in certain environments and then fail in others. The principle also lays the groundwork for range-trading, mean reversion trading strategies, which give rise to breakout strategies that can lead to large profits at the exact genesis of a new move in the market.

Part 2 focuses on modern-day strategies and charting tactics to compliment your analysis from the foundational price principles. Chapter 4 explains how to identify effective candle patterns on the charts, and contains a unique step-inside perspective of each candle pattern described, cutting to the heart of why the pattern is important. You will undoubtedly be familiar with some of the popular price patterns in Chapter 5, but I explain not just how to recognize and trade the pattern, but how the pattern derives its application from one of the foundation price principles described in Part 1. I explain why it is not enough simply to recognize a pattern—particularly in today's sophisticated markets. Much has changed in the more than 70 years since early chartists quantified these patterns. In Chapter 6, I explain how to draw Fibonacci retracement grids, how to find Fibonacci price confluence, and how a Fibonacci retracement grid assists your trade identification, entry, and exit decisions, all while keeping the examples current and simple to understand; Fibonacci analysis need not be complex. I conclude the section on modern-day strategies by explaining the Life Cycle of a Stock move, from accumulation through realization, and into the final stage of distribution, explaining insights into how professionals behave against the crowd at all stages. The chapter includes a quick description on how Elliott Wave complements Charles Dow's original work on trends, and how both techniques combine in today's world of active trading.

No book on trading strategies would be complete without a discussion on edge, execution tactics, trade setups, and how to put the information into practice in real-time under conditions of uncertainty and heightened emotion. Part 3 begins in Chapter 8 with a detailed discussion on risk management, edge optimization, trade execution tactics, and expectancy. Unlike other books on trading tactics, I explain the importance of combining these factors into a strategy that fits your unique personality, making a careful distinction between conservative and aggressive tactics in all the trades you take. Chapter 9 combines all that we have learned in *The Complete Trading Course* into the four components of every trade, as well as the two broad categories of trade setups and the four specific types of trade setups, all of which reduces the uncertainty of a trading decision into four categories of breakouts, retracements, reversals, or fades. The final chapter encourages you to use what you have learned and create your own specific trade setups with a discussion on how to do so, and a detailed explanation of the Impulse Buy trade, Impulse Sell, Cradle Buy trade, and Cradle Sell.

With a firm knowledge of basic price principles, specific trade strategies for today's markets, information on edge and execution, and a clear discussion of trade setups, you will be fully equipped to take your trading to the next level and formulate your own personal strategies in your trading plan that lead you on your lifelong journey to trading success.

Acknowledgments

Writing a book is far more difficult than writing a blog post! While one person can create and maintain a blog, it is absolutely impossible for one person to do all the work necessary for a book to come to life. I especially want to thank Kevin Commins, Meg Freeborn, and Claire Wesley along with the whole staff at John Wiley and Sons for their encouragement, feedback, and time they put in assisting me with the manuscript.

In the trading community, I want to express my thanks to Tim Bourquin of Trader Interviews.com and the hard-working staff members at the MoneyShow.com who host the popular Traders Expo conferences. It was through these Expos, both as an attendee and a speaker, that I was introduced to the professional world of trading which allowed me to make many contacts and enabled me to connect with the market professionals who molded me into the trader and market analyst I am today. Specifically, thank you to Linda Raschke who first alerted me to the early founders of technical analysis and key price principles, and whom I continue to be inspired by to this day. I also owe a lot of my professional success to Andrew Horowitz of the Disciplined Investor web site and podcast series—I cannot express how thankful I am for all your support, encouragement, and all the hours we have spent talking markets, both from a fundamental analysis and technical analysis standpoint. A special thanks also to Dr. Brett Steenbarger who taught me the importance of developing as a trader, and for the selfless insights he provided each day through his TraderFeed blog and books—thank you also for the initial push to write the book. Mike Bellafiore of SMB Capital was instrumental in sharing his insights with me about writing a book, and for his continued support and encouragement as the manuscript took shape. Thank you also to Toni Hansen and again to Linda Raschke for helpful tips on public speaking.

In the financial blogging community, thank you to everyone who has linked, commented, and visited the Afraid to Trade blog. Thank you to TraderMike for the very first link that started traffic coming to the blog early in 2007. Much appreciation to John Forman for his patience with me, along with Rob Hanna, Scott Andrews, Hale Stewart, Jeffrey Lin, Charles Kirk, Phil Pearlman, Brad Stafford, and so many others who had to endure my delayed emails as this manuscript came to completion. Thank you to the many blog readers for your encouragement and supportive emails and Tweets. I would not have kept up the early blogging activities were it not for you all. Thank you as well to the many members of the StockTwits community and your daily enthusiasm and passion for trading. Thank you to Jim Slagle and the whole crew at GreenFaucet.com for the Technician's Edge column, and to Karen, Josh, Paul, and everyone at TraderKingdom.com/ Mirus Futures for the webinar opportunities.

I wanted to share a special appreciation for all the staff and members of the Market Technician Association, and for their hard work at developing and educating professional technical analysts. All that I had learned previously through so many sources finally fell into place as I progressed through the formal CMT program and coursework, and I am thankful for your support and networking as well. Many thanks to Rick, my local CMT study-partner and all the many late hours for more than two years we spent studying the material, then continuing the study sessions once the CMT coursework was complete. You got me addicted to coffee, but without our study sessions and research meetings, I would not have been able to obtain the professional insights you provided, and had so much fun in the process.

Finally, thank you to my parents, George and Debby. Words cannot express my gratitude for your continued support and love. Without Dad and his initial encouragement early in my life that I should "learn business and investing," when I told him I wanted to be a psychologist then later work in politics, and our many debates about stocks and the market, none of this would have been possible at all. It's hard to be a full-time trader, but having your full support made me feel that anything was possible—and many years later, I still believe it is.

The Complete Trading Course

PART I

Foundational Principles

CHAPTER 1

Supremacy of the Trend

Where do you start when you first look at a stock chart? Are your eyes drawn to the indicators first? Perhaps your chart has too many indicators and you don't know where to start. With so much information for the technical analyst to discover, new traders often do not know where to begin or what should guide them in structuring their price charts. Sometimes it can be helpful to remove the indicators and focus squarely on price itself—after all, you've certainly heard the axioms "Price is King" and "Only price pays."

This introductory chapter will examine why trend analysis is so important to formulating your trading plan. Using your assessment of the current trend structure as guidance for which indicators to use and which to ignore, you will then be able to envision a clearer pathway ahead for the next swing or directional move in price, and thus be better equipped to take advantage by trading the expected move.

After all, you must start your decision-making process somewhere and you must be as objective as possible, as opposed to subjective analysis which is prone to opinion, bias, and error. While technical analysis is more of an art than a science—which leaves the chart open to interpretation—you build your foundation from time-tested principles that guide your analysis each time you review a chart and seek opportunities for profit. This chapter lays the foundation for successful analysis and trading, starting with the underlying principle of technical analysis—the trend.

WHAT IS A TREND?

Before making any decisions about buying or selling a particular stock or market, you must first assess the current price trend as a backdrop to further analysis. Afterward, you will be better able to assess the longevity, magnitude, and probabilities of the current trend continuing. Before applying any intermediate or advanced analysis methods, you should always start with a firm understanding of the basic concepts of supply and demand, as revealed through the price charts. The best way to begin your analysis is by simply quantifying the current trend objectively, be it up, down, or sideways. While it seems so simple, many traders skip this step and jump right to the indicator signals, not understanding that some popular indicators work well when a trend is established but then fail when a sideways trend occurs. By objectively assessing the trend in place, you will then be prepared to take the next step in your analysis. Let's start with the basic question, "What is a trend?"

Breaking it down into simplest terms, a trend is a series of price swings traveling in the same direction over time. Most traders assess the strength of up-trends in order to find buying opportunities in a prevailing trend that has been confirmed. In the context of a prevailing up-trend, traders will be looking to put on new positions on pullbacks to expected support levels.

TREND

Trend is the prevailing tendency of the price of a security or market to move in the same direction over time. In the stock market, trends are often divided into long-term or secular trends, intermediate term trends, and short-term trends.

Up-trend: A series of higher price swing highs and higher price swing lows over a given period of time.

Down-trend: A series of lower price swing highs and lower price swing lows over a given period of time.

In his book *Technical Analysis Explained*, Martin Pring gave us the best definition of technical analysis—the method of making decisions to the likely future price movement of a stock based on the past and current chart—with the following definition, which underscores all of our efforts as traders:

> *The technical approach to investments is essentially a reflection of the idea that prices move in trends which are determined by the changing attitudes of investors towards a variety of economic, monetary, political, and psychological forces.*
>
> *The art of technical analysis is to identify trend changes at an early stage and to maintain an investment posture until the weight of the evidence indicates that the trend has reversed.*

For traders, the most important parts of the definition are the "identify trend changes at the earliest stage" statement as well as the "weight of the evidence" portion. These two concepts underscore all of the decisions you make as a trader or an investor. Let's break them apart individually.

Identifying Trend Changes Early

One of the most commonly accepted principles of technical analysis states that the trend, once established, has greater odds of continuing than of reversing. If we accept this principle as true, then the most profitable, lowest risk opportunities will come by trading retracement-style set-ups in the direction of a confirmed, prevailing trend. Many new traders try to call tops and bottoms in a stock and thus fight established trends, which often results in monetary losses and psychological frustration. While all traders want to be the first to call reversals in markets, and indeed traders can make a public name for themselves by accurately calling major turns in a market, it is important to realize that for every correctly called market top or bottom, there are dozens if not hundreds of inaccurate calls of tops or bottoms that lie scattered in the graveyard of market analysis and in personal trading accounts. Some traders destroy their accounts by stubbornly fighting a trend, clinging to their opinions of what the market should be doing as opposed to what the market is actually doing. Traders lose money when they try to force their will on a market, and traders who fight prevailing trends can suffer major losses as they trade against the probabilities from the onset.

On the other hand, a trend cannot persist forever; as such, downtrends evolve over time into up-trends, and then mature up-trends must devolve again into down-trends as the market cycle continues throughout history. Chapter 7 describes the typical lifecycle of a price move from bottom, to top, to bottom again. Those who do well over their trading careers are the ones who understand this principle and act accordingly when the weight of the evidence has shifted, rather than remaining committed to a losing position. The majority of this book will be dedicated to identifying trend reversals as early as possible as you assess the weight of the chart evidence, which implies never looking at one indicator or variable in isolation, but as a composite whole to the best of your ability. While your goal should always be to determine trend structure, you must simultaneously be aware of potential signals that a trend in its mature stage might be reversing. No matter what your emotions or other anecdotal evidence suggest, you must be able to change your expectations once the price chart gives a trend reversal signal, and not stubbornly assume that the current trend will continue forever. Sometimes traders learn this lesson with one painful experience, as a child learns not to touch a hot stove, though other traders may need to be reminded throughout their career that the best trades often come in the direction of the prevailing trend, rather than against it.

You must be prepared to sell your position and take profits when the trend changes from up-trend to early down-trend, just as you must also be able to act on any positive reversal in a down-trend which is showing signs of reversing into an up-trend. It takes confidence to buy after a sustained down-trend, just as it takes a strong fortitude to sell a position with profit once a market signals odds favor a turn to the downside. Those who identify confirmed reversals at the earliest reasonable stage possible will outperform those who are not as systematic in determining the health of a trend in existence and the probabilities of continuation or reversal of the prevailing trend. We will be discussing this concept in great detail.

Waiting for the Weight of the Evidence

As mentioned earlier, you cannot wager consistently on a trend reversing. Doing so will often result in numerous losses and unnecessary frustration. Most of the easiest trades come from positioning yourself in the direction of a prevailing trend, usually during pullbacks or retracements to support or resistance levels, and assuming that the trend will continue rather than reverse. In those terms, you can think of almost all the trades you take as either betting on a prevailing trend continuing or of a mature, lengthy trend reversing. Do not make this decision lightly.

Many of the most successful traders have solid rules for assessing the markets or stocks they trade, and their methods can be summarized as assessing the evidence—whether from fundamental, technical, or quantitative methods—and making a determination of the probabilities of a market continuing to rally or reversing into a down-mode. No single method is perfect, and no one method can ever call all tops and bottoms in a market.

Over the lifetime of your trading or investing career, you will do better to use noncorrelated methods to assess the probabilities from an unbiased approach to the best of your ability. In this book, I will be sharing how to combine leading methods into a unified approach for assessing the probability of the next likely swing or directional move in price. In so doing, you will be assessing the weight of the evidence using methods that you understand and that interest you. Do not feel as though you have to learn every single method of any trading system or strategy perfectly. By the same token, do not give any one method absolute dominance over others. When you observe noncorrelated methods and indicators such as moving averages, candles, divergences, and price patterns pointing in the same direction, you will increase your odds of a successful trade outcome more than if you used any one of these methods in isolation.

For example, if you see a reversal candle, it can be a bearish signal to exit a position. However, if you fail to assess the weight of the evidence, or the context in which the reversal candle occurs, you might be exiting a profitable position too early, or worse, if you chose to put on a short-sale position (attempting to profit from a market decline) based on a single candle, you might subject yourself to an unnecessary loss had you taken more time to assess the trend structure, volume signals, confirming indicators, or any number of analytical methods before making a final trading decision.

It can simplify your task immensely if you think of trading as a measurement of the probabilities of a trend continuing or of reversing, and taking specific entries and exits based on the developing structure that the price chart reveals to you. You will enter at more favorable levels, place stops at key points at the price where an idea will be proven incorrect, and play for realistic targets with exits that are generated by the weight of the evidence that solves the "exiting too early or too late" problem that most traders face.

METHODS FOR DEFINING TRENDS

"What is a trend?" seems like such an easy question to answer but, as you'll see, the answer can be as simple as "higher highs and higher lows" or as complex as a linear regression analysis or other statistical calculations. Despite the complexity (not to mention usefulness) of some mathematical models, the best way to define a trend can still often be the simple principles defined by Charles Dow in the early 1900s.

Charles Dow was one of the earliest researchers of technical analysis, and modern traders study his principles of what developed later into the Dow Theory of technical analysis. Dow noted that an uptrend required a higher high and a higher low to be valid, just as a downtrend required a lower low and lower high to be valid. Dow noted that volume confirmed the trend, such that in the context of an uptrend, volume rose during the upward swings in price and declined during the downward corrections or retracements, just as volume rose during the downward swings in a downtrend and declined during the corrections or upward retracements in the context of a trend. Modern day traders have layered complex methods over these simple, basic principles.

Recall that early technical analysts did not have the benefit of computer charts as we have today. Instead, they calculated charts each day by hand and placed a high emphasis on trend structure as defined by price itself. This is called the Pure Price Method and it is still used today as one of the most accurate and objective methods of defining a trend. In addition to the Pure Price Method, contemporary traders use the Moving Average Method to assess the structure of a short-term, intermediate term, and long-term moving average, paying specific attention both to the orientation of the averages themselves, and the relation of price to these averages.

The preferred method combines both the Pure Price and Moving Average methods, as each give similar signals and exact prices where a trend officially reverses. It will be these official classifications that remove the subjectivity or confusion most traders experience when attempting to label trends on price charts.

The Pure Price Method

Let's start with the simplest concept and move to more detailed definitions. As its name implies, the Pure Price Method removes all indicators from the charts and builds the foundation for trend analysis on the price itself. The method is only concerned with locating swing highs and swing lows while comparing prior highs to recent highs and prior lows to recent lows. You can use a candle chart, standard bar chart, or even a line chart to define trends using this method; sometimes a line chart can be the best place to begin when objectively analyzing trend structure. The goal is to remove bias and get a clear picture of the steady rising or falling rhythm of the price of the stock or market you are analyzing and thinking of trading.

As most traders can recite without thinking, an uptrend is defined as a series of higher price highs and higher price lows while a downtrend is defined as a series of

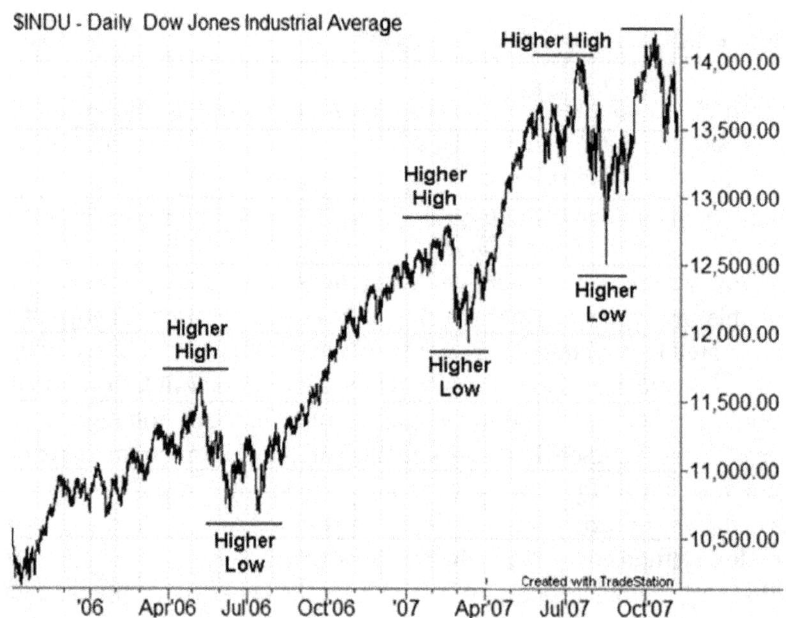

FIGURE 1.1 Dow Jones Industrial Average Daily Chart from 2006–2007

lower price highs and lower price lows. Using this phrasing as our departure point, let's see this definition in action.

Figure 1.1 shows a snapshot of the Dow Jones Industrial Average rising through 2006 to the October 2007 peak. According to the Pure Price method, we are only concerned with key swing highs and swing lows to develop our definition of the trend. Any change in the series of higher highs and higher lows will be a warning sign of a potential reversal ahead, but until we see price either form a lower swing low or a lower swing high, we must assume that the uptrend in place will continue and trade accordingly in the direction of the prevailing trend. We will learn trading tactics in later chapters, but this principle lays the foundation for all other analysis we layer onto the price trend structure.

What Constitutes a Swing? On the surface, the Pure Price method is deceptively simple, but the challenge comes from your definition of what constitutes a price swing. Can one bar (day or week) be a swing? Does price have to move a certain percentage to classify as a swing? Does a swing have to last a certain number of bars? These are just some of the questions a trader must define in advance when labeling price highs and lows.

Like most things you will discover as a trader, there is a balance you must achieve when defining what constitutes a price swing. If your definition is too narrow, you will label too many swings and arrive at false conclusions, calling a potential trend reversal far too early. If your definition is too broad, you will not label enough swings and likewise arrive at false conclusions and call changes in trend far too late. This is where eyes can be deceiving and simple mathematical models can provide clarity.

FIGURE 1.2 Dow Jones Industrial Average Daily Chart from January 2006 to October 2006—Swing Duration and Percentage

Let's first start with time or duration. What you label as a swing depends on the timeframe you are analyzing. On a five-minute intraday chart, a single price swing may last 30 minutes to two hours or more. On a daily chart, a single swing might last weeks to months. On a weekly chart, a single swing might last months to one year. Your chosen timeframe provides guidance for you in assessing the time component in classifying what a swing actually is. Let's focus mainly on daily and weekly charts.

In Figure 1.1 we see a two-year span of time on the daily chart. During that period, we can label four up-swings and three down-swings. Notice how the up-swings are longer in both time and price range than the down-swings. In an uptrend, you would logically expect up-swings to both last longer and cover more ground in price than the down-swings, or counter-trend swings. Figure 1.2 gives us a closer look at the time period from January 2006 to August 2006 for specifics of the time and price concept of defining a swing.

The daily chart perspective reveals a series of higher highs and higher lows from January 2006 from 11,000 to the May 2006 peak above 11,600. On a lower timeframe chart, these would certainly count as swings within a lower timeframe uptrend. However, do we count these when looking at the daily chart itself? For almost all traders, the answer is no. Why? Doing so would take a definition of swing that was too narrow, leading to a costly whipsaw and false classification of a downtrend taking place in June 2006 (assuming that the early March swing down from 11,600 was a lower low then the 5-bar swing up to the late March 11,300 swing high was a lower high and that the May swing under 11,000 took out the lower low, defining a trend change).

It is better to classify the entire move from early May at 11,600 to mid-July 2006 at 10,700 as a single down-swing in price, labeling the double-bottom pattern that formed as a single swing low on your chart instead of labeling this up-swing as a lower high. The bounce rally in June 2006 from 10,700 to 11,200 that lasted 15 days and moved up 5 percent was also not enough to be classified as an up-swing in price. When making the final decision, take into account time in number of bars on your chart and percentage change, depending on your timeframe. Classifying swings seems easy, but it is a skill that you will master with time and practice.

Remember, if your definition of swing is too narrow (in that one to five bars can comprise a single swing) then you will be classifying too many swings which will lead to false classifications in the context of a larger, broader uptrend. The following grid reflects generally accepted classifications for swing definition for the daily timeframe of stocks or a market.

Consider the following parameters for using daily charts:

Price Percentage Change

- Less than 5 percent is probably too narrow
- From 5 percent to 15 percent is average and usually works best
- Greater than 15 percent (depending on the stock) is probably too wide

Time Duration or Number of Days

- Less than one month is almost always too narrow
- From one to six months usually works best
- Six months or one year is probably too wide

For the weekly chart, you would have larger parameters in all categories while for intraday charts you would have smaller parameters in all categories. While most swings will be obvious to you on a chart in hindsight, you will likely struggle as you start to apply this method in real time when you are confronted with price moves that fall just beyond the comfort level of classification.

Trend Reversals Now that you know how to label price swings as the building blocks for uptrends and downtrends, the next task is to find the exact spot on the price where a trend reverses from an uptrend to a downtrend and vice versa. While the Pure Price method can never call an absolute top and bottom, the lag time satisfies Martin Pring's threshold of the "weight of the evidence." In other words, pointing to a chart and declaring a new high that occurs in real time to be the top of the market would not be taking into account the weight of the evidence. However, waiting for price to form a lower low, rally to form a lower high, and then decline to break under the recently formed lower price low would argue that the weight of the evidence for trend continuity has shifted to favor a reversal, and would thus change your definition of uptrend to a newly developing downtrend. In other words, there is a specific process price must complete in order to declare a trend officially reversed. Of course we will be using other indicators and methods, but we must start with the foundation and build from there.

By definition, a trend reversal using the Pure Price method occurs one of two ways, assuming an uptrend is currently established. The easiest outcome is for price to break its series of higher highs and higher lows by first making a new swing low, breaking under a prior swing low, and then rallying to form a lower high beneath the recently established swing high. The reversal is only confirmed when price turns back to the downside and breaks under the newly established low in price, officially reversing the uptrend to a new downtrend.

The alternate method of trend reversal occurs when price is in an established uptrend and first makes a lower high at a lower price than a recent peak and then swings down to break to a new low beneath a prior price support or swing low in price. This method can call a trend reversal quicker but also can have its fair share of whipsaws until price breaks under the newly established low.

Let's see an example of these concepts in Figure 1.3.

The image on the left shows the first method, where price in the context of a rising uptrend first swings down to a lower low and then swings up to a lower high. At this point, odds are reduced for trend continuation, but price has not triggered the official signal that the weight of the evidence suggests an official reversal in trend. The signal, or precise trend reversal point, occurs exactly when price takes out the newly formed lower low to confirm that a new downtrend has begun. As a trader, you'll often find it better to wait for confirmation rather than to jump the gun and try to call tops and bottoms early, especially in an established uptrend. However, once price does form a lower high and then break beneath the prior low, then we can feel confident in our assessment that the trend has reversed. Chapter 2 explains how momentum factors in to our assessment of trend reversals.

The image on the right side of Figure 1.3 shows the second scenario where the price reversal first begins with a lower swing high and then immediately moves down for a lower swing low. The aggressive or early trend reversal spot (Spot 1) occurs immediately as price breaks under the low as labeled, which itself is not yet a lower low (as it made

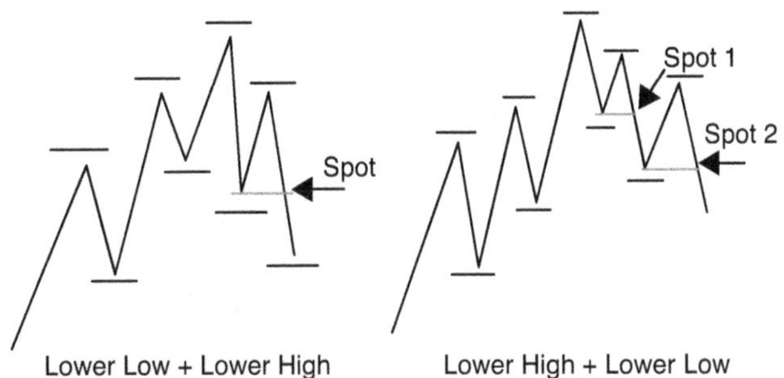

FIGURE 1.3 Two Methods of Pure Price Trend Reversals and the Exact Spots to Confirm Trend Reversals

a higher low than the previous swing low). This scenario can be more puzzling than the first scenario that leads with an observable lower low.

However, when price forms a second lower high and then breaks to a new swing low under the prior new swing low which is labeled Spot 2 in Figure 1.3, we can be confident that the trend has reversed, as we stood by patiently for the full weight of the evidence to come in. By this time however, the downtrend is well-established and we have exited our long position or entered a new short-sale position at a less-than-favorable price than had we taken the more aggressive Spot 1 signal, but that only underscores one of the main realities of trading: You pay for confirmation.

There is a balance between gathering too much information (leading to late entries but higher confidence) and not enough (leading to early entries with lower confidence that have greater odds of being incorrect). We will discuss the finer nuances of these trade-offs in the discussion on aggressive and conservative trading tactics in Chapter 8. Figure 1.4 reveals a real-world example of how the Dow Jones Index transitioned from an uptrend to a downtrend after peaking in October 2007.

Starting with the left side of the chart, we observe higher highs and higher lows all the way up to the final peak above 14,000 in October 2007. Using the Pure Price Method, we see an 'all-clear' signal to continue expecting the uptrend to continue. In fact, as price swung to a higher low in November 2007 we still had an all-clear signal as price formed a higher low and began to rally.

The first warning sign from the Pure Price Method developed as price peaked near 13,750 in December 2007 and then turned quickly lower to take out the newly established

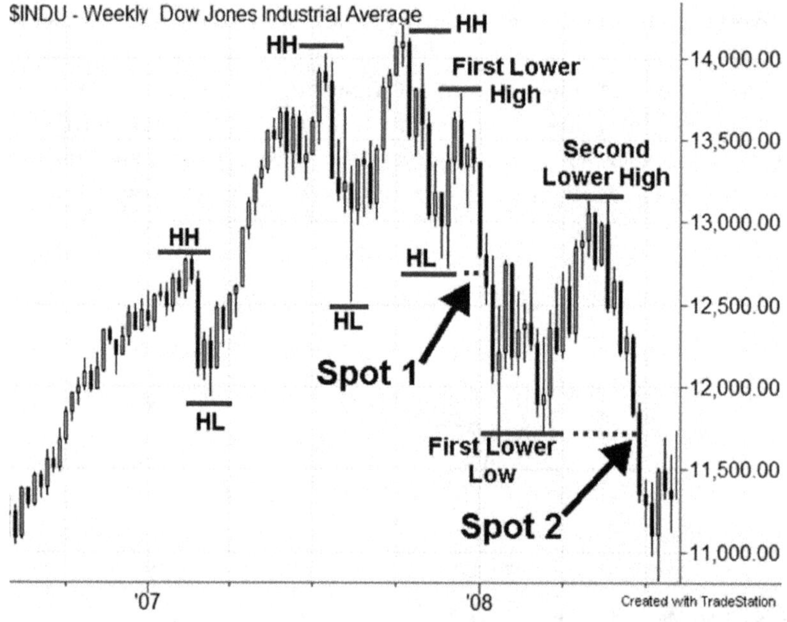

FIGURE 1.4 Dow Jones Weekly Chart: Transition from Uptrend to Downtrend

higher low from November at the 12,750 level. Trend reversals that occur so suddenly can feel like a sudden bolt of lightning in that one moment we see no warning sign on the chart, but a few bars later, an early trend reversal signal develops suddenly. Markets that form an about-face by forming a lower high first and then swing violently to take out the higher low can leave traders confused about what to do next, as opposed to the alternate, safer trend reversal method where a lower low forms first then price calmly forms a higher high and then falls cleanly lower to take out the lower low.

In this case, the Dow Jones formed its lower swing high and then suddenly turned down, giving an early trend reversal signal at Spot 1 which officially puts the price in a "lower high, lower low" trend reversal. Price then rallies to form a second lower high at the 13,000 level in May 2008 which locked in the lower high. The final signal, for those waiting for it, came when price broke the lower low established in early 2008 (labeled "First Lower Low") which placed us in a downtrend beyond a shadow of a doubt. For reference, price continued making lower lows and lower highs until bottoming in March 2009.

Using the Pure Price Method, you had an early trend reversal signal in January 2008 at the 12,750 level with a final, official signal as price broke the first lower low (after forming two lower highs) in June 2008 at the 11,750 index level.

While no method will consistently alert you to peaks and bottoms in all stocks at all times, it pays to use Martin Pring's Weight of the Evidence model for analyzing potential trend reversals. Now that we have established the foundation using price itself, let's move to a similar method that uses a short-term and an intermediate term moving average as either a stand-alone or confirming method for spotting trend reversals in stocks and indexes.

The Moving Average Method

Many traders use some sort of moving average on their charts to define trends and reveal price structure. Even investors who use fundamental analysis in selecting stocks to buy might glance at a price chart to see if the current price is above or beneath the 200-day simple moving average, which is a widely watched average even by those who don't often follow price charts. Such investors will define price as being in an uptrend simply if the current price remains steadily above the 200-day simple moving average (SMA) or being in a downtrend if price is beneath it. That's certainly an oversimplification of how to define a trend, but it's better than not looking at a chart at all!

You can add sophistication along with a consistent analytical method to your trading plan by using moving averages to help you define trends, either as a stand-alone method, or preferably in conjunction with the Pure Price Method. The Moving Average Method uses a short-term, intermediate term, and long-term moving average to assess the developing trend structure in price.

For the short-term moving average, consider using a 20-period average which would be 20 trading days or roughly one full month on a daily chart, or 20 full weeks on a weekly chart, which would track price over five months. The 20-period average is a popular choice because it averages or smoothes the price changes over the course of a single month, and many traders react to retracements to the 20-period average. For the intermediate term moving average, consider using a 50-period moving average which would track 50 trading days on a daily chart, or 50 full weeks, which would be roughly equivalent to the 52 weeks in a full calendar year.

For the long-term moving average use the popular 200-day simple moving average on your daily charts to study the relationship of price being above or beneath this popularly followed average. There are roughly 252 trading days in a calendar year, so the 200-day simple moving average approximates price over the course of a year. To be more exact, you can use a 250-day simple moving average if you so choose, but the 200-day average is a far more popular and effective choice. Comparing the relationship of price to these short, intermediate, and long-term moving averages reveals the Moving Average Orientation.

THE MOST BULLISH OR BEARISH ORIENTATION POSSIBLE

When assessing trends using moving averages, it is important to understand the chart image of the strongest confirmed uptrend.

The most bullish orientation consists of price being above the 20-period moving average, the 20-period moving average being greater than the 50-period moving average, and both the 20- and 50-period moving averages being greater than the 200-period moving average.

Using the same logic, the most bearish orientation would show price beneath the 20 period moving average, the 20-period moving average beneath the 50-period moving average, and both the 20- and 50-period moving averages being beneath the 200-period moving average.

Figure 1.5 shows us the transition from the Most Bullish Orientation possible to the Most Bearish Orientation from July 2007 to February 2008. Starting in July, we see price above the 20-day exponential moving average (20 EMA), the 20-day EMA above the 50 day-exponential moving average (50 EMA), and both of these averages being above the 200-day simple moving average (200 SMA). Price then takes a sudden dip from 14,000 to 12,600 into August 2007 as the 20-day EMA crosses briefly under the 50-day EMA yet price bounces (fails to close) above the 200-day SMA.

The uptrend then continues as price makes one final higher high in October 2007, peaking above 14,000 before reversing, breaking back under the 20 and 50 EMA but this time closing under the 200-day SMA in November 2007 at the same time the 20-day moving average crossed bearishly under the 50-day moving average (the short term average crossed under the intermediate term average). Moving Average crossovers are precursors to trend reversals, but like the Pure Price Method, need confirmation that price has officially reversed trend.

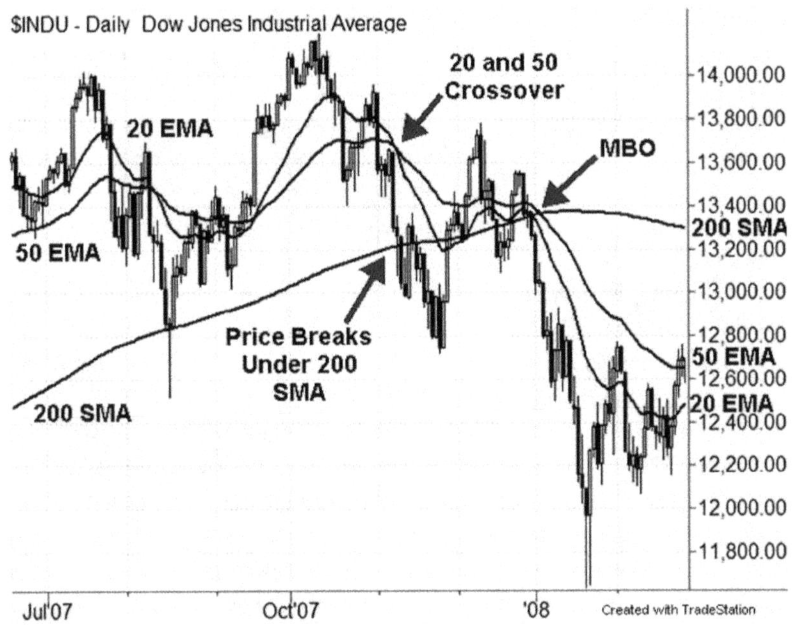

FIGURE 1.5 Dow Jones Daily Chart: Transition from Uptrend to Downtrend using the 20-, 50-, and 200-day Moving Averages

Price rallied back to 13,600 in December 2007 (though the 20-day average remained bearishly under the 50-day moving average) and then fell sharply down through the triple-convergence of the 20-, 50-, and 200-day moving averages at the 13,300 level as the new year dawned in January 2008. This time, both the 20 and 50 period moving averages crossed under the rising 200-day moving averages, heralding an official trend reversal in early January as the chart adopted the Most Bearish Orientation possible.

Recall that the Pure Price Method called for an early trend reversal at the exact time when price formed a lower swing low (November's 12,800 low), rallied to form a lower swing high (December's 13,800 peak), and then declined to take out the prior low from November, creating a succession of a lower high followed by breaking to a new low. In this example at the peak of 2007, both the Pure Price Method and the Moving Average Method (at least on the daily chart) gave a long-term sell signal simultaneously.

Neither one of these methods in isolation are magic and neither one will give you a perfect buy or sell signal at the absolute top. However, both methods satisfy the weight of the evidence requirement when making trading and investment decisions regarding trend reversals. You will find your results improve when you use the two methods in conjunction, rather than in isolation. The goal is to assess the chart evidence in an unbiased fashion and identify objective rather than subjective turning points that can be classified at exact prices. You can identify the exact price when an uptrend officially shifts into a downtrend (or vice versa) using either method.

Simple versus Exponential Moving Averages There is a difference in what type of moving average you use on your chart. While most traders use simple moving averages, other traders prefer to use exponential averages when assessing trend structure. Simple moving averages weight each day equally, making the price 50 days ago equal to yesterday's price in the calculation of a 50-day moving average. Simple moving averages tend to be smoother and reflect a true average of price changes over time. As a result, simple moving averages are slower to respond to swift recent changes in price and have a longer lag time as a result.

In contrast to a simple moving average, an exponential moving average places more emphasis on the recent bars and a lesser importance on the past. In fact, exponential averages can also be described as exponential weighted moving averages, which take into account recent price changes faster than simple, equal-weighted moving averages. As a result, EMAs tend to react quicker to sudden recent price changes; furthermore, traders often value EMAs due to their quicker reactivity and reduced lag than simple moving averages. This is another compromise you must make as a trader: Exponential averages react quicker to recent changes but may result in more whipsaws than simple averages, which react slower to recent changes but are less prone to false signals.

While there is little difference between a 20 period EMA or SMA, the difference is magnified the longer the period you use. Experiment for yourself to find the right combination for you. In most charting examples, unless specified, I will be using the 20 EMA, 50 EMA, and 200 SMA. On my charts, I always color the 20 EMA green, the 50 EMA blue, and the 200 SMA red. I use the 200 SMA instead of the 200 EMA because most traders watch and react to the 200 simple moving average, which tends to have more importance than a 200 EMA, but this is still a matter of personal preference and experience.

Trend Reversals Like the Pure Price Method, we are looking for objective evidence and an exact price (or date) to identify a trend reversal, which will always be signaled shortly after an absolute top or bottom has formed. Using the Moving Average Method, the following must take place for a market to shift from an uptrend to a downtrend on a daily chart:

- Price must first break under the 20-day then the 50-day moving average
- The 20-day average must cross under the 50-day moving average
- Price must cross under the 200-day moving average
- The 20- and 50-day averages must then cross under the 200-day average
- Price officially shifts to a downtrend when all criteria have been fulfilled.

Figure 1.5 shows the usual progression from uptrend to downtrend using the moving average method as a guide. These steps need not be sequential, as a trend reversal is signaled when all criteria have been met.

To confirm a trend reversal on the weekly chart, it is often only necessary to watch for a bearish cross of the 20-week average under the 50-week average while price remains under these averages. You will often wait far too long if you wait for price and the shorter

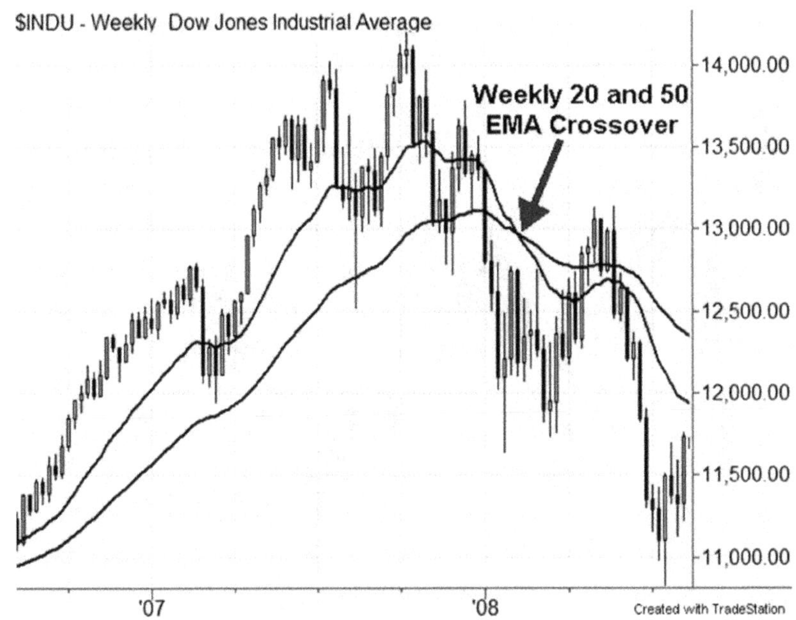

FIGURE 1.6 Dow Jones Weekly Chart: Transition from Uptrend to Downtrend Using the 20- and 50-week Exponential Moving Averages

term averages to cross under the 200-week moving average, so give greater importance to the crossover of the 20- and 50-week moving average, rather than waiting for price to cross under the 200-week average for final confirmation.

Let's view one more example of the Weekly Chart of the Dow Jones Industrial Average as it peaks in October 2007. Compare Figure 1.6 with Figure 1.4, both of which are identical charts that highlight the two main methods of trend classification.

Unlike the daily chart which uses three moving averages, the weekly chart trend reversals are best identified with the 20- and 50-week moving averages. You may find yourself waiting too long for price and the shorter term averages to cross under the 200-week moving averages, especially after a powerful uptrend has completed. Notice how the 20-week EMA crosses under the 50-week EMA in February 2008, one month after the daily moving average chart confirmed a downtrend.

While the classifications of price swings will not differ greatly using the Pure Price Method on daily or weekly charts (swing highs and lows should be similar), you can get a lead or a lag using the Moving Average Method on daily versus weekly charts, but the lag usually is only a few months. The same logic is true when a market transitions from a downtrend into an uptrend, as seen in the reversal in 2003 in Figure 1.7.

After peaking in January 2000 above 11,600, the Dow Jones Average fell steadily into a downtrend until bottoming officially (triple bottom) in March 2003 at 7,400. However, when did the Moving Average Method on the daily chart officially signal the end of the downtrend?

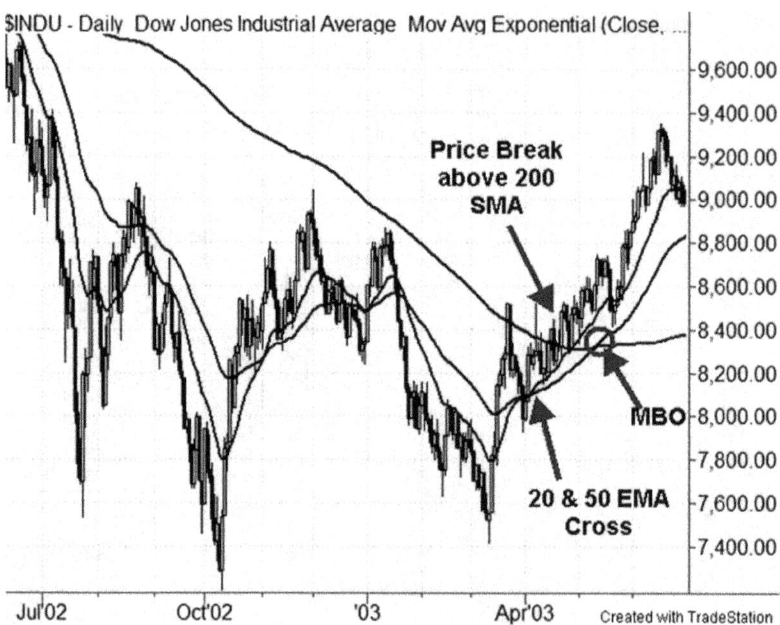

FIGURE 1.7 Dow Jones Industrial Average Showing a Transition from Down to Up in Mid-2003

The official change is labeled Most Bullish Orientation (MBO) to represent the official trend reversal which fulfilled all requirements: the 20-day EMA crossed above the 50-day EMA in April 2003 while price broke and closed above the 200-day SMA shortly after in late April. To complete the reversal, both the 20- and 50-day EMAs crossed bullishly above the 200-day SMA in May 2003 while price traded at the 8,600 level.

How did the Pure Price Method signal a reversal? The index was in a steady progression of forming lower swing lows and lower swing highs until it formed a higher swing low for the first time in March 2003 off the 7,400 level. Price then rallied in a single swing to take out the high established in December 2002 at the 9,000 level, which then created both a higher low and official higher high, flipping the trend to the upside by breaking back above 9,000 to a new swing high in June 2003. Notice that the Moving Average Method had a slight lead to calling an official bottom, but again this is not always the case.

Using the 'weight of the evidence' model, both the Pure Price and Moving Average Methods signaled an official trend reversal together in May 2003. Price formed a higher low then took out a recent higher high (an uptrend is defined as a series of higher highs and higher lows) and the daily triple-moving averages crossed bullishly while price remained above them all, creating the Most Bullish Orientation possible.

With both methods signaling a trend reversal, the objective evidence called for a bullish investment and trading posture going forward as a new trend emerged. Traders who remained short after May 2003 did so squarely against the odds. Using the Pure Price and Moving Average Methods, you'll no longer have to guess when a trend has reversed.

Instead, you'll know the point of maximum probability using simple, objective evidence that a trend has reversed. The methods are not perfect, but certainly work better than gut feelings, intuition, or trying to catch falling knives (that is trader speak for trying to buy every single new low in hopes of a trend reversal, which often leads to large losses and unfortunately the end of some trading careers).

PINPOINTING THE TREND REVERSAL IN 2009

Can you spot the objective trend reversal, using both the Pure Price and Moving Average Methods as the market transitioned from downtrend to uptrend off the March 2009 bottom? Study the chart in Figure 1.8 before reading the answer.

At what exact index level did the trend officially reverse from down to up? Let's take a look. The 20- and 50-day EMAs crossed bullishly in April 2009 but because of the severity of the recent sell-off and downtrend in 2008, it took three more months for price and both moving averages to cross back above the 200-day average, doing so in mid-July 2009 to signal an official trend reversal (using the Moving Average Method) at 8,500. That signified a potential turn in trend, but a 20/50 moving average crossover does not officially reverse a trend in play, though it is a required precursor for any trend to reverse.

The Pure Price Method signaled an official trend reversal shortly thereafter when price crested above the June 2009 swing high just shy of 9,000. We can label the

FIGURE 1.8 Dow Jones Daily Chart: Identify the Exact Point of a Trend Reversal

two-month correction phase from May to July as a down-swing, which formed a higher low at the 8,000 level as price swung back to take out the most recent high (creating a new swing high) at the 9,000 level which also broke above the January 2009 high for extra measure. The new series of higher lows and higher highs confirmed an official trend reversal just after the Moving Averages crossed to the Most Bullish Orientation possible—the first time since we saw them cross negatively in a downside trend reversal as seen on the daily chart in Figure 1.5. Do we thus call the downtrend reversed officially in mid-July 2009 when price rose above the 200-day SMA and above the June swing high at 8,700? Officially, yes, but let us see one final component that places the weight of the evidence so convincingly in favor of the bulls as to be objectively impossible to refer to price above 9,000 as remaining in a downtrend.

Price rose to the 9,000 index level in January 2009 to form a key swing high prior to the final low in March. Thus, the 9,000 level represents a past swing high that would be further, or perhaps final, bullish evidence of a reversal if buyers pushed through this level. The powerful swing off the July 2009 low did just that, with price breaking above not only the most recent swing high at 8,700 in June 2009, but the prior high six months in January at 9,000. To be absolutely sure that price had completed all requirements from the Pure Price Method and the Moving Average Method, the objective and final declaration from a change in trend from down to up triggered on July 30, 2009 when price broke and closed above the January 2009 high of 9,088.

As of July 30, 2009, price formed a series of higher highs and higher lows, crossed above the 200-day simple moving average, rose after the bullish crossing of the 20- and 50-day EMA, and finally closed above the past swing high from January 2009. This example reveals the logical and objective chart analysis you should use when classifying trends, which reveals to you the type of trading strategies to use for the highest probability, lowest risk set-ups.

Now that you know where to begin by assessing the trend structure when you first look at a chart, let's add an extra dimension to your analysis: assessing the strength or weakness of a confirmed trend in place. To do this, we will study the momentum principle, which helps us assess the probabilities of a confirmed trend continuing, or setting up for a potential future reversal. In other words, learning how to interpret price momentum can clue you in early for a potential trend reversal ahead of waiting for the official price and moving average method to give you a pure signal, and thus you will identify early warning signs of potential reversal ahead of the official signal from price alone.

CHAPTER 2

Momentum's Leading Edge

To recap, the first thing you should assess when studying a price chart initially is the trend structure. This can be done objectively via the Pure Price Method or the Moving Average Method, preferably in conjunction. Once you establish that price is in a rising or falling trend, the second step is to assess the magnitude or power of that trend. To do this, you'll need the leading edge that momentum can give you, both to identify confirmations in the early stages of a trend and non-confirmations in the form of momentum divergences as the trend matures in its latter stages. In this way, momentum provides two benefits to your analysis, first in confirming the health of a new trend in development, and second in assessing the likely end of a mature trend via divergences in advance of the official but delayed signal the Pure Price and Moving Average methods reveal to you.

That's not all momentum can do for you—the momentum helps you set specific trades, namely the impulse-related trade setups like flags and Impulse Buy setups we discuss in Chapters 9 and 10. In this chapter, you will learn how to interpret the momentum conditions of a price move, identify momentum bursts as confirmations of early trends, and locate divergences as early warning signals that a mature trend is showing signs of a potential future reversal.

THE SCIENCE OF MOMENTUM

Before we examine how to apply the concept of momentum to our price charts, we first need to define momentum and how it reveals itself on the price charts in any market or timeframe.

Think back to high school or college physics when you studied Newton's Laws of Motion. If it's been too long since you've had your last course in physics, here is a basic summary of these three principles as we understand them today:

- **Law 1 (Inertia):** Objects at rest remain at rest (stationary) until another force acts upon them. Similarly, objects in motion tend to stay in motion until some other force acts upon them.
- **Law 2 (Momentum):** An object will accelerate proportional to the force that acts upon it (as in, the stronger the force, the more momentum and thus motion generated). Force equals mass times acceleration or $f = m(a)$.
- **Law 3 (Action/Reaction):** Every action has an equal and opposite reaction.

These are certainly oversimplified definitions to these important concepts, but for trading purposes, we only need to understand the main ideas of these principles and apply them to the charts. For traders seriously interested in a deeper discussion of how the worlds of physics and finance interact, I recommend two works: *The Physics of Finance* by Kirill Ilinski or the easier to understand *My Life as a Quant: Reflections on Physics and Finance* by Emanuel Derman.

We will define objects as prices and forces as the buying or selling pressure that investors and traders place on the price of stocks in terms of supply and demand for limited shares (or contracts in the futures markets).

For example, a rush of buy orders after a positive earnings announcement in a stock serves as a force that moves the object—the price—higher in relation to how aggressively the buyers purchase shares, when combined with those who are short (short sellers) being stopped out of their positions and forced to buy shares to cover their short positions (the basis of short-squeezes). These initial bursts of momentum, in the form of a buying/selling or supply/demand imbalance, move price forward in trends. Price tends to stay either stationary (range-bound) or moving higher or lower in a stable trend until some outside force, which reveals itself as a supply/demand imbalance, disrupts the equilibrium or balance.

Stated in stock market terms, prices tend to remain range-bound (trendless) until a news event or other form of momentum via a supply/demand imbalance propels the price forward in an impulse and trend motion. We will discuss the Price Alternation Principle, which addresses Newton's Third Law, appropriately in Chapter 3.

Ball-Tossing Momentum

One of the easiest examples to use when comparing real-world physics and momentum principles to the stock market is to discuss the physics that occur when you throw a ball into the air.

Imagine you are holding a tennis ball in your right hand. The ball will remain stationary (at rest—Law 1) until some other force (your hand) acts on it to start the ball moving. Now, imagine yourself throwing the ball high into the air. The ball will continue rising until some other force (gravity) acts upon it. Your hand and the strength with which you throw it serve as the beginning force that sets the ball in motion, and the ball will travel higher if you exert more force in your initial swing than if you exerted less force as you move your hand higher to release the ball (Law 2). The air (resistance) and gravity (force) will counteract the force you used to throw the ball into the air, eventually becoming stronger as the momentum you used to throw the ball into the air decreases. The ball will slow down before reaching the highest point at apogee, pause for a split second, and then begin falling back down to earth, returning hopefully to your outstretched hand to catch it.

In that simple example, we just demonstrated the First and Second Laws of Motion! The concepts of physics do not have to be difficult. Again, the ball would have remained in your hand until you threw it into the air (first law). How hard you throw the ball determines how high the ball travels in the air (second law). The ball would have stayed in perpetual motion had you thrown it up while floating in outer space (no gravity or wind resistance), but you were on Earth when you threw the ball, so the forces of gravity and air molecule resistance acted against the ball to slow down the trajectory to the upside and eventually return the ball back to earth.

That's great, but how does throwing a ball relate to buying and selling stocks? That's what this chapter will reveal. To get us started, imagine that the price of a stock is relatively flat or range-bound for a period of time. Now, imagine that the company suddenly releases better-than-expected earnings or in some way due to positive news becomes the focus of an intense buying campaign, driving the price higher. This is called a Momentum Burst, or impulse, which sets the stock moving higher in a trend or upward trajectory. The stock will continue moving higher as a result of the supply/demand (sellers/buyers) imbalance until some other force serves to weaken, then reverse the trend, which often reveals itself on the price chart in the form of a rounded reversal price pattern or negative momentum divergence. Usually, the trend will end just like the ball you threw, which means that price moves often end through a weakening of buyers or loss of momentum at the highs (which show up as negative divergences) before the stock pauses, then returns to lower levels as a new downtrend develops.

MOMENTUM IN THE STOCK MARKET

Now that we have a quick review of the scientific concept of momentum, let's apply this directly to the stock market. We define momentum in simpler terms when describing price on the charts, with the simplest definition being "momentum represents a change in price over time." Large changes represent large spikes in momentum—also known as acceleration—and hint that price will continue traveling in the direction the momentum burst occurs. You want to see momentum spikes or sharp acceleration occur at the start of a new trend, either before or shortly after a trend reversal has occurred using the definitions and tactics in Chapter 1, or breaking out of a sideways trading range as we will see in Chapter 3. Initial bursts of momentum after lengthy divergences represent a kickoff in price that often leads to a pure trend reversal and tradable opportunity for low-risk profits.

In an article for the *Journal of Technical Analysis* entitled "Momentum Leads Price," Timothy Hayes explained that momentum leads price through detecting acceleration and deceleration. Using an example of two cars, Hayes showed that if two cars leave the same destination with the same acceleration and stop accelerating at the exact same time, then both cars would continue coasting forward and slow at the same rate, all things being equal. However, what would happen if one driver accelerated for a longer period before taking his foot off the accelerator? That car would subsequently coast forward for a longer period of time and travel farther than the other car whose driver released the accelerator earlier.

Such a comparison of cars and acceleration is similar to stocks and their momentum qualities, such that stocks with higher momentum often travel higher in price relative to stocks with lower momentum readings, using the momentum to coast to higher prices than stocks with lower momentum. It is thus very important to assess the momentum environment when assessing opportunities in specific stocks to trade.

GAPS REVEAL MOMENTUM

Observe momentum by itself without indicators by looking at sudden changes in price. A gap or sudden large price move is by definition a momentum impulse, highlighting the force (of supply or demand) acting on the price of the stock or market. Let's see a simple example of a positive earnings announcement in Amazon.com's stock (AMZN) serving as a momentum burst (Figure 2.1).

FIGURE 2.1 A Gap as a Momentum Impulse in Amazon on October 23, 2009

Prior to the gap in mid-October 2009, Amazon was range-bound (trendless with a slight upward bias). However, the positive earnings announcement sent traders rushing to buy the stock (and short-sellers rushing to cover their short positions), which appeared on the chart as a momentum impulse. This is similar to Newton's First Law of Motion which states that "objects tend to stay at rest until a force acts upon them," which in this case was a rush of buyers creating the force, driving price higher. Taking into account Law 2, "an object will accelerate proportional to the force that acts upon it." To the extent that this positive earnings surprise caused a rush of buyers to purchase shares of Amazon, the stock will be expected to continue higher in price as the initial force of momentum—like throwing a tennis ball into the air—leads to a higher trajectory and uptrend in price. Stronger initial impulses can be expected to drive price higher than weaker initial impulses—all things being equal.

In plain English, this means that the spike in price and the corresponding volume spike, which often accompanies any sort of momentum burst or impulse, sent prices higher and led us to expect a continuation of upward prices into the future. Stated differently, after observing a momentum impulse in price, we expect continued higher prices in the future, translating into low-risk trading opportunities such as buying shares on pullbacks to support levels in the context of a rising trend. Like the ball rising immediately from the initial momentum burst the moment it leaves your hand and then continuing to rise, we would expect stock prices to continue rising higher in the aftermath of a major impulsive event that sends price higher either in a breakout or continuation trend motion. Positive momentum bursts in price reveal that a prevailing uptrend is healthy and should continue higher into the future, rather than reverse.

Let's see another example of a momentum burst (impulse), both to the upside and downside in Electronic Arts (ERTS) during the transition from 2004 to 2005 (Figure 2.2).

As revealed in Amazon, a gap was the initial impulse burst that led to higher prices yet to come in the future. Electronic Arts shows the same concept in December 2004 when price began to accelerate in a momentum burst confirmed by an accompanying rise in volume. From December 10–14, 2004, we see three days in a row of one-sided action, showing a sharp acceleration of price to the upside, revealing our momentum burst (or force acting on the object—price). Such momentum bursts hint to us that odds favor even higher prices yet to come. We'll learn in later chapters that it is best to put on a position immediately following the first retracement after we see a spike in momentum (I call this the Impulse Buy trade), but we first must understand why these make good trade setups by learning the foundation concept of momentum.

We can see an example of the concept in a breakaway gap to the downside in March 2005 with a downside impulse leading to lower prices yet to come. On March 22, 2004, price opened down $9.25 or almost 14 percent lower, showing us a clear momentum impulse, or burst, to the downside, serving as a force that kept prices traveling lower. Notice the large spike in volume: almost 40,000,000 shares traded that day, when the average for the prior days was near 5,000,000 shares per day. Price reached an absolute bottom of the move in May 2005 at $47.45.

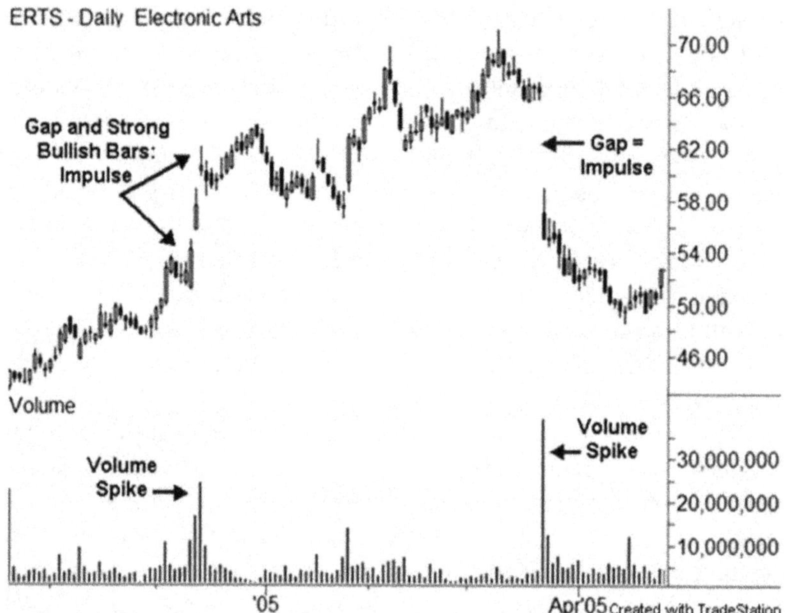

FIGURE 2.2 Two Gaps showing two Momentum Impulses in Electronic Arts, 2004/2005 Daily Chart

Of course, not all gaps result automatically in a continuation of the trend. Breakaway Gaps and Common Gaps do so, but Exhaustion Gaps (those that form at the end of a lengthy trend) do not. Breakaway Gaps occur at the start of a new trend near the time of a confirmed trend reversal, while Common Gaps (also known as Measured Gaps) occur usually near the middle state of a trend. Exhaustion gaps are a different story, as they occur at the end of a lengthy trend and fill immediately. Breakaway Gaps rarely fill, while Exhaustion Gaps fill almost immediately; in fact, that is the distinguishing characteristic between them. It also shows the importance of taking into account the maturity of a trend when assessing momentum readings.

Amazon and Electronic Arts showed an example of a Common (Measured) Gap when the price broke in impulse fashion to the upside, while the second gap on March 23, as seen in Figure 2.2, in Electronic Arts showed us an example of a Breakaway Gap to the downside after price had formed volume (and momentum) divergences, as price rallied to new highs. We will discuss divergences as forecasting trend reversals later in the chapter.

THE MOMENTUM INDICATOR

Before we describe indicators, it is important to understand that momentum is a concept of physics that is applied to the price chart of stocks. There are a variety of methods, or indicators, that help you assess the current momentum condition of a stock price in motion, but the goal is to assess the momentum environment, specifically if momentum is increasing or decreasing within the context of a new or mature trend.

Though it may sound confusing, there is a specific indicator named Momentum, but this indicator is not the same thing as identifying the physics concept of "momentum" that we are trying to assess. There is only one concept of "Momentum" though there are many chart indicators you can use to assess momentum, one of which is labeled the "Momentum Indicator." It's not as confusing as it initially seems.

Most charting platforms include a simple indicator appropriately named momentum. The momentum indicator compares the price today with the price X days in the past to show not just whether price is higher or lower than in the past, but to what extent. In fact, the Momentum Indicator is perhaps the simplest but ironically not most effective indicator when studying the physics concept of momentum as applied to the stock charts. The indicator compares the price today with the price a certain number of days in the past and tallies the result each day as a line to assess whether momentum is rising or falling. The momentum indicator formula compares the current price with the price a specified number of days past, usually 14 as the default, and then plots the value each day as an oscillating line around zero. A reading of zero indicates that the price today and the price 14 days ago are equal.

MOMENTUM INDICATOR

An indicator that shows price today minus price X days ago

For simplicity, let us say that X days ago is 14 days, so we want to know how much higher or lower price is today than it was 14 days ago. That is what the indicator shows for the current reading. For example, if price today is $50.00 and price 14 days ago was $47.00, then the formula would show $50.00 minus $47.00 equals $3.00. Thus, the current reading would show $3.00. If price was $53.00 14 days ago and price is $50.00 today, then the indicator would show −$3.00, showing that price has declined $3.00 from the value 14 days ago.

For the purpose of momentum as a physics concept (and not an indicator), the current value of the indicator is of little to no significance to us. What is most important is the highs and lows of the oscillator itself when compared to respective price highs and lows. Other textbooks will tell you to buy when the indicator crosses above the zero-line (indicating positive momentum) and to sell when the indicator crosses under the zero-line (indicating negative momentum) but that is not what we are discussing here. We are not using the indicator to give us buy or sell signals; rather, we are most interested in comparing the highs and lows of the indicator as they relate to swing highs and lows in price in order to reveal the current condition of the physics of momentum on the price charts. You discover insights into momentum—the concept—through comparing oscillator highs and lows with corresponding price highs or lows.

FIGURE 2.3 Using the Indicator Momentum to Compare Oscillator and Price Swings—NML = New Momentum Low

Let us see an example using the S&P 500 as the market turned from bull to bear in early 2008 (Figure 2.3).

Comparing the Oscillator and Price for Confirmation

Compare oscillator swing highs directly with corresponding price swing highs, and oscillator swing lows to corresponding price swing lows. You may find it beneficial to draw vertical lines on your chart to see exactly where the price and oscillator highs and lows align. The oscillator should behave similarly to price, and serve to highlight swings in price. In other words, if price makes a new swing low, then we expect the momentum oscillator also to make a corresponding swing low as a confirmation of the price low. If you are seeing new price lows correspond with new oscillator lows, then you observe a confirmation of indicator and price that suggests that you can expect lower prices yet to come. Using the same logic, if you see new price highs and these new highs are confirmed with new oscillator highs (look directly down at your oscillator when price is making a new high), then see this as a confirmation and thus expect higher prices to continue in the uptrend.

We see this occurring as expected in the chart in November 2007 and January 2008 in Figure 2.3 as price forms a new swing low with the oscillator forming a corresponding oscillator swing low with price. I drew vertical arrows in the chart to focus your attention on comparing the price low with the momentum oscillator low. We can establish a logical rule based on this concept, which will later form the basis for trade setups (classic retracement trades, bull or bear flags, and impulse buy or sell trades):

PRICE VERSUS MOMENTUM EXTREMES

New Momentum Oscillator Highs plus New Price Highs

When the Momentum Oscillator forms a new swing high (relative to the recent past) at the same time that price forms a new swing high, then this serves as a confirmation of the recent price high and suggests that a higher price high is yet to come. We can buy the first pullback into support for a potential trade setup.

New Momentum Oscillator Lows plus New Price Lows

When the Momentum Oscillator forms a new swing low (relative to the recent past) at the same time that price forms a new swing low, then this serves as a confirmation of the recent price low and suggests that a lower price low is yet to come. We can short sell the first pullback into resistance for a potential trade setup.

In Figure 2.3, we saw our first new price low and new oscillator low at 1,400.00 in the S&P 500 during November 2007. Price then retraced higher to form a lower swing high (this is called the first reaction or first retracement) and then fell to a new price low that was forecast—or hinted—via the confirmation signal given by momentum. Price and momentum both made new lows, so we would anticipate a future new price low yet to come. Price swung to a new low in January 2008 at the 1,300.00 index level with the momentum oscillator also forming a corresponding new low. What do we assume next?

Again, we see a new price low (new swing low—refer to Chapter 1 for a discussion on price swings) which was confirmed again with another new oscillator low in the momentum oscillator. For reference, the price swing low in January 2008 is roughly 100 points lower than the December 2007 price swing low, and the January 2008 momentum oscillator low is roughly 55 points lower than it was in December 2007 (it hit a low of –105.00 in December and a new low of –160.00 in January).

We would thus expect new price lows yet to come, as hinted by the confirming signal in the oscillator, along with price. The trade setup is to sell short the first reaction or retracement into resistance after price and the momentum oscillator form a new low together (in unison). This retracement takes us back up to the 1,400.00 index level in February, giving us a chance to short sell. We do see a drop to a new index low as expected, breaking to 1,250.00 in March 2008, but something strange happens to the oscillator.

Price just made a new swing low, but the oscillator did not—look carefully at the swing low under 1,300.00 in March 2008. This is our first positive momentum divergence on the chart, meaning price made a new low but the oscillator diverged, or did not confirm the price low under 1,300.00 by forming a new low in the oscillator. The divergence opens up a new world of analyzing the momentum oscillator, which warns us of a potential reversal in trend instead of continuation. Remember, momentum reveals the health or weakness of a trend, and while momentum highs in an uptrend highlight trend strength, negative momentum divergences that form in the context of a mature trend are often warning signs of trend deterioration and potential future reversal ahead of the official signal given from the Pure Price or Moving Average Methods.

Divergences as Non-Confirmations

A divergence occurs when price and the oscillator disagree, or more specifically, when price has formed a discernable new swing low but the oscillator has formed a noticeably higher swing low, both relative to the recent past. Be sure you are comparing the exact same swing in price to the oscillator; draw a horizontal line if you are not sure. First, let's officially define a divergence.

NEGATIVE VERSUS POSITIVE DIVERGENCE

While momentum extremes help forecast future prices in the continuation of a trend in place, momentum divergences highlight a weakening in the trend and potential for a future reversal in price.

Negative Divergence: New Price High but Lower High in the Oscillator

In the context of an established uptrend, price forms a new swing high as expected, but the momentum oscillator actually forms a lower swing high, which serves as a non-confirmation of the recent price high. This serves as a warning signal, but not yet a downside trend reversal signal unless confirmed by price in the form of a break in a rising trendline or moving average.

Positive Divergence: New Price Low but Higher Low in the Oscillator

In the context of an established downtrend, price forms a new swing low as expected, but the momentum oscillator actually forms a higher swing low, which serves as a non-confirmation of the recent price low. This serves as a warning signal, but not yet a positive trend reversal signal unless confirmed by price in the form of a break in a falling trendline or moving average.

Divergences can be tricky to spot at first, but once you understand how to identify them, you'll start seeing price and indicator divergences more clearly. Let's look at some examples of Price and Momentum Oscillator divergences for a reference.

FIGURE 2.4 Highlighting an Example of a Negative Momentum Divergence in Johnson and Johnson Daily Chart

In Figure 2.4, we see the daily chart of Johnson and Johnson (JNJ) as price swings to three higher highs above $65.00 per share in late March and April 2010. If you are just looking at the price by itself, all looks well in an established uptrend. However, if we add the indicator Momentum and verify whether or not the oscillator confirms or disconfirms the recent price highs, we see that indeed the oscillator is forming lower highs as price pushes to higher highs. We have a negative momentum divergence developing: caution!

As we will see in detail through Chapter 7, trends have life cycles and do not persist indefinitely. Negative divergences between price and an unbound momentum oscillator often develop prior to a trend reversal from up to down and serve as potential early warning signs that the trend is in its latter stages and likely to reverse soon. Traders should adopt a cautious stance when observing negative divergences after a lengthy trend has persisted for a relatively long period of time, depending on the timeframe of the chart. A long time may be defined as a few days on the 15-minute intraday chart, while a long time might mean three years or more on a weekly chart. Negative divergences may resolve with a small downside action lasting hours on an intraday chart, but the resolution of a negative divergence on a weekly frame might take months or even years.

We will discuss trading tactics using divergences in Chapter 8 when we discuss trade execution tactics and Chapters 9 and 10 for specific trade setups. For now, focus on learning what a momentum divergence is, where it is likely to occur, and what it means for traders on any timeframe looking to establish a new position or take off a profitable old position in a particular stock.

Recall that the momentum oscillator confirms a price high when the oscillator forms a new swing high at the same time a new price high forms. This suggests that the trend remains strong and that higher prices are likely yet to come in the future. Divergences send the opposite message, and act as warning signals to reveal that a trend may be losing steam. If price swings to a new high but the momentum oscillator fails to register a new oscillator high, then you might choose to tighten any trailing stop loss orders or be prepared to exit your position on any break of a prior swing low, moving average, or rising price trendline.

It is very important that you discern a negative divergence as a warning signal and not a sell-short or reverse position by itself. A caution light is not a red light; in fact, caution only means to slow down. To initiate an actual sell-short position from a price divergence, you need additional chart information such as price breaking under a rising trendline, short-term moving average, or some other technical signal such as a reversal candle or a price pattern entry signal such as the break under a neckline in a head and shoulders pattern (see Chapter 4 on price patterns). Divergences form the initial condition that gives you the confidence to execute a safe reversal trade when other confirmation factors develop on the chart; after all, divergences help us discern the weight of the evidence in terms of analyzing potential trend reversals.

Figure 2.5 reveals an example of a positive divergence that marked the March low in 2009 in the S&P 500 broad market index.

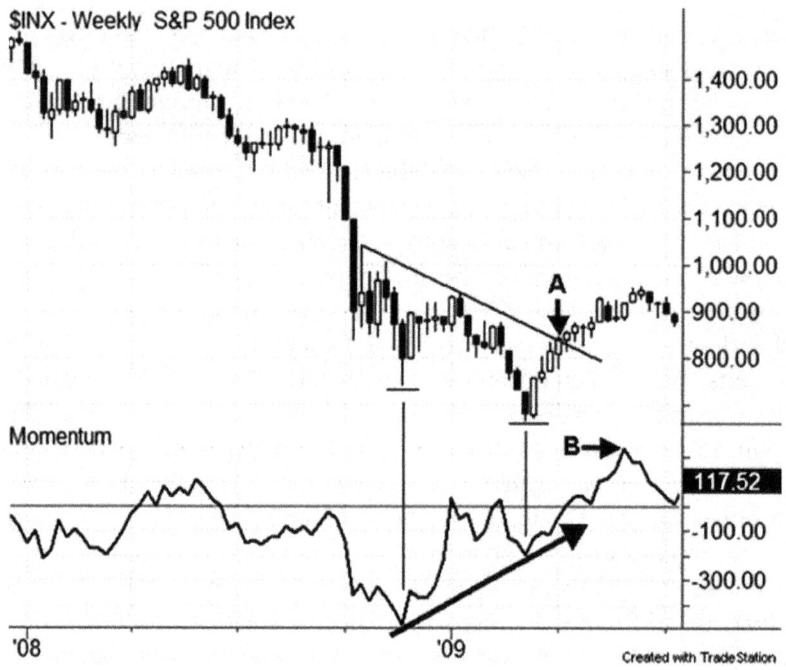

FIGURE 2.5 Positive Divergence then New Momentum High Marks Bottom of Market in March 2009

If you were following price alone, you probably were certain that we would see lower and lower prices far into the future for the index, and from a pure price trend continuity standpoint, you would certainly assume that lower prices were yet to come. An official trend reversal from down to up requires an initial higher high, then higher low, and finally a break above the most recent higher high. In March 2009, there was absolutely no evidence present from price that the stock market downtrend was in jeopardy of reversing to a new uptrend. However, the momentum oscillator revealed that short-sellers should be cautious, as the oscillator formed a clear positive momentum divergence with the final price low.

Look closely at price to see that the index formed a new low in October 2008 with the momentum oscillator confirming the new price low under 800. That signaled that odds favored a lower price low yet to come as the downtrend had greater odds of continuing into the future, being confirmed not just by the price trend structure, but by the momentum principle. Early 2009 resulted in the new expected index low forming in March as the index took out the 800, then the 750 level last seen in November 2009. Using the momentum principle, we should have expected this new price low due to the confirmation of price and the momentum oscillator both forming new lows simultaneously.

However, when price pushed to its new low, we see that the momentum oscillator formed a clean higher low. For reference, the indicator low in November 2008 was –482.00 while the indicator low in March 2009 was –196.00. The respective index lows were 741.00 in November 2008 and 666.00 in March 2009. The positive momentum divergence warned short sellers to take a defensive position, tighten up any trailing stops, and keep a close eye on the trendline connecting the swing highs from late 2008 and early 2009.

Price broke the trendline at the 850.00 level in April 2009, which I have labeled as point A on the chart. This was an objective place to take profits if you were holding a short position, and then stand aside for a potential trend change that could be in development. Shortly after price broke the trendline, a new price high formed above 900 in June 2009 that was confirmed with a new momentum oscillator high, which I labeled point B. Now we see a distinctly bullish development, in that the index formed a positive momentum divergence at the March 2009 low, broke the descending trendline shortly after, then price swung to a new swing high, which was confirmed with a new high in the momentum oscillator. Notice the new swing high in the oscillator—this is labeled a kickoff in price, and is often an early signal of a very likely trend reversal yet to come.

Refer to Chapter 1 on trends in Figure 1.8 to see the official trend reversal, marked by a higher price high, higher price low, then price taking out the prior high—all of which occurred after the 20- and 50-day exponential moving averages crossed bullishly. Now with your new knowledge of momentum, you can add that a positive momentum divergence preceded the trend reversal months in advance. Also, a negative momentum oscillator divergence preceded the stock market top in 2007. Momentum often has a distinct leading edge over official trend reversals in terms of clear divergences at major turning points in a market.

THE RATE OF CHANGE INDICATOR

To highlight that we are describing a concept of momentum and not necessarily a single oscillator, I want to highlight other indicators you can use when discerning changes in the physics of momentum via the price charts. Remember, we are discussing a principle of physics and applying it to stock prices as changes in supply and demand act as forces that move the object of price along. Just as you can use different tools to measure momentum in the real world, you can use different indicators to measure momentum in the stock market.

Recall that the indicator named momentum takes a simple comparison of price today in relation to price a set number of days in the past. The line you see as your momentum oscillator is a running total of changes in price. You want to know how strong past swings in price are to the current swing. If the current swing is larger in intensity or duration than the immediate swing that preceded it, then you are likely observing a new momentum high and therefore you will expect to see further price highs yet to come because momentum is increasing, driving prices higher and revealing a healthy trend in motion.

On the other hand, if you see the current swing is shorter in price difference or length than the prior swing, even though price formed a new swing high, then you could be observing a deterioration in momentum (or supply/demand imbalance) which suggests that the trend could be ready to reverse as the buyers are losing the upper hand to the sellers; the uptrend is losing steam.

You do not need momentum oscillators to show you the momentum conditions of a price trend once you gain experience, but oscillators serve as excellent reference tools even for trained technicians; oscillators highlight divergences that we may miss if we only studied price charts themselves.

If your charting software does not contain the indicator named Momentum, then you can use the more popular indicator labeled Rate of Change, which is almost identical to Momentum. The mathematical formula for the Rate of Change oscillator is almost identical to that of the momentum oscillator, with one small change: while the Momentum oscillator plots price comparisons as actual price differences, the Rate of Change oscillator plots price changes as a percentage.

RATE OF CHANGE (ROC)

The formula for ROC is:

ROC = [(Close Today - Close N Periods Ago) / (Close N Periods Ago)] × 100

Stated differently, the Rate of Change Oscillator takes the same formula for momentum—stated in the numerator of the fraction—and divides by the close a fixed number of periods ago and then multiplies that fraction by 100 to arrive at a percentage value. The default value for periods is 14.

Let's look at two mathematical examples. Today, price is $50.00. Fourteen days ago, price was $40.00. Using the indicator momentum (price today minus price 14 days ago), then we arrive at a value of $10.00, which would appear on our chart for the oscillator value.

If we use the Rate of Change formula, we take the close today ($50.00) then subtract the close 14 days ago ($40.00) as our numerator which is $10.00 (where the first example stopped) and then divide that number by the close 14 days ago, which is $40. Thus, $10.00 divided by $40.00 is 0.25. Now, we take that ratio and multiply by 100 to convert the number into a percentage, which gives us 25 percent. In other words, the price today is 25 percent higher than it was 14 days ago.

Using the formula for Momentum, we can say that price is $10.00 greater than it was 14 days ago, or using the Rate of Change indicator, we can say that price is 25 percent greater today than it was 14 days ago. What we see on our charts as the oscillator will be the rolling difference as each day passes. Rather than the absolute numbers or percentages, we are most interested in the shape of the oscillations as they relate to the price oscillations; namely, we want to see new oscillator highs confirm new price highs, or note whether price forms a new high and the oscillator registers a lower high in a negative divergence.

If we see price form a new high but our oscillator form a lower high, then this is a negative divergence, which is a sign of a loss of momentum and potential evidence for a future trend reversal yet to occur. The Momentum Oscillator and Rate of Change Oscillator will form similar, though not identical, oscillations with price. It will be up to you to examine these particular indicators and adjust the look-back period settings to see what parameters are most to your liking.

Let's take another look at the charts used in Figures 2.4 and 2.5, only this time we will use the indicator named Rate of Change instead of the one labeled Momentum (see Figures 2.6 and 2.7 for a comparison to Figures 2.4 and 2.5).

Refer to Figure 2.4 to see the daily chart of Johnson and Johnson with the Momentum Indicator as a guide. Note that the Rate of Change and Momentum Oscillators are almost identical in following price and forming divergences with price. We see the same three-swing negative oscillator divergence with the subsequent new price highs for Johnson and Johnson in early 2010, along with the new price and momentum high that occurred in mid-March which hinted that higher prices were yet to come in the stock.

To refresh, when price and the oscillator form new highs simultaneously, it often is an all-clear signal that the trend is likely to continue and we will see higher prices yet to come. However, if we start to see negative divergences between the price and the oscillator, we should then be cautious and prepare to take profits or even decide to short sell if we see further deterioration in price and the breaking of trendlines or moving averages. The main idea is that we are using unbound momentum oscillators to give us clues to the state of the concept in physics about the momentum of a trend—or stated in market terms, a window into the supply/demand imbalance—increasing or decreasing—between buyers and sellers.

FIGURE 2.6 Negative Divergences with the Rate of Change Oscillator in Johnson and Johnson Daily Chart in early 2010

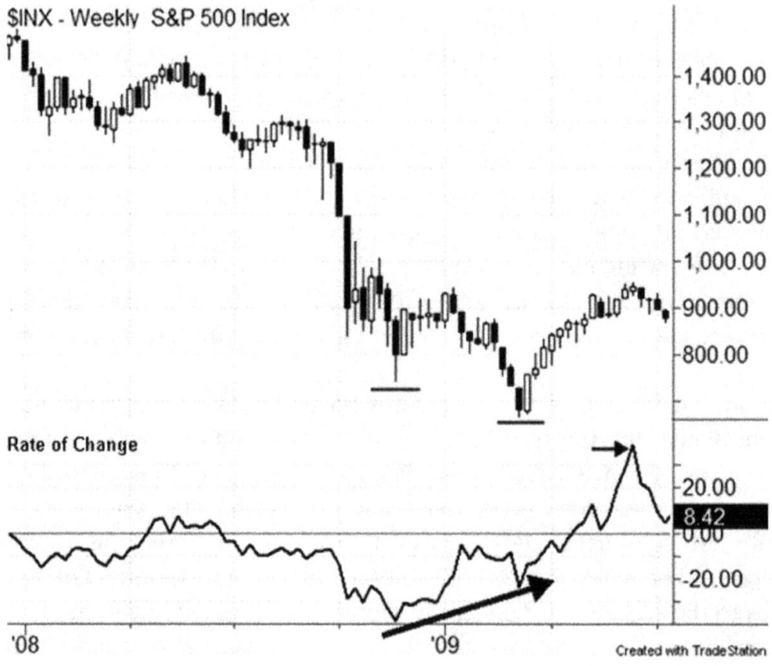

FIGURE 2.7 Positive Divergence then New Momentum High as seen with the Rate of Change Oscillator

Now let us compare the market bottom in March 2009 on the weekly chart between the Momentum Oscillator in Figure 2.5 and the Rate of Change Oscillator as seen in Figure 2.7.

The indicators are almost identical and highlight the new momentum low in November 2008 (hinting that a lower price low was yet to come in the future) and the positive momentum divergence that formed at the actual price low of 666 in March 2009, which was a caution signal to bears and early warning signal that the trend might be in the early phases of a positive reversal. Notice also that the new oscillator high formed the Kick-off in June 2009 as price moved to a new high, serving as a confirmation and hinting that higher prices were likely yet to come in the future.

THE 3/10 MACD OSCILLATOR

The Momentum Indicator highlights price changes as unaltered price differences over time, while the Rate of Change Indicator highlights changes as a percentage change over time. In both oscillators, we are comparing price now to price in the past to create an oscillator, and we aim to find confirmation or non-confirmation in price and the oscillator to reveal insights about the physics of momentum and likelihood of a trend continuing or reversing.

Another way to discern momentum characteristics in the stock market is to use the Moving Average Convergence Divergence (MACD) indicator. The MACD indicator plots the difference between two moving averages as an oscillator which can be used to assess momentum spikes as confirmation and divergences with price as non-confirmations.

The default setting for the MACD indicator, as explained by its creator Gerald Appel, is 12, 26, 9. The first two numbers in the parameters refer to the two Exponential Moving Averages—which use a shorter-term and an intermediate-term average of price. The difference, or subtraction, between these two averages creates the actual MACD Line that is plotted as an indicator on a price chart. The final number refers to the smoothing constant of the MACD line that is called the signal line.

In the context of this discussion, we will not be discussing how to use the MACD Indicator in standard form, but with reference specifically to its ability to highlight momentum characteristics in the market. Also, we will be placing emphasis on the MACD line itself instead of the signal line. You can find more information on the MACD in Gerald Appel's book *Technical Analysis, Power Tools for Active Investors*, or through a variety of sources for this popular indicator.

MOVING AVERAGE CONVERGENCE DIVERGENCE (MACD)

The formula for MACD is:

MACD Line = Faster EMA Value - Slower EMA Value (EMA is Exponential Moving Average)

Moving averages calculate the average price over time and are useful in discerning trends. When the faster (or shorter) moving average (in this case, the 12-period EMA) is greater in value than the slower (or longer) moving average (the 26-period EMA), then we can assume that price is moving in an upswing, perhaps in the context of a rising uptrend.

The distance between these moving averages reveals the momentum characteristics of the market environment we are studying. A large impulse in price, such as a gap or sustained upward move, will cause the shorter-term average to react much more quickly than the longer-term average, and therefore the distance between the short and long moving average will rise. This is how the MACD indicator becomes a momentum oscillator; we assess the physics concept of momentum via the differential between a short-term and intermediate-term moving average.

When price swings narrow or price consolidates and the distance between the shorter-term and the longer-term moving average contracts, then this can highlight a state of momentum divergence to us through the MACD oscillator. What we are interested in knowing via the oscillator is how great the distance is between the two averages, which will reveal to us changes in momentum over time. Recall that the MACD line, or the solid oscillator line we see, is the price difference between the fast- and slow-moving averages. The signal line, often shown as a dotted or hash-line, is the smoothed average—usually nine periods—of the MACD line. The signal line is less important in highlighting momentum confirmations and divergences.

Let's use the same chart of Johnson and Johnson as we did in Figures 2.4 and 2.6 and reveal what the default MACD value of 12, 26, and 9 highlight on our chart (see Figures 2.8 and 2.9). Figure 2.9 shows a faster MACD that we will come to describe as the 3/10 MACD Oscillator for future reference.

We see the same three new swing highs in early 2010, but this time we are using a new oscillator on our chart. This is the default MACD value with the MACD line solid and the signal line (less important) as hash marks. Notice that the MACD Indicator spikes to a new chart high in late March when JNJ makes a new swing high at $65.50, serving as a confirmation of the price high and creating the expectation that all is well with the trend and we should see a new price high yet to come.

We do see that new price high in early April as price nears $66.00, but this time the MACD solid line (difference between the 12- and 26-day exponential moving averages) does not rise to a new oscillator high, but instead forms a lower high, forming your negative divergence. As price swings one more time to a new high above $66.00, the MACD indicator has formed a lower swing high, just like the Momentum Oscillator and Rate of Change Oscillator did, but perhaps not as clearly. Price then fell to the downside after the negative divergence formed.

Figure 2.8 reveals how to use the default MACD indicator that is standard on most charting programs. However, as is the case with almost all indicators, if you shorten the parameters for input, you can enhance the indicators and make them more reactive or sensitive to price, which can call your attention to changes earlier. As an example, a 20-day moving average is more reactive (changes more quickly) to price than a 50-day moving average.

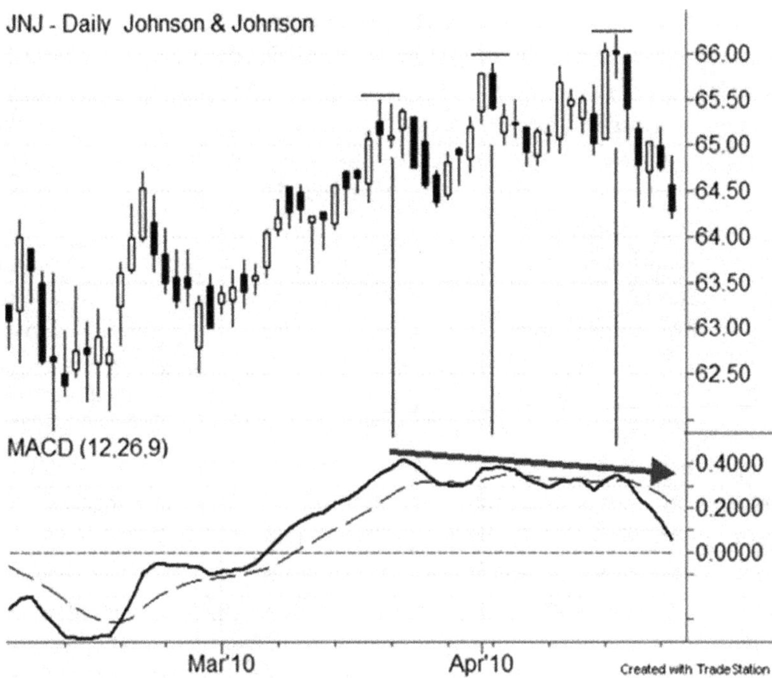

FIGURE 2.8 Negative Divergence in Johnson and Johnson using the default 12, 26, 9 MACD Indicator

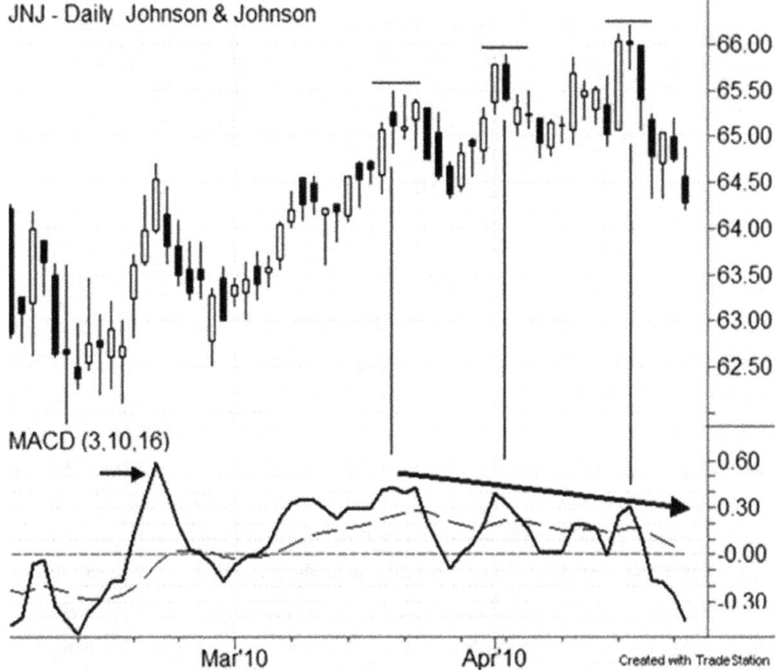

FIGURE 2.9 Negative Divergence in JNJ using the custom "faster" 3, 10, 16 MACD Indicator

The same logic holds true if you decrease the periods for the moving averages you use for your MACD indicator. There is a MACD setting that makes the indicator more suited to detecting subtle changes in the momentum environment of a trend, which can clue you in to signals earlier than the default indicator. Linda Bradford Raschke of LBR Group (www.lbrgroup.com) popularized the setting of 3, 10, and 16, respectively, which emphasizes the momentum function of the standard MACD Indicator and creates a new indicator named the "3/10 Oscillator."

Instead of comparing the difference between a 12- and 26-period exponential moving average, you can greatly shorten the periods of the indicator to compare the difference between a three-period and 10-period exponential moving average. Most charting software programs allow you to edit the parameters for your indicators to create the 3/10 Oscillator. To do so, change the default 12, 26, 9 to the new values of 3, 10, 16. Alternately, to remove the signal line completely, you can change your MACD settings to 3, 10, 1, which will only show the MACD line (difference between the 3 and 10 moving averages) as your sole momentum indicator, making it more similar to both the Momentum Oscillator and the Rate of Change oscillator. We are concerned only with oscillator highs and lows as they compare to price highs and lows.

The official 3/10 Oscillator used by Linda Raschke uses simple moving averages in its calculation instead of the standard exponential moving averages that the classic MACD uses, but not all software programs will allow you to change the type of moving averages your MACD indicator uses. Unless otherwise stated, I will be using the custom 3, 10 MACD setting that uses simple moving averages rather than exponential moving averages. You will see this labeled on the chart as the MACD SMA Indicator, created in TradeStation. To replicate this indicator, change the EMA setting to SMAs and input MACD settings 3, 10, 1. Other charting packages, such as StockCharts.com, require you to input 3, 10, 0 for your MACD settings to eliminate the signal line from the oscillator, leaving only the distance between the 3 and 10 period moving averages for the creation of the oscillator. While small, there are subtle differences in using exponential or simple moving averages in the calculation. Experiment with the settings over a variety of charts to find the combination that suits your preferences best. Figure 2.9 shows the same Johnson and Johnson chart using the 3/10 MACD Oscillator (exponential moving averages).

While the 3/10 MACD Oscillator version shows the same three-swing negative divergence price as all other oscillators, the main difference now is that the 3/10 version spiked to a new indicator high in February 2010 instead of forming the final indicator high in mid-March as the other three indicators highlighted. That is because the 3/10 Oscillator, highlighting the difference between a three-day and 10-day exponential moving average, was much more reactive to the four-day rally in mid-February than the other three momentum-locating indicators we have seen so far. Notice that the default MACD indicator registered its final high in March. However, being more reactive to price, the 3/10 Oscillator revealed the negative divergences more clearly than the default MACD indicator.

We see the benefit of the faster reflexes of the 3/10 Oscillator in comparing the differences at the March 2009 bottom, as seen in Figure 2.10.

FIGURE 2.10 Triple Swing Positive Divergence Revealed through 3/10 MACD Oscillator

Because the 3/10 Oscillator is more reactive with price than the other oscillators, the indicator highlighted a positive divergence on each of the swing lows from October to November 2008 then March 2009 while the other three indicators treated the November 2008 low as a singular event not distinct from the October low. Remember that our goal is to compare price swings with immediate oscillator swings, and sometimes it can be helpful to have a more responsive or reactive momentum indicator like the 3/10 Oscillator.

For another reference, Figure 2.11 shows the same chart of the 2009 trend reversal process as seen on the default MACD Indicator with values 12 and 26 for the moving average differences.

Using the default MACD Indicator, we see the same reading the Momentum and Rate of Change indicators revealed to us, highlighting only a single swing divergence between the November 2008 low and the March 2009 bottom.

Why is this distinction important? As you may have guessed, multiple swing positive or negative momentum divergences, as revealed through an oscillator, are more important and carry more weight than a single swing divergence. Remember, we're trying to put together the likely probabilities of the next swing unfolding in price, and then assessing the odds of the trend continuing or reversing via insights from momentum. We will use information to trade within the price swings when we find a specific low-risk, high probability entry given the trend and momentum characteristics on the chart.

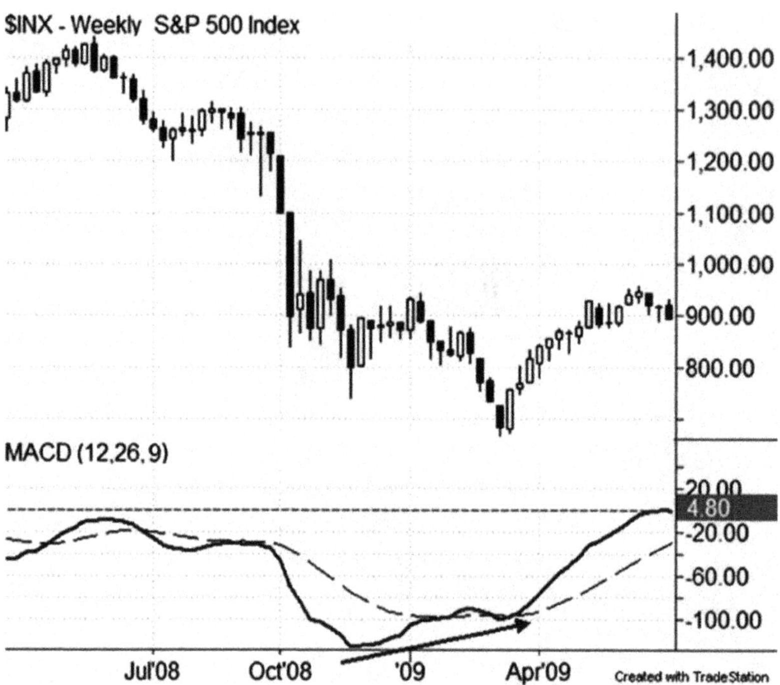

FIGURE 2.11 Single Swing Positive Momentum Divergence Revealed through the Standard 12, 26, 9 MACD Oscillator

While a single swing momentum divergence is a warning signal, a triple (or multiple) swing momentum divergence is a stronger signal that the trend is likely to reverse as momentum declines near an eventual price peak. Single swing divergences are often take-profits signals for traders, while multiple swing divergences can serve as a reversal-style trade entry signal, usually when combined with a reversal candle, price pattern, or some other chart signal from classic technical analysis. As such, we want our momentum oscillator of choice to highlight momentum confirmations and divergences as soon as possible in order to assess the trend health (or deterioration) quickly.

The purpose of the indicator is to highlight the momentum characteristics of the trend using the principles of physics as they relate to objects in motion. We are not using indicators to find overbought or oversold conditions in the market, nor are we using the indicators themselves to generate isloated buy or sell signals (such as a cross above or beneath the zero line). In using momentum oscillators to discern momentum, the zero line becomes irrelevant and we focus only on oscillator extremes (highs and lows) as they relate to respective price extremes (highs and lows). First we assess the trend, then we assess the health of the trend, and from that assessment we make decisions about where to buy and sell based on the price itself, though we will discuss specifics of entry and exit in later chapters.

WHERE MOMENTUM IS STRONGEST

As we have reached the end of Chapter 2, you now have the knowledge of the importance of identifying trend structure and confirming your assessment by identifying the momentum conditions that support a current trend in place. Understand that the momentum principle builds upon your analysis of a prevailing trend in two ways: we look for momentum to be strongest at the start of a new trend, particularly with a 'Kick-off' in the oscillator to form confirmations with price, and then as a trend matures over time we look for non-confirmations of recent prices through momentum divergences, which hint that odds now favor a reversal in trend as momentum weakens ahead of actual reversals.

As a trader, you must develop a narrative of price as revealed through the price chart that tells the story of the underlying supply/demand relationship between buyers and sellers. Specifically, you want to know the current price trend as well as the strength of a price trend in motion. Momentum is strongest at the earliest stage of a trend and weakest at the latter stages just prior to a trend reversal, in the same way that a ball accelerates fastest when leaving your hand and slows down its rate of ascent prior to its final peak and return to earth. We can say that the ball formed a negative momentum divergence at the high (apogee) prior to returning to earth, which is similar to a classic move in a stock price trend. Momentum tends to fall ahead of the actual price fall, or in the case of the tennis ball, momentum declines while the ball still rises to its peak.

By identifying the trend structure and assessing the underlying momentum principles that exist under the surface of price (namely in your momentum oscillator), you can find specific trade setups that correspond well with key points in the trend structure and enhance your trading results and confidence of a successful trade outcome.

While the Trend Continuity and Momentum principles are essential to your education as a trader, there is one more foundation price principle you must understand, and we turn now to the Price Alternation Principle in Chapter 3. After all, price on a chart can travel up, down, or sideways, and we have not effectively addressed sideways motion yet.

CHAPTER 3

Price Alternation Principle

So far, we have covered the Trend Continuity Principle and the Momentum Principle that underscore price behavior. These help build a foundation for why we expect certain price moves in the future, which provides an edge to use for entering and exiting low-risk trades. In this chapter, we will discuss the third foundation principle of price behavior, which is described as the Price Alternation Principle. This principle covers the periods of time a stock is trading in a sideways trading range as opposed to a persistent up or down trend on the charts.

While separate from the trend continuity and momentum principles, the price alternation principle helps us to understand range alternation between contraction phases and expansion phases in the price structure. After all, you've almost certainly heard that price on charts can travel in three types of trends: up, down, or sideways. Most traders discover that the easiest opportunities for profits come from up or down trending moves. In fact, many traders gain steady profits during up-trending periods but then lose money consistently as a stock devolves into a lengthy sideways trend.

This chapter will explain how to recognize and position yourself within the context of a trading range on the charts. We will learn how to identify horizontal support and resistance price lines, how to trade within them, and what to do when price breaks free of its trading range. Finally, the Price Alternation Principle lays the foundation for all the price breakout trading strategies you will employ as a trader.

DEFINING THE PRINCIPLE

The Price Alternation Principle simply states that price alternates between two distinct phases: range contraction and range expansion. One could also define these phases as a trend phase and an anti-trend phase. The two separate phases help us discern what indicators to emphasize and which to ignore, as certain indicators are better suited for a sideways range-bound or a trending range expansion environment. This principle explains why some indicators work well for a period of time and then generate a string of losing trades, which new traders often report as being one of the most frustrating aspects of trading. It answers the question "Why does a particular indicator work really well for me and then all the sudden generate a string of constant losses?"

PRICE ALTERNATION PRINCIPLE

Price alternates between the states of range expansion and range contraction.

Range Contraction: When price has formed a sideways compression phase that either takes the form of a rectangle with clearly defined horizontal trendline boundaries or a triangle pattern with converging trendlines.

Range Expansion: When price breaks outside the boundaries of a range and enters a period of sustained upward or downward movement, characterized with a momentum impulse or directional trend movement.

The price alternation principle addresses those periods between directional trend moves in price where a market or stock consolidates a recent directional trend move into a temporary or lengthy sideways correction phase, where price is said to digest or consolidate after a recent directional move.

It is helpful to think of the principle in terms of using the current phase to anticipate the next change in price. Recall that the momentum principle states that if price and momentum form a higher high together, then we can expect a higher high in price yet to come after an immediate pullback. Similarly, by monitoring the current price structure, we can then anticipate the next likely move in price according to this principle. If price is in a contraction phase with clear trendlines right now, then we can expect a price range breakout to develop soon in the future to carry price in a sustained directional move—up or down—once price breaks outside of these price trendline boundaries. Such an expectation creates an edge that allows us to anticipate and then place price breakout trades from range compression environments, such as trading triangle, rectangle, or other specific price pattern breakouts. This principle underscores the logic of trading triangle and rectangle pattern breakouts which we will discuss in Chapter 5 on specific price patterns.

First, let us formally define the two states of price behavior before we see examples of the concept.

PRICE CONTRACTION PHASE

As we begin our discussion on the price alternation principle, let us first start with describing the state of price consolidation. Throughout the discussion, we will use the words contraction and consolidation interchangeably to mean a period of low volatility, low range price movement. A market in consolidation contains clearly defined boundaries of support and resistance price levels, which are easily identified by hand-drawn price trendlines. In fact, the best indicator you can use to highlight support and resistance during a trading range period is self-drawn price trendlines.

You don't need complex mathematics or indicators to reveal important reference levels on the chart. Price areas that have held as key support or resistance in the past often hold as future support or resistance levels, and these should be obvious but they can be obscured by numerous indicators on the price chart itself.

Figure 3.1 shows the three terms you need to know when describing a market in a consolidation phase.

Figure 3.1 is a pure price chart that emphasizes how to label the three main points of reference in a trading range or price consolidation. As we will see from the example in Figure 3.2, \$54.00 per share represents the upper resistance line, the price where buyers and sellers deem price to be expensive; \$52.00 represents the fair value or midpoint price where buyers and sellers agree that the price is fair; and \$48.00 represents the lower

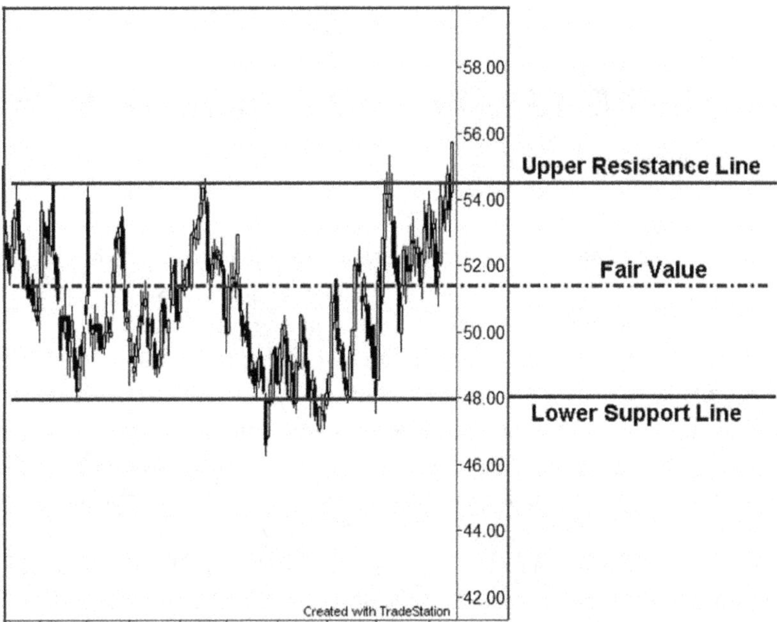

FIGURE 3.1 Definitions Used in Describing a Consolidation Phase

FIGURE 3.2 ERTS During a Clear Consolidation Phase in 2007

support line where buyers and sellers generally agree that price is cheap, or a bargain to buy because it is beneath the agreed fair value price.

PRICE CONSOLIDATION PHASE

There are several terms used to define the price consolidation phase, including the upper resistance line, the midpoint or fair value line, and the lower support line.

Upper Resistance Line: The higher resistance trendline at which buyers and sellers deem the price to be too expensive to purchase, which is usually where buyers take profits and refuse to pay a higher price to acquire more shares and sellers enter new short-sale positions in anticipation of price declining to the fair value line or lower.

Midpoint or Fair Value Line: The average price between the upper resistance line and lower support line where buyers and sellers agree on the current price of a share of stock. This price represents equilibrium or balance between buyers and sellers and is considered a reasonable price to use as a reference for what is cheap or expensive.

Lower Support Line: The lower support trendline at which buyers and sellers deem the price to be inexpensive, cheap, or under fair value. This is often the price where buyers will step into the market to purchase shares and short sellers will buy back to cover short positions with the expectation that price will return again to the fair value line or higher.

Figure 3.2 shows us the actual stock price chart and the context surrounding the labeled trading range or price consolidation that formed through most of 2007 in Electronic Arts (ERTS).

In this example, we see price in a clear expansion or directional trend phase during the latter part of 2006 that then devolves into a sideways trading range throughout the majority of 2007. By April 2007, the boundaries between buyers and sellers become clear as to what market participants deem expensive and cheap in terms of buying and selling shares of ERTS. The chart is also a good representation of the price alternation principle, in that a phase of range contraction or compression follows a phase of price range expansion, or directional trend movement.

Once you observe two tests of a trendline, it is often safe to draw a trendline and extend that line into the future. By March 2007, we could observe three quick tests (touches) of the $54.00-per-share level, along with three tests of the $48.00-per-share level, which defined a potential trading range with established reference boundaries for the upper resistance and lower support boundaries. As long as price remains within these horizontal trendlines, traders can take advantage of these boundaries by buying as price tests the lower support trendline and then selling, or aggressively selling short, as price rises to the upper resistance line. That is the most common strategy a trader uses when trading within the confines of a trading range or price consolidation phase.

In general, a trader would place a stop-loss order slightly beyond the upper or lower trendline, giving a bit of breathing room for sudden breaks outside the barrier that fail to sustain an actual breakout move. This happened a few times when price broke down from the $48.00 level, only to rise back into the trading range in what traders call a "bear trap." A bear trap occurs when price breaks down through a known reference support level, but then almost immediately rises back within the confines of the trading range, thus trapping those traders who established a short-sale position on the suspected breakout. Similarly, a bull trap occurs when price slightly breaks above the upper resistance line and returns back under the horizontal trendline.

If one strategy is to trade within the confines of the price consolidation boundaries, then what might be the alternate strategy once a trader recognizes a clear trading range phase exists? The alternate strategy is to wait in anticipation of a breakout and enter a position on a clean breakout from the trading range boundary, in anticipation of the second stage of the price alternation principle: a price expansion phase.

PRICE EXPANSION PHASE

We can expect a range expansion phase to follow a range consolidation phase. As traders, we look to make the quickest profit most efficiently, and price breakouts, or price-range expansion plays, often accomplish this goal of being in the market (a trade) the shortest amount of time to capture the largest price move available.

Established price trading ranges contain well-defined boundaries where traders generally agree on reference prices that are fair, expensive, or cheap. Traders know where to enter a position, where to sell it, and where to place a stop in the event that a range breakout move occurs to take price outside the trading range. In essence, these boundaries become self-fulfilling prophecies that create the expected moves up off of support or down from overhead resistance.

In a range expansion phase, traders lose these easily defined reference areas and become uncertain as to whether to enter a new position for a profit, take an old position off for a loss, or stand aside and wait for a better entry. Traders often report that they cannot buy a breakout move because they feel they are chasing the move, which means they feel uncomfortable buying a new price extreme because they suspect the exact moment they enter a position will be the moment the market movement will reverse, trapping them suddenly with a losing position. Unfortunately, they stand on the sidelines without a position as price continues higher and higher as they watch the move expand beyond where they thought price would travel.

It is very important to make this distinction: in a trading range, range boundaries are well-defined and traders can plan positions logically, while in a range expansion breakout phase, logic escapes them and emotion takes over as participants no longer have the comfort of clean reference levels to guide their trading decisions.

A market in expansion continues to expand until buyers and sellers reach a new equilibrium in price and then establish new boundaries or reference levels as to what is expensive or cheap in reference to the new equilibrium. It's helpful to define range compression phases as states of equilibrium between buyers and sellers and range expansion phases as states of disequilibrium or uncertainty. Think back to the physics of motion when describing prices in motion and the balance, or imbalance, between buyers and sellers as being the impulse that drives prices of stocks higher and lower over time. A market with a higher supply/demand imbalance will develop a larger range expansion move than one with a smaller imbalance.

The key point to remember as you understand the concept is that range contraction phases reflect stable boundaries of low volatility, while price expansion phases reflect uncertain boundaries and high volatility. Figure 3.3 shows us what happened to Sears Holdings (SHLD) in mid-2007 after a rising price consolidation phase gave rise to a sharp price expansion phase to the downside.

Note that price contraction phases in a stock do not have to take the form of perfect horizontal boundaries. The fair value price, and thus the upper and lower trendline price boundaries, can rise or fall over time in an angled direction (slope) as the market participants determine what represents the fair value price trendline. In the case of triangles, which we will see in Chapter 5, the fair value line remains constant while the upper and lower trendlines converge toward the fair value price trendline or midpoint.

From October 2006 to June 2007, Sears Holdings (SHLD) maintained a rising consolidation phase on its daily chart as drawn in Figure 3.3 with the upper resistance line rising over time from \$185.00 to \$195.00 and the lower support line rising over time from \$170.00 to \$180.00. With the exception of a few price spikes outside of these boundaries,

FIGURE 3.3 Range Expansion and Contraction Phases in Sears Holdings Daily 2007

buyers and sellers contained the stock price between these two lines during a range consolidation phase after the large price expansion move from $135.00 to $180.00 per share from July to October 2006. Remember, price alternates between periods of range expansion and contraction, as you can see in the daily chart.

Buyers and sellers had the stable reference lines to guide their trading decisions until price firmly broke down from the rising support line at the $180.00-per-share level in June 2007. When price breaks outside of established trendlines, buyers and sellers lose their concept or anchor of what is cheap or expensive. Price can fall rapidly in a range expansion environment as buyers and sellers seek to establish equilibrium, and sometimes that equilibrium will be at a much lower price. In this case, price fell from $180.00 in June 2007 to $130.00 per share in August 2007 as buyers and sellers then began to establish another trading range or equilibrium environment at the $137.00-per-share level. Notice the large price gap in July 2007 that accompanied the range expansion move to the downside and the higher volatility environment of the range expansion impulse move down.

Surprise economic news or announcements often serve as the catalyst that drives price outside these boundaries and triggers a range expansion move from a sudden supply/demand imbalance. Remember our discussion on Newton's Laws of Motion in Chapter 2, where the first law stated that an object at rest tends to stay at rest until another object or force acts upon it. We can relate laws of motion to price motion by defining a trading range as prices being in a state of rest or equilibrium and any force, be it a news event, earning surprise, or any market-moving event that affects buyers' and sellers' perception of fair value, as being the catalyst to set prices in motion in a range breakout expansion phase. We then tie in the second law of motion, defined as the Momentum Principle in Chapter 2, to help us conceptualize a market in motion and how a market moves in the same (trend) direction until another force, often revealed through momentum divergences, slows the move until buyers and sellers find another equilibrium price zone which then gives rise to a new trading range consolidation phase at a higher or lower level.

It is vitally important to understand how these concepts give rise to price movement which then gives us specific expectations about the next likely move in price, and thus enter, manage, and exit positions with a solid conceptual framework that underlies our trades. We will discuss how to use this concept to set up trades in later chapters, but for now, understand the logic behind price consolidation phases and price expansion phases.

Here is another example to highlight the concept of range consolidation and expansion, as seen in Figure 3.4 of eBay's (EBAY) daily chart from 2009.

Starting with the transition into 2009, we see a descending range consolidation phase between buyers and sellers of eBay stock with the trendlines and fair value area drawn. Price then breaks to the upside in a sharp and quick range expansion move, including two daily price gaps, in April 2009. Participants then form a small trading range or

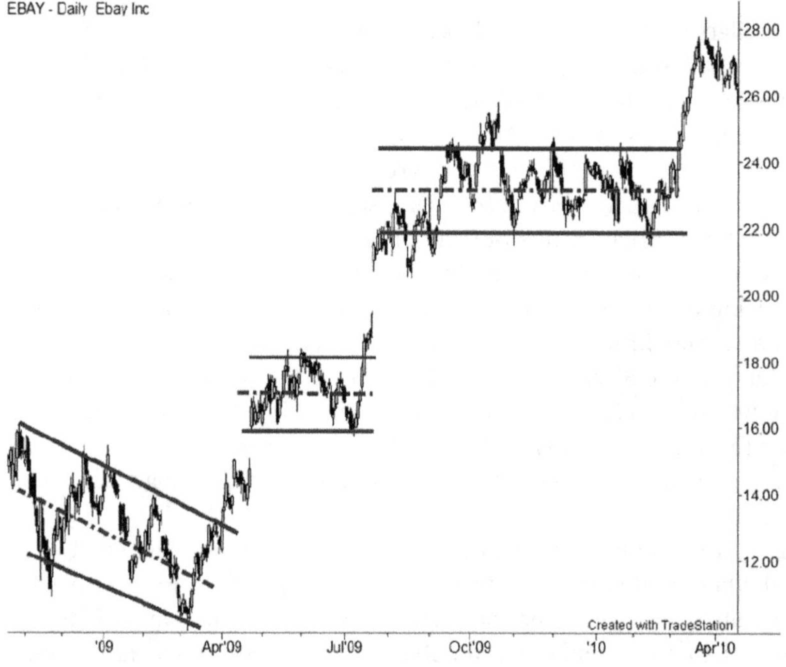

FIGURE 3.4 Range Expansion and Contraction Phases in eBay Daily 2009

consolidation phase—which resembles an island—from May to July, and then buyers overtook sellers in another sudden range expansion impulse move up, including a large gap in July. Buyers and sellers then find equilibrium or fair value at $21.00 per share with the upper resistance line residing just above $24.00 per share and the lower support line resting at the $22.00-per-share level. This trading range continued from August 2009 to March 2010, at which point buyers again overtook sellers in another sharp range expansion impulse move to the $28.00-per-share level in March 2010.

The chart of eBay reveals that price in expansion phases can be volatile periods comprised of overnight gaps as buyers and sellers struggle to find value without the help of established boundaries. A range expansion phase changes the parameters of what is cheap or expensive. For example, in early 2009, $14.00 per share reflected an expensive price for buyers of eBay stock. However, after a range expansion phase a few months later, buyers and sellers agreed that $16.00 per share was cheap and beneath fair value. That definition itself changed after the sharp expansion in July, at which point the former upper resistance line at $18.00 was now deemed well beneath the new price level defined as cheap: $22.00 per share.

The quest to find value can be violent, with large range expansion days and overnight gaps as a market enters a feedback loop, which is the next concept we will discuss to help us understand sudden price moves that occur in a stock. But before we define feedback loops, let's take a step back and define how buyers and sellers interact to move prices.

VIEWING THE MARKET AS BUYERS AND SELLERS

While there certainly are a myriad of forces that act upon a stock, it can be helpful to narrow down those forces—market participants from hedge funds, mutual funds, swing traders, day traders, long-term investors, retirement account investors, professionals, and amateurs—into the broader categories of buyers and sellers. Throughout this discussion, I will use the terms "buyer" and "bull" interchangeably to mean an individual (or fund) that purchases shares in anticipation of a future upward move, just as I will use the term "seller" and "bear" interchangeably to mean an individual (or fund) who wishes to sell shares already purchased or to bet on a price decline through the activity of short selling in hopes of buying back a stock at a lower price.

If we oversimplify the market into buyers and sellers, we arrive at the following concepts or broad labels for market participants. A buyer, or a bull, purchases shares in hopes that the price of the stock will be higher in the future so that he or she can sell those shares at a higher price for a profit. The individual will also sell the purchased shares at a loss if the price of the stock falls beyond where he or she is comfortable holding on to the position, perhaps at a predetermined stop-loss price. Thus, we can think of a buyer today as a future seller.

On the other hand, traders sell-short a stock at a price today that they hope to be able to buy back to cover the borrowed shares they sold short at a profit in the future.

Buyer

A person who buys shares of stock in the hopes that the share price will rise. A buyer can also be defined as a future seller.

Seller

A person who sells stocks that are already purchased, hopefully at a profit, but also potentially at a loss if the value has declined.

Short seller

A person who sells stock short, borrowing shares, in the hopes that price will decline so as to buy back the shares at a lower price for a profit. A short-seller will also be forced to 'buy to cover' if price rises unexpectedly. Thus, a short seller can also be defined as a future buyer.

Short-sellers hope to profit from declines in stock prices. Thus, we can classify a short seller today as a future buyer. A short seller will buy back borrowed shares at a profit if the share price declines in the future, or will also be forced to buy back the shares to cover the short position at a loss if the price of the stock rises to the predetermined stop-loss price, or if the broker issues a margin call for the borrowed shares.

We can then separate actions from intentions to further understand how prices move and how market participants affect the price of stocks. A new buyer willingly buys shares of a stock, hoping price will rise so he or she can sell it in the future for a profit An old buyer willingly sells the shares purchased previously if the price of the stock rose and the buyer is taking profits, perhaps at a predetermined price target. On the other hand, an old buyer unwillingly, or forcefully, must sell his or her shares at a loss in the event that the price of the stock has declined beyond the predetermined stop-loss price, or when the pain of loss is greater than the hope of the position recovering if the individual has let the stock fall beyond the predetermined stop-loss price. Two buyers may sell their shares at the same price, though one may sell happily with a profit while the other sells unhappily with a loss.

A new short seller willingly initiates a new short-sell position when he or she believes that the price of a stock will decline in the future, and if so, the short seller willingly buys back the borrowed shares at a profit. On the other hand, if the price of the stock rises either beyond the predetermined stop-loss price, or beyond the pain threshold where the individual can no longer bear the pain of losing money if price has moved far beyond an established stop-loss price, then the old short seller will be forced buy back shares unwillingly to cover the borrowed shares at a loss.

A trader has leeway about where to enter a position, and can do so after great deliberation, perhaps only when all signals align. If the trader feels the stars do not align on the chart, then no one will force the trader into a position. Traders are far less likely to panic into a position than they are to panic out of a position, and you can use this knowledge to your advantage if you can identify this behavior on the price charts: it is critical to make this distinction.

While traders will likely enter at different levels when they believe everything is perfect timing for a position, most traders tend to cluster their stop-loss orders together at the same price level, especially within the context of a sideways trading range. In the event that a market enters this cluster of stop losses that affect traders positioned the wrong way, a sudden impulse burst may occur to ignite a price breakout of a trading range, creating a feedback loop, forcing one group of traders to rush for the exits as another group rushes to enter new positions for the developing breakout.

FEEDBACK LOOPS

Price movements in stocks occur mainly due to supply and demand imbalances between buyers and sellers, and it helps to oversimplify market participants as such. As in physics, once an object is set in motion, it is easier to keep the object moving than it is to stop and reverse the object. In life, we are aware of two distinct cycles or feedback loops that we call virtuous cycles (or circles) to describe a string of good events that lead to other good outcomes or alternatively vicious cycles (or circles) that are a string of bad events that lead to further negative outcomes. These feedback loops also occur in the stock market. One of the best sources to learn more about feedback loops in the stock market is from Robert Shiller's discussion in his book *Irrational Exuberance* regarding the buying frenzy that took stocks to unfathomable highs via positive feedback loops, particularly technology stocks, in the run-up to the 2000 peak.

Positive Feedback Loops

Positive feedback loops refer to one event leading to a similar outcome, and then those outcomes lead to similar events that produce the same outcome. Keep in mind that, despite the term 'positive,' the outcome and perpetual motion might not necessarily be considered positive or good: it depends on your perspective and current position. The term "positive" refers to perpetual motion, rather than in the context of anything good or bad.

In the stock market, a positive feedback loop is characterized by sustained price movement in one direction, usually as one side of the market dominates the other, such that higher prices lead to increasingly higher prices just as lower prices lead to increasingly lower prices. Market participants react to new prices and then react again to newer prices, and then react in the same way to even newer prices in a perpetual loop that propels price movement in a sustained direction.

In a breakout expansion price move to the upside, the positive feedback loop may begin initially with a price breakout above an upper resistance line at which time both new buyers push the price higher beyond the breakout level which in turn causes those who hold short positions to buy back to cover their positions at a loss, particularly if they placed a stop just above the resistance line. Once price has broken above the resistance price, it may lead buyers who did not participate in the initial breakout to buy price once they feel safe that the stock is indeed breaking above the resistance level and will not lead to a bull trap. As new buyers push prices higher, old short sellers cover additional short-sold positions, convinced as well that price is truly breaking above resistance. Their buying to cover their short position at a loss further drives the price higher. Perhaps the price breakout triggers alerts or shows up on other traders' scans, which causes more bulls to step in and buy the stock, which now is caught in a positive feedback loop and thus breakout impulse move to the upside. The higher prices cause more short sellers, who remain stubbornly short despite price moving beyond their initial stop-loss price, to cover, thus driving the price even higher. A positive feedback loop in price will continue until sidelined bulls cease buying price (no more buyers), bulls currently in a position begin taking profits perhaps at an upside price target (old buyers become new sellers), or those who remain short have bought back all of their borrowed shares at a loss (old bears cease buying to cover).

Though this example shows a positive feedback loop to the upside, the situation occurs in reverse when a breakout impulse move sends price lower in a positive feedback loop where bears are shorting to profit from future declines in price, which leads bulls to sell their shares at a loss, which then triggers more bears to short the down-move in progress, which in turn triggers more bulls (old buyers) to liquidate their shares as price travels steadily lower.

In simplistic terms, think of a positive feedback loop to the upside as bulls buying willingly along with bears buying to cover positions unwillingly, often at a loss. A positive feedback loop to the downside is thus characterized by bears short-selling willingly and bulls selling shares (liquidating) unwillingly, usually at a loss. Another way to think of a positive feedback loop might be to state that higher prices lead to higher prices, which then lead to higher prices; or to the downside, lower prices lead to lower prices, which then lead to lower prices. Understanding positive feedback loops helps you to understand why price can move in a lengthy trend range expansion move over time, especially when breaking free of a lengthy, established sideways trading range.

Negative Feedback Loops

It is very important that you distinguish between directional bias in a positive and negative feedback loop. A negative feedback loop does not mean that price is heading lower in a breakout move. Instead, negative feedback loops describe what happens during a price consolidation or contraction phase. We can restate the price alternation principle in terms of feedback loops. Instead of saying price alternates between periods of range expansion and contraction, we can declare that price moves between periods of negative and positive feedback loops.

During a range contraction phase, price boundaries are clearly defined between the upper resistance line, lower support line, and the value area or midpoint price. This gives both bulls and bears—buyers and sellers—a clear reference for what to expect and how to position when price comes into one of these price reference levels. As such, a price rise into a known resistance area does not lead to short sellers covering, as a higher price would do during a positive feedback loop. Bears generally do not panic as price rallies into an overhead resistance level, but only when price breaks unexpectedly above that reference level. Instead, the higher prices attract new short sellers in combination with old buyers who purchased shares at lower prices taking profits at the upper price resistance level. As such, the higher prices attract sellers, which then lead to lower prices. As price then falls to the lower support line, old short sellers cover their positions at a profit and new bulls buy stock in anticipation of a bounce higher off support. Thus, lower prices lead to higher prices.

This is the best way to conceptualize a negative feedback loop: higher prices bring out sellers, which drives price lower, which brings out buyers, which drives price higher. Or to further simplify the definition, we can say higher prices lead to lower prices, and lower prices lead to higher prices—usually during the context of a trading range or consolidation environment. Contrast this with a positive feedback loop where higher prices lead to higher prices and vice versa during a price expansion phase.

FEEDBACK LOOPS

Feedback loops refer to cycles of events that create perpetual motion as buyers and sellers interact with each other via developments on the price charts.

Positive Feedback Loop: Higher prices lead to higher prices which lead steadily to higher prices in a range breakout mode to the upside. Bulls purchase shares willingly and the higher prices cause bears to buy-back shares to cover positions unwillingly. Similarly, lower prices lead to lower prices, which lead steadily to lower prices in a range breakout mode to the downside. Bears sell shares short willingly and the lower prices cause bulls to sell shares unwillingly.

Negative Feedback Loop: Higher prices lead to lower prices which lead to higher prices in the context of a trading range or consolidation phase. A price rally into resistance causes bears to sell shares short willingly for an expected future profit as buyers sell shares willingly, taking profits into resistance. As price then falls to a lower level, short-sellers buy-back shares willingly at a profit and bulls buy shares willingly in anticipation of a future rally off support.

Figure 3.5 shows Apple Inc. (AAPL) through two cycles of negative and positive feedback on its daily chart throughout 2008 and 2009.

Though Apple is a volatile stock, it is not immune from the price alternation principle. Figure 3.5 shows us two instances of range expansion in a positive feedback loop, along with two phases of range contraction in a negative feedback loop in the one-year period from mid-2008 to mid-2009.

Beginning in mid-2008, we see that buyers and sellers have established a declining value area along with a declining upper resistance and lower support lines. Price moved between these boundaries until sellers ejected the price lower starting with a breakout in

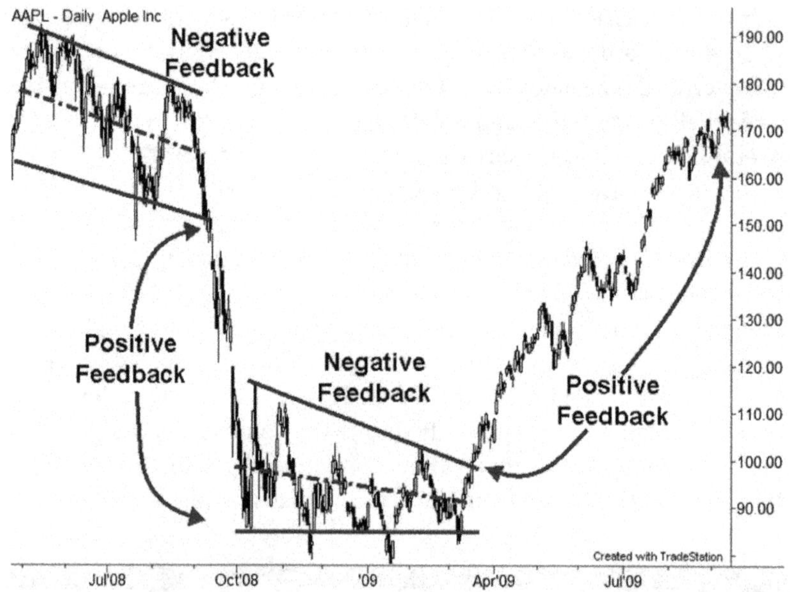

FIGURE 3.5 Positive and Negative Feedback in Apple Inc. during 2008 and 2009 Daily chart

September 2008 at the $150.00-per-share level. This range breakout and price impulse to the downside perpetuated a positive feedback loop as short sellers sold shares to profit from the down move and buyers sold stocks to limit losses as price plunged to the downside. Buyers who failed to limit their losses experienced larger losses, which intensified the selling pressure for those holding shares as price continued its range expansion play to the downside.

However, price cannot remain in a range expansion phase forever. Eventually price will stabilize as the lower prices entice new buyers to purchase shares in an attempt to 'catch a falling knife' or buy as close to the lows as possible. In fundamental analysis terms, eventually price will fall so far beneath fair value that long-term investors will begin a campaign of accumulation as the stock trades beneath their assessment of long-term fair value of what a share of Apple should be worth, taking into consideration all company valuation statistics.

Price entered a bottoming process that stretched from October 2008 to the range breakout in March 2009. This bottoming process revealed a new fair value price at the $90.00-per-share level, with a lower support line stabilizing horizontally at the $85.00-per-share level and an upper resistance line stabilizing but declining at the $100.00-per-share level. Buyers and sellers pushed price between these boundaries in a negative feedback loop, where higher prices encouraged selling above $90.00 and lower prices under $90.00 encouraged buying.

This range consolidation or contraction phase ended with the price breakout in late March 2009, which put shares of Apple again on a positive feedback loop, this time to the upside as buyers were rushing to purchase shares as price trended higher and short sellers were forced to cover any remaining short positions in the stock to limit mounting losses. Price formed a very short-term range consolidation for the month of June 2009 with a fair value price at $140.00, but buyers continued to push price higher in a continuation of the positive feedback loop and range expansion phase that began in March 2009.

The Case of Sears Holdings (SHLD)

Like Apple in Figure 3.5, shares of Sears Holdings (SHLD) exemplified the concept of the Price Alternation Principle with a similar transition from the range phases as buyers and sellers interacted. Instead of showing the full chart, we will focus on how price transitioned through these phases and what trading opportunities a savvy trader or investor could have employed with a firm knowledge of this principle.

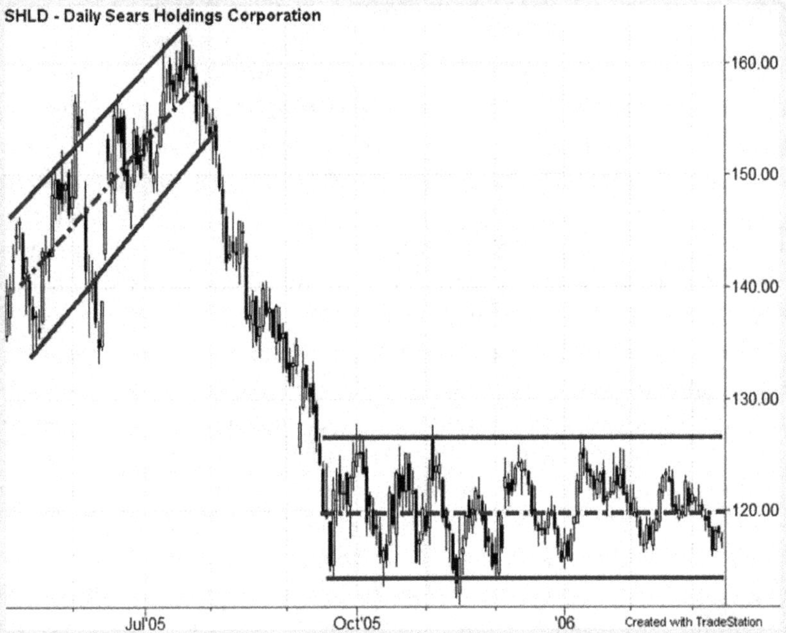

FIGURE 3.6 Range Contraction and Expansion in Sears Holdings through 2005

Figure 3.6 shows us the first phase of the price movement in Sears Holdings on its daily chart for the majority of 2005. Remember that price in a negative feedback or rangebound environment does not have to take the form of a horizontal rectangle; instead, the fair value and upper/lower reference boundaries can be rising or falling. Observe the three components of a trading range when assessing whether the market is in a negative or positive feedback phase: fair-value median line, upper resistance line, and lower support line. If you can draw parallel or converging trendlines with price highs and lows, then you

(Continued)

are likely correctly observing a range consolidation or negative feedback loop occurring in price.

With the exception of two sudden breaks in early June 2005, buyers and sellers kept price contained within the respective rising boundaries as shown from May to July 2005. We expect price to remain within these trendlines, and thus generate trading opportunities for short-term traders, until we see a clean breakout from the established boundaries, which would signal the start of a new breakout or range expansion phase in price. Alternately, traders who wish to take on longer-term positions can avoid trading within a negative feedback environment and wait to establish a position when price breaks through the boundaries and embarks on a range expansion phase.

Price broke the rising lower support trendline and prior swing low at the $150.00-per-share level in early August 2005, signaling a possible short-sale position (or a put purchase for those who prefer trading options on high-priced stocks) with an entry under $150.00 per share. A trader would likely place a stop-loss order near the $155.00 level, which would protect from a larger loss in the event that the breakout was a bear trap. We will discuss the specifics of trade execution, stop-loss placement, and trade management in Chapter 8.

Holding short, a trader could target the prior price support line at the $135.00-per-share level, perhaps expecting a potential bounce higher from that prior price zone. Price did bounce higher for one week, then collapsed back under $135.00, initiating a new confirmation that the positive feedback loop was dominant. Remember, supply and demand imbalances affect price movements, and our goal through using the chart is to assess the dynamics of the relationship between buyers and sellers. In this case, buyers had an opportunity to support price at $135.00, but their failure to do so was an immediate signal that bears were still dominant and that traders who bought at the $135.00 level were now forced to sell their shares at a loss, further exacerbating the positive feedback loop of selling pressure to the downside. Remember, positive feedback loops are characterized by bears short selling willingly and bulls selling to limit losses unwillingly.

Despite the fear and emotions of bulls caught in a downside range expansion phase, price cannot fall to zero unless the company declares bankruptcy or is delisted from an exchange. Barring those two possibilities, the positive feedback loop eventually will break and a new phase of range consolidation or compression will occur. You cannot anticipate where a new trading range will form in advance, but once you see price test a price level two times, you can assume that a trading range is likely forming.

In this case, price tested the $125.00-per-share level three times in the October 2005 period while simultaneously testing the $115.00-per-share level three times also during the same period. It is thus safe to assume that buyers and sellers have established a fair value region between $115.00 and $125.00, with the specific fair-value price being $120.00 that creates an upper resistance reference line at $125.00 and a lower support reference line at $115.00. Position traders—those wishing to play for large targets over time—may consider exiting their short-sale positions established near the $150.00

breakout at the lower support zone of $115.00, perhaps in October or November 2005. These same traders would remain sidelined (not in a position) while buyers and sellers held price between the $125.00 and $115.00 trendlines as a negative feedback loop developed in price. Each time price rallied to $125.00, buyers sold to lock in profits and bears were encouraged to put on a short-sale position to target the lower support line at $115.00. As price traded back down to the $115.00 level, bears were encouraged to cover (buy) their short-sale positions at a profit as bulls were encouraged to buy shares at an established lower support line. This is the hallmark of a negative feedback or range consolidation environment in price.

Price remained within this boundary for the remainder of 2005 and into early 2006. The boundary lines were firmly established with short-term traders playing positions within the $115.00 to $125.00 trading range and position traders waiting patiently for either an upside break to buy or a downside break to short for another range expansion play or positive feedback loop to develop.

Psychology and Trading Ranges

It's best to wait for a confirmed breakout of the trading range rather than trying to guess which direction price will break. This is because if you choose incorrectly, you will be trapped in a potentially violent range expansion phase and lose much more than your stop-loss price. There is also an unrecognized danger to trading within an established range. Once you are certain that price is trading within the boundaries of an established range, you will often achieve a very high win-rate percentage of successful trades if you buy at the lower support line and then sell at the upper resistance line and then sell short at the upper resistance line and buy back to cover your short at the lower support line. A range contraction phase cannot last forever, just as a range expansion phase cannot last forever. When—yes, when, not if—price breaks out of the trading range, you will immediately incur a losing position because your trade was in expectation of the trading range continuing instead of price breaking out of the range, and thus your stop will be outside the boundaries of the trading range. Here is a good example of where psychology trumps probability if you are not careful. A trader who has just experienced six winning trades in a row might doubt the breakout, and thus ignore taking a stop loss when the strategy calls for a stop to be taken. As price continues to move in breakout mode, overconfidence causes the trader to hold short from a position made at the upper resistance line.

If this is a true range breakout, one of two outcomes are likely to happen: first, price is likely to rise rapidly and suddenly as buyers put on new breakout positions and those holding short—not trapped by their emotions—rush to cover their short positions at a small and quantified loss. Second, price is likely to gap significantly higher, leaving all short sellers trapped in a position where price gapped through their predetermined stop-loss price, and now might suffer the classic "deer in the headlights" syndrome of panic where they wonder if they should sell now and accept a larger loss than expected, or continue

(Continued)

holding short in anticipation of price falling back to fill the gap. Neither situation is good for the trader who remains trapped.

Your ability to understand this situation and the Price Alternation Principle in general will make the difference in your ability to take the proper steps if trapped on the wrong side of a range expansion move. Price continues to expand when traders who are trapped on the wrong side of a range breakout move cannot take the emotional pain or rapidly increasing financial losses of price in a positive feedback loop. As more losing traders succumb to this pain and exit their positions with larger losses than they expected, these same traders continue to push price in the direction of the range breakout, which therefore increases the pain of the other traders caught in the wrong direction who stubbornly are still holding on to their positions.

Let us now return to our example of the price movement in Sears Holdings to assess what happened next in price. Figure 3.7 gives us the answer.

FIGURE 3.7 Range Breakout Move in 2006 for Sears Holdings

On the Ides of March, March 15, 2006, Sears Holdings broke sharply upward through its upper resistance line at $126.00 per share, triggering the start of a range breakout expansion phase in price that would later take price back to the $165.00 level seen almost a full year later. Let's envision this move through the thoughts of two separate traders: one who understood the Price Alternation Principle and one who did not.

Two Trader Perspectives

Our first trader understood the range alternation principle and had been waiting eagerly for a price breakout one way or the other to put on a breakout swing or position trade.

The first chance came on the initial break on March 15th, though taking a position right as price breaks out is an aggressive entry tactic. Aggressive traders seek to enter a position as soon as possible, while conservative tactics encourage waiting for confirmation before making an entry. Price formed a strong buy candle that closed at $132.00, which was a stellar $15.00 move up, including the gap, from the prior close on March 14th of $117.00. Conservative-style traders looking for more confirmation can wait for two bars to close outside the breakout level, which occurred the next day on March 16th as price rallied more than $7.00 to close at $139.50. A trader could have looked to enter a position on the next trading session if not already committed long for a breakout play.

A conservative trader, combining the Price Alternation and Momentum principles, could have waited to put on a position when price retraced downward slightly. While this strategy is successful, a powerful breakout from a range consolidation zone may not produce a perfect retracement for you to enter, particularly if the market enters a sharp positive feedback loop where higher highs lead to higher highs without retracements. It will be up to you as you develop your techniques to determine when to enter a breakout position, though we will discuss trade entries in Chapter 8.

Whether our trader entered immediately on the breakout, two closes after the breakout, or on the retracement back to $130.00 in the weeks after the breakout, our trader was committed long to play for a potential range breakout expansion phase, or positive feedback loop in price. The trader was greatly rewarded, as price moved back to the $160.00 level with two minor retracements, which provided good entries in the context of an upward trending market (see Chapter 1 on trend continuity). The trader would continue holding long in a position trade until he was convinced a potential trend reversal or second consolidation phase was forming, which is not shown on the chart.

Our second trader did not fully understand the Price Alternation Principle, but saw a market that had clearly established boundaries and began to trade both short and long within the confines of the trading range. This trader had racked up quick, easy profits and was ready to position into the seventh profitable trade in a row. The trader entered this on March 9 as price returned yet again to the $115.00 level and planned to exit on a retest of the $125.00 level, just the same as for identical setups recently. On the morning of March 15, the trader couldn't believe it! The profit was there, and so a rush to hit the sell button to lock in gains. This was the seventh winning trade in a row! With price now opening up above $125.00, the trader immediately entered a short sale and wrote down in the trading journal a plan to sell if price rallied to $127.00 or $130.00. It wouldn't matter, because there was no way price could get that high—not after the last six instances where sellers pushed price lower at the $125.00 level.

A few hours into the trading day, Sears Holdings rallied to $127.00, then to $130.00. Nervous, our trader was uncertain what to do. Buying back to cover here would lock in a painful $5.00 loss. So the trader decided to continue holding short, assuming this was another typical bull trap. At the close of March 15, the price was above where the plan called for exit, at $132.00.

(Continued)

As the next day's trading session began, the price rose to $133.00, $135.00, and higher. This could not be happening! This was now a $10.00-per-share loss, which translated into $10,000.00 per every 1,000 shares the trader was short. Still unsure of what to do, and certain that price had to come back down, the trader held on though Sears Holdings closed that day just shy of $140.00 per share.

Over the next few weeks, the trader felt justified as the losing position decreased as price fell back toward the entry at the $125.00-per-share level. Another bullet dodged! Price traded back down to $130.00, but all of a sudden, Sears Holdings gapped higher again on April 5. Why didn't our trader cover then? A $15.00 loss had been endured, which now was only a $5.00 loss and back within the risk-controlled parameters.

We'll leave the story there, because our trader was not alone. There were hundreds of other traders who took the same position short and endured the same psychological and financial pain. For some, the threshold of pain was lower than others, and they covered as price began to rise back to $140.00 in early April. Others, either with a higher threshold of pain or a greater sense of stubbornness, held short as price rose back to $145.00, $150.00, all the way to $160.00.

This story helps explain why positive feedback loops exist and how emotions can blind you to what's happening within the price structure. One of the reasons that technical analysis successfully helps assess future potential moves for price is because charts show repeating patterns, and traders—whether bulls or bears—recreate these patterns over time because we react to similar situations in similar ways. An understanding of psychology can help you realize why these patterns form and how you can position yourself to profit from these patterns. Always remember that people—traders and investors—create the chart patterns you see and these patterns reveal insights into the psychology—fear and greed—of the market participants. Your ability to realize these patterns, and your ability to overcome the psychological traps as described in this example, will carry you far on your lifelong journey as a trader.

CHOOSING THE RIGHT INDICATORS

Have you ever wondered why a certain indicator will generate a series of great trades and then all of a sudden begin to trigger a series of failed trades in a row? Have you ever trusted an indicator and then been betrayed by it suddenly? That's likely because certain popular trading indicators that work well in a range consolidation environment will fail miserably when price breaks out in a range expansion environment. This is particularly true with popular overbought and oversold oscillators such as the RSI and Stochastic oscillators. Let's take a quick look at what indicators work best with the two different phases, and how the Price Alternation Principle reveals which indicators to use and which to avoid.

Range Contraction Indicators

Price has a tendency to remain within a consolidation phase longer than it does range breakout expansion phases, and because of that, you may become accustomed to signals from an indicator that is optimized for a range contraction phase in price. This is especially the case when traders purchase black-box trading systems optimized with past-price performance data. When price breaks out of the range and embarks on a range expansion phase, those same indicators on which you became dependent will then fail as price changes character in a breakout mode. This specifically refers to the class of indicators that are overbought/oversold oscillators such as the Stochastic or Relative Strength Index (RSI). Let's now compare these two indicators in a range compression and range expansion phase.

Stochastic and Relative Strength Index: Overbought and Oversold Oscillators The stochastic index and relative strength index (RSI) are two of the most popular oscillators that traders use on their charts. The buy and sell signals are clear to new traders, and deceptively simple. These indicators calculate the current price and measure the past to show price in terms of a percentage of the recent trading period. Traders identify overbought zones if the oscillator registers in the upper range and identify oversold zones if the oscillator registers in the lower range. Traders look to buy positions when the oscillator reveals an oversold signal and then sell shares—or perhaps sell short—when the oscillator registers an overbought reading. For the stochastic, traders consider an indicator value above 80 to be overbought and for the RSI, traders identify an indicator value above 70 to be overbought. For oversold levels, traders look to 20 on the stochastic and 30 on the RSI as the threshold to deem price oversold, and thus look to put on a buy position or cover-short position. A mechanical trading system might look to buy shares when both oscillators register oversold and then sell (or consider selling short) those shares when both oscillators register overbought. Traders can increase or decrease the sensitivity of the indicators by raising or lowering the look-back periods the indicator uses in its calculation. Though the default look-back period for both oscillators is 14 bars, a trader can increase the sensitivity, generating more signals, by shortening the period less than 14, or decrease the sensitivity, generating fewer entry/exit signals, by increasing the period greater than 14. Keep in mind that on a daily chart, 14 bars refers to 14 days while on a weekly chart, 14 bars refers to 14 weeks.

In Figure 3.8, arrows on the RSI and Stochastic with a shortened look-back of five bars (days) indicate when the oscillator enters the overbought or oversold territory. Arrows on the Sears Holdings price chart, which represent trade entries and exits, indicate only when both the RSI and Stochastic are showing the same overbought or oversold reading simultaneously.

Figure 3.8 revisits the same Sears Holdings daily price chart during its range consolidation period throughout the end of 2005. As price enters the trading range officially, both the RSI and stochastic oscillators generate two buy signals that fail to rise to the

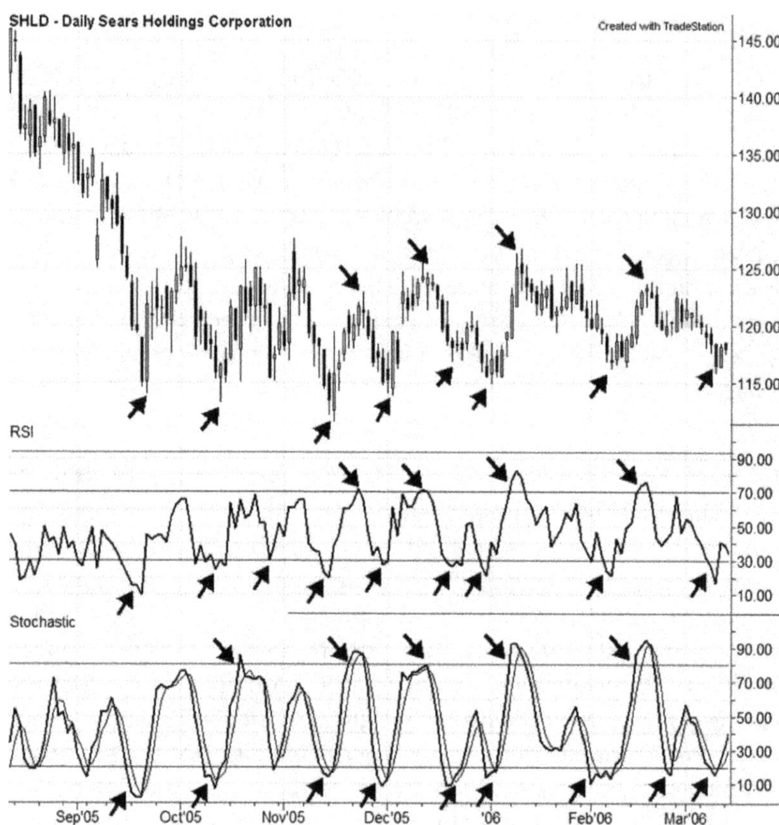

FIGURE 3.8 Signals from the RSI and Stochastic Oscillators in Sears Holdings during the 2005 Trading Range

overbought level to generate a sell signal in early October. However, after these two buy signals, the RSI and stochastic enter their zone of maximum effectiveness as price begins to trade within the confines of the established trading range between $125.00 and $115.00.

From November forward, the oscillators generate very accurate and profitable trading signals, as shown. The main idea is that overbought and oversold oscillators perform best within the confines of an established trading range during a negative feedback, range contraction phase. These can lure traders into a false sense of security or cause them to over-trust the oscillators as magical indicators that point the way to the future. They do not. The indicators are designed to highlight overbought and oversold regions in price, and thus generate suggested positions for you to take. If price remained forever within the confines of a trading range, we would never need any indicator beyond these two oscillators to give us trading signals.

However, price does not remain in a state of range consolidation forever. Let us now pull back the perspective and focus on the numerous failed signals that these oscillators generate while price is in a range expansion phase.

Simultaneous signals in the five-period RSI and stochastic oscillators during the context of the 2005 range expansion sell-off in price and the 2006 range expansion rally are indicated in Figure 3.9. An arrow on the price chart, which represents a corresponding buy or sell signal, appears only when both the stochastic and RSI signal an overbought or oversold position at the same time.

As you can see, during the 2005 sell-off range expansion phase, both indicators generated four disastrous buy (get long) trades in a row. The oscillators signaled that price was in an oversold condition, but in a range expansion phase, price in an oversold condition continues its decline into an even larger oversold condition. This is because of the difference in positive and negative feedback loops and how the oscillators are designed. These overbought or oversold oscillators perform best in a negative feedback environment where price moves between a defined trading range boundary in a range consolidation phase. In a range expansion phase where lower prices lead to lower prices, what is oversold leads to an even deeper oversold condition.

You may have heard the statements "in a bear market, there is no support" and "in a bull market, there is no resistance." You can now rephrase that in terms of positive

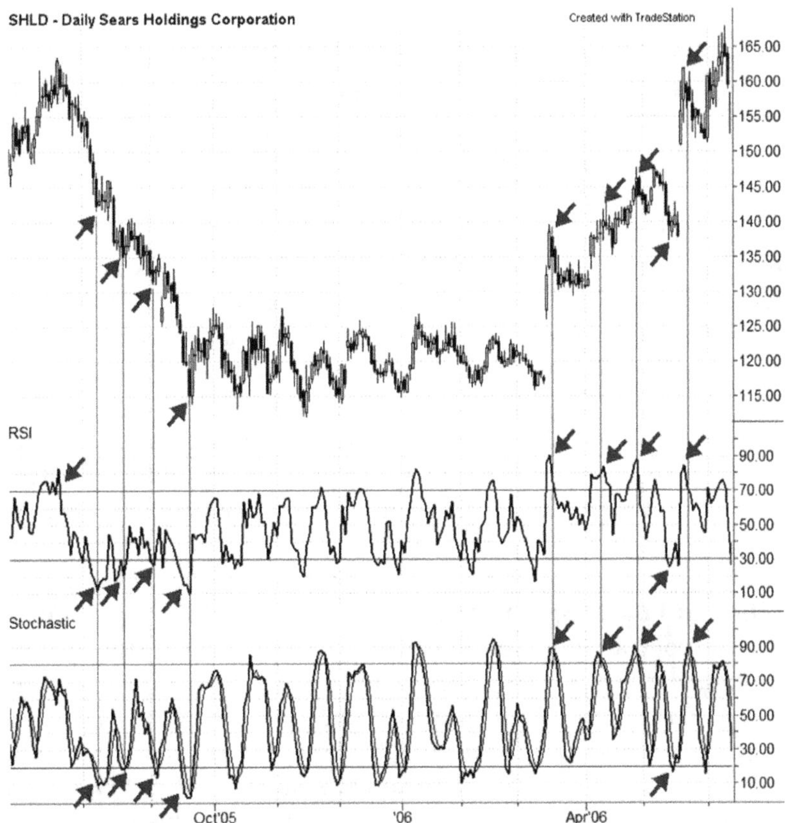

FIGURE 3.9 Signals from the RSI and Stochastic Oscillators in Sears Holdings during the 2005–2006 Price Expansion Phase

feedback loops: "in a positive feedback loop to the downside, there is no oversold" and "in a positive feedback loop to the upside, there is no overbought."

The four signals from the RSI and stochastic in Figure 3.9 would have you buying price at $140.00, then $135.00, then $130.00, and finally $115.00. Notice that these oscillators never gave you an exit signal, and never registered overbought to give you an exit signal. That's because of the way the indicators work. I'll spare you the detailed mathematical explanation of why this is so, but just understand that these oscillators seek to tell you where price is within the most recent look-back period, and if price never rises within the context of a downward trending move, then the indicator can never rise to the overbought condition to give you an exit signal.

The failure of overbought/oversold indicators is also seen during positive feedback loops as price is in a rally phase, as seen by the range expansion period in 2006 in Sears Holdings. Although as seen in Figure 3.8, oscillators perform exceptionally well in a trading range environment, they fail spectacularly in a range expansion environment. Immediately after the breakout, both the RSI and stochastic gave immediate "take profits" or "sell short" signals at the $135.00/$140.00 level but only gave a quick, one-day oversold signal on May 15, 2006 after giving two additional overbought signals as labeled.

During the range expansion phase in Sears Holdings, the stochastic and RSI gave four failed sell-short signals and one overbought buy signal (May 15, 2006). If you study this and similar charts, you may even cynically come to the conclusion that during a range expansion phase, it's best to take the opposite signal than the oscillator generates, meaning sell-short oversold indications in a range expansion phase to the downside or buy overbought indications in a range expansion rally.

Instead of doing that, it's better to eliminate oscillators from your charts during a range expansion phase. You often obtain better entry and exit signals from pure price trendlines than you do from overbought or oversold oscillators during trading ranges. Still, traders who enjoy using indicators must be aware of the conditions when a specific indicator works best or when the indicator is likely to generate false signals. It helps to think of indicators as tools. A hammer works well when striking a nail into a wall, but would not work for turning a screw into an object. You'll obtain more effective trading signals from oscillators during trading ranges instead of breakout range expansion phases.

Bollinger Bands: Volatility and Standard Deviation Indicator Many traders also include the popular indicator Bollinger Bands on their price charts. Despite their popularity and effectiveness, Bollinger Bands find their maximum usefulness in a trading range contraction environment and subsequently fail to generate effective signals in a price breakout environment. John Bollinger created the popular indicator and published a book on the topic entitled *Bollinger on Bollinger Bands.* For those interested in learning more about this indicator, visit his official web site at http://www.bollingerbands.com.

The Bollinger Band indicator takes into account the last 20 periods (or other input setting you choose) and plots the average price, which is the same as the 20-period simple moving average. From there, the indicator calculates the standard deviation of price during the period and then displays two standard deviations above the average price and two standard deviations below the average price. If you brush off your college statistics textbooks, you may remember that in a normal distribution, 95 percent of the observances—in this case prices—will be located within two standard deviations from the mean.

Traders often mistakenly assume that if price is now trading outside of the upper or lower Bollinger Band, then there must be a 95 percent chance that price will return back into the Bands and most likely back to the average price. This is a fallacy because price does not lend itself to the constraints of a normal distribution. Nassim Taleb's book *The Black Swan* explains why price has a tendency to move many times beyond the typical two standard deviations, also called sigma, from the mean. For reference, you may also hear Bollinger Bands called Sigma Bands if a chart shows more than one standard deviation from the mean.

Statistics aside, the Price Alternation Principle has its own explanation of why price does not lend itself to the parameters of two standard deviations from the mean at all points in time. During range contraction or negative feedback periods in the market, Bollinger Bands, like oscillators, generate highly accurate and profitable trading signals as price moves up into the upper band, reverses, and then moves down toward the lower band. Price then touches the lower band and then reverses to travel back to the upper band, giving traders who position themselves accordingly stable profits.

However, once price ejects from the stability of the trading range in a negative feedback loop, price then begins to remain above the upper Bollinger Band or beneath the lower Bollinger Band for the duration of the move as a positive feedback loop develops, never moving to the opposite side of the indicator as expected. It is during these times that traders who use Bollinger Bands identically in all market environments will suffer potentially devastating losses.

Though there are other ways to use the indicator, the most common method most traders use is to determine that if price is at or outside the upper Bollinger Band, then they should take profits by selling shares, or consider putting on a new short-sale position. If price is at or trading beneath the lower Bollinger Band, a trader might look to cover a short-sale position or buy shares to establish a new long position.

Let us see an example of a trading range where Bollinger Bands are very effective in generating profitable trading signals. Figure 3.10 shows us the same example of Sears Holdings in 2005 as price remains in a negative feedback, range compression environment.

Arrows at each of the classic trade entry and exit signals show the positions most traders take when using Bollinger Bands. Traders take buy signals when the price touches or extends briefly outside of the lower Bollinger Band and then take sell signals as price touches or extends briefly outside of the upper Bollinger Band. Bollinger Bands reveal two standard deviations above and beneath the mean, or 20-period moving average.

Like the stochastic and RSI oscillators, the Bollinger Bands generate two buy signals in September and October without a corresponding exit signal. However, once price

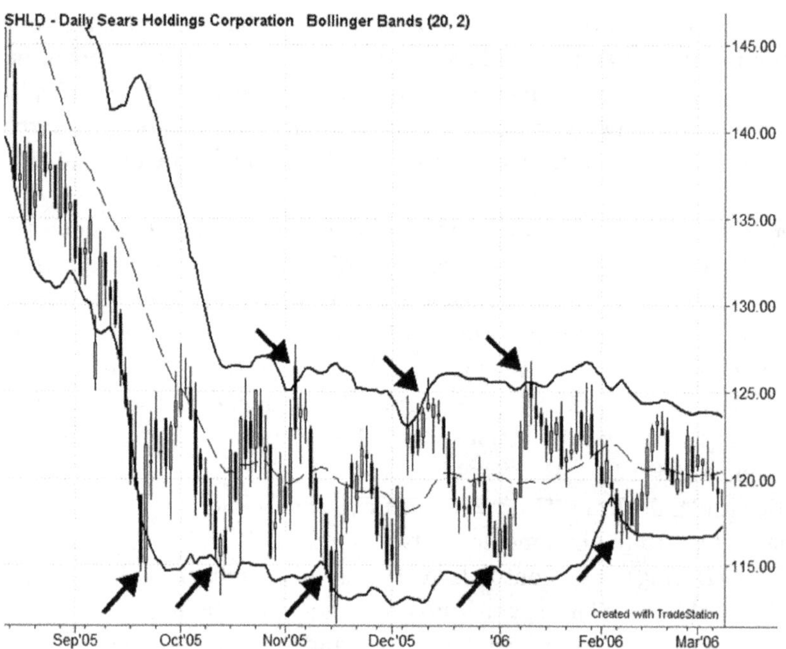

FIGURE 3.10 Signals from Bollinger Bands in Sears Holdings Work during Range Contraction

officially establishes a trading range and negative feedback loop, the Bollinger Band indicator accurately positions us for profitable trades both long and short. Arrows highlight these positions.

As you might already suspect, in the range breakout or price expansion phases of positive feedback between buyers and sellers, the Bollinger Bands, like the overbought/oversold oscillators, generate a string of losses for traders who use these indicators in the classic method.

In Figure 3.11, I have highlighted only the signals that the Bollinger Bands indicate during the two periods of range expansion or positive feedback loops in SHLD's daily price chart. From August to September 2005, price touches or trades beneath the lower Bollinger Band at least five times as price falls from $150.00 to $115.00. A trader who depends exclusively on the Bollinger Band indicator would buy Sears Holdings five times and suffer debilitating losses as a positive feedback loop drove prices lower and lower in a range expansion move.

The same scenario occurs in the opposite direction as price ejects into a range breakout, positive feedback rally loop from March to June 2006. Like the prior decline phase, the Bollinger Bands generate five sell-short (or take profits) signals as price rallies from $130.00 to $165.00 in four months. The Bollinger Bands do give one sudden buy signal in mid-March just as the stochastic and RSI indicators did. You may also notice that on each breakout of the upper Bollinger Band, price did retrace back to the rising 20-period moving average, which would result in profitable trades. However, if you waited for price

FIGURE 3.11 Signals from Bollinger Bands in Sears Holdings Fail during Range Expansion

to move all the way back to the lower Bollinger Band, as would be the trading signal during a range contraction phase, you would not have a chance to exit your short-sale position and would similarly endure large losses as price continued higher in a positive feedback loop to the upside.

Indicators are useful for highlighting potential trading signals, but the RSI, stochastic, and Bollinger Band indicators work best during a range contraction phase and then mislead the trader into large losses during a range breakout trend phase.

Range Expansion Indicators

If there are indicators that do well in range consolidation phases but fail in range breakout expansion phases, there must be indicators that perform well in range expansion phases but then fail in range contraction phases. One such indicator that performs exceptionally well in range expansion moves, also called trend continuity moves, are moving averages as discussed in Chapter 1 on the trend continuity principle. Recall that the Moving Average Method helps define trends, as moving averages are very useful for trend definition and position management.

In a range breakout price expansion, traders often look to establish positions on pullbacks or retracements to key moving averages. These averages also serve as reference points for traders to assess the health of a trend and potential for trend reversal. Let us see how moving averages can guide our trading decisions in the context of a range breakout phase, but lead us woefully astray during a range contraction phase.

Moving Averages From Chapter 1, we noted how traders use moving averages to define trends in the market. Traders often use a short-term, intermediate-term, and a long-term moving average for reference within a trending environment. If the short-term average is greater than the intermediate-term average and both averages are greater than the long-term average, then we would declare that market to be in the most bullish orientation possible. In the opposite structure, if the short-term average is lower than the intermediate-term average and both averages are beneath the long-term average, we would declare that market to be in the most bearish orientation possible.

While you can use any combination of moving averages to satisfy the short-, intermediate-, and long-term averages, I prefer using the 20-exponential, 50-exponential and 200-simple moving averages for my charts. Traders would then look to buy shares on pullbacks to the rising 20- or 50-period moving averages in the context of a range breakout expansion trend phase to the upside, or short pullbacks to the declining 20- or 50-period moving averages in the context of a declining range breakout trend phase.

If price breaks under the intermediate-term average, or the 20-and 50-period averages cross bearishly (the 20 crosses under the 50-period average), then we would interpret this as an early warning of a potential trend reversal yet to come. The same interpretation holds if we see price in a downtrend break above its 50-period average, or the 20-period average cross bullishly above the 50-period exponential moving average (EMA)—we would look at this as an early sign of a potential trend reversal.

Alternatively, if we start to see price consolidate and the short-term and intermediate-term averages converge, then this would signal to us that we are likely entering a range consolidation phase in price and to decrease our reliance on moving averages for trade entries and exits. During a trading range, price will chop above and beyond flat moving averages as if they did not exist. Just as the stochastic and RSI fail in range breakout modes, moving averages will fail in range consolidation modes.

Let us see an example in Figure 3.12, again using Sears Holding for a unified reference of comparison, of how moving averages give great signals during a range expansion phase but then fail to do so during a range contraction phase.

To recap, when price is in a trend move, we look to short retracements in price to the declining 20- or 50-period exponential moving average, and during a trend move to the upside, we look to buy pullbacks to the 20- or 50-period moving average. In Figure 3.12, I label four short-sell signals as price retraced either to the 20- or 50-period moving average, while the averages remained in a bearish orientation that began with a bearish crossover in mid-August 2005. Each retracement led to a profitable short-sale trade.

However, as price ended its range expansion phase and consolidated in a range contraction phase beginning in October and November 2005, the moving averages converged and price traded up and down through these flat moving averages. Price remained in this range contraction phase until the March 2006 breakout, and shortly after the 20- and 50-period moving averages took on a bullish structure and price began forming good

FIGURE 3.12 Buy and Sell Signals using the 20- and 50-day Exponential Moving Averages during Range Expansion Phases SHLD Daily

retracements back to the 20- or 50-period averages, in turn setting up new buy signals. I have highlighted four buy signals starting with early April 2006 that triggered as price retraced to these averages.

During a range breakout phase, look for moving averages to generate low-risk buy or sell signals and to be effective indicators for price structure. However, during a range consolidation phase, moving averages completely lose their value to generate buy and sell signals, as price no longer respects the averages for support or resistance. Look for a clean distance between the short-term and intermediate-term averages as they rise or fall during a range expansion phase and then observe the flattening or consolidation of the moving averages during a range contraction phase in price.

The ADX Indicator: Revealing the Difference in Contraction and Expansion

By now, you're probably wondering if there is any indicator that works well in both range expansion and contraction environments. You may also be asking if there is a specific indicator to tell if you are in a range contraction or expansion environment beyond pure price trendlines. Just remember that there is no perfect indicator for all market conditions, and that almost all indicators are a derivation of price. You will often find the best answers by observing price itself, in terms of drawing trendlines to highlight key price levels and monitoring price as it interacts with those levels.

However, there is an indicator that can give you clues about whether price is in a range contraction or expansion phase, but like all price-based indicators, there is a slight delay in its signal because the math has to catch up with the price action. The ADX may be one of the most mysterious and least understood indicators, but it also can be very helpful in revealing the type of feedback phase—positive or negative—that a particular stock or market is experiencing.

Wells Wilder created the Average Directional Index (ADX), and introduced this indicator to the world in his book *New Concepts in Technical Trading Systems* in 1978. Sparing you the math, the indicator calculates the strength of a trend in place, or reveals the absence of a trend.

The ADX is the average of two separate calculations: the positive directional index which measures the strength of rising prices and the negative directional index which measures the strength of falling prices. If there is a large directional move to the upside, the positive directional index will rise and the negative directional index will fall, thus increasing the average of the two, which comprises the value of the ADX indicator. However, the situation is the same in a falling trend. During a sustained price decline, the negative directional index will rise and the positive directional index will fall, and the larger the distance between the two, the larger the ADX value will be.

This is what is confusing to most new traders: the ADX does not reveal the direction of a price move, but instead reveals its intensity, or specifically the tendency of price to move in one sustained direction. During a range consolidation phase, we do not see directional price movement and the ADX value will decrease as the positive and negative directional indexes converge. Traders generally accept that an ADX value above 30 indicates that price has developed a range expansion phase or trend move, while any value under 20 indicates the lack of a trend. A value under 15 indicates a sustained period of range contraction and a value over 30 indicates a sustained period of range expansion. Once again, let us turn to our example in Sears Holdings (SHLD) through expansion and contraction phases to observe how the ADX indicator performs, as seen in Figure 3.13.

Turning back to our familiar example, we see that the ADX begins the chart in July 2005 under 20 which indicates that price is likely in a range contraction phase. Price then breaks sharply under the lower trendline at the $155.00 level in early August and then the ADX Indicator breaks above the 30 value threshold in late August to indicate that price has now moved into a range expansion mode. The ADX stays elevated above 30 until dropping back under the 30 level in early October as price begins to form a trading range consolidation.

Generally, an ADX reading between 20 and 30 indicates a market in a potential transition phase, so most traders wait for price to break under the 20 value threshold to declare a market officially in a range consolidation phase. The ADX drops under 20 in early November as we can clearly draw trendlines as highlighted in earlier examples at the $125.00 and $115.00 levels. Throughout the entire range consolidation phase, the ADX

FIGURE 3.13 The ADX Indicator during Range Expansion and Contraction Phases in Sears Holdings

remains under 20, and actually stays most of the time under the 15 threshold to define a lengthy range compression phase.

However, price breaks upwards from the consolidation on March 15, 2006, and the ADX rises above the 20 threshold two days later on March 17. The official range expansion signal comes from the ADX on April 5 as the indicator broke above the 30 threshold to signal that price has likely entered a range expansion phase. Throughout the rest of the chart, the ADX remains elevated above 30, peaking near 43 on May 1, indicating the presence of a strong range expansion phase.

Figure 3.14 reveals how the ADX indicator performed during eBay's three range contraction and expansion phases in 2009.

The three range consolidation phases are labeled and horizontal lines are also drawn when the ADX indicator crossed above the 30 threshold to signal a likely range expansion phase in price. Arrows on the ADX indicator highlight where the indicator crossed either beneath 20 to indicate a range consolidation phase or above 30 to indicate a range expansion phase.

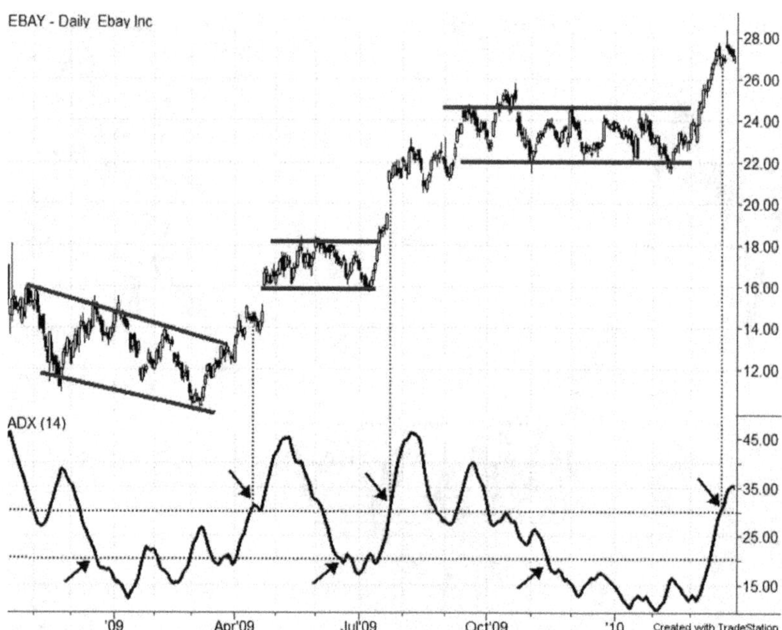

FIGURE 3.14 The ADX Indicator during Range Expansion and Contraction Phases in eBay

The ADX Indicator first dipped under 20 in December 2008 as price consolidated in a slightly downward sloping trading range that led to a quick range expansion phase in April 2009. The ADX indicator rose above 30 shortly after the early April price breakout and then quickly dipped back under 30 then 20 to highlight the May to July range consolidation phase in price. Price gapped higher out of the range, breaking above $18.00 per share and the ADX followed quickly by rising again above 30, only to fall once again under 30, then 20 in November 2009. This time, price remained in a sideways negative feedback loop or range consolidation environment until the breakout on March 5, 2010 and the ADX rose back above 30 to confirm the range expansion mode on March 23, almost a full month later. Remember that all price-based indicators contain a lag or delay due to the mathematical calculations that take place. You're often in a better position to recognize range breakouts by monitoring price and acting on any sudden breakout through the upper resistance line or lower support price as opposed to waiting for an indicator to reveal to you a price breakout or increasing value in the ADX.

In addition to highlighting on your chart likely periods of range expansion or contraction, the ADX is useful for traders who search specifically for compressed stocks that are likely to make a range breakout soon. Using any scanning program, you can scan the universe of stocks for those with ADX values under 20 and then examine their respective stock charts to see if you can draw trendlines to highlight a range contraction phase in price. If so, you can keep those stocks in a separate watchlist and set alerts to notify you when a stock has broken above or beneath a trendline price you set. This way you will be able to keep track of stocks that are potentially ending a range consolidation phase and embarking on a range breakout phase.

Now we have discussed the three foundation price principles and are ready to use these as a stepping stone to build trading strategies, guide our analysis, and find trading opportunities. The next four chapters will build upon these principles using classic methods for identifying low-risk, high probability trade setups to enter and manage. Chapter 4 describes how to read candlestick charts and the popular signals that price reveals through one-bar moves, while Chapter 5 uncovers popular price patterns. From there, Chapter 6 explains how to use Fibonacci retracements to find hidden support or resistance levels within the context of a trending move, and Chapter 7 defines the life cycle of a price move, and where we can expect to find the best trading setups in the broader context.

PART II

Strategies and Tools

CHAPTER 4

Candlestick Charting

Candlestick charts offer a depth of information on supply and demand that visually leaps off the chart at the trader, offering insights that simple bar or line charts do not reveal. Not only can candlestick charts reveal better insight into the current supply and demand balance than traditional bar charts, they can also help us confirm or even trigger entry into a trade setup. As we will see, we do not need to learn intricate or obscure candle patterns, but need only to identify insights into the changing supply/demand relationship between buyers and sellers, particularly at expected turning points such as major support or resistance levels on the charts. A candle trigger can be the final piece of the puzzle that calls for position entry within the context of where the candle signal occurs.

This chapter will explain the benefits of candlestick charts, describe some of the most effective signals, and explain how reversal candles can be used as trade triggers to draw us into trades with other sources of confluence across non-correlated methods such as we will discover in the next few chapters.

BENEFITS OF USING CANDLESTICK CHARTS

Many beginning traders start analyzing stock price charts by viewing simple bar charts, which are default in most charting websites or software programs. Bar charts graphically represent the open, high, low, and close of a stock price or index as a single line with the height or range of the bar representing the difference between the open and the close. A left hash-mark represents the opening price on a given timeframe and a right hash-mark represents the closing price.

While bar charts may be sufficient for longer-term investors who only want a quick view of the current price trend before adding a stock to a portfolio, shorter term traders benefit from the clearer signals and additional information candle charts reveal at key market reversals. In fact, the strongest benefit of using candlestick charts is to highlight key shifts in the supply and demand relationship that occur at expected market turning points in the trend.

When a candle reversal signal appears at an expected market turning point, a trader can enter a position after the candle has formed and then place a stop under the low of the candle. Traders often seek as much information as possible from noncorrelated methods or strategies before putting on a high-probability, low-risk trade. We never strive for perfection before putting on a trade, but only that the odds of a successful trade be as much in our favor as possible. Interpreting candle reversal signals is a valuable tool in any trader's arsenal. A specific candle signal often gives us the trigger needed to enter a position at a confluence support or resistance zone in anticipation of a turning point in price.

By using candlestick charts, you can expect the following benefits:

- Quickly reveal insights into changes in supply and demand
- Easily spot potential turning points in price as they occur
- Confirm other signals as price moves into a support or resistance zone
- Enter a trade objectively as price rises above or below a reversal candle
- "Step inside a bar" to reveal information present on lower timeframes

CONSTRUCTION OF CANDLESTICK CHARTS

Figure 4.1 compares the construction of a price bar and a price candlestick. The open, high, low, and close of the timeframe is shown in both images.

The amount of data contained in each candle depends on the timeframe of the chart you analyze. A weekly candle contains five trading days, with the open price reflecting the opening price on Monday morning and the closing bar reflecting the closing price on Friday afternoon, while the high and low of the bar would reflect the high and low price of the entire week.

The open of a monthly candle begins the morning of the first day of the month and the close of a single monthly candle ends on the close of the final trading day of the month. The high and low of the candle mark the respective high and low price of the entire month. The same logic applies to a daily candle along with intraday candles that

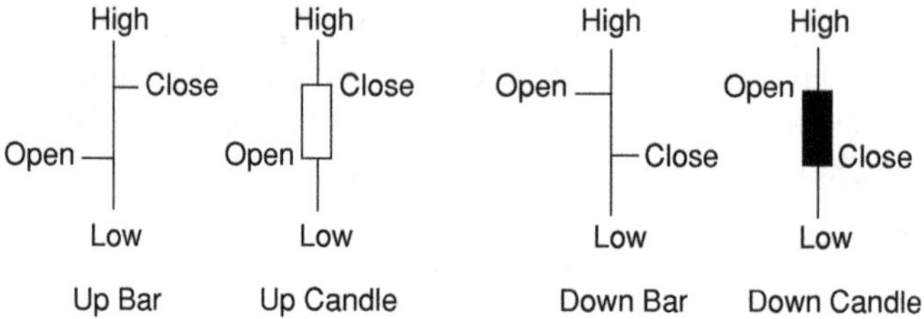

FIGURE 4.1 Construction of Bar and Candle Charts

form from 15-minute, 30-minute, or even 1-minute charts. Candlestick charts and bar charts present the exact same price data, however the candle chart adds an extra visual dimension to the difference between the opening and closing price of the bar. In essence, the candle chart creates a distinction in the difference between the open and close that is not viewed as easily on a simple bar chart.

Unlike a bar chart, which reflects the open and close with hashmarks, if the close of the bar is higher than the open, meaning that price rose during the period, then a candle would be white or hollow (or sometimes colored green). However, if the close of the bar is lower than the open, meaning price declined during the period, then the candle would be black or filled (or sometimes colored red).

WHY CANDLESTICK CHARTS TRUMP BAR CHARTS

Candlestick charts highlight the difference between the opening and closing price more clearly than bar charts. By emphasizing the most pertinent information, candle charts provide quick insights into the supply and demand relationship which can alert you to price reversals sooner than bar charts alone.

In addition to the distance between the open and the close of the candle being important, a trader is interested in the wick or shadows, which reflect the volatility of a particular bar and distance between the high and low as compared with the open or close. Long upper shadows reflect bearish price rejection, which is important when these candles, such as shooting stars or gravestone doji, occur at a key resistance level that also contains a negative momentum divergence or other indicator sell signal.

By learning how to interpret a candle chart instead of a bar chart, a trader gets a deeper glimpse into the buying and selling pressure of the market and receives earlier alerts to the potential for a price swing that is occurring at the time a particular candle forms. In trading, the sooner we receive a signal that the probabilities, as revealed from price and indicators, favor a change in trend or in the current price swing, the better we will be able to exit a profitable position at the most favorable price, and put on a new position with a tighter stop as close as possible to the expected turning point in price.

Figure 4.2 shows a standard bar chart of the S&P 500, while Figure 4.3 represents the same information, only with the benefit of a candle chart. Compare these two charts carefully.

In the S&P 500 daily chart showing the beginning of 2009, we see how standard bar charts reflect the daily range, open, high, low, and close. However, as seen in the same chart using candles, we emphasize the difference between each day's opening and closing price as a way to highlight the buying or selling pressure. Though the information is the same, the candle chart visually reflects more information about the underlying price moves. Though you might not see the value of the candle chart immediately, come back to this example after reading this chapter and see if you recognize additional insights from the candle chart. The candle chart also labels some common candlestick signals at key turning points in price that are not seen as easily in the bar chart alone.

FIGURE 4.2 Daily S&P 500 Index—Bar Chart

FIGURE 4.3 Daily S&P 500 Index—Candle Chart

Which chart is more visually appealing to you?

We will describe the particular candlestick signals labeled in the chart above. A specific candle signal appeared at most of the key turning points in swing highs and lows in price as the market moved in a downtrend to the March 2009 lows. The final low in 2009 revealed two 'neutral' candles and one 'extreme' reversal candle, giving an early signal that odds favored a shift toward buyers in the supply/demand relationship.

It is important to distinguish between the opening and closing price of a bar because this information gives clues into the current supply and demand relationship that existed during the time period the bar was created. A price that closed strongly above the open indicates bullish strength, while a price that closed strongly below the open reflects bearish weakness.

If the closing price is roughly equal to the opening price, then we would know that supply and demand were neutral, or in balance, for that particular bar. Pay particular attention to the range of a bar in comparison to previous bars to give insight into the volatility of the candle. Remember that price alternates between range expansion and contraction on all timeframes. Candles give swift insight into expansion and contraction periods on lower timeframes.

Some candles reveal a small price distance between the high and low of the bar, which reflects a non-volatile period while other bars exhibit large ranges which reflect periods of range expansion. Tight range, low volatile candles can reflect a market that has the potential to reverse, particularly if the narrow range candle forms at a known support or resistance area.

Strong, large range candles, particularly those that open at one extreme and close at the opposite extreme, might indicate that an expansion move or reversal in trend is developing, especially when these bars form either after neutral candles or also at a known price support or resistance level. We will learn how to interpret small and large volatility candles and what specific insights we can gather when considering entering or exiting a trade.

If a candle closes at the upper part of the range, or at the high of the bar, then this is a signal of bullish strength, just as a candle that closes at the lower part of the range is a signal of bearish weakness. Candle charts clarify this distinction and allow us to focus closer on the supply and demand relationship as revealed through price on the chart. Such insights clue us in earlier to shifts or reversals in price, giving us a low-risk trading opportunity when located in context.

BASIC TERMS USED TO DESCRIBE CANDLESTICKS

When analyzing candlestick charts, traders use specific terms to describe the key characteristics of the chart. Figure 4.4 and the following definitions explain this candlestick language.

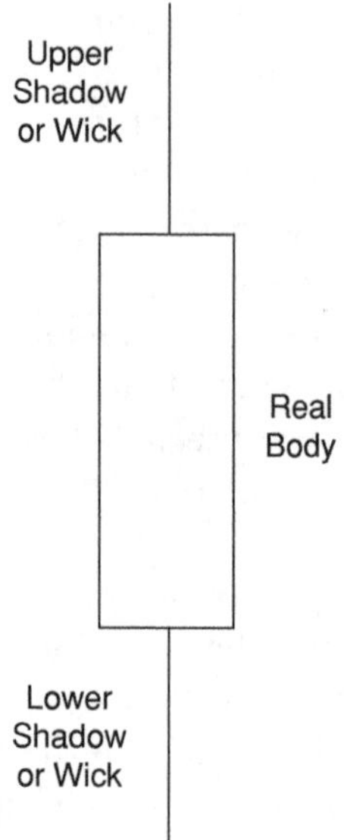

FIGURE 4.4 Terms Used in Candle Construction

When describing candles, we observe the real body of the candle which gives us insights into the intensity of the buyers during an up candle and the sellers during a down candle. The real body is the distance between the open and the close of a specific candle, where a major price distance between the open and close shows up as a visually noticeable bar, while a very small change between the open and close reveals itself as a flat line, or no real body. If the real body of an up candle is longer than prior candles, we glean insights that buyers are increasing their aggression to purchase shares and that we could expect continuation of higher prices, just like a longer real body of a bearish down candle suggests that sellers are more aggressive and that lower prices could be in store for the future.

CANDLESTICK TERMS

Real Body: The distance between the open and the close. Real bodies are hollow when the close is higher than the open and filled when the close is lower than the open.

Upper Shadow or Wick: The distance between the close and the high of an up candle or between the open and the high of a down candle.

Lower Shadow or Wick: The distance between the open and the high of an up candle or between the close and the high of a down candle.

If the real body is narrow or smaller than prior candles, this would suggest that the buyers and sellers were coming into balance, or were equally aggressive such that neither side could move price. Candles with very small or non-existent real bodies could be a sign of possible indecision, or balance between buyers and sellers and might be a precursor to a potential reversal in the future of the prior price direction, especially when such candles form at known support or resistance levels.

The upper and lower shadows of a candle, also called wicks (think about an actual candle with long real body and a small wick at the top) give us insights into the volatility of a time period. A wick forms when the high or low of the candle is different from the open or close of the candle. For example, an upper shadow forms when the high of the bar is greater by a noticeable difference than the top of the real body, just as a lower shadow forms when the low of the bar is lower by a noticeable difference than the real body. Long shadows can be a clear sign of price rejection and can also be associated with key turning points in a market, especially when long shadows form at key support or resistance levels.

COMMON SIGNALS

Now that you're familiar with the benefits of using candlestick charts versus standard bar or line charts, it's important to know that there are two major types of candlestick signals: extreme and neutral. As mentioned, candles reveal the intensity of the imbalance between supply and demand. Extreme candles with long real bodies reflect intensity on the part of buyers or sellers, while neutral candles with very small or even non-existent real bodies reflect lack of intensity on the part of both buyers and sellers. By assessing the intensity factor of buyers or sellers, you can then use that knowledge in context to assess the odds of a price move continuing to move in the same direction or possibly reversing to a new direction.

Extreme Candles: Marabozu

The most bullish candlestick opens at the low of the bar and closes at the high of the bar, while the most bearish candlestick opens at the high of the bar and closes at the low of the bar—in both cases exhibiting larger range expansion than previous bars.

Figure 4.5 shows an example of these most bullish and most bearish candlesticks, which have full real bodies and almost no wicks or shadows.

Unlike bar charts, certain candlesticks have unique names which traders use to clarify the concepts of supply and demand. The bullish candle shown in Figure 4.5 where the open is the low of the bar and the close is the high of the bar is labeled a Marabozu. These particular candles show that one side of the market dominated the other side, and can be excellent signals for entry when confirmed with other methods. Marabozus are extreme range expansion bars that have little to no upper or lower shadows and very wide real bodies.

A candle that opens at the low and then steadily rises to form a wide bar which closes at the high is called a Bullish Marabozu, which gives a glimpse inside the supply and

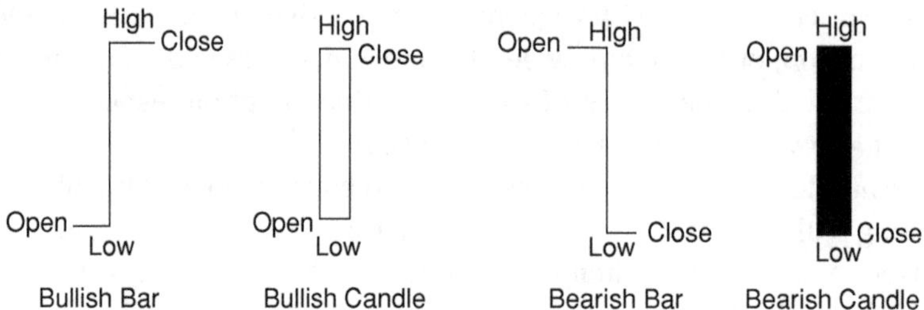

FIGURE 4.5 Marabozu Candles and Standard Bars

demand relationship between participating buyers and sellers. This relationship shows that buyers were dominant over sellers during that particular time period which could have forecasting ability into future price action if indeed the relationship has clearly shifted to the buyers. If looking at a daily chart, these would indicate trend days on the intraday charts. These powerful candles suggest that odds favor higher prices yet to come because buyers overpowered sellers during the period the candle formed.

The opposite of a Bullish Marabozu is a Bearish Marabozu, which implies that sellers were more aggressive than buyers and dominated the period in which the candle formed. If a Bearish Marabozu forms at an upper resistance level or in the context of a larger downtrend, then this single candle sends a message that odds favor lower prices ahead.

In Figure 4.6, Google (GOOG) gives a great example of a strong, powerful bullish Marabozu and how that candle as seen on the daily chart is constructed by smaller bars on the intraday charts.

Google's stock begins the trading day rising from the $500.00-per-share level and continues higher with minimal pauses until buyers push the price to close at the highs of the session at $517.00. This is a good example of the logic of extreme candles that open

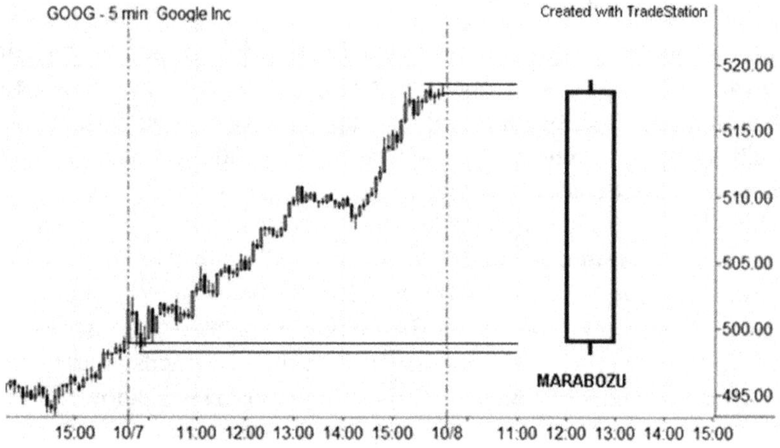

FIGURE 4.6 October 17, 2009 Shows the Internal Construction of a Daily Marabozu Chart for Google by Showing the Five-minute Intraday Bars

at one end and close at the opposite end. Buyers dominated the sellers for the entire session, and this insight gives us clues that the bullish dominance may continue into the next trading day. Intraday traders label such days as trend days.

The opposite of a bullish extreme Marabozu candle is a bearish Marabozu candle, which conveys a bearish signal for prices, indicating that sellers dominated the action for the duration of the bar. Google (GOOG) forms a Bearish Marabozu candle a few weeks later in October 2009 after Figure 4.6 showed the Bullish Marabozu.

In the creation of a bearish Marabozu, the high of the day occurs at the open as sellers dominate the action in a trend day down to close at the low of the session. In Figure 4.7, there is a tiny lower shadow or wick which indicates that price closed slightly off the low of the session. However, the main idea is that sellers were dominant on the intraday chart, pushing price lower from the opening session into the close. In both the bullish and bearish Marabozu candles, it is important to understand the logic of the formation of the candle, which represents a powerful move on a lower timeframe, such as the intraday chart for a daily candle, the daily chart of a weekly candle, or the weekly chart for a monthly candle.

Extreme candles send the signal that odds favor continuation in the direction the candle closed, under the principle that trends have greater probabilities of continuing than of reversing. A single candle contains many bars of lower timeframes that reflect the balance or imbalance between sellers and buyers, which affects how price moves.

Traders can find bullish extreme candles at the end of a downtrend, which would signal a strong price reversal to the upside, as was the case on the daily chart of the S&P 500 with the bullish Marabozu reversal candle on March 10, 2009. Powerful candles signal that buyers have taken control and would be expected to push prices higher, leading traders to buy on any price move higher than the close of the Marabozu candle to play for a potential trend reversal.

FIGURE 4.7 A View inside the Intraday Creation of a Marabozu Candle Google (GOOG) October 30, 2009 (with slight lower shadow)

FIGURE 4.8 The Daily Chart of Google (GOOG) Showing the Bullish and Bearish Marabozu Candle Examples

In addition to being reversal signals into key support levels, or in the context of a downtrend, extreme candles can also be considered continuation signals if they form away from a key support or resistance level. The underlying signal of extreme candles is that one side of the market is dominant over the other, and may continue to be dominant in the next few candles of the chart.

Figure 4.8 shows the daily chart of Google and the two Marabozu candles that formed as a result of the intraday charts as seen in Figures 4.6 and 4.7.

The Bullish Marabozu of October 17, 2009 (Figure 4.6) occurred after price was in an upswing that began in early October, while the Bearish Marabozu that formed October 30, 2009 (Figure 4.7) occurred after a price resistance formed at $560.00 per share. In this example, both Marabozu candles formed as continuation patterns near the central part of a price swing instead of serving a purpose as a reversal candle.

There is a similar candle pattern to a Marabozu that serves exclusively as a reversal signal, and it is a two-bar candle pattern known as the bullish and bearish engulfing candles.

Reversal Candles: Bullish and Bearish Engulfing

Another extreme candle that has a large range and often opens at one extreme and closes at the other is called an Engulfing candle. An Engulfing candle visually overtakes (or engulfs) the real body of the prior candle, and in some cases, even overtakes the high and the low of the prior candle. Engulfing candles are associated with a market that has experienced a sudden shift in the supply/demand imbalance, and can mark the exact turning point in price.

Often, an Engulfing candle will expand beyond the range of a prior neutral candle with a small range. This implies that price boundaries and expected support and resistance levels are changing. As such, engulfing candles are a two-bar signal, unlike the Marabozu, which is a single candle bar. Engulfing candles can also reveal an exhaustion phase on one side of the market, where all buyers are satisfied or all sellers have sold their shares, which creates a vacuum, which is filled with an Engulfing candle.

There are two specific types of engulfing candles: Bullish Engulfing and Bearish Engulfing.

Bullish Reversal Candle Pattern: Bullish Engulfing Bullish Engulfing candles often appear at the end of a downtrend, and for a true bullish engulfing candle to be valid, we would need to see price in a prevailing down move as sellers overtook buyers as price fell to lower levels. However, if buyers and sellers come into balance as seen on a lower timeframe chart, then a sudden bullish shift in the relationship can create a trend day that can be the precursor for a strong retracement back to the upside at a minimum, or a true trend reversal if this marks an intermediate-term low in prices.

Figure 4.9 shows the intraday timeframe chart of Electronic Arts (ERTS) on the 15-minute frame in early February 2009 as a bullish engulfing formation developed. Sellers dominated buyers as price fell to lower levels in a downswing in price. However, on February 3rd, price opened with a sudden downside thrust as sellers drove prices to new lows under $14.50 per share. However, buyers found this price to be a good value and began buying shares, shifting the relationship between buyers and sellers to

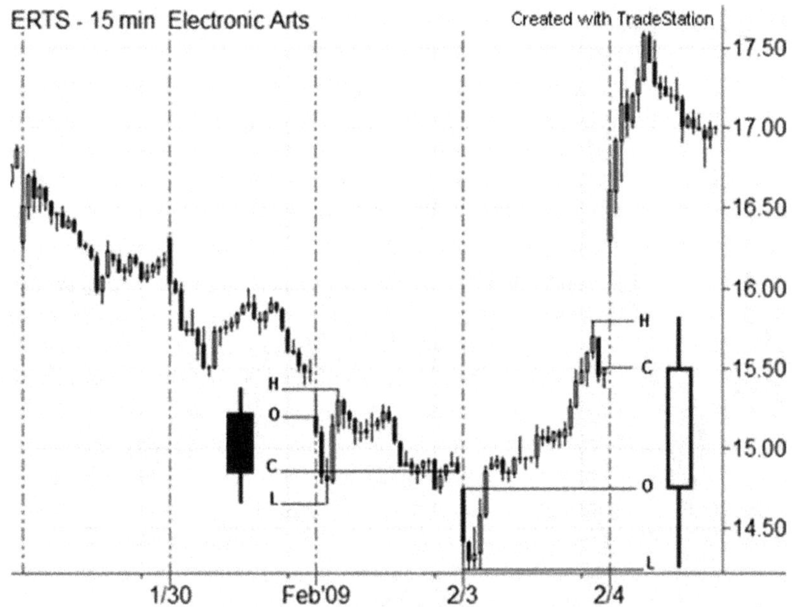

FIGURE 4.9 Bullish Engulfing Forming in Electronic Arts 15-minute Chart

the upside. Eventually, short sellers were forced to buy back shares as price continued to rise, which resulted in a positive feedback loop (see Chapter 3). As February began, the range contracted to form the candle labeled on the left, with open, high, low, and close shown.

As aggressive buyers pushed price higher, February 3 revealed a session where the low of the day and the high of the day completely engulfed the prior day's high and low. This chart reveals the construction behind a bullish engulfing candle as it forms on the lower timeframe chart. The candle represents a dramatic change in the relationship to favor the buyers, and alerts us that we can potentially expect higher prices yet to come from this development.

This reveals how candles on the daily or weekly frame allow us to 'step inside' the price action on the lower timeframes of the intraday charts. Let's step back to the daily chart, shown in Figure 4.10, to see this same pattern on the higher timeframe.

We can observe that the $15.00 level reflected a prior support zone in December 2008. As price came back to this level, traders could have been anticipating a potential reversal back to the upside if this level held as support again. A bullish engulfing candle pattern formed at the $15.00 support level, and traders could have found other sources of confluence to establish a trade at this level, expecting a reversal in price. Notice the power of the positive feedback loop, and bullish impulse that took price from the low of the trading range at $15.00 per share to the upper resistance line at $19.00 per share in four days. The bullish engulfing candle was the first clue that odds shifted to favor buyers, and that traders might benefit from buying shares of Electronic Arts to play for an upside return to the $19.00 level.

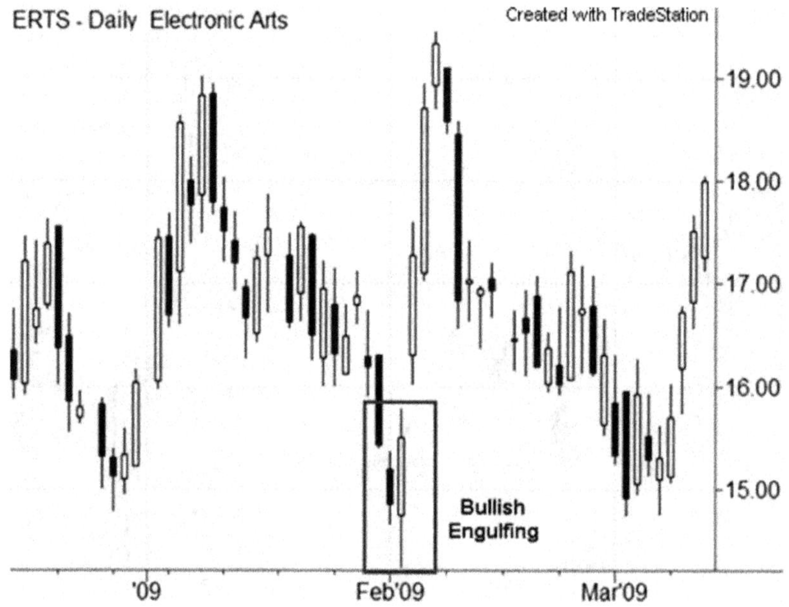

FIGURE 4.10 Bullish Engulfing Marks a Turning Point on the Daily Chart of Electronic Arts

FIGURE 4.11 Bearish Engulfing Marks a Turning Point on the Daily Chart of Yahoo

Bearish Reversal Candle Pattern: Bearish Engulfing The logic in the formation and signal of the Bearish Engulfing candle is similar to that of the bullish engulfing, only that a Bearish Engulfing candle must form after an upward move in price and the candle signal is enhanced if it forms at an overhead expected resistance level in price. We turn to Yahoo Inc (YHOO) in Figure 4.11 for an example of a bearish engulfing candle.

From late September to October 2009, Yahoo stock formed key resistance at the $18.00-per-share level, as shown from four prior attempts to overcome this level when the bearish engulfing candle develops. In late October, price rallied again to challenge the $18.00 overhead resistance level, and a bearish engulfing candle formed, signaling that odds favored a move back down to test the prior support zone at $16.50 for a minimum downside price target. Having observed the bearish engulfing candle in late October 2009, we can now view Figure 4.12 to step inside this candle signal to reveal the intraday balance between buyers and sellers, which created this reversal candle.

Unlike the chart of Electronic Arts above, Figure 4.12 does not reveal the broader context in which the Bearish Engulfing candle develops. Reference the daily chart of Yahoo in Figure 4.11 to uncover the context leading up to the bearish engulfing candle on October 23, 2009. It is very important to understand the logic of why certain candles have the association with price reversals that they do, which allows you to make more informed trading decisions with higher probabilities of success. The key is understanding lower timeframe supply and demand relationships, which candles can reveal clearly.

Remember from viewing the daily chart that the $18.00-per-share level was a month-long resistance level. Price rallies just shy of $17.80 on October 22, and then falls sharply in the morning session on October 23. Sellers became dominant over buyers and the supply/demand relationship began to shift, as evidenced by the wide-range Marabozu bars. Price rallied mid-day and then closed toward the low of the session. More importantly, price had engulfed the range of the prior day's activity, giving the candle chartist a signal that odds favored lower prices yet to come.

FIGURE 4.12 Bearish Engulfing Forming in Yahoo 15-min Chart

A trader could have seen this development and entered a short-sale position when the sellers pushed price under the low of the bearish engulfing candle at \$17.10 and then placed a stop above the high of the candle at \$17.80, or above the known resistance level at \$18.00 per share. Chapter 8 further details trade-execution tactics using candles, but the main idea is to understand how these candles reveal insights into the supply/demand relationship on lower timeframes and give trading signals when confirmed with other forms of analysis that reveal expected support or resistance levels.

Neutral Candles: Doji

While candles reveal insights into underlying buying strength or selling pressure by visually emphasizing the range along with the open and close, there is another type of candle that signals equilibrium or indecision between buyers and sellers. These particular candles form when the open of the bar is equal or almost equal to the close of the period, which suggests that neither buyers nor sellers were dominant. The general name for candlesticks where the open is roughly equal to the close of the bar is called a doji. Figure 4.13 shows the comparison between a bar chart doji and a candle doji. Figure 4.14 then steps inside a price chart of the ETF-traded SPY intraday chart to highlight how a doji on the daily chart forms in the intraday timeframe. Notice that the figures are identical. A bar chart and a candle chart reflect an identical image when the open and close are equal.

Candle charts clearly reveal the difference between the open and close of a bar, but not all candles or bars have a difference in the open and close of the period. Interestingly, a candle chart and bar chart will reveal the same image when a doji forms. Fortunately, we also receive an insight into the supply and demand relationship when the open and close of a bar are identical or nearly identical in price. Rather than being inherently bullish or bearish, the bar highlights balance between buyers and sellers. Traders often identify doji candles with key turning points in price because supply and demand

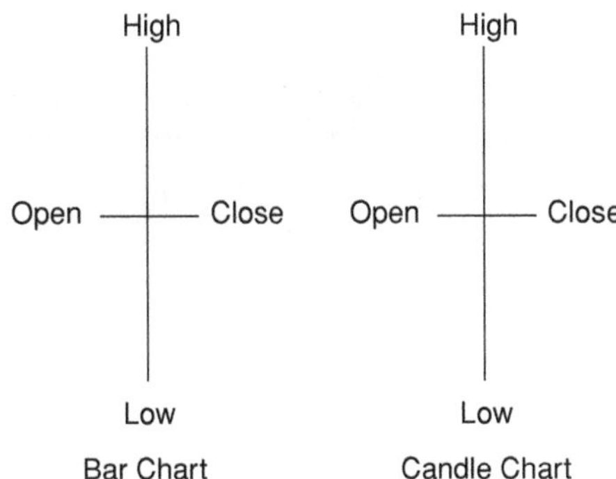

FIGURE 4.13 Bar Chart and Candle Chart Neutral Bar Doji

balanced during that time period, and any movement to tip this balance could result in the beginning of a short-term reversal in price.

Many traders use doji candles to trigger an entry if these candles form at key support or resistance levels. Doji candles are most closely associated with the concept of indecision, and doji candles can be said to reflect a period of indecisiveness between buyers and sellers—neither buyers nor sellers won the supply/demand battle. Doji that form at a potential resistance level after a price rally can offer a low-risk, high-probability trade entry or trade exit because these candles are associated with exact turning points in price.

Neutral Candle: Spinning Tops Similar to a doji, a spinning top contains a slightly larger real body than a doji, though both candles reflect indecision or equilibrium between buyers and sellers, and as such are associated with temporary turning points in price.

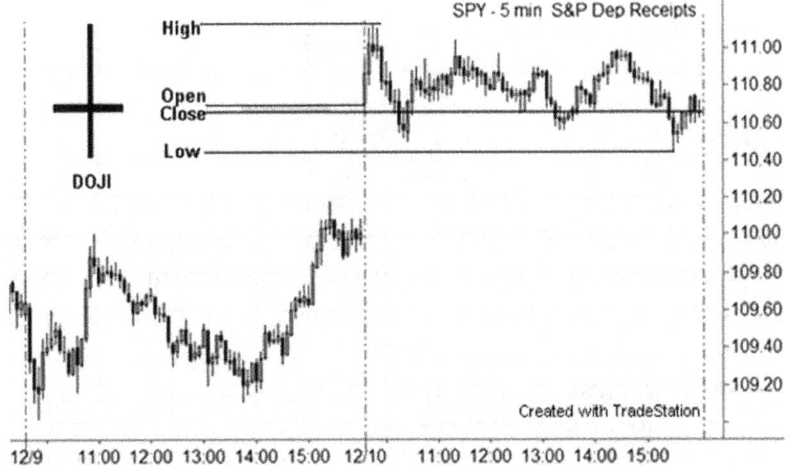

FIGURE 4.14 The Formation of a Daily Chart Doji as Seen on the Exchange-traded SPY Five-minute Chart on December 10, 2009

FIGURE 4.15 Formation of a Spinning Top Candle in the S&P 500 Index 15-minute Chart

While the open and close of a doji are almost equal, the open and close of a spinning top candle show a small distance, as seen in Figure 4.15. which reveals the 15-minute chart of the S&P 500 Index during early February 2009. Remember the previous chart of the S&P 500 shown in Figure 4.3? Figure 4.15 steps inside the creation of the spinning top labeled on the daily chart of the S&P 500 Index in early 2009.

The spinning top candle formed at the peak of a counter-upswing in price that ended near the 870.00 price level as the downtrend continued. As seen in the 15-minute chart, price rallied until February 9 when buyers and sellers found balance and the intraday trend paused, stabilized, and then reversed to the downside.

An intraday trader could have sold short the S&P 500 (using the exchange traded fund SPY) as soon as price broke beneath the intraday low of 861.00, which formed the low of the candle and of the short-term intraday range in price. A trader using the daily chart similarly could have put on a short-sale position when price broke beneath the low of the spinning top candle also at 861.00, in anticipation of the downtrend continuing, thus playing for a much larger target in a swing trade than the intraday trader would achieve. Both traders would have considered placing stops above the high of the spinning top candle, or intraday range, above the 875.00 level.

Momentum Shift: TriStar Doji Pattern As if one doji were not enough, there is a special name given to a cluster of three doji candles that form on a price chart, and the triple-doji signal gives a stronger indication for a potential short-term turn in price. We refer to three doji candles that form together in a row as the Tri-Star Doji pattern.

Tri-Star patterns are rare, but traders often spot them more easily; in fact, sometimes traders report that these patterns leap off the charts at them. No pattern guarantees a successful trade outcome, but these patterns can give useful signals when they form on a daily or weekly chart.

As discussed in Chapter 3, price alternates between periods of range expansion and range contraction on all timeframes. The Tri-Star doji candle pattern reflects tight range contraction on a lower timeframe that is expected to break into a price range expansion phase yet to come. As seen in Figure 4.16, the S&P 500 daily chart formed two range consolidation periods that created the two Tri-Star doji patterns, both of which preceded a range expansion move in price and short-term price reversals.

Tri-Star doji pattern signals increase confidence for traders anticipating either a range expansion move or a price reversal, especially if this pattern forms at an expected support or resistance area along with a corresponding positive or negative momentum divergence. The signal is bullish in July when forming after a down-move and bearish when forming after an up-move in August; thus, the tri-star pattern is neither bullish nor bearish in isolation, but the price chart context reveals the inherent bullishness or bearishness of the candle pattern.

A trader would buy after the high of the highest doji that created the Tri-Star pattern is exceeded and place a stop beneath the low of the lowest doji. Likewise, if a tri-star doji pattern formed into key resistance after an upswing in price, a trader may sell short as price broke beneath the low of the lowest doji and then place a stop above the high of the highest doji.

FIGURE 4.16 Two Tri-Star Doji Patterns Form in July and August 2009 on the Daily Chart of the S&P 500 Index

As seen in the tri-star doji that formed in August 2009, it can be helpful to place stops slightly above candle highs instead of one or two pennies above a high. It is best to place stops beyond prior price resistance levels instead of directly at those levels. A very tight stop would have resulted in a loss as price made one final push two points to a new marginal high of 1,039 before falling to a low of 990 in September, emphasizing the point that traders often benefit from placing stops beyond known support or resistance levels, rather than locating them exactly at a key price level. We discuss execution tactics and stop-loss placement logic in Chapter 8.

Higher Price Rejection Candle: Gravestone Doji While a standard doji candle shows the high and low of the candle to be roughly equal, there are two special types of doji that reflect clear price rejection of a certain level. The first special doji is a gravestone doji, which has a much longer upper range than a standard doji. These doji candles show a long upper wick, which reflects that price rose to a higher level and then declined to close at the same price as the opening period, revealing a rejection of the higher prices earlier in the session. In other words, buyers pushed price higher early in the period, but by the close, sellers pushed price lower back to where the period opened for no net price gain or loss. Gravestone doji are visually distinctive because the open and close are near the low of the session, while the high is often a wide range above this area.

Gravestone doji that occur after an extended price rally, or at a critical overhead resistance level, imply that odds favor a possible reversal to the downside, as sellers overtook buyers during the session and pushed prices to lower levels. Specifically, the sellers rejected higher prices and the supply and demand relationship returned to balance at the close of the session just as it existed at the open of the session.

It is easy to associate the potential signal given from a gravestone doji, because of the negative connotations associated with a gravestone. The candle is named because it resembles a tombstone, with the open and close of the candle appearing at or near the low of the session though the high was noticeably higher than the low of the session.

As eBay Inc (EBAY) prepared to enter 2009, a rally formed from mid-November to mid-December, and a gravestone doji formed with price rejecting the $15.50 high. After buyers pushed price higher, sellers stepped in to drive prices lower, creating a long upper wick which sends a bearish signal for the future. Figure 4.17 reveals the gravestone doji on the daily chart of eBay, and then Figure 4.18 drops to the 10-minute intraday chart to show exactly how buyers and sellers interacted to create this candle on the daily chart.

The $15.50 level served as key resistance after a rally higher into this level. The intraday chart in Figure 4.18 shows exactly how this candle formed, and the logic behind its potential to serve as a price reversal signal.

The stock price of eBay continued higher into the afternoon on December 17, 2008, but formed an afternoon high of $15.50. Sellers became aggressive and pushed price back to the morning's opening price near $15.10 to form the special doji with a long upper wick. Immediately after price formed the gravestone doji on the daily chart, sellers became dominant and pushed prices lower through the next week. Price rallied back to

FIGURE 4.17 Gravestone Doji on the Daily Chart of eBay in December 2008

the $15.50 area in early January 2009 only to form another long upper shadow at the established resistance level before price fell in a stronger downswing.

Lower Price Rejection Candle: Dragonfly Doji The other specially named doji is a dragonfly doji, which is the opposite of its gravestone doji brother. Unlike the gravestone doji, a dragonfly doji is associated with bullish reversals in price, as the open and

FIGURE 4.18 Inside the Gravestone Doji in eBay—A Look at the 10-minute Intraday Chart from December 17-18

FIGURE 4.19 Dragonfly Doji Example on the Daily Chart of Sears Holdings on July 13, 2009

close of the bar are roughly equivalent and occur at the high of the session. Imagine a dragonfly flying higher and you will understand the logic of this candle, especially if it forms after a price swing to the downside into an expected support area.

In Figure 4.19, Sears Holdings (SHLD) gives us a good example of a dragonfly doji on its daily chart. Price formed a downswing that began in early June and continued into mid-July. Sellers pushed price down to the $55.00-per-share level, where buyers found value and began supporting the price.

The 10-minute intraday chart in Figure 4.20 shows us exactly how sellers pushed price lower, buyers and sellers came into alignment with a price consolidation at the $57.00 level, and how sellers were quickly and suddenly overtaken by buyers on July 13th which marked a key swing low in price that provided an opportunity to trade long when the dragonfly doji was complete and price rose above the high of $57.50 which completed the candle pattern.

Price Rejection Candles: Hammers and Shooting Stars

We have seen how the upper or lower shadows of doji candles can be helpful in identifying price rejection at key support or resistance levels, which can clue us in to key turning points in price swings. While a doji candle with a long upper or lower shadow has a similar opening and closing price, there is a separate but similar candle that forms a similar long shadow, but has a slight difference between the open and the close of the candle. Traders often call these candles hammers if they occur at a support level or shooting stars if they form at a resistance level.

FIGURE 4.20 Sears Holdings Reveals the Intraday Creation of a Daily Chart Dragonfly Doji—July 13, 2009

As we will see, the difference between a bullish hammer and a dragonfly doji is the same logic as the difference between a doji and a spinning top. The main idea is to pick up on the bullish or bearish clues that a particular candle reveals within the context of the price chart, rather than get confused by the specific terminology traders use when describing candles.

Bullish Lower Price Rejection: Hammer It is often best to think of candles generally instead of specifically, meaning it is best to understand how candles reveal the dynamics of supply and demand on lower timeframes, which gives clues into the future move in price rather than missing a signal because a candle did not conform exactly to specifications. As such, hammers and shooting stars fall under the same logic as gravestone and dragonfly doji: These candles reflect intraday price rejection and could be the start of a new swing in price if these long wicks form at key support or resistance levels.

The hammer candle would be most similar to a dragonfly doji in both logic of formation and indication of a potential bullish reversal in price, especially when this special candle forms into a key support level after a downswing in price.

While the hammer and dragonfly doji both have long lower shadows (wicks), the main difference is that the hammer shows a small price distance between the open and close while the dragonfly doji shows little to no price change between the open and the close. Technically, the hammer sends a bullish reversal signal regardless if the open is higher than the close, or if the close is higher than the open. Traders generally think of hammers as having a higher close than open, making it a hollow bullish bar, but many candle experts teach that hammers can either be hollow or filled, meaning that the orientation of the close to the open is irrelevant as long as the distance between the two is roughly two times the distance of the wick or greater.

The best hammers form after a downswing in price which comes into an expected or confluence support zone, perhaps as a positive momentum divergence forms. Traders buy after the high of the hammer is exceeded and often place stops under the low of the candle or other relevant support area.

Like the dragonfly doji, the hammer reflects a bullish price rejection of lower prices, which forecasts a positive shift in the supply/demand relationship. The important characteristic of the candle is the long lower shadow which reflects not only an inability of sellers to drive prices lower, but a willingness of buyers to enter the market at lower levels, potentially finding value at lower prices.

Yahoo Inc (YHOO) shows an example in Figure 4.21 of two hammer candles in late January 2009, and also how the $11.00-per-share level served as a key support zone. Figure 4.22 zooms in on these two candles to highlight the development of a bullish reversal forming at the $11.00-per-share level.

Officially, the candle that formed on January 26 would be a hybrid between a dragonfly doji and a true hammer, as the open and close were slightly larger than the equality expected in a doji, but not enough to qualify for the "real body is two times the lower shadow" rule of a hammer. Instead of becoming frustrated by specific labeling of a particular candle, focus on the underlying message of the candle, whether it be bullish, bearish, or neutral. Our goal is to spot the signals that give us clues into the supply/demand relationship between bulls and bears, especially in regard to reversals in the relationship.

As we step inside the intraday frame in Figure 4.22, we now see how these candles developed. Price formed a bullish engulfing candle on January 23 which was the first

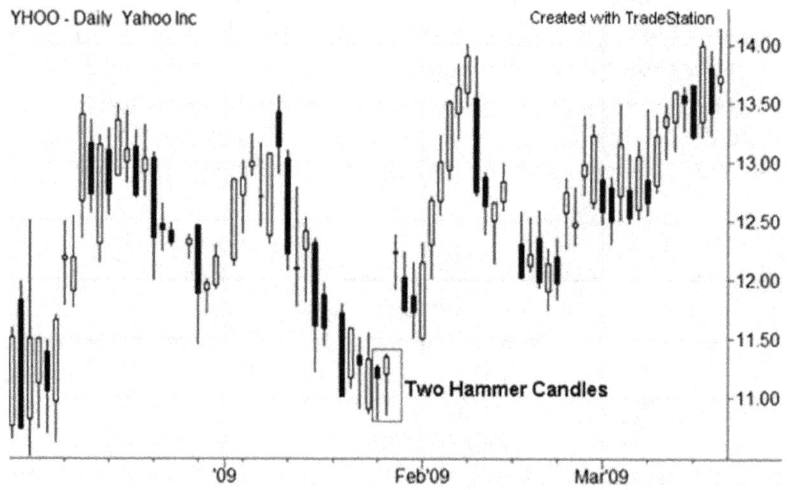

FIGURE 4.21 Daily Chart of Yahoo in January 2009 Reveals two Hammer Candles

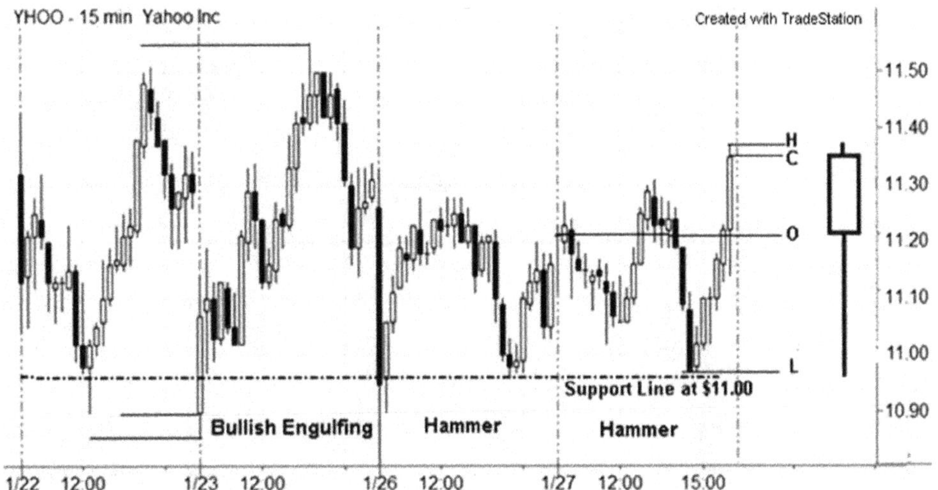

FIGURE 4.22 The 15-minute Chart of Yahoo from January 22–27, 2009 Reveals a Key Support Level at $11.00 and three Specific Candles: a Bullish Engulfing on January 23, and two Hammers

clue that buyers were finding value at lower prices and willing to drive prices higher. However, sellers entered by the close of the session and then pushed prices lower into the morning of January 26. Buyers and sellers then kept price in a range, with buyers entering to create support at the $11.00 level and sellers pushing price lower, creating resistance at the $11.25 level.

The daily chart does give a powerful signal that odds favor a potential move higher yet to come. How? Price formed a bullish engulfing candle, quasi-hammer candle (long lower shadow), and official hammer candle, all of which formed long lower shadows at the $11.00 level. Price then gapped higher the next morning and quickly rallied to $14.00 before turning lower, highlighting that buyers became dominant over sellers. A savvy trader might have seen this development on the daily chart and entered as price tested the $11.00 level either on January 26 or 27 and placed a tight stop under $10.90, or perhaps entered long into the close on January 27 as the upper range boundary at $11.30 was broken and the hammer completed.

We can also see a similar construction of a hammer on Exxon-Mobil (XOM) on the five-minute frame on November 24 in Figure 4.23. Instead of seeing multiple bars as revealed on the chart of Yahoo above, the Exxon-Mobil chart reveals a pure intraday structure that forms a daily hammer.

Price opened on the morning of November 24 at the $75.70 level and sellers quickly pushed price lower under $70.00 per share. However, buyers found value at the lower prices and quickly rejected the morning lows formed by the sellers. Buyers pushed prices higher into the close, creating the hammer bar drawn on the right side of the chart.

By integrating the daily chart with the lower timeframes and seeing the push and pull interaction between buyers and sellers, traders can understand potential shifts in

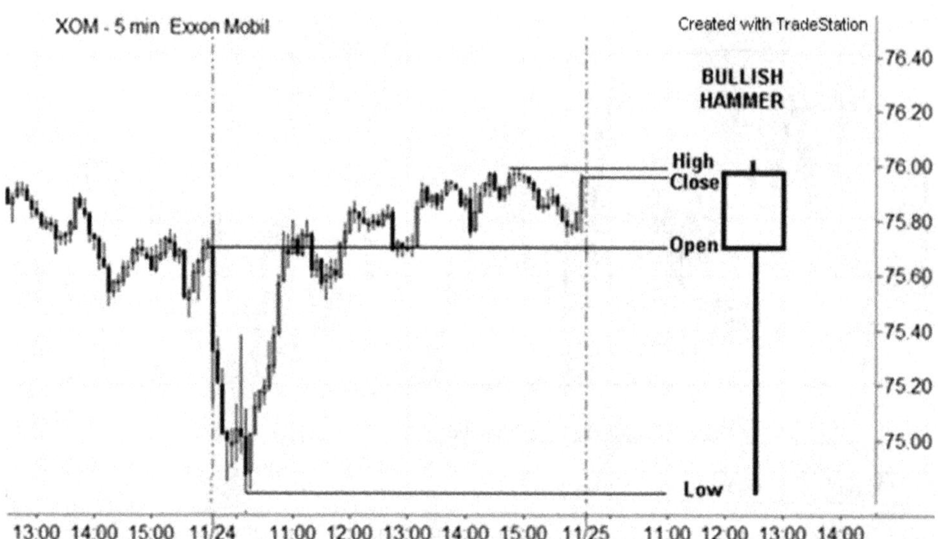

FIGURE 4.23 Bullish Hammer Formation in Exxon-Mobil Five-minute Chart on November 24, 2009

the supply/demand relationship clearly which then creates low-risk opportunities for profit, especially when combined with other forms of analysis that uncover support and resistance levels.

Bearish Upper Price Rejection: Shooting Star The same logic that applies to bullish hammer candles applies to their opposite bearish signal—shooting stars. A shooting star is similar to a gravestone doji, except that the distance between the open and close is slightly greater than that of a doji candle, which ends in near price equality.

Shooting stars form long upper shadows which reflect price rejection of higher levels, and signal low-risk trading opportunities when they form after an upswing in price into a key resistance level, particularly if a negative momentum divergence develops. The best trading signal would contain all three (or more) elements (shooting star candle, trendline or moving average resistance, and negative divergence).

In Figure 4.24, Johnson and Johnson (JNJ) shows another hybrid candle signal between a true shooting star (in which the distance between the open and close is roughly two times that of the wick) and gravestone doji. Don't pass on a potential signal that does not conform specifically to exact definitions from textbooks. You will deprive yourself of a potentially good opportunity if you demand perfection.

As price moves into August 2009 after a two-month upswing, price forms a shooting star at the $62.50-per-share level. Price quickly retraces after this candle forms, as a profit-taking swing unfolds which drives prices lower.

Stepping inside the shooting star candle seen in Figure 4.24, the intraday chart of Johnson and Johnson in Figure 4.25 allows us to understand the logic and intraday formation of the shooting star candle signal. The importance of any candle signal is not

FIGURE 4.24 Shooting Star candle on the Daily Chart of Johnson and Johnson—July 30, 2009

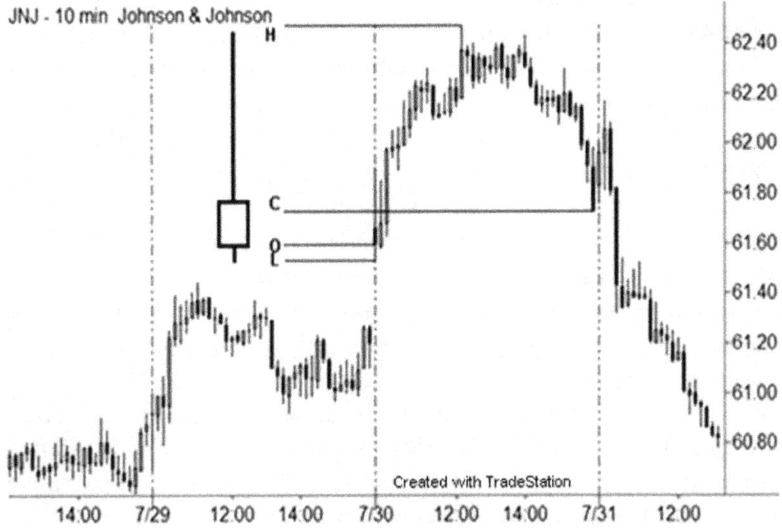

FIGURE 4.25 An Inside Look at the 10-minute Intraday Chart of the Daily Shooting Star in Johnson and Johnson—July 29–30, 2009

the signal itself, but the insight the candle gives into the lower-timeframe supply and demand relationship and how that helps uncover the broader picture of price structure and potential turning points.

In a shooting star candle, price is in an established uptrend with buyers overtaking sellers. In this case, the open and low are almost equivalent, and buyers continue to push price higher into mid-day. However, a rounded reversal price pattern forms as the balance of supply and demand gently tips to the sellers, who push price lower into the close of the day. The result appears as a bearish shooting star on the daily chart, which offers a potential short-term price reversal signal. A trader could enter short as the low of the candle at $61.60 was broken, which occurred early on the next morning's session, and then place a stop above the high of the candle above $62.40.

Upside-Down Candles: Hanging Man and Inverted Hammer Before concluding our discussion on shooting stars and hammer candles, it is important to make a quick note about inverted signals that these candles can form. These particular candles reveal why trend context is so important in making a trading decision.

A hammer is a bullish reversal candle with a long lower shadow that occurs after a price decline and is associated with price rejection at a support zone. The logic is that price is likely to rise because buyers have overtaken sellers and demand is stronger than supply, and we would expect a continuation of the rally upwards off of established price support.

However, an identical formation can also occur at the peak of an upswing in price into a key resistance level. A hammer candlestick that forms at the end of an upswing is labeled a hanging man, and carries much darker connotations than a hammer. Hanging man candles have the same bearish reversal expectations as shooting stars, only the candle is flipped upside down.

In the same inverse logic as the hanging man, a shooting star candle that forms after a lengthy downswing or into a key support level is labeled an Inverted Hammer. While this less-creative name is not as graphic as hanging man, the inverse logic is the same. The inverted hammer is identical to a bearish shooting star with a long upper wick, but the upside-down candle forms at the end of a downswing.

You may take inverted hammers and hanging man candle signals in the same way you would interpret shooting stars and hammers, only the context will be flipped. If you are uncomfortable or do not understand the logic of these upside-down candles, you might pass on a particular trade and move on to the next trade that you interpret more clearly. Many traders report difficulty in buying shares after a bearish-looking candle like a shooting star forms into a support level, or short-selling shares after a bullish-looking candle like a hammer forms into known resistance.

These upside-down candles reveal why context is so important. Never take candle signals in isolation, but instead, always look to the broader context before making any trading decision. The broader context includes the prevailing trend, known support or resistance levels, any non-confirmations (such as positive or negative divergences in momentum, volume, or market internals), and any indicator signals such as an overbought or oversold oscillator.

Even if you see a common candle signal such as a hammer or a doji, but it appears out of place, you might consider passing on a trade setup. In other words, every day will form a candle on your daily chart. However, only a handful of candles should grab your attention, and those would be the ones that form at confluence or expected support or resistance levels. If price does not form a common candle pattern that you understand the logic of the formation as it gives insights into the supply/demand relationship, then you are receiving no signal from the candlestick chart. You do not need to become a candlestick expert to use candle charts—just as you need not become an indicator expert to use indicators. Place all signals in the broader structure or context of price principles and price behaviors.

THREE TRADING SCENARIOS

It is helpful to envision a candle as a graphical representation of the supply and demand balance between sellers and buyers that exists over a given period of time, such as a month, week, day, or intraday period. For this example, let us discuss a weekly time period which reflects five days worth of price data. We will look at three different scenarios. Read the scenarios first and envision what the candle will look like. Then, see Figure 4.26 for the answers and the respective candles that formed for each of the three scenarios.

A Very Bullish Week

Assume that the price of a given stock begins Monday morning at a price of $100.00 per share. By Tuesday, the price has risen to $102.00 per share and by Wednesday, the price closes at $105.00 per share. Buyers are dominant over sellers as evidenced by steadily rising closing prices each day. On Thursday, the price closes at $107.00 per share and by the close of Friday afternoon, the price of the stock rests at $110.00 per share, which is the highest price of the week.

The candle created by this five-day period would be the most bullish single candlestick called the Marabozu, where price opened at the low of the week and price closed at the high of the week. The insight we would gain from seeing this candle on a weekly chart would be that buyers dominated the week from Monday's open until Friday's close, which could hint at further bullish action yet to come if the buyers continue their aggression over sellers.

A Neutral Week

We again start the week at $100.00 per share and move higher on Monday and Tuesday to close at $102.00 per share. However, this time Wednesday is a sharp down day which takes the price down $4.00 to close at $98.00 per share, which is lower than when the week began. Seeing the $98.00 level as a bargain, buyers step in and push the price slightly higher to close Thursday at $99.00 per share. By the close on Friday, buyers again stepped in to push the price higher by $1.00 to close at the original $100.00 level where price opened on Monday morning. The candle created by this week would be a doji candle with the open and close being equal in price, while price would show a $4.00 range with $102.00 per share being the high and $98.00 being the candle low. Neither buyers nor sellers were dominant this week as evidenced by the equal close.

A Bullish Reversal Week

Let us again start Monday morning at $100.00 per share and by the close of Monday's trading, price has declined $4.00 to $96.00 per share. The week is off to a bearish beginning, which is continued also into Tuesday, with the price falling another $2.00 to close at $94.00. At this point, the situation is looking bleak for buyers. However, by Wednesday's close, buyers stepped in to push the price slightly higher to close back at $96.00. Thursday is another up day for the stock, and this time buyers are showing aggression as they push the price $4.00 higher to close yet again at $100.00. At this point, we have a long lower shadow which indicates price rejection of lower prices as evidenced by the higher move. By Friday's close, buyers have taken charge and driven the price higher by $2.00 to close the week at $102.00, having come back from an early decline at the beginning of the week.

The shape of this candle displays a bullish bias because the candle formed a long lower shadow, which indicates that sellers drove price lower initially and then aggressive buyers prevented lower prices by finding value at lower levels. Demand outweighed supply and price rose off a lower level. The name for this type of candle is a hammer candle, and it is often associated with bullish price reversals. Hammers provide clues into possible bullish market reversals when they form at confluence support levels. Lower shadows or wicks inform us that buyers rejected lower prices, or found value at the lower levels, and could be expected to push price even higher.

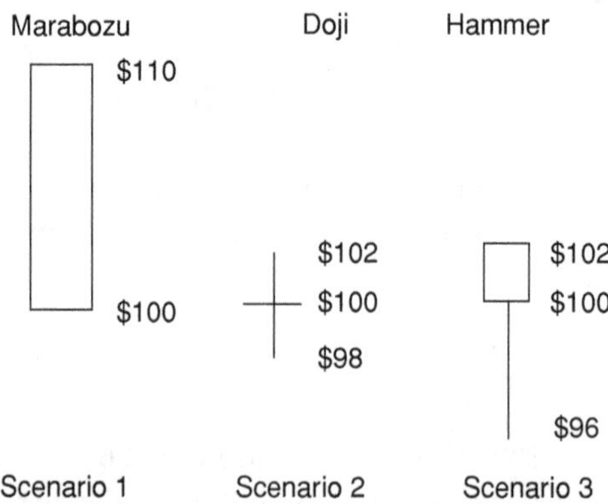

FIGURE 4.26 A Bar Chart and Candle Chart Neutral Bar Doji

A LITTLE KNOWLEDGE GOES A LONG WAY

Authors have written full books on the subject of candle charting, and some traders have become experts in the area. For example, Thomas Bulkowski compiled extensive data on 103 candlestick patterns in his book *The Encyclopedia of Candlesticks.* I have only discussed 13 of the more common, popular candles that are in the vocabulary of most traders.

You need not become an expert in candle charting to gather information and employ the benefits from candle patterns on your charts. However, there are great resources available for you if you desire to learn more. Steve Nison is recognized as the individual who introduced candle charts to American traders, and he has written extensively on the subject with such books as *Japanese Candlestick Charting Techniques, Beyond Candlesticks: New Japanese Charting Techniques Revealed,* and *The Candlestick Course.*

Candle charts have their place in a complete trader's plan because they give quick insights into the supply/demand relationship in price. They can also be helpful in confirming a trade setup while triggering an entry or stop-loss when a signal occurs at a point of confluence with other strategies.

A trader will benefit from finding a key reversal candle such as a bullish engulfing or doji pattern that forms at an expected support zone such as a prior price support level, moving average, Fibonacci retracement level, or trendline. Traders can enhance the odds of a successful trade by identifying a positive momentum divergence or other indicator buy signal that forms simultaneously at this price level. The remainder of the book will discuss other methods for finding confluence before placing a trade, but many trades will be officially triggered with a buy or sell signal when a common candle reversal signal forms and price officially breaks above or beneath the respective high or the low of the candle.

CHAPTER 5

Examining Price Patterns

So far, we have discussed three main price principles, along with basic candlestick charting on our quest to discover higher probability trade setups and determine how to profit from the next likely swing in price. This chapter will continue the journey by describing how popular price patterns help you uncover opportunities in the seemingly random movements of the markets.

However, simply finding a price pattern is not enough; rather, you will enhance your trades if you combine the principles, insights from candle charts, volume, momentum, and—as we will soon see in Chapters 6 and 7—Fibonacci principles, along with the life cycle of a price move. All of the concepts combine to form a complete strategy to increase the odds of success as you develop trading experience. Combining as much chart information as possible allows you to have a greater degree of confidence that the trade setup you are about to take has a high probability of meeting the price target that you expect.

This chapter will describe popular classic price patterns, show how the patterns are based on one of the underlying principles, and explain exactly what to know about each pattern to increase the probability of a successful trade. By the end of the chapter, you will be able to see the logic of pattern formations, rather than just recognizing them on the price chart. That will take some practice, but first, let's get to work defining these popular patterns!

WHAT ARE PRICE PATTERNS?

If you have been trading for any length of time, you've certainly heard of at least one of the dozens of popular patterns traders use. With names as colorful as a dead cat bounce, cup with handle, head and shoulders, and many other lively titles, price patterns are sure to grab your attention as a trader, if anything, to arouse your curiosity as to what the pattern means. You may even decide to classify some of the price patterns you discover on your own—there is no limit!

Simply defined, a price pattern is a repeatable formation that has been observed in the past by many traders and has been classified with specific parameters. Traders label patterns by drawing lines, arcs, squares, triangles, circles, parabolas, or any other geometric tool on the price chart itself. New traders, and even experienced traders, often recognize patterns best on a pure price chart devoid of indicators. A price pattern provides a logical entry price as a trigger, profit target price in the event the pattern succeeds, and stop-loss price in the event the pattern fails to generate the expected price movement. Like anything in trading or investing, there's no guarantee of a successful outcome, but a pattern can give objective prices to anticipate when odds favor pattern completion or pattern failure.

The art of using price patterns to develop trading decision stems from the idea that history repeats, and thus patterns repeat—this is one of the main principles of technical analysis. Therefore, when a trader begins to recognize a common price pattern developing in real time, he or she can anticipate the resolution of the pattern to unfold similarly to the way it has in the past, allowing the trader to envision the next move ahead in price. In this way, traders can use patterns as potential roadmaps today to the immediate future, in the event that price continues to form the classic pattern as expected from start to finish.

In price patterns, you gain the immediate benefit of trading price itself in generating your initial trading decision, rather than analyzing potentially contradictory indicators that are derived from price, and thus lagging indicators by definition. If you use price-based indicators alone to generate trading ideas, such as buying a stock that is showing an oversold stochastic or RSI indicator, you are one step behind the price itself because all price-based indicators are mathematical derivations of the price of a stock, and are thus based on lagging calculations.

In addition, using oscillators or other price-based indicators leaves you wondering exactly where to enter, place a stop, or aim for a price target. If you trade using an overbought and oversold oscillator, your price target is unknowable because you will exit your trade when your indicator tells you that price is now overbought. You are relying on indicators for trading decisions, rather than price itself and are one step removed from the action.

With price patterns, you decide where to enter, where to place a stop, and where to aim for an expected price target using price itself. Remember the old saying "Only price pays"? Traders who incorporate price pattern analysis into their trading decisions pay homage to that time-tested statement.

In popular trading literature, authors classify price patterns generally into continuation or reversal patterns, but that has often led traders to confusion when a pattern that is defined as a reversal pattern fails and price then moves in an unexpected direction, which can result in large losses for traders positioned the wrong way. For example a descending triangle, which is often classified as a bearish reversal pattern, is considered to fail if price breaks to the upside instead of breaking to the downside as expected.

While it's not possible to cover every single pattern that exists in the trading literature in a single chapter, this chapter's purpose is three-fold:

1. Tie price patterns to foundation principles
2. Explain how these principles enhance your confidence in the pattern
3. Challenge your thinking on how to trade common patterns

For a full discussion on price patterns, there are four main texts which traders use as a reference:

- *The Encyclopedia of Chart Patterns* by Thomas N. Bulkowski
- *Martin Pring on Price Patterns* by Martin Pring
- *Technical Analysis and Stock Market Profits* by Richard Schabacker
- *Technical Analysis of Stock Trends* by Robert Edwards and John Magee

Before I begin discussing price patterns, I felt it was necessary to make a distinction between blind reliance on a pattern and intelligent integration of the larger chart structure when taking a trade based on a chart pattern.

To be clear, you first have to learn the patterns—the classic definitions and expectations—before you can master how to trade chart patterns. Once you have developed some experience in the art—and often frustration of having a perfect pattern not work out as you expected—you will then begin to see the patterns as a way to see how other traders or investors are reacting to the pattern, as well as the supply/demand relationship that is setting up as the pattern forms. Patterns are similar to candle charts in that they reveal insights into the supply/demand relationship that exists between buyers and sellers. Thinking about why a pattern might be forming, along with the context in which the pattern forms, is far more important than excitedly pointing out a pattern and then rushing to put on a position when a popular price pattern forms on a chart.

It's important to remember that patterns are not magic profit pathways to the future, but rather insights into a temporary potential window into the future that can simultaneously give you insights into the minds of traders who are forming the pattern and the frustration—evident on the charts—when a popular pattern fails. It seems that in today's educated trading world, everyone knows the patterns, but the ones who are profiting from the patterns are the ones who can see beyond the patterns and into the minds of traders taking the setup. Specifically, experienced traders profit not just from successful obvious patterns, but from obvious patterns that fail and thus trap traders on the wrong side of the market. That is the most important distinction you can make. If something looks too good to be true, it probably is, and the pattern will likely fail; it is one of the strange paradoxes of trading. However, there can actually be better opportunity in a pattern failure, which can give you a quick, profitable trading opportunity that other traders do not see, provided you have quick reflexes and the ability to see patterns for what they are, meaning they are not perfect windows to the future.

TRADING PATTERNS: TWO SCHOOLS OF THOUGHT

Adam Grimes, a trader at SMB Capital and Director of Tactical Investments at Waverly Advisors, explained in a blog post the distinction between the two prevailing modes of thought—namely between the amateur and the expert—when trading price patterns. I wanted to share a portion of that discussion as we begin examining price patterns. Here is what Adam says:

> *I believe there are serious flaws in the way most of us start learning technical analysis. Usually a set of patterns is presented to the student, with the idea that once you have learned to recognize these patterns, all you have to do is go find them in the market, put on your trades, and then dream of the profits that will roll in. As Mike Bellafiore, co-founder of SMB Capital, tells every trader who walks through the door: the world does not work like that. There is more to successful, consistent trading than simply recognizing a set of patterns.*
>
> *There are two radically different schools of traditional technical analysis, and both spring from the writings of two men in the 1920s and 1930s. Richard Schabacker was a successful trader, investment advisor, and author whose approach was based on classifying many variations of patterns. His books include variation after variation on continuation patterns, trend change patterns, consolidation patterns, etc. After studying thousands of these patterns and then seeing them in action, the student is supposed to be able to gain some intuition about the future direction of prices.*
>
> *Richard Wyckoff was another author whose approach was completely different. He focused on trying to understand why the market was doing what it was doing. The "why" was much more important than the "how"—the concept was more important than any specific pattern—the thing itself more important than the form of the thing.*
>
> *Rather than equip the student with a large set of potential patterns, Wyckoff believed it was important to understand how the motivation of buyers and sellers showed itself in the patterns of price and volume.*
>
> *To my thinking, this is a much more valuable approach, but it seems like 90 percent of the books, web sites, and courses today focus on patterns like "cup and handle", "head and shoulders", etc.*
>
> *One possible reason for this is that everyone reads Edwards and Magee's* Technical Analysis of Stock Trends, *which itself springs from the Schabacker school of thought, but it's also much easier to teach specific patterns than to teach real understanding of supply and demand. Without that understanding of supply and demand, any approach to trading is ultimately doomed to fail.*

Source: Adapted from Grimes, Adam. "Technical Analysis: A Little Background and History." SMB Training Blog. May 5, 2010. http://www.smbtraining.com/blog/technical-analysis-a-little-background-and-history

We as traders must realize that price patterns are not magic, and what's important is the supply/demand factors, as well as the underlying context in which the pattern forms.

Today, it's not enough to take a trade based on a single chart pattern alone; rather, we need to look at the broader picture to determine the odds of a pattern succeeding or failing, both of which give traders opportunities.

We will discuss how to trade these patterns when we discuss execution tactics in Chapter 8 and combine the bigger picture in a later chapter on integrating concepts, patterns, and indicators into specific trade setups, some of which derive their edge directly from an existing price pattern. For now, similar to the prior chapter on candlestick charting, we need to learn the basics of price patterns so we can build upon that knowledge to generate high-probability, low-risk setups.

INTRODUCTION TO THE MOST POPULAR PATTERNS

In his book *The Encyclopedia of Chart Patterns*, Thomas Bulkowski quantifies 52 patterns, some of which consist of one to three bars while others may last many bars. Some patterns, like the head and shoulders reversal pattern, are in the common trading knowledge that even non-chartists would recognize, while other patterns, like the shark-32, are obscure patterns that not even expert market technicians can define on the spot! Like candles, you need only learn the basics to be successful, rather than know the intricacies of every single price pattern—or candle pattern—that exists.

Just like any form of charting analysis, you can delve as deeply into the material as you wish, but the benefit will be not from the depth of knowledge of the intricacies of chart patterns, but in integrating the most common patterns into a larger framework of supportive methods and confirming signals from non-correlated styles of market analysis.

You will benefit most from understanding the edge that is inherent in most price patterns. By edge, we refer to the inherent price levels that a pattern provides as an entry, stop-loss, and target, where the target is always larger than the stop-loss. In the event that you can consistently find a pattern with a two-to-one reward (target) to risk (stop-loss) from the entry point, then you will consistently make money over time even if 50 percent of the patterns that you trade fail. That's because you can expect to make twice what you lose on the trades that you win.

If you risked $500.00 on each trade and lost that amount when the pattern failed, but profited $1,000.00 each time the trade succeeded, then you would have a pattern-based edge that resulted in consistent profits with a 50 percent win rate of your trades. Out of 10 trades taken, five would lose, costing you $2,500.00, but five would win, profiting $5,000.00. A 10-trade string that results in a gain of $5,000.00 minus loss of $2,500.00 results in a net gain to your account of $2,500.00, minus commission and slippage. This is how you would approach trading patterns from an edge-based standpoint. We will discuss the finer details of a trader's edge in Chapter 8.

Your goal is not to work as hard as possible and get every signal in alignment to produce a very high win rate. Rather, your goal is to identify patterns that generate a minimum of a two-to-one reward-to-risk ratio or better. Most trading literature suggests a three-to-one edge is minimum, but you must develop your own style from your personal experience and risk tolerance. Perfection in win rate is never the goal with any style of trading. As such, focusing on edge reduces the psychological discomfort or frustration that will befall you when a perfect pattern that meets all the textbook definitions unexpectedly fails, resulting in confusion.

The focus of the patterns in this chapter is on popular trading patterns rather than the lesser-known patterns. Why? We want to know what the mass public is thinking, and how they might behave when they see a popular pattern. To an extent, the benefit you receive as a thoughtful, well-reasoned trader will be in assessing self-fulfilling prophecies that result when popular patterns form. At times, when price triggers an entry for a popular pattern in a popular stock, traders will behave in a predictable fashion and enter at the same point, place a stop at the same point, and exit at the same point.

You'll soon learn the benefit of failed patterns, where the public enters a well-known pattern, places their stops at the exact same level, and then all rush for the exits at the same time as the pattern mysteriously fails. This is the logic of how positive feedback loops develop, such as those we discussed in Chapter 3. You'll be in a better position to profit if you fully understand that patterns are not magic, but are temporary windows of probability, not certainty. Many traders believe that price patterns are magic, and thus get very frustrated when a pattern fails. Don't be like the public!

With that in mind, let's survey a few of the most popular trading patterns that have grabbed the attention of the public, and thus give us insights into the supply/demand relationship.

HEAD AND SHOULDERS

If you took a poll of the general trading public and asked them to list their favorite pattern, chances are the head and shoulders would make the top three. In many cases, it might even be the number one most-recognized pattern because even financial commentators on popular financial news broadcasts have been known to describe a head and shoulders pattern forming on an index or a popular stock. They even bring in technical analysts to describe the pattern and draw it on the charts and explain to the general public what is ahead for the market, usually a reversal, when this pattern develops.

Defining the Pattern

What exactly is a head and shoulders pattern? Let's turn to AIG's daily chart as the stock formed a lengthy pattern in 2006 (see Figure 5.1).

If you're wondering if the price scale is an error, it's actually not. AIG issued a one-to-twenty reverse split to shareholders on July 1, 2009, which meant shareholders saw their total shares invested decrease such that for every 20 shares they owned before July 1, they would now own one share for those 20 shares. A person who owned 100 shares

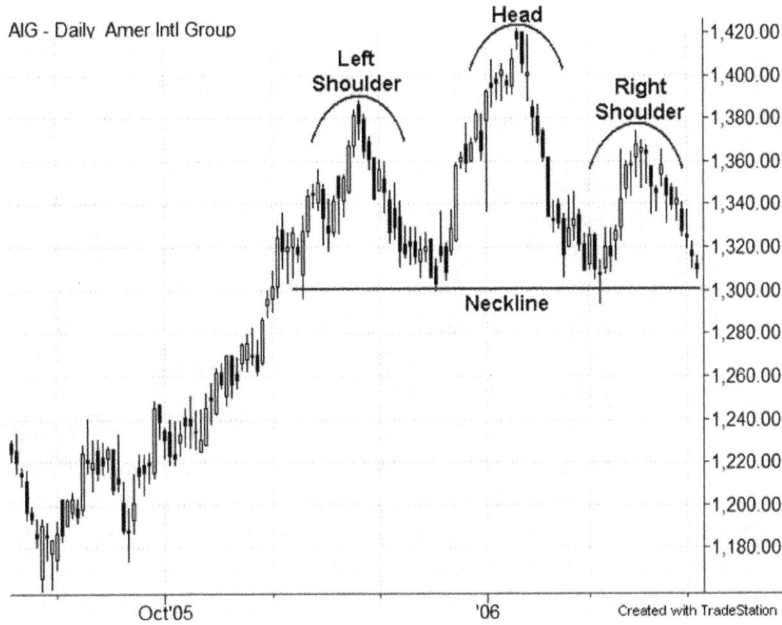

FIGURE 5.1 AIG Head and Shoulders. Daily Chart: 2005-2006

at $1.00 would now own only five shares worth $20.00. The value of their investment remained the same after the split.

As a result, the share price of $1.00 at the time was multiplied by 20, which resulted in a stock price of $20.00. Due to the split, there was no change in market capitalization, however for those of us looking at historical charts such as this one of AIG, we see the price scale inflated by a factor of 20, which means that the $1,300.00-per-share level, the neckline of the pattern, actually was equivalent to $65.00 per share, which is how investors saw the price in 2005 and 2006. This chart provides us an interesting history lesson in reverse splits as well as showing us a near-perfect head and shoulders pattern.

The classic head and shoulders pattern requires four points to define the pattern. The left shoulder is the initial swing high (a higher high in an uptrend) that gives way to a standard retracement, which is seen as a buying opportunity into support in the established uptrend. No danger exists on the horizon during the left shoulder, and we would expect volume and momentum to register new or equivalent highs as on prior swings. Price would not break trendlines or moving averages during this time. The key to remember on the left shoulder is that investors can see no hint that the pattern is forming in real time and no bearish signals yet.

The head is often the final peak in the up-trending market. We cannot know this is the final peak as it forms, but many times the head portion will form on a negative divergence in volume or momentum, which should be your first clue as a trader that things are not as bullish as they seem. Sometimes the head will actually be the terminal fifth wave in Elliott wave notation as we will discuss in Chapter 7 and so advanced traders might start to sell shares while the general public, who do not pay much attention to negative divergences or Elliott wave counts, see no danger and continue to buy shares as the price rises and rises. Notice that we have competing behaviors from professional and amateur traders as the head portion forms in the prospective pattern: professionals are exiting (selling) positions (the right side/decline portion of the head) while amateurs see no danger at all and continue buying shares.

Experienced traders sense that a reversal is nearing, and will behave more conservatively. However, amateurs who see nothing but the prior rise in a lengthy uptrend, are unaware of the potential reversal pattern forming. The sell-off from the absolute peak might break under key rising trendlines or the 20- (or 50-) period exponential moving average, both of which are early warning signs that a trend may be getting ready to reverse.

The right shoulder forms in part from amateurs continuing to buy the stock despite the warning signals that are mounting. Price rallies a final time as traders buy shares as they see price coming into a prior support level, which is the low formed from the bottom swing of the left shoulder—the neckline. However, the picture of who is holding shares is changing. Head and shoulders patterns are clean distribution patterns where professional traders take profits (sell shares) to late-comers who have waited to buy when they are convinced price will continue to rise forever, which occurs at the later stages of a trend. Price rises, but soon fails to make a new swing high as the right shoulder completes. By this time, you have probably seen a clean rising trendline break and price has almost certainly broken through the 20- or 50-period EMA, and now we see a clean lower high put in place, which is the first step before a confirmed trend reversal according to the Pure Price Method (see Chapter 1).

By the time the right shoulder has formed, experienced traders already anticipate a break of the neckline and are prepared to get short to take advantage of the pattern forming and triggering an entry, which would be as soon as price broke the neckline trendline. Notice the dynamic in supply and demand. Professional traders are distributing throughout the whole pattern (see Chapter 7), amateurs are buying shares because they do not see the danger (only the rising trend), and chart-specialist traders (technical analysts) are getting ready to go short (put on new short-sale positions) in the event that price breaks and closes under the neckline, or fourth component of the pattern. Traders who will enter a new short-sale position under $1,300.00 will place a stop either directly above the right shoulder at $1,380.00, or above the head (the absolute high) at $1,420.00. Keep in mind that if the pattern fails, these same traders who tried to get short will be forced to cover (buy, adding a force of demand) in the event that price rallies above $1,380.00 or $1,420.00.

If price does break under the neckline, what is likely to happen? The rush of new short sellers will be a force of supply to drive price lower by their actions (putting on new positions). Many amateur traders who did not see the pattern forming will have placed their stop loss orders under the support zone that comprises the neckline. This is also a form of supply, which is old buyers selling old positions for a loss, usually in a panic.

The combination of new short sellers and old buyers who are being stopped out can create a positive feedback loop (see Chapter 3) which can send price much lower as a result of the dynamics that formed the pattern: professionals selling (perhaps for fundamental reasons), technical analysts selling (because of the break under the neckline and negative divergences), and amateur/inexperienced traders panic selling because they are losing money and their expectations of higher prices are being dashed.

Where might this positive feedback loop end? Or stated differently, what will stop the flood of sellers? All of the chart books that describe the head and shoulders pattern place the target at the same location. To derive the price target for the pattern, which is the place where short-sellers will then buy to cover the shares that they shorted (a force of demand), take the distance from the top of the head to the neckline and then subtract that value from the breakdown price of the neckline.

Price Targeting in the AIG Head and Shoulders Example

In our example in Figure 5.1, AIG's split-adjusted neckline formed at $1,300.00 per share. The top of the head—or the peak of the rally—formed at $1,420.00. If we subtract $1,300.00 (neckline) from $1,420.00 (top of the head), we arrive at a distance of $120.00. To complete the projection, we then subtract this distance ($120.00) from the breakdown of the neckline ($1,300.00) to arrive at a pattern price target of $1,180.00. At that price, the chart traders who went short from this pattern will begin to buy back their shares at the target zone.

This zone may also correspond with other investors, perhaps fundamental investors (not using charts to make investment decisions) who determine that the share price is now cheap compared to what it should be (or used to be), and thus they will begin buying the shares at the reduced price that happens to correspond with the chart traders buying back shares (demand) to cover.

To recap, a trader will enter a short-sale position when he or she observes a left shoulder, head, right shoulder, and then a break under the neckline (entry). The same trader will place a stop either above the right shoulder (which is a conservative strategy) or above the top of the head/peak (which is a more aggressive strategy). The traders will play for a target that is equal to the distance of the head from the neckline, which is subtracted from the neckline.

To confirm that you are truly seeing a head and shoulders develop, watch for a potential fifth-wave clear Elliott Wave count when combined with negative volume, momentum, or breadth (market internals if looking at an index such as the S&P 500), divergences as the head forms.

Look for price to break under established rising trendlines and the 20 or 50 exponential moving averages to increase your confidence that you are witnessing a market in a trend reversal stage. Look for new momentum lows and volume spikes to form as price breaks under the neckline (horizontal support) which confirms that the momentum and trend is shifting to the downside, and also watch for a confirmed trend reversal using the pure price method (lower high, lower low).

What happened to AIG? Did it ever break the neckline and trigger a short-sale trade? Yes, but it threw in one curve ball before giving an official signal—that is why I chose this

FIGURE 5.2 AIG Head and Shoulders Resolution. Daily Chart: 2005–2006

example of a text-book pattern with a real-world curve-ball. Let this be a reminder that patterns are never as perfect as the textbooks say, but still give excellent opportunities for those willing to position themselves accordingly. For the resolution, see Figure 5.2.

I mentioned that patterns are rarely if ever as perfect as the textbooks teach. In this case, AIG formed one more rally or bounce off the neckline horizontal trendline support at $1,300.00, forming a second right shoulder before breaking the neckline. Chartists call this a double shoulder head and shoulders. Price triggered an official entry on the April 2006 break under $1,300.00 per share. At this time (or even before this), you could have determined the price projection pattern target to be $1,180.00 as defined above. Traders would have put stops above the second right shoulder at the $1,380.00 level and entered on a breakdown under $1,300.00 to play for a target (take off the position) at $1,180.00 which actually wasn't an ideal reward-to-risk relationship, certainly not the two-to-one that makes pattern trading worthwhile from an edge-based standpoint. However, the trade did meet its price objective and actually formed a second pattern during the decline. Can you spot the bear flag pattern that formed while traders were short AIG to target the $1,180.00 level? If not, we'll discuss the flag patterns later so you can come back and find it. Yes, smaller patterns can form within larger patterns.

Once price hit the target level, those who were trading short to play for the head and shoulders target began to buy back their shares to cover their short positions, adding demand to the market and stabilizing the price at the $1,180.00 level.

Understand the underlying supply/demand relationship that developed as this pattern completed. Walk through the chart, stepping inside the shoes of the professionals (distributing), technical chart traders (waiting for a break, then taking the breakdown, then exiting at the target), and the amateur trader who bought near the highs (usually on the head or right shoulder) and could not understand why they bought shares in a company with a rising trend, yet the price started falling; feel their pain as they consider whether or not to keep holding on to a losing position while the stock keeps falling, and keep in mind they don't know where the pain of loss will end, meaning they are experiencing the pain of loss and are selling all the way down at different levels as the pain of a losing position is too much to endure.

Refer to Chapter 3 on the Range Alternation Principle to identify this as a horizontal trend channel with an overhead expensive resistance line at the $1,400.00 level, lower cheap support line at $1,300.00, and value area (midpoint) at $1,350.00. Another way to view the head and shoulders portion is as a consolidation pattern that should lead to a range expansion move once investors break the lower support line as a positive feedback loop develops, sending price to find value (buyers) at a lower level.

Head and shoulders appear on all timeframes, from monthly charts down to one-minute charts, but the intraday patterns will not involve as many participants as the higher timeframe patterns on daily or even weekly charts. Remember that the psychology of the reversal will be proportional to the scale of the pattern. Larger-scale head and shoulders patterns will involve many more market participants and many more emotions, from skilled experts to brand new trading novices than the intraday patterns. While the parameters and definitions are the same for all timeframes, the psychology (greed, fear, hope, despair, confusion, frustration) and participants are different. The same is true for all chart patterns.

INVERSE HEAD AND SHOULDERS

As a reference, the opposite pattern to a bearish Head and Shoulders Reversal pattern at the highs is a bullish Inverse Head and Shoulders Pattern at the lows. In order to cover more patterns in a single chapter, I won't go into as much detail as for the standard head and shoulders description, but do realize that, while the targets, labels, descriptions, stop-loss, and entry are identical (but in reverse), the psychology is dramatically different when a market transitions from a bear market downtrend into a consolidation period and then into a bull market uptrend than when the market reverses from up to down. Instead of going through a distribution period, a stock is experiencing an accumulation period marked by active purchasing of shares by the professionals instead of selling to lock-in profits. Traders enter long at the breakout from the neckline, place a stop-loss either beneath the right shoulder swing low or the low of the head, and then target an identical move, except this time the distance from the head to the neckline is added to the breakout from the neckline instead of being subtracted.

Different Emotions from Bear to Bull

One major reason that the psychological dynamics of supply and demand are different is because the amateur trader or small retail investor is less likely to short stock than they are to buy it, and so we do not see the same panic to buy to cover their short sales for a loss when the market is rising as we see the panic to sell the previously purchased that decline in value as price falls. Usually, tops are made with euphoria and optimism from the smaller investors while bottoms are made with disgust, anguish, despair, and fear from the general public. The forces that carry a stock up are not the panicked, desperate forces that carry it down. Keep this in mind when trading bullish and bearish chart patterns and how it fits into the Life Cycle of a price move as explained in Chapter 7.

Let's look at the example from Boeing (BA) from its recovery rally during 2009 in Figure 5.3.

Like AIG, Boeing did not form the perfect textbook inverse head and shoulders as it transitioned through an accumulation phase and reversal from a downtrend to an uptrend throughout 2009. Price formed a left shoulder with no sign of trend reversal in sight in late 2008 at the $35.00-per-share level, then formed a new swing low under $30.00 per share in March 2009 which would later become known as the head of the pattern that was forming. Price broke the dominant trendline (not drawn) as it rallied above $40.00 per share in late April 2009 (along with the 20- and 50-day EMAs, not shown) as the head completed and price retraced up to the forming horizontal trendline which would

FIGURE 5.3 Boeing Daily Chart Inverse Head and Shoulders 2009

later be known as the neckline at the $53.00-per-share level. Price also formed positive momentum divergences on this final push to a new low, indicating that odds were shifting to favor a potential trend reversal.

Price retraced one more time, forming a higher low in July at the $40.00-per-share level before rallying to break to a high of $55.00 in late September 2009, which triggered an official entry to buy shares for a potential head and shoulders confirmed breakout. Like AIG, price had a final trick up its sleeve, falling unexpectedly back under the neckline, but not falling low enough to trigger a stop loss of traders who located their stops under the right shoulder at the $40.00 level. We had a second break above the neckline in December, triggering a second-chance entry and then the positive feedback loop developed, with those who were short the stock being forced to cover as new longs, including chart traders playing the neckline break of the inverse head and shoulders pattern, buying—both of which drove the price higher. Price rallied almost without a meaningful retracement until the stock hit the expected price pattern projection target of $76.00 per share, which added the distance from the neckline to the low of the head ($23.00) to the breakout price of $53.00 per share. Price found resistance and then sold off sharply from that level, in part due to chart traders who were taking profits from the price projection target of the pattern (among other reasons of course).

AIG Example: Inverse Head and Shoulders

Here is a view of the same chart of the same period, but adding a trendline, the corresponding 20- and 50-day exponential averages along with the 200-day simple moving average, and the 3/10 MACD Oscillator—which highlighted the dramatic positive momentum divergence at the low (see Figure 5.4).

I have referenced four specific points in the chart using letters A, B, C, and D. Let's make sense of this chart one element at a time:

A. Trendline Break: Price breaks above the trendline as drawn, connecting multiple swing highs in the context of the prevailing downtrend.

B. Positive 20- and 50-day EMA Cross: The 20-day EMA is the dashed line while the 50-day EMA is the solid line. One of the first steps toward a trend reversal, which usually occurs about the same time as we see a trendline break, is a bullish cross of the 20-day EMA—a shorter average—above the 50-day EMA—a longer average. Price also began rallying above these averages. Notice that price stayed consistently beneath these averages during the downtrend. As the head develops, professional traders and chartists are starting to see signs of a reversal. Notice also the clear positive momentum divergence that formed on the absolute low under $30.00 per share. The 3/10 Oscillator shows a triple-swing positive momentum divergence when comparing the oscillator low to the corresponding price lows. An arrow highlights this development.

C. 200-day SMA Cross: Price broke and closed above the 200-day simple moving average, which is the defining line between a bull and bear market to some analysts.

FIGURE 5.4 AIG Head and Shoulders Resolution. Daily Chart: 2005–2006

A close above the 200-day moving average is one of the last bullish confirmations to occur that indicates that odds have shifted to favor a trend reversal and that it is now safe to begin trading long and risky to continue selling the stock short.

D. Neckline Break: Price finally crosses the horizontal resistance line that comprised the neckline of the inverse head and shoulders pattern, triggering an official entry for those chartists who only trade chart patterns.

The purpose of this example is to combine the prior chapters and layer a price pattern on top of the analysis. A stock must transition from a bear market to a new bull market and often undergoes not only a consolidation phase (range alternation), but shows specific signals that the trend is changing, such as the indications mentioned above (trendline breaks, positive momentum divergences, EMA crossovers and breaks, and so on).

Notice also the negative momentum divergence, shown with an arrow from January to March 2010, which preceded the sell-off that occurred at the price pattern projection target of $76.00 per share. Even if you were not trading the head and shoulders pattern, you could have labeled this target and then observed the negative momentum divergence that formed as price continued to new recovery highs in 2010. This describes another way that price projection targets can be helpful, especially when combined with other signals.

A trader long Boeing into the $75.00 level could have taken profits as a result of the inverse head and shoulders target being hit in conjunction with a lengthy negative momentum divergence, while more aggressive traders could have put on a new short-sale position, with a stop-loss just above $75.00, as price turned down from this level, perhaps when combined with a bearish reversal candle (a doji and shooting star reversal candle formed at the $75.00 level, though that is not clear from the chart).

Now do you see why it is more important to assess the larger picture of what is happening with the stock rather than rushing out and buying a stock because it happens to be forming an interesting-sounding pattern? It takes extra work to identify a stock in a transition phase, but the extra work is worth it in the form of the consistent profits and higher confidence that come from specific entries and low-risk locations to place stops if an unexpected event occurs.

BULL FLAG

Bull and bear flags also would likely make the top three in a poll of most popular trading patterns, most likely due to their popularity and ease of recognition. Flags are much more common than head and shoulders patterns, and also occur on all timeframes, from monthly charts down to the one-minute charts.

Flags are impulse patterns that derive their forecasting ability (for the next likely swing) from the principle that momentum precedes price. Recall from Chapter 2 that momentum has a leading edge on price. Stated in trading terms, if we see price and momentum form a high simultaneously, we would then expect a higher high yet to come in price. It takes great force to propel an object into motion (in our case, a sudden imbalance in the supply/demand relationship) but it takes less force to keep a moving object in motion. Bull flags are a great example of how this concept of motion and physics plays out on the price charts.

There are three specific components to a bull flag, as labeled in Figure 5.5:

- The initial impulse (the pole)
- The retracement (the actual flag)
- The measured move (an equal reaction swing to the pole)

As in physics, an object tends to stay at rest until a force interacts with the object, setting it in motion. That is the logic behind the pattern of the bull flag. It's not our goal to predict when the initial force will interact with the object, or in this case, when the sudden supply/demand imbalance will propel price higher in a sharp impulse move. It's like the left shoulder of the head and shoulders pattern—you can't know the pattern is forming until it is nearing completion.

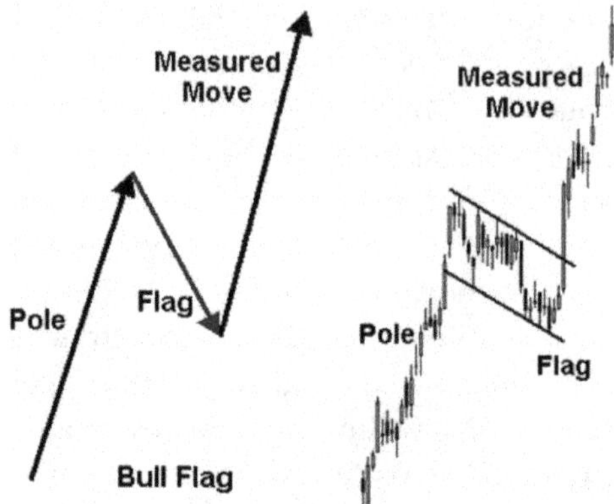

FIGURE 5.5 An Ideal Image of a Bull Flag

Another analogy that helps understand the bull flag (or bear flag) reaction is like a stone being dropped into a calm pond. There is an initial burst of energy that sends the waves moving, and then those waves later become ripples as the energy is dispersed. The initial thrust (supply/demand imbalance) that begins a flag pattern is the rock being dropped into calm waters, and the actual trade setup is similar to riding a wave or ripple that originates from the initial move.

Recall the second portion of the momentum principle: when price and momentum form a new high, odds favor a higher high yet to come in price after an initial pullback. The flag portion of the pattern represents this initial pullback in price, and the trade that we take, buying the breakout of the flag, is taking advantage of the higher high yet to come component of the momentum principle.

Rules for Trading a Bull Flag

What are the general rules for trading a bull flag? Chart traders want to put on a new position in one of two locations when they believe they are trading a bull flag pattern that has developed on the chart. Aggressive traders want to buy shares as close to the bottom of the flag as possible, as price often moves within a descending short-term parallel trend channel, or as price forms a reversal candle at the bottom of the parallel trendline channel. This strategy allows for a closer stop, which enhances the edge of the pattern (see Chapter 8).

The more conservative trader would enter a position long only when price broke the upper parallel trend channel as price officially broke outside of the flag portion of the pattern, perhaps on a strong bullish candle (like a marabozu or bullish engulfing). While there are advantages for waiting for confirmation to be sure that you are trading a flag pattern, the disadvantage comes in the form of a more distant stop-loss, which is still placed under the lower boundary of the descending parallel trend channel.

The bull flag target is one of the easiest price projection target calculations you can make. Simply measure the horizontal price distance of the pole portion of the formation—the initial impulse from low to high prior to the retracement—and then add this value to the bottom of the parallel trend channel when price officially breaks out of the trend channel and begins rising. Doing so will reveal the upper price projection target.

Alternatively, some traders insist on projecting the measured move target from the upper trend channel directly at the break-out price rather than the lower trend channel from the bottom of the retracement. Again, there is no magic formula that makes all patterns work perfectly, so you will have to experiment with a few flags on your own to find which of the two methods for price projection works best for you and your trading style. For the purpose of the discussion here and forward, I will be projecting the price target from the low of the trend channel at the price swing low of the retracement instead of the upper trend channel.

A trader would look to exit the position as price approaches or achieves the upper price projection target, particularly if a reversal-style candle forms such as a doji, shooting star, or bearish engulfing. A very aggressive trader might even look to initiate a short-sale position at the price target, placing a stop loss just beyond the target and playing for a retracement back to a rising moving average or other lower, unspecified small target.

Why a Bull Flag Works

A bull flag is an impulse pattern that reflects the reactions from investors and traders to an initial impulse, or sudden shift in the supply/demand relationship. Perhaps the initial impulse begins as some sort of short-squeeze or range breakout play, but the impulse sets the stage for future reactions in price in the direction of the initial impulse.

Traders who were long prior to the initial impulse might see the impulse rally giving them an unexpected windfall profit, and so they will sell the shares they own at any weakness, which usually explains in part the downward reaction that comprises the flag portion. Take into account also that other traders may be initiating a short-sale position to take advantage of a price move that is overextended from its shorter-term moving average such as the 20-period EMA. They may also exit from a signal via an overbought indicator reading—a sell signal—in a popular oscillator like the stochastic or RSI. The combination of buyers taking sudden profits and new short-sellers trying to take advantage of the mean-reversion principle (prices that are overextended tend to return to an average price) helps explain why price might retrace or sell off after an initial rally.

However, the supply/demand balance has shifted after the initial impulse, and after traders have sold their shares or have already gotten short (pushing the price down), a new dynamic or shift in the supply/demand relationship takes over as traders begin to buy as price falls back to a support level (such as a moving average or Fibonacci retracement price). At the same time, those who took a short-sale position begin to buy back shares to cover their short sale for a profit.

Now, we have a combination of bears buying back to cover and new bulls buying stock, either because the fundamental situation of the stock has changed (perhaps an earnings report or some other announcement caused the initial impulse spike that created the pole), or because they are reacting to a bull flag that they believe is forming on the chart. Remember, chart patterns can be self-fulfilling prophecies. Either way, price begins to rally in a similar impulse move as it did for the pole, and price rallies up to the target with traders buying either at the support level, above the breakout from the declining trendline that comprises the flag, or somewhere after the breakout, as traders feel they are missing the move so they rush in to buy shares.

Like the head and shoulders, traders who are specifically buying because they see a bull flag on their chart will then take their profits as price approaches and tests the price projection target. Because the target is easy to calculate, many traders will be aware of this target level in advance and might consider selling just because price has reached the upper price target, especially if traders observe any reversal candle or other confluence resistance level. Traders may even decide to take profits, similar to that of the end of the initial impulse, when they start to see price fall after a sudden rise; they want to lock-in profits they have gained. As usual, aggressive short sellers might try to take advantage of the situation and initiate new short-sale positions, all of which serve to alter the supply/demand relationship in favor of supply (selling).

Putting a Bull Flag in Context

Bull flags are popularly described as continuation patterns, and most commonly appear in already established uptrends. It is rare, though possible, to see a bull flag form in the context of a prevailing downtrend; you are more likely to see bear flag retracements up that lead to continuation moves down in a downtrend. Again, the context where the pattern forms is important.

Bull flags are less common within the context of a lengthy trading range, or range compression period in price. In fact, the failure rate of bull (or bear) flags is higher when a bull flag develops in what looks to be an initial impulse that forms completely within the confines of a well-established trading range. Within the context of a larger range, price is less likely to achieve the upper price projection target.

However, it is possible to see a bull flag form after an immediate breakout from a trading range or range contraction period in price. In this sense, you can actually position yourself to trade not only the breakout from the established trading range, but also a potential bull flag that develops, from the initial retracement, after a breakout impulse occurs. Remember that the initial impulse indicates a sudden imbalance—in favor of the buyers/demand—in the established supply/demand relationship.

Look for price to form a new momentum high in the 3/10 Oscillator, Rate of Change, Momentum, or other unbound oscillators to confirm the recent high that has formed in price. Make sure that price is indeed forming a new swing high, or else you might not be looking at a bull flag in formation. Look for the combination of new indicator swing high along with a new price swing high, not necessarily making an absolute new high, but a high above recent swing highs in price and the indicator.

Enhancing a Bull Flag

After the initial impulse occurs, there are two additional components you can watch to increase the odds of trading a bull flag successfully.

The first level to watch is the initial retracement. Remember you have two possible entry points from the pattern itself. An aggressive trader wants to buy shares as close as possible to the expected bottom of the retracement phase, while a conservative trader wants additional proof that price is indeed forming a bull flag, and thus will wait until price has began its initial move up from a support zone and broken above the upper parallel trend channel that comprises the flag.

Buying after price has broken above the upper trendline is simple, but you can enhance where you enter a position closer to the lows, which gives you a double advantage: first, your stop-loss will be closer to your entry if you buy close to the swing low as opposed to waiting for the confirmed break above the upper channel. Second, your target, and thus potential profit in the trade, will be a larger distance from your entry than if you waited for confirmation via a break above the trend channel. By placing a smaller stop and playing for a larger target, you enhance the probabilities of a successful outcome over waiting for confirmation and a later entry when trading bull flags.

Using a more aggressive strategy will result in more stop losses being hit than if you waited for confirmation. A trader who waited for confirmation would put on fewer positions than one who entered long on a market that did not rally off support as expected. Each individual trader must determine the tradeoff between a superior reward/risk relationship and a higher accuracy rate (a result of waiting for confirmation).

Let's look at a few ways to enhance the odds of finding a reasonable swing low price to enter a position as close to the low as possible, while still having a reasonable stop-loss order in the event that price continues falling and does not trigger an official bull flag entry.

First, there is the parallel trend channel itself. No matter the timeframe on which you are trading, the definition of a bull flag calls for a declining parallel trend channel to form, which connects the prices during the retracement portion of the flag formation. If you see that price has spent some time in a short-term parallel trend channel after an initial impulse, and is currently at the low of the channel, you can enter a position close to the low of the parallel trend channel.

Second, if we add another layer of confirmation to the pattern, you would only enter a position long at the lower trend channel if a corresponding reversal candle, such as a doji, bullish engulfing, spinning top, or hammer formed as price rallied off the low of the parallel trend channel. You might not be able to name the candle, but look for a lower shadow to form which may actually extend slightly beneath where you drew the trend channel. If price breaks above the high of this candle, then enter a position immediately and place a stop just beneath the low of the candle.

Third, you can look to see if price has retraced to any corresponding short-term moving average, specifically the rising 20-period exponential or simple moving averages, for an extra layer of confirmation. The same logic is true for self-drawn price trendlines. Some traders will enter a position just because price has retraced to a rising moving average or established price trendline in the context of an uptrend. A flag can retrace to a rising short-term moving average and thus trigger traders to enter positions, driving the price higher, along with providing a good reference level under which to place stops (the moving average). Although it's not as common, look for the potential for the parallel trend channel to intersect with a rising moving average.

Fourth, you can draw a Fibonacci Retracement grid from the low of the impulse swing to the high of the impulse swing—the pole. I discuss specifics of how to draw Fibonacci grids in Chapter 6, so use that as a reference if you are unfamiliar with Fibonacci retracements. Usually, the retracement portion of the flag will retrace up to 50 percent (the halfway point) of the impulse before finding support. You don't even need to draw a Fibonacci grid to find the half-way point. Measure the distance from the current swing high to the prior swing low and then determine the midpoint of the swing. This will be your reference point. However, it's often helpful to have the 38.2 percent and the 61.8 percent Fibonacci retracement numbers handy when making a trading decision. You can enter your position as you see a reversal candle form at the 50 percent retracement price and then place your stop under the 61.8 percent retracement price for added protection. If price retraces greater than 61.8 percent of the initial impulse, then that deeper-than-usual retracement reduces the odds that we will see the full target of a measured move achieved, so you might want to go ahead and exit a position, or not put on a bull flag position (if not long already) that retraces deeper than the 61.8 percent Fibonacci line.

Fifth, you can look for a three-wave, ABC-style retracement to comprise the retracement or flag portion of the pattern. Identifying simple three-wave retracements is the easiest form of Elliott Wave (discussed in Chapter 7) analysis, as the theory teaches that retracements against an impulse or uptrend take the form of a three-wave move, where the A-wave is a mini-down move, the B-wave is a mini-up move, and the C-wave is the final mini-down move that suggests that the correction has run its course and that the main uptrend will be resuming at the final point in the C-wave. If you look closely at the ideal flag, captured in candlestick form, in Figure 5.5, then you can see the mini-three wave progression, ABC, that comprised the retracement portion of the larger pattern. Waiting for a three-wave sequence to appear can prevent you from thinking that price has found a bottom too early in what is actually a B-wave rally that then resolves into a tiny C-wave down. You can enhance your confidence and increase your edge if you can clearly observe a mini-three wave structure unfolding within the flag retracement portion.

The perfect entry into a bull flag pattern would be one that derives from an initial impulse swing up in the context of an established uptrend, where the flag portion pulls back to the 50 percent Fibonacci retracement price in an ABC three-wave progression that also happens to correspond either with the lower parallel trendline channel of the flag itself or a rising short-term moving average that also forms a bullish reversal candle at the confluence support area. You would take the trade entry after a bullish reversal candle has completed and price has broken the high of that candle on the next bar. You would then place a stop either under the 61.8 percent Fibonacci retracement of the initial impulse, or under the most recent swing low from the reversal candle.

While you may never find all of these ideal conditions in alignment in your personal trading, you will likely find at least two or three components in alignment when you are observing a potential bull flag in real time. Entering as close to the low of the swing of the retracement as possible will give you the greatest reward-to-risk relationship for a larger, defined target with a smaller, defined risk.

Coca-Cola Example: Bull Flag

Coca-Cola's daily chart through 2009 gives us a good example of the bull flag forming with some of the enhancements mentioned above (see Figure 5.6).

Instead of seeing an ideal version of a bull flag, Coca-Cola (KO) gives us a chance to see a six-month bull flag formation in the real world. I've also added the 50-day simple moving average along with the Rate of Change momentum oscillator to show some of the examples of how to enhance a standard bull flag pattern. I also drew a Fibonacci retracement grid (described in Chapter 6) to measure the price retracement—flag

FIGURE 5.6 A Confluence Bull Flag Example in Coca-Cola Daily Chart through 2009

portion—from the high to the low of the pole. Finally, I labeled abc to show the three-wave Elliott style correction that can guide your decisions as to when to enter a bull flag trade.

In context, Coca-Cola was in a prevailing daily chart uptrend after forming a bottom at $38.00 per share along with the broader stock market in March 2009. Price consolidated from June to September 2009 (an example of the Price Alternation Principle as described in Chapter 3) and then broke out of the upper resistance at $53.00 per share in early September. Price then rallied sharply in a single swing that simultaneously formed a new price high and new ROC oscillator high (labeled NPH and NMH respectively). According to the momentum principle, when price and a momentum oscillator form a new high simultaneously, odds favor a higher high yet to come in price after an initial retracement. In this case, the retracement developed into a bull flag price pattern.

We can label the pole portion as the entire swing, with a small retracement, from $49.00 to $55.00 per share. The chart above is a good example because there is a small retracement of four days in late September that does not constitute a full swing, but rather a mini-retracement in the context of a larger price swing. It's rare that you will see a perfect bull flag that rallies every single bar in the pole, so allow for a few bars of retracement when determining where the pole ends and begins.

Price retraced, starting with a gap, in mid-October to form an abc three-wave correction that lasted until November began. Recall that it is important to assess supply and demand, as well as the logic of both bulls and bears, when contemplating taking a trade based on a price pattern. The retracement portion often reflects the orderly, not panicked, selling from bulls who purchased shares at lower prices and then realize the share price has rallied quickly, so they begin to lock in (sell) profits on any weakness after a sharp rally. Short sellers may decide to enter new short-sale trades as overbought/oversold oscillators register an overbought condition, or play for mean reversion by shorting a stock that is deemed overextended beyond its 50-day moving average.

Once price retraced back to the rising moving average, these short sellers will likely cover their position, buying back their shares for a profit, while traders who see the potential bull flag will also begin buying shares as price retraces to an expected support level, such as the 38.2 percent Fibonacci retracement at $52.83 or the rising 20-day moving average, also at the $53.00 level. The main idea is that a shift in the supply/demand relationship occurs at expected support levels as traders buy shares, either to cover short positions or initiate new long positions, into an expected support level.

If you are trading this pattern, this is the spot that you should get long: when price retraces to the confluence of the 38.2 percent or 50.0 percent Fibonacci retracement and a key rising moving average (like the 20-, 50-, 100-, or 200-day averages). In this case, price touched the exact confluence of the 38.2 percent Fibonacci retracement and the rising 50-day simple moving average on November 3, 2009, giving aggressive traders an immediate buy signal at $52.83. These traders would place their stops either just under the 50 percent Fibonacci retracement at $52.00, which serves as a logical point because $52.00 is a round-number psychological support zone and the price is just beneath the rising 50-day moving average. Traders willing to accept more risk from a wider stop would place their stop under $51.00, which was the 61.8 percent moving average. In the event that you bought shares at $52.83 and price continued to fall, breaking under the 61.8 percent retracement, the odds of price completing a full price target for the bull flag, or that a bull flag is developing, are reduced, so you would want to exit your position when the odds deteriorate.

Aggressive traders look to enter on the immediate pullback to a known price level, and they will buy shares without waiting for confirmation that price is rallying. This allows them to enhance their risk/reward relationship, in that they have a much closer logical stop (the $51.00 area) and are playing for a much larger target, which is a projection or measured move of the pole—in this case $7.00, which is the high of the pole at $55.50 minus the low of the pole at $48.50 added to the expected low of the swing at $52.80. Entering at the $53.00 level allows for a $2.00 stop to play for a $7.00 target, for a $7.00 to $2.00 reward-to-risk relationship, or a three and a half-to-one reward-to-risk ratio. Anything above two to one is desired.

However, where would a conservative trader enter the flag position? Those traders who need extra confirmation would notice the price retracement to the 38.2 percent Fibonacci area and the 50-day moving average, but would want proof that price was likely to support at this area. They could wait for a reversal candle to form or for price to break officially above the descending trendline at the $54.00-per-share level.

On November 4, 2009, a clear doji candle formed, with the high of the doji at $54.00 even, which happened to rest just beneath the declining trendline as drawn, comprising the flag pattern. A conservative trader would enter when price rose above the high of the doji and also broke the high of the trendline. In this case, the doji high corresponded with the trendline, but in other cases where a reversal candle forms under a trendline, a trader must decide if price breaking the high of a reversal candle is sufficient evidence for a likely trade entry, or if waiting for a break above the upper trendline is enough evidence to risk their capital. As we will see later, no two traders are identical in their risk-seeking profiles, and so it's best to think of trade setups as having multiple entries depending on your risk-tolerance level. Either way, price did officially break above the doji high and the trendline at $54.00 on November 5 with a powerful bullish confirmation candle, triggering entry at any point in the day. A fill (trade entry) could have occurred anywhere between $54.00 and $54.48 (the high of the day).

While waiting for proof increases the odds that we will be putting on a successful trade, what happens to the risk/reward relationship for the conservative trader? In most cases, waiting for proof will deteriorate your risk/reward relationship and harm your edge while increasing accuracy. How can that be so? We will discuss edge in a later chapter, but for this example, the conservative trader would enter a position at the $54.00 level, place a stop under $52.00 (perhaps as low as $51.00), and then play for the exact same upside bull flag target to $59.00. With their entry at $54.00 and a stop at $52.00, the conservative trader has deteriorated their edge to a $5.00 reward for a $2.00 risk. In terms of the ratio, this becomes a two and a half-to-one reward-to-risk ratio. It's still better than the two to one that is usually required as a minimum for putting on a trade, but is worse than the three and a half to one that the aggressive trader enjoys. If the conservative trader located his or her stop under $51.00 per share (the 61.8 percent retracement), then the reward-to-risk relationship would be a $5.00 target with a $3.00 stop or a one point six-to-one reward-to-risk relationship, which deteriorates the edge to less than the two-to-one reward-to-risk relationship.

Keep this discussion in mind when thinking of taking trades based on price patterns, and how conservative or aggressive strategies affect the entry and reward/risk relationship of the trade. Patterns give you an inherent signal for entry, stop-loss, and a target, but how you employ them, enter your trade, manage your trade, and exit your trade will be based upon whether you are a conservative, moderate, or aggressive trader.

The resolution? Coca-Cola rallied for the next month, enduring another mini-retracement on the way to its target, which price hit on December 11, 2009, as a clear negative momentum divergence formed along with a shooting star/doji candle on December 14. Once price meets a target, it can change the supply/demand relationship. In the event that other bearish signals form, such as negative divergences or reversal candles, it can further tip the balance to the sellers and help send price lower. Aggressive traders could have shorted near the $59.00 level in anticipation of some sort of price retracement as the $59.00 target was hit—and that is exactly what happened. Price quickly retraced into January 2010 to see the $55.00 level again. Both conservative and aggressive traders should have exited a bull flag position as price touched $59.00, completing the price pattern trade.

TRIANGLES

I mentioned that head and shoulders and flag patterns would likely take one of the top three spots on a trader's favorite price patterns list. It's likely that triangles would also occupy one of the top three spots for the same reasons—triangles are easy to recognize, give clear entries and targets, and they occur with relative frequency so traders can see many examples of triangles.

The head and shoulders is based on both the trend reversal and momentum divergence principles, the flag is based also in the trend continuity and momentum burst/impulse principle, but on what principle do we base triangle patterns? Triangles are clearly range contraction patterns that derive their logic from the Price Alternation Principle described in Chapter 3. Restated, the principle declares that price alternates between periods of range contraction and range expansion. We can thus use this principle to help us forecast the next swing in price and trade it as such. Triangles are short-term contraction patterns that often precede a short-term, tradable price range expansion phase.

An Important Caveat on Directional Biases

There is one major caveat to know when working with triangles. In the trading literature, you will find ascending triangles described as bullish continuation patterns and descending triangles described as bearish continuation patterns. In my experience, you do yourself a disservice if you classify triangles as such. Why? Let's assume you see an ascending triangle in the context of an uptrend and you enter a buy position prior to the breakout from the triangle, which is the official signal to enter. In other words, you assume the triangle will break to the upside and so you position yourself early in expectation of an upside break. However, the triangle does not break to the upside, but instead breaks to the downside and you're now facing a rapidly moving downward impulse that either stopped you out or leads to a very large loss if you did not take a stop loss. Either way, you walk away confused as to what happened and why the triangle did not do what it was supposed to do.

The triangle did exactly what it was supposed to do based on the Price Alternation Principle, which was expand after a period of range contraction, but you tried to outthink the triangle by predicting in which direction the triangle was going to expand. Ultimately, we should not try to predict which direction price will break from a range compression pattern (including rectangles along with triangles)—this is where new traders get in trouble. We should understand that the pattern is based on the Price Alternation Principle and expect that a period of range expansion, in either direction, follows a period of range compression, as described in Chapter 3. The Price Alternation Principle does not reveal to us in which direction price will ultimately break. While bull/bear flags along with head and shoulders patterns do have directional biases, based on the prevailing trend, triangles do not have inherent directional biases based on the Price Alternation Principle.

That's not to say that ascending triangles cannot meet their upside breakout targets—many times they will or that descending triangles will not break to the downside—they do. However, when thinking of these patterns in terms of risk/reward and edge, it's best to treat them without directional bias and take advantage of the principle of range expansion following range contraction instead of the complexity of trying to predict which direction price will break.

In fact, you'll likely find that some of the best trades will come from triangles that break opposite of their expected directional bias. Why? Because traders who think that ascending triangles will always break to the upside will be forced to sell their shares as they stop-out when the ascending triangle breaks unexpectedly to the downside, and these traders stopping out, when combined with sellers entering new short-sale positions as a result of the confirmed triangle pattern entry, will create a positive feedback loop that propels price to achieve the unexpected downside target. Strangely enough, price tends to move faster when one side of the market is being squeezed, or forced to stop-out unexpectedly. Knowing this is a major benefit when anticipating where or how to enter a potential triangle trade.

Symmetrical Triangles

Symmetrical triangles are very easy to spot, as traders can observe a distinct narrowing in the price range as it forms to a central point. As price swings narrow, you can draw simple trendlines on your chart to highlight the range compression that takes place.

The easiest way to conceptualize a symmetrical triangle is to think of price winding down to an exact value area, or exact fair value price. Under the range alternation principle, a rectangle style trading range has an overhead resistance price at which shares are deemed expensive, a lower support price at which shares are deemed cheap, and a central value area which price is deemed fair value. In a range pattern, price bounces up and down between these levels until some other force acts on the equilibrium to send price breaking out—up or down—into a new price range expansion move.

Now, instead of visualizing the upper and lower levels as horizontal lines, envision them as contracting toward the fair value price. The best way to think of it is that price is narrowly arriving at a fair price that is deemed reasonable to both buyers and sellers. Remember, if price is deemed too expensive, buyers will not pay the high price, and if price is deemed too cheap, it will attract a rush of buyers to purchase shares on sale. If a price is at exact equilibrium between buyers and sellers, then participants have neither a need to rush to buy shares nor a need to sell shares for a profit. Buyers and sellers meet each other halfway in a state of agreement or equilibrium.

In a symmetrical triangle, the upper resistance line declines over time toward the midpoint or fair value line, while the lower support line rises over time to meet the fair value line. A symmetrical triangle is an example of price efficiency between buyers and sellers.

We know from the Price Alternation Principle that this equilibrium cannot last forever, and when some new piece of information disturbs the calm balance, we can expect some sort of impulse move to send price bursting up or down depending on how that information has affected buyers and sellers and changed their perception of fair value. This would be akin to an initial burst in the supply/demand relationship that serves as the force that sets an object into motion that has been at rest. Figure 5.7 reveals an ideal version of a symmetrical triangle.

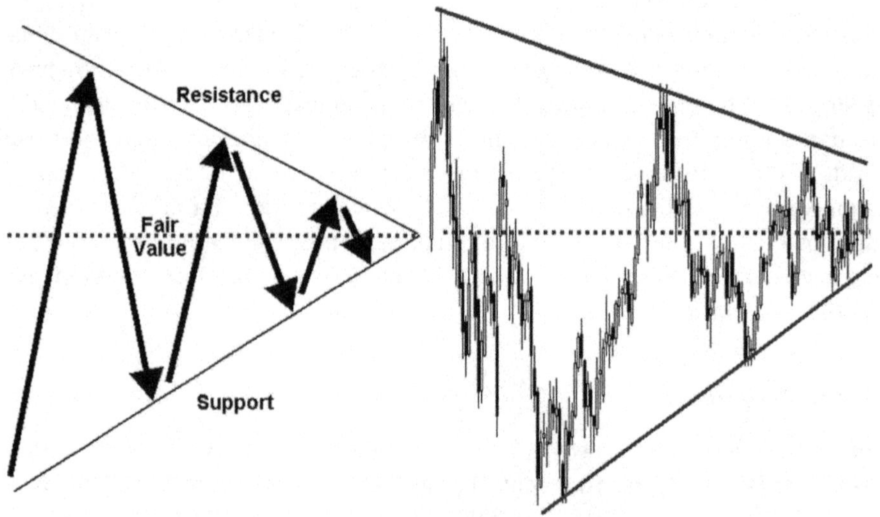

FIGURE 5.7 An Idealized Example of a Symmetrical Triangle

Look back to Chapter 3 where we defined the upper trendline as an overhead resistance expensive price level while the lower trendline was a lower support cheap price level. The fair value, or midpoint price, represents the value area between prices deemed expensive or cheap. In a symmetrical triangle consolidation pattern, unlike the rectangle, the trendlines converge and angle toward the fair value price as time progresses.

Specifically, traders deem what is expensive to be decreasing and what is cheap to be increasing until price arrives at the fair valuation level. At that point, price often breaks out of the pattern in a range expansion phase in price where we have a volatile impulse that creates a positive feedback loop as both buyers and sellers are thrown off balance with regard to prior-existing reference levels of expensive and cheap. In the event of an upside break, buyers are rushing in to drive the price higher while sellers, or those who are holding short-sale positions, are forced to buy to cover, which also drives price higher in an expansion move.

Rules for Entry, Stops, and Targets

As a trader, you can take advantage of these range breakout plays. The rules for entry usually center on buying shares as soon as price breaks solidly above the declining upper trendline, or short selling shares as price breaks under the rising lower support line. Research by Thomas Bulkowski and other technicians indicate that price often will break out of a symmetrical triangle ahead of the price at which the trendlines converge, which is labeled the apex. From the point where the triangle begins, research shows that most triangles break out of either the upper or lower trendline anywhere from 66 percent (two-thirds) and 75 percent (three-fourths) of the way to the apex, though some triangles break out at the apex.. As with all patterns, nothing is guaranteed to happen, and a trade is based on the historical probabilities along with edge—a smaller stop in relation to a larger target. Again, even if half of the trades fail, if we consistently play for at least a two-to-one reward-to-risk relationship, we have a monetary edge.

In regard to where to enter the triangle, we turn back to conservative versus aggressive tactics. An aggressive trader would put on a position immediately as price began to break above the upper trendline or beneath the lower trendline without waiting for confirmation. Conservative traders have a variety of entry strategies, including entering only as price breaks above a strong bullish breakout candle like a bullish engulfing or marabozu, or beneath a strong bearish candle like a bearish engulfing.

In addition to adding candle analysis, traders can employ a two-bar or three-bar close rule, meaning a trader will only enter after two or three bars have closed outside the upper or lower trendline as drawn. A conservative trader may also use a price or percentage function, meaning price has to close a certain dollar value or percentage value (depending on the timeframe) before entering—for example, $1.00 or $2.00, or 2 percent. A trader might also use a multiple of the current Average True Range (ATR) for determining when to enter. For example, if the current daily ATR value is $2.00 and the price is currently trading at $50.00 per share with the apex of the symmetrical triangle also trading at $50.00 per share, then a trader will demand that price rise at least one ATR value or even two ATR values before entering. This would place the trade entry at $52.00 when price has moved one ATR value, or at $54.00 when price has moved two times the current ATR value.

Traditionally, a trader will place a stop just beyond the opposite trendline once he or she has entered a position in expectation of a range breakout. For example, if the horizontal value area for a fair price is $50.00 per share, and the declining resistance line currently rests at $51.00 and the rising support line rests at $49.00, then a trader would enter when price rises above $51.00 and place a stop under $49.00 per share.

In the event that a triangle breaks out earlier than expected, or if the respective trendlines are a lengthy distance apart that would make placing a stop at the opposite trendline unpalatable, then a trader can choose to place a tighter stop at the apex or fair value price of the triangle, which would be $50.00 in the immediate example.

Where would a trader place a price target when playing for a range breakout symmetrical triangle trade? The traditional target is to measure the height of the triangle, which is the greatest distance between the upper declining resistance line to the lower rising support line from where the triangle pattern trendlines began. Take this distance and then add it to the breakout price, similarly to the head and shoulders or flag patterns, to calculate the expected price pattern target.

In the previous example, with an apex at $50.00, let's say that the triangle pattern began to form with an upper price at $55.00 for overhead resistance and a lower price of $45.00 for the lower support line. The distance, or height of the triangle, is thus $55.00 minus $45.00 or $10.00. We take the $10.00 and then add that value to the apex or midpoint of the pattern at $50.00 per share to arrive at a final price projection target of $60.00 per share. If we enter our position at $51.00 and then place a stop at $49.00, then we effectively are playing for a $9.00 target with a $2.00 stop-loss risk price, which gives us a ratio of $9.00 to $2.00 or four and a half-to-one reward-to-risk ratio, which is quite high—much better than the standard two-to-one minimum requirement.

As we will learn when discussing edge in Chapter 8, there is a tradeoff between high reward-to-risk relationships like this. The tradeoff between a high ratio is often a lower win rate, or accuracy rate of the trades which you'll often find is the case. Triangles, and breakout trading patterns in general, tend to be less reliable patterns because of the potential for false breakouts, known as bull or bear traps. However, even if 50 percent of the triangle trades that you take fail by hitting the stop-loss instead of the target, if you consistently take the same setups with higher-than-average reward/risk relationships, you will profit more from the fewer trades that succeed than from the more numerous trades that fail.

The key to understanding these patterns is to realize that the Price Alternation Principle, when price reacts as expected with a fast, volatile range expansion move that originates from the breakout, will result in quick profits that often are a multiple of three or four times your initial stop-loss price, which is often on the opposite side of converging trendlines.

FIGURE 5.8 Symmetrical Triangle Example in Gold Futures Prices through 2009

Let's see an example of a long-term symmetrical triangle that formed in gold throughout 2009 (Figure 5.8).

Gold prices remained in a long-term uptrend moving into 2009, yet price formed a consolidating trading range from January to September that formed a symmetrical triangle pattern, with converging highs and lows that moved toward the apex in early September at the $950.00-per-ounce-level.

Instead of the consolidating taking more of a rectangle shape with a clear horizontal resistance line and horizontal support line, these price boundaries converged toward the midpoint or value area at $950.00. Traders could have been anticipating putting on a position on a break above the resistance trendline or beneath the support trendline as shown. In early September, price officially broke and closed out of the triangle pattern forming two bullish power candle days in a row that took price above the prior swing high from June at the $1,000.00-per-ounce level.

Remember back to the chapter on the Price Alternation Principle, and you can visualize the range contraction period that marked the triangle giving way to a range expansion period that formed after price broke out of the established "expensive/cheap" boundaries that converged toward the fair value price. An aggressive trader would establish a long position as soon as price broke above the $970.00 level which reflected the upper resistance line at that time and then measured the distance from the start of the pattern—the height of the triangle—and then added that value, which was roughly $225.00, to the breakout zone at the $970.00 level just above the fair value price of $950.00. For the purpose of this example, I'm using round numbers to make the example clearer. Taking the height of $225.00 and adding it to the breakout price at $975.00 gives us a price pattern projection target of $1,200.00. A trader would place a stop on the opposite side of the triangle trendline, in this case the lower trendline at the $925.00 level, or for a tighter, more conservative stop, at the apex value area of $950.00 per ounce.

Price continued up to the $1,200.00 target, rallying from $1,050.00 to $1,200.00 in a single month—November—at which point triangle pattern traders would sell their positions with a profit and successfully completed pattern. Gold actually rallied slightly higher than its official $1,200.00 target before falling back to the $1,050.00 level. Again, some traders will decide to sell short once a classic price projection target is achieved.

Ascending and Descending Triangles

For all practical purposes, you should treat an ascending triangle the same way you would a symmetrical triangle. All triangles are consolidation patterns that derive their predictive nature and price projection targets from the Price Alternation Principle. While most traders view triangles as continuation patterns, it's best to see them as neutral and be equally prepared to trade an upside or a downside breakout from the converging trendline boundaries.

If the triangle behaves as expected, meaning the range consolidation phase gives way to a sudden impulse in price into a range expansion phase, you would be saddled with a large, unexpected loss in the event you guessed incorrectly as to which direction the triangle would break.

It may indeed be statistically true that ascending triangles have a greater than 50 percent chance of breaking out to the upside, but remember, it's best to base your trading decisions on long-standing price principles such as the Price Alternation Principle, Trend Continuity Principle, or Momentum Principle. As such, I suggest treating ascending and descending triangles with a neutral directional bias, the same as a symmetrical triangle, and trading them as such.

The logic is similar to that of the symmetrical triangle, except that in the case of an ascending triangle, price will form a horizontal overhead resistance level above the value area while the lower support trendline will rise to converge with the horizontal level, forming a triangle pattern that moves toward the apex, or convergence of the trendlines. Similarly, a descending triangle will form a horizontal support line along with a descending upper resistance line that eventually will converge at the apex of the pattern.

Let's move from our example in Figure 5.8 and see a descending triangle in the context of gold's larger uptrend.

While Figure 5.8 showed a complete symmetrical triangle example in gold prices, Figure 5.9 shows a descending triangle example and ends with the breakout from the descending upper resistance line.

FIGURE 5.9 Descending Triangle Example in Gold Futures Prices through 2006

A descending triangle contains a clear horizontal support line, which can be referred to as cheap (or on sale) to market participants, which can cause them to buy at the horizontal support level and thus drive the price higher. However, unlike a rectangular consolidation pattern, the upper expensive resistance line resembles a descending trendline, as investors deem price to be expensive at sequentially lower levels over time. That is one reason investors often view descending triangles as inherently bearish.

The official trade entry signal comes as price breaks under the lower support line, in this case at the $650-per-ounce level which is clearly defined as support, or the upper resistance level which occurred at the end of October 2006 at the $690.00 level. In this example, price broke out of the descending triangle to the upside, giving you a chance to buy into the context of a prevailing uptrend at a low-risk entry level. You would place your stop under the clear support level at $650.00 and set your price target in a similar method as you did for the symmetrical triangle. Take the height of the triangle and then add that value to the breakout price of the pattern. The triangle begins at the $820.00 level and ends at the $650.00 level, which gives us a height of $170.00 per ounce. We then add our $170.00 height to the breakout price at $690.00 to give us a price pattern projection target of $860.00.

Although the chart does not show it, price continued to rise almost without pausing to meet the $860.00 target in September 2007, less than a year from when the breakout occurred. Price again overshot the target slightly, peaking at $894.00 before falling sharply back to the $820.00 level.

Sears Holdings Example: Intraday Ascending Triangle

All price patterns are applicable on all timeframes, as Figure 5.10 reveals, as it shows the 30-minute intraday chart of Sears Holdings (SHLD). Patterns even form and complete their targets on timeframes as low as the 1-minute chart!

The price of SHLD was in a sharp impulse move up from the $106.00 level on April 21 to peak and form a line of horizontal resistance at $125.00 from April 23 to May 1. Traders and investors formed a horizontal resistance line at the $125.00-per-share level, as they deemed this level to be "expensive" to buy shares at that price. However, the level deemed cheap, or the lower support zone, began on April 23 with a series of higher lows that formed a clean rising trendline as drawn.

FIGURE 5.10 Intraday Ascending Triangle Example in Sears Holdings—April 2010

By May 1, it became clear that price was most likely forming a consolidation pattern that took the form of an ascending triangle. However, just as soon as you realized that price was contained within a consolidation pattern with a median or fair value price at the $122.00 level, sellers took price lower, breaking under not just the lower rising trendline, but the prior swing low of $121.00 per share from April 30, triggering an official price pattern short-sale entry trade.

I used this example to underscore the point that if you were 100 percent convinced that price had to rise and had bought shares long while the triangle formed, either because the prior trend was up or because you felt that all ascending triangles broke to the upside, you would be trapped in a sharp sell-off that began with a morning gap and immediate sell-off that took price from $122.00 to $118.00 right off the market open. If you regarded this pattern as neutral, you would have avoided this painful loss and would be in the right mindset to put on a short-sale trade, if you so desired, to play a range breakout trade.

In this case, the entry was as soon as you could get short once price cleanly broke under the rising trendline, which occurred at the $122.00 level. Your most realistic entry came at the $118.00 level, which placed a stop likely within the triangle at the $122.00-per-share level or above the upper resistance line at $125.00. To project your price target, you would measure the height of the triangle, $125.00 minus $116.00 gives us $9.00, and then subtract this value from the price breakout zone at the $121.00-per-share level. Subtracting $9.00 from $121.00 gives us a lower price projection target of $112.00. In the event that you entered short at $118.00, that left you with a price target distance of $6.00 with a stop-loss at $122.00, which was $4.00 away. That's not at all an ideal reward-to-risk ratio, being $6.00 to $4.00, or one and a half to one.

This also underscores the point that it is best to enter into a triangle breakout as soon as possible, and you could have done so right off the open as price began to trade under $120.00. Shorting exactly at $120.00 would have given you a superior reward-to-risk ratio of $9.00 to $2.00, or four and a half to one. Every penny matters when you are taking a trade, and the longer you wait for confirmation as the price moves toward the target and away from the stop-loss, your reward-to-risk ratio deteriorates.

Sears Holdings hit its price target of $112.00 per share officially on May 6, 2010, two days after the breakout trade triggered. Price actually fell further after this chart ends. Remember, with price patterns, generally your stop is at a fixed location and your target is also at a fixed location. The closer you enter to where you would locate a stop makes a big difference in your reward-to-risk ratio. We will discuss these details when we discuss Edge and Probability in Chapter 8.

USING PRICE PATTERNS IN THE REAL WORLD

Price patterns are important to traders, but they are by no means perfect. If you expect all patterns you see on a chart to work perfectly according to textbook standards, you will soon be disappointed. However, when you tie price patterns to underlying principles of price behavior, understand that patterns offer a brief window of a possible pathway forward to a target in price, and that the edge from patterns comes from the low risk/higher reward relationship contained in the inherent stop and target placement, you will likely find that trading specific price patterns can be a rewarding practice.

As is the purpose of this book, all concepts are enhanced through confluence, rather than in isolation. Look for as many convergences in principles and price levels as possible before putting on a trade. In so doing, you will pass on the sub-par patterns that develop and trade only those that align with other price principles or concepts you have learned in your experience. Envision patterns as a brief window into the supply/demand relationship that exists among traders of all styles and experience levels, similar to the way a candle reveals insights into the current supply/demand relationship between buyers and sellers and what that might indicate for the future.

Keep in mind that some of the best trades come from what we call busted patterns, or patterns that grab the attention of a large majority of traders, and then fail, taking the massive stop-losses of those who have entered which creates a predictable equal but opposite reaction than is expected. Positive feedback loops often develop unexpectedly when a popular price pattern fails as traders are trapped.

For now, study these patterns along with additional patterns you have learned in the trading literature, but never take a pattern at face value or believe with 100 percent certainty that the pattern will resolve exactly as the textbooks say it will. We trade in the real world, not the theoretical, and we need to adjust our expectations accordingly and be nimble without being biased to a single position.

We have briefly touched on how Fibonacci retracements can enhance a bull flag trade, but Fibonacci retracement grids go far beyond that application. Our next chapter explains how to draw and apply Fibonacci retracements within the context of trending environments to locate hidden support or resistance confluence levels in price.

CHAPTER 6

Fibonacci Tools

So far, we have discussed price principles, price patterns, and basic candlestick charting as a means to discover higher probability trade setups. Now we move into our first advanced price charting method, known as Fibonacci Analysis. Traders use basic Fibonacci retracements to find support or resistance in a trending market, and these key prices can help uncover hidden points of potential support or resistance levels not seen using basic charting methods. Most software programs or charting web sites make Fibonacci tools available to traders, and thus increased the popularity of using even simple Fibonacci techniques.

In this chapter, we will discuss how to use Fibonacci retracements to find key support or resistance levels that may form alignment with other price levels, how to uncover hidden confluences of Fibonacci retracement levels, and how even simple Fibonacci tools can help confirm other methods of identifying price support or resistance, which leads to enhanced trade entry and exit.

WHAT IS FIBONACCI IN TRADING?

Traders in 2010 still use insights from a number series described by Leonardo Fibonacci of Pisa, an Italian mathematician from the thirteenth century as described in his book *Liber Abaci* (which translates as "The Book of the Abacus"). Most modern mathematics students know the Fibonacci sequence as the classic 1, 1, 2, 3, 5, 8, 13, 21, 34, 55, 89, 144, 233, and so on, where the next number in the sequence is the result of adding the prior two numbers together. For example, 5 plus 8 equals 13, and 8 plus 13 equals 21. The Fibonacci sequence initially explained growth and decay sequences in nature, such as the growth in generations beginning with a single pair of rabbits, and has now been expanded to include larger growth and decay cycles of much larger structures, including financial markets.

The numbers themselves are not as important to modern traders, who are more concerned with the specific ratio between the numbers that develops the idea behind the Fibonacci charting strategies used today. Dividing one number by the immediate larger number in the sequence results in the ratio 0.618, such as the number 55 divided by 89 equals 0.618, which forms a stable relationship when dividing any number by one Fibonacci number higher. With the exception of the beginning numbers in the sequence (5 divided by 8 is 0.625, any number in the infinite sequence above 34 results in the 0.618 relationship). The 0.618 number becomes important when using the Fibonacci retracement tool common on most software programs.

Dividing a given number by the next smaller number in the sequence results in the ratio 1.618, as in the example 89 divided by 55 equals 1.618, or 55 divided by 34 equals 1.618. This relationship and ratio holds true no matter which number in the sequence is divided by a lower number. As such, the ratio of one number to the next Fibonacci number is 1.618 times itself, or stated differently, to identify the next larger number in the series, one then multiplies a current number by 1.618, as in the example 89 times 1.618 equals 144. The ratio 1.618 has importance for traders looking to use Fibonacci price projection or extension tools on their charting software to uncover potential range expansion price targets.

The application to modern traders has less to do with the actual Fibonacci numbers than the 0.618 and 1.618 relationships themselves. As explained by Charles Kirkpatrick and Julie Dahlquist in *Technical Analysis: The Complete Resource for Financial Market Technicians* (2007), the .618 and 1.618 ratio between numbers holds true regardless of the departure point as long as the two numbers sum to the third number in an infinite sequence. Kirkpatrick and Dahlquist begin their example with the random whole numbers 14 and 285 as a departure point instead of the 1, 1, 2, 3, 5, 8 numbers that begin the official Fibonacci sequence. Over a period of 7 to 8 iterations of adding the original two numbers, the ratio converges to the same 0.618 relationship between a given number and the next larger digit, and the 1.618 ratio of a given number and the next smaller digit in the sequence.

Try it for yourself with any two random starting digits, such as in the example 25 and 50. $25 + 50 = 75$; $75 + 50 = 125$; $125 + 75 = 200$; $200 + 125 = 325$; $325 + 200 = 525$; $525 + 325 = 850$; $850 + 525 = 1{,}375$ to infinity. The sequential number 850 divided by 1,375 equals 0.618, and the sequential number 850 divided by the higher sequential number 1,375 equals 1.618. The application to the markets and beyond therefore comes from the mathematical ratio itself and not from the starting numbers.

Now that we have a basic understanding of the 0.618 and 1.618 ratio numbers which are important not only to mathematicians, let us now move into the realm of describing how modern traders use these ratios to create Fibonacci tools to uncover potential turning points in the market.

FIBONACCI RETRACEMENTS

While many traders are familiar with Fibonacci tools, others have never heard of the concept as it relates to technical analysis or charting. The simplest way to apply the 0.618 ratio is in the common Fibonacci retracement tool on most charting software programs. Recall that in an upward trend move, price forms higher highs and higher lows, or stated differently, price forms upward impulses and downward retracements. Traders anticipate where these retracement swings to the downside will stop and then price will resume rising in its established uptrend. Some of the easiest trades come from buying pullbacks in an uptrend to a key support level, such as a short-term moving average, rising trendline, or prior price support levels.

Another trading tool is the simple Fibonacci retracement tool, which is designed to find the end of a downward retracement into support so that traders may buy shares as price begins to rise upward from a potential support level. Traders use the 0.618 ratio and derivations of this ratio such as the popular 0.382 ratio to find potential turning points in a market. Traders use percentages such as the 61.8 percent retracement level and the 38.2 percent retracement level. The 38.2 percent level derives from the remainder or what is left over after measuring 61.8 percent of a move. In terms of ratios, think of the 0.382 as being left-over after finding the 0.618 segment, or specifically 1 minus 0.618 equals 0.382. This is why you see the 38.2 percent retracement on standard Fibonacci retracement tools. While not officially a Fibonacci ratio, almost all traders pay attention to the 50 percent retracement level in addition to the 61.8 and 38.2 percent levels, which is why most default retracement tools show three lines in the chart. Thus, the 61.8 percent, 38.2 percent, and the 50 percent retracement lines are what you can expect to see most frequently when doing any type of Fibonacci retracement analysis on the price chart.

Drawing Fibonacci Retracement Grids

Most software programs incorporate Fibonacci tools into their basic or free set of indicators, such as the charting web sites StockCharts.com and FreeStockCharts.com. The following describes the purpose and rules for drawing a classic Fibonacci retracement grid on a chart to reveal potential support levels in an established uptrend.

The purpose for drawing a Fibonacci Retracement Grid is to find potential support or turning points that will end a downward retracement swing in an established uptrend. The trader looks to buy shares if price forms a reversal candle at a major Fibonacci retracement level, or if a Fibonacci Level forms a price confluence with a moving average, trendline, or other form of support.

The following steps represent the sequence to draw a Fibonacci Retracement Grid:

1. Establish that price is in a confirmed uptrend
2. Observe a recent price swing high and note that price is retracing down from a recent swing high in price

3. Use the Fibonacci Retracement tool to start the grid by clicking on the most recent swing low in price and dragging the grid to the most recent swing high in price
4. Observe the 38.2, 50.0, and 61.8 percent retracement levels the software labels on the price chart for potential downside targets and areas to identify potential price confluences with other methods, with the purpose being to buy when price has retraced into support and may be resuming the established uptrend

For finding overhead resistance levels in a downtrend, repeat the procedure above but start the Fibonacci grid at the most recent swing high in price in an established downtrend and end the grid at the most recent new swing low in price to uncover the 38.2, 50.0, and 61.8 percent overhead resistance levels. Look to sell short when price retraces into one of these overhead resistance levels, particularly if the level forms a confluence with a moving average or trendline along with a reversal candle.

Examples of Identifying Price Support

The following examples of Fibonacci retracement grids designed to identify price support will be helpful in understanding this concept. Keep in mind that the technique will be opposite for finding overhead resistance levels to short-sell in a downtrend. Let us start with a pure Fibonacci example using a theoretical uptrend beginning at $1.00 and moving to $100.00 (an extreme example), and we want to know the potential retracement levels of the prior swing from $50.00 to $100.00. Figure 6.1 shows the established uptrend and the recent retracement to a lower support level, where a Fibonacci Retracement grid can be helpful.

In Figure 6.1, we first observe an uptrend as evidenced by higher price highs and higher price lows. The most recent swing took price from a swing low of $50.00 to the most recent swing high of $100.00 per share. The most recent swing was a $50.00 move to the upside, and we want to know where potential levels of support might be, and so we use the Fibonacci retracement tool.

Starting with the most recent $50.00 swing low, we begin our grid and then end the grid with the most recent swing high at $100.00. The software then draws the 38.2, 50.0, and 61.8 percent retracement levels. Some software programs might draw the grid starting with the high and ending with the low, so be sure to consult the user manual of the charting software program you use. The goal is to have the 38.2 percent retracement in an uptrend be near the recent high in an uptrend to find support, and for the 38.2 percent retracement to be near the recent low in a downtrend to find resistance.

The 50.0 percent retracement is the easiest to understand, as this is the halfway point of the prior swing. In a strong uptrend, price can retrace up to 50 percent of the prior swing to be considered healthy. However, any price retracement greater than 50 percent of the prior move could signal a deeper than normal retracement is underway, and that the next level to expect support is at the 61.8 percent level.

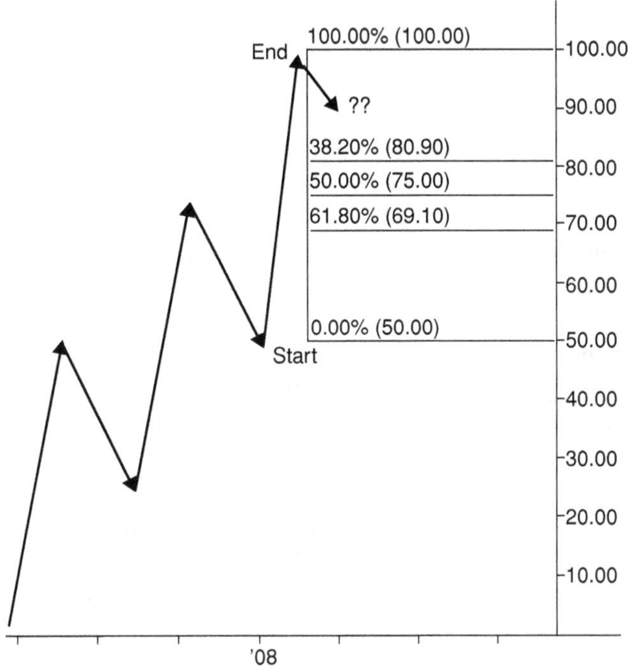

FIGURE 6.1 A Pure Price Example of a Fibonacci Retracement Grid

If price retraces greater than 61.8 percent of the prior move, then many traders would be comfortable stopping out in anticipation that price was forming a reversal swing to the downside instead of a standard retracement to test lower support levels. As such, many traders regard the 61.8 percent level as a very important level to watch as a boundary line to determine the potential for a reversal to form instead of a retracement.

In this example, the price swing is $50.00. Half of this value is $25.00, and when either subtracted from the $100.00 high or added to the $50.00 swing low, the result is $75.00 per share, which is conveniently labeled on the chart. In this example, the $75.00 level also forms a confluence with the most recent prior swing high, meaning that we have a confluence of support from the 50 percent retracement grid and a prior swing high. If price retraces to this level and a reversal candle or a positive momentum divergence forms at the $75.00 confluence support level, we would be interested in buying the market to anticipate a resumption of the uptrend, leaving us to profit from any move to the upside from an expected support level.

Other than the 50 percent halfway retracement level, we then turn to the two Fibonacci Levels as drawn by the retracement grid, starting with the 38.2 percent line which appears at $80.90 in this example. It is possible that price will continue retracing downward and find support at this higher retracement level, and we might want to buy the market if we start to see signs of a reversal forming at the $81.00 level in the form of positive divergences or reversal candles. We would also look for any rising trendlines or short-term moving averages such as the 20-period simple or exponential moving average to align at the $81.00 level. If so, we would consider buying the market at the 38.2 percent Fibonacci retracement price of $80.90.

The final well-known Fibonacci-based retracement zone comes in at the 61.8 percent retracement level. The 61.8 percent level reflects the 0.618 ratio of the recent $50.00 swing to the upside, such that $50.00 (the distance of the prior swing) times 0.618 (the Golden Ratio) equals $30.90. Taking the swing high at $100.00 and subtracting $30.90 gives us the 61.8 percent retracement at $69.10. As a cross-check, adding this same value to the $50.00 swing low gives us the $80.90 price, which is the same as the 38.2 percent retracement level.

After observing price as being in an established uptrend and finding the price retracing downward from the key swing high of $100.00, we use our Fibonacci retracement tool to find the $80.90, $75.00, and $69.10 price levels to be potential support zones. Should other non-related methods, such as moving averages, trendlines, or prior price support levels align with one or more of these levels, then we could expect increased odds of a potential turn in price back to the upside, giving us a potential trade setup.

While specific trade execution tactics will be discussed in Chapter 8, we would confirm a trade entry if we observed a reversal candle such as a bullish hammer, bullish engulfing, or doji candle at the expected support level. In addition, if we observed a positive momentum divergence either on the same timeframe or on a lower timeframe, odds would be increased for profitable trade setup. No method alone can guarantee success, but finding confluences across multiple non-correlated methods increases the odds of a successful trade outcome and helps with the accuracy edge in our strategies.

UTX Daily Example

In Figure 6.2, we see a real example of a Fibonacci retracement grid and the outcome of a deep retracement of a prior swing to new highs in United Technologies (UTX) in mid-2007.

Although not specifically showing it, United Technologies was in an uptrend since the 2003 lows and had recently formed a key swing high just shy of $78.00 per share. In July, price began a downswing to test lower levels, and nimble traders drew the following Fibonacci Retracement grid to find potential support levels to watch for a potential entry. Initially, price found support in early August at the 38.2 percent level at $72.41, but after a week of trading higher, price then suddenly fell to the deeper potential support level of the 61.8 percent retracement at $69.06. Traders often place stop-losses under the 61.8 percent level of a retracement, and the United Technologies chart in Figure 6.2 is a good example of how this can be a helpful tactic for those who were bullish on United Technologies.

The candle on August 16, 2007 took price sharply lower in a sudden gap lower as price fell throughout the intraday trading session. However, by the close of the day, buyers found that the 61.8 percent retracement level contained the low of the trading day, and also the retracement lower as a bullish hammer candle formed at the close of the

FIGURE 6.2 Daily Chart of a Fibonacci Retracement Grid in United Technologies during mid-2007

session. Traders associate bullish hammer candles, with the long lower shadow reflecting price rejection of lower prices, with price reversals. True to its bullish signal, the hammer candle preceded the next upswing in price as buyers took price back above the 38.2 percent retracement level and later to new highs above $78.00 in a resumption of the uptrend, though this chart does not show the new highs which formed a final swing high of $82.50 on October 2, 2007, a few weeks after the end of this chart.

United Technologies Weekly Example

Let us move to a longer-term example of a weekly Fibonacci retracement grid also in United Technologies, forming off a powerful upswing in price that began over the course of many months instead of weeks in the prior example.

Starting with the March 2003 low of $26.75 and ending with the February 2004 price swing high of $48.92, we draw a standard Fibonacci Retracement grid on the weekly chart of United Technologies. In this example, price formed a large downward week in late February 2004, beginning a standard downward retracement in price against a powerful uptrend that took price from a swing low of just under $27.00 to $49.00, almost doubling in price over the period of a year.

FIGURE 6.3 Weekly Chart of a Fibonacci Retracement Grid in United Technologies during 2003–2004, with a Marabozu Candle at the 38.2 percent Retracement Level

Traders expected a natural retracement in price, but the question became a matter of finding where to expect price to find support and resume the uptrend. Traders who drew the following Fibonacci grid as shown in Figure 6.3 found $40.45, $37.84, and $35.21 as potential downside targets and levels to watch for any sign of price reversal. Because price moved in a single swing off the early 2003 lows, there were few if any places to look for prior price support levels, so the Fibonacci retracement grid became especially helpful in uncovering hidden potential support levels.

The first test of support came in late May 2004, as price retraced to the first potential support zone at the 38.2 percent Fibonacci retracement at the $40.46-per-share level. We do not know in advance where a retracement level will end, and price will resume its uptrend, but we can look to Fibonacci levels as sequential levels for a potential turn in price. The first level is the 38.2 percent zone, and in this case, that was the terminal point for the downward retracement in price.

Traders who also used candlestick charts observed the bullish marabozu extreme candle that formed just after a spinning top neutral candle at the 38.2 percent retracement zone at $40.45, giving them an early clue that price could find support at this level and resume its upward climb. Those who took the time to observe the daily chart at this same juncture in price saw a clear doji candle that formed on May 21, which was a neutral candle that signaled the potential for a market turning point, especially at a key support level. Traders could have bought United Technologies when price rose above the high of the weekly Marabozu candle at the $42.00-per-share level or more aggressively, bought as price rose beyond the high of the daily doji on May 21 that closed at $40.92 to target a resumption of the uptrend and eventual retest of the prior highs just shy of $50.00 per share or beyond.

The chart also shows the custom MACD Indicator (using simple moving averages instead of the standard exponential moving averages), with input settings 3, 10, 1, which reveals a positive momentum divergence occurring as price formed a bullish Marabozu candle at the 38.2 percent Fibonacci retracement price of $40.45 per share. See Chapter 2 for a discussion on the custom MACD indicator, or the 3, 10 Oscillator and positive indicator divergences. Recall the price principle momentum leads price, and that positive momentum divergences are associated with positive reversals in price, especially in an established uptrend. Our job as traders is to piece together the puzzle as we perceive it and put on trades that have the odds in their favor of successful outcomes.

In the event that price fell through the $40.00-per-share level, traders would be on the lookout for any reversal candle that formed at the 50 percent half-way retracement level at $37.84. Traders who bought United Technologies at the $40.00-per-share level would also place stops conservatively under the 38.2 percent retracement perhaps at the $39.00 level, or more aggressively under the 50 percent halfway retracement at $37.84.

In this way, traders can use Fibonacci retracement levels not only to confirm a potential support zone, but as a location to place stops while in an established position. Should price retrace lower than the 61.8 percent level at $35.22, traders would then start to doubt the potential for a continuation swing back to test new highs, and might consider the possibility that a reversal swing to the downside is occurring instead of a classic retracement in price, and move on to looking for the next opportunity.

HOW TO IDENTIFY FIBONACCI RETRACEMENT CONFLUENCE ZONES

Once you master the concept of simple Fibonacci price retracement grids, you will likely begin asking yourself "Where do I begin my Fibonacci grid if I see more than one swing low to begin drawing the retracement grid?" This is an excellent question, and the quick answer is to start grids at the immediate swing low in price and draw to the immediate swing high.

However, instead of ignoring prior swing lows, astute traders find value in drawing identical Fibonacci retracement grids that end at the most recent swing high to multiple beginning points based on prior swing lows in an established uptrend. Using this technique, traders are able to find hidden confluence or convergence levels of Fibonacci grids that can provide valuable information available to those who use this method.

A traditional Fibonacci retracement grid starts at a key swing low and ends at a key swing high in an uptrend to find a lower support level, or alternately, starts at a key swing high and ends at the most recent swing low in a downtrend to find an overhead resistance level. When price undergoes a lengthy uptrend or downtrend, multiple swing levels form which create multiple departure points to create Fibonacci grids.

Instead of finding the three primary retracement levels to expect a price reversal, Fibonacci retracement confluence grids drawn off multiple swing lows to a common swing high help find the more important potential turning points in a market. The goal is to observe any exact price retracement level confluences, and then observe any resulting retracement levels that overlap relatively close to additional retracement levels. In taking the extra time to find convergence zones, you can gain a quick edge over traders who use single retracement grids exclusively.

Drawing Fibonacci Confluence Retracement Grids

Similar to the rules of classic Fibonacci retracement grids, a trader who draws multiple grids off key swing lows attempts to find confluence zones of major Fibonacci retracement levels. Instead of drawing a single retracement grid as drawn above, a trader would draw a retracement grid that ends with the most recent swing high in an uptrend but begins at two, three, or more key swing lows in an established uptrend. To find overhead confluence resistance levels in a downtrend, a trader would end with the most recent swing low and then begin a classic Fibonacci retracement grid at two, three, or more swing highs in an established downtrend.

The purpose of drawing a Fibonacci retracement confluence grid is to find hidden, important levels of convergence starting with more than one standard Fibonacci Retracement grid. Instead of finding the three main retracement levels, a trader is interested in finding price levels where two or more main Fibonacci grids align closely or exactly.

The following steps represent the order a trader should take to draw multiple Fibonacci Retracement Grids:

1. Establish that price is in a confirmed uptrend.
2. Observe a recent price swing high and note that price is retracing down from this high in price.
3. Use the Fibonacci Retracement tool to start the grid by clicking on the most recent swing low in price and dragging the grid to the most recent swing high in price.

4. Continue drawing similar Fibonacci Retracement grids in the same manner from prior key swing retracement lows in price.
5. Observe the levels that align closely and watch for price to move toward these levels.
6. Consider establishing a buy position in the event that other forms of analysis such as reversal candles, momentum divergences, or other forms of support align at or near the confluence price level.

For finding confluence retracement grids in a downtrend, repeat the same procedure but begin each new grid at prior swing highs in a downtrend and end each grid at the most recent swing low in price in order to uncover confluence overhead resistance levels to establish short-sale positions on any momentum divergence, reversal candle, or other method of charting that uncovers resistance levels or sell signals.

Examples in an Uptrend

With the procedure for finding confluence zones established, let's discuss some examples of how to apply this concept.

Sears Holdings (Weekly) First, let's begin with a weekly chart of Sears Holdings (SHLD) from 2004 to 2006.

As with all examples, we can see what happened after price rallied off support, so keep in mind that we do not know the outcome of a trade setup while it is forming.

Let's transport back in time to mid-2005 to identify how the confluence in Figure 6.4 formed. We have confirmed that price is in an uptrend and has reached a key swing high at $160.00 per share as a shooting star candle formed, which was then followed by a mild bearish engulfing candle. We can be confident that a retracement swing is the next likely course of action for the daily chart.

We want to answer the question, "Where will price find support," or specifically "Where will I want to put on a buy position at a favorable entry to trade a potential bounce off support?" We can use the classic Fibonacci Retracement tool.

Start with the key swing high of $160.00 and then look back to prior swing lows on the chart. Most traders only draw a Fibonacci retracement grid to the obvious swing low, which is usually the genesis of the trend, and then stop there. Take the extra step and draw as many grids as is reasonable based on prior price swing lows. Starting with the swing low in early 2004 at $25.00 per share, we have our dominant or long-term Fibonacci retracement. We then move up to the next immediate swing low from the retracement to the $40.00-per-share level in May 2004. From there, we draw a third Fibonacci retracement grid from the $60.00-per-share level on the August 2004 pullback. We can draw a fourth and final retracement grid on the January 2005 pullback to the $90.00-per-share level.

Figure 6.4 marks each swing low with the word start to indicate where to draw the Fibonacci retracement grid each time to the end of the $160.00 expected swing high. Our goal now is to look at our Fibonacci retracement grid lines to find any overlapping prices

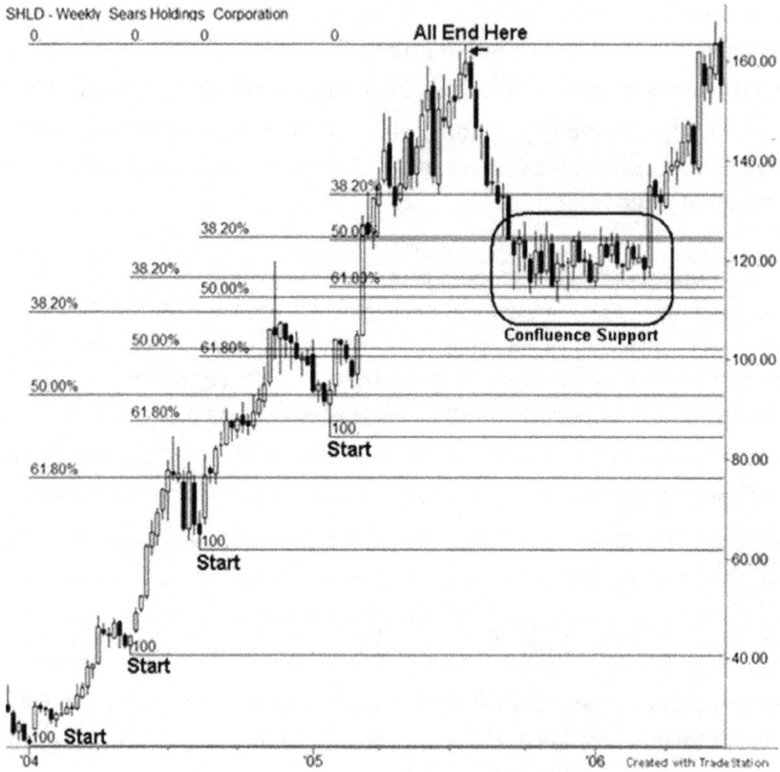

FIGURE 6.4 Weekly Chart Example of Identifying a Hidden Fibonacci Confluence Support Zone in Sears Holdings

which will draw our focus to those levels as potentially hidden support zones that could provide a low-risk entry if confirmed with other methods, such as positive divergences, trendlines, or other forms of price support.

Remember, let's pretend that we can't see the future, and can't see that price will support at the confluence level that arises at the $115.00 level. Working our way up the chart, we see the first confluence rests at the $100.00-per-share level, which is an overlap of the 50.0 and 61.8 percent retracement from the starting points shown.

The level above the tight $100.00 confluence reveals four retracement lines in a loose confluence of two 38.2 percent retracements, one 50.0 percent retracement, and one 61.8 percent retracement (look closely at how these confluences form from the retracement grid). That naturally draws our attention as chartists to expect a potential support area and rally from the convergences at the $115.00 area. Closer to the swing high, we see another tight confluence at the $125.00 area from the overlap of the 38.2 percent and 50.0 percent retracement lines. The chart reveals no other major or minor confluences to watch.

Moving ahead in time, we see that price interestingly remained between the tight confluence at $125.00 as resistance and the looser or wider confluence of four lines at the $115.00 area. Once you see this happening, you can then prepare to buy the stock if it forms reversal candles, positive divergences, or other bullish developments at the $115.00 level. Alternatively, as you see price is remaining within a tight trading range between these two levels, you could stand aside and wait to play a potential breakout rally that would be expected to continue should buyers push price above the $125.00 confluence.

Remember that price alternates between periods of range contraction and range expansion, and we see that price is forming a lengthy consolidation period, which took the form of a rectangle price pattern, between two of the three dominant Fibonacci confluence zones. This Sears Holdings chart is the same situation we observed in Chapter 3 when discussing the Price Alternation Principle.

Once price broke above the upper confluence at $125.00, then you could have put on a buy order to play the potential breakout and trend continuation move that ultimately did take price in the next swing back to challenge (and exceed) the prior $160.00 level.

That was your goal anyway, wasn't it? You wanted to find a support zone to buy this stock in a rising uptrend while controlling your risk. You would have placed a stop conservatively under the middle confluence at the $110.00 level, or if you favor wider stops, then you would have chosen to place a stop under the tight confluence at $100.00.

Mini-Gold Futures (Weekly) Let's now move to the gold market to see a confluence Fibonacci example in mini-gold prices (@YG) in Figure 6.5, which spans from 2002 to 2007.

This time I kept the trendlines to show the Fibonacci grids more clearly. In this example, we assume that the May 2006 swing high to the $840.00 level is a key high, but we also suspect gold remains in an uptrend and want to know where price is likely to find support on any pullback to a large-scale Fibonacci support area. Start each retracement grid at key swing lows during the recent uptrend and connect each of your four grids to the $840.00 swing high as shown.

I chose this example to show that sometimes you might get lines that form only one convergence or perhaps none at all. In this example, we see weak convergences above $650.00, so we cannot reasonably count those as confluence support areas.

However, if we start from the lower end of the chart and work our way higher, we do see two distinct convergence lines, with the first overlap forming at the $640.00 level and the second nearby overlap forming at the $655.00 level. We also see that price retraced to the $650 level and formed a slight double-bottom price pattern before rallying higher, allowing aggressive traders to enter at this level, provided there were other buy signals (the two lower wicks or shadows on the candles were clues that buyers were active and rejected any price under $650.00). If you chose to enter as price challenged the $655.00 Fibonacci confluence, then it would be encouraged to place a stop under the lower confluence at the $640.00 level. In the event that sellers pushed price under this confluence, odds would favor a deeper retracement swing, if not a full price reversal, and we would not want to trade long after a deep retracement and potential reversal of trend.

FIGURE 6.5 Weekly Mini-Gold Prices showing two Fibonacci Retracement Confluences

Although I froze the chart slightly after price formed its rally off of the confluence support area, prices continued to rally in the prevailing uptrend to test not only the prior $840.00 swing high, but soared to reach $1,225.00 by December 2009.

You can apply this concept to daily charts of any market as well as the weekly chart as seen in the prior examples. Intraday or swing traders can also use Fibonacci confluence grids on their intraday timeframes, but it takes quicker reflexes and plenty of practice using this concept so that it becomes second nature.

Intraday Examples of Dual Fibonacci Confluence

The rules and guidelines are the same whether you are seeking to find Fibonacci confluences on any timeframe, but you have to be much quicker to do so while price is moving on your intraday charts. Here are two examples in the popular SPY exchange traded fund, which would be similar to trading the e-mini S&P 500 futures intraday along with any stock, index future, or index fund.

SPY Five-minute Chart: May 14, 2009 Remember, the goal of finding a Fibonacci Retracement Confluence zone is to locate a potential support area to put on a buy

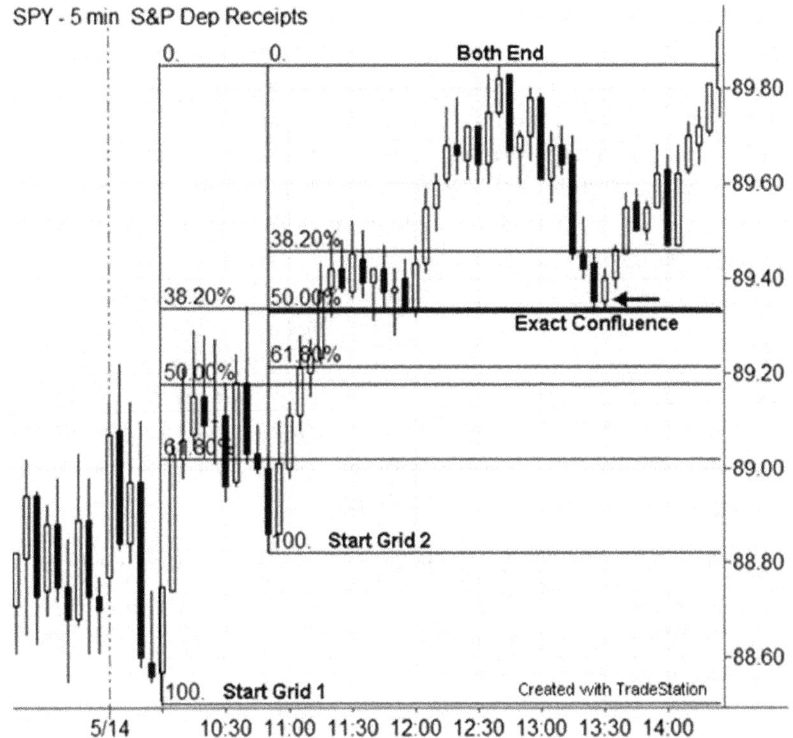

FIGURE 6.6 Intraday Dual Fibonacci Retracement Confluence Grid in SPY Five-minute Chart on May 14, 2009

position in an up-trending stock, or to find a resistance level to short-sell a down-trending stock. We are always interested in the next likely swing, which allows us to play the price movement we expect while managing risk with a close stop and a larger target, which is often a new swing high (or low) or the retest of a prior high or low.

While these examples show the outcome after price has tested and moved off the Fibonacci level, remember that you will not have this benefit in your real-time trading, so keep this in mind when studying these charts.

In Figure 6.6, we see price forming an intraday swing high just above $89.80 in a prevailing up-trending move. We want to know where we can enter a buy order to try to profit if the trend continues. To enter safely, we need to know where a likely support area exists.

In this example, observe the two Fibonacci retracement grids starting with the two immediate prior swing lows at $88.50 and $88.80 and connected both grids to the $89.80 intraday high. We want to know where it might be safe to buy into a confluence Fibonacci support zone.

Using the two grids, we find that an exact Fibonacci retracement grid confluence exists at $89.35, which is valuable information to know. We drew the grid because we suspected price would be forming a retracement swing after forming the bearish engulfing bar beginning at the $89.80 level. A trader can draw a single Fibonacci grid or a confluence Fibonacci retracement grid as soon as he or she suspects that price has formed a key swing high and then will be retracing lower to find support.

In this example, a trader had a span of 10 bars (50 minutes) to draw the grid after the bearish engulfing candle formed until price tested the confluence support level and formed a spinning top style candle at the exact confluence price of $89.35. Intraday traders must have quick reflexes and a thorough knowledge of how to use the tools they have selected for their trading method.

Traders would look to buy when price breaks the high of the spinning top candle at 1:30 p.m. EST (13:30) at $89.42 to trade long (buy) for a move back to test the afternoon high of $89.80 at a minimum, while placing a stop-loss either conservatively five cents under the exact confluence, or aggressively under the next loose confluence area at $89.20. As the chart shows, price rallied strongly off the confluence area to give profits to those who bought as the pullback swing ended and the trend continued in an upward, rally swing to test and exceed the intraday swing high.

SPY Five-minute Chart: December 8 and 9, 2009 Figure 6.7 is an additional example of the Fibonacci Confluence tactic as shown in the SPY intraday frame, only this time we will describe a multi-day setup that took advantage of a retracement swing into confluence resistance in a downtrend.

This time, price is falling in a downtrend on our intraday five-minute chart in the SPY and we want to find overhead resistance areas to put on a short-sell position to take

FIGURE 6.7 Downside Intraday Dual Fibonacci Retracement Confluence Grid in SPY 5-min chart on December 8 and 9, 2009

advantage of a low-risk entry into an established downtrend. We can either use a single Fibonacci retracement grid to do so, or we can take advantage of the two prior swing highs, instead of a single swing high, to find potential convergences of retracements. This time we will look further back to find key swing highs from which to draw retracement grids.

Starting with the swing high of $111.52 on December 7, we draw our first grid to the $109.02 swing low two days later on December 9. The 38.2 percent retracement rests at the $110.00 area which is helpful to know, but we can gain an added benefit from drawing one more quick Fibonacci retracement grid from the closing high of $111.00 on December 7. We now see that the 50 percent retracement from the $111.00 level overlaps the 38.2 percent retracement from the $111.50 level. Now that's even more helpful!

As a reminder, traders often look to round number resistance from numbers such as $100.00, $101.00, $110.00, and so on, making the double Fibonacci retracement confluence at the $110.00 level on December 9 align with the round number price of $110.00. We have three quick pieces of evidence to suspect that price will find resistance at the $110.00 level, giving us a short-sale entry, particularly if we find that a doji, bearish engulfing, or shooting star candle forms at this level.

Look closely to find that a shooting star with a long upper shadow formed at 11:00 a.m. EST into our confluence Fibonacci target. You could have drawn this target as soon as price began to rally off the $109.00 swing low, particularly as a spinning top or doji-style candle formed, hinting that odds favored a retracement swing up into resistance to unfold.

As was the case, price did find resistance at the tight confluence at $110.00, but in the event that buyers drove price higher, you could have located your stop-loss above the next confluence level at the $110.27 or $110.30 level, which not only was a loose Fibonacci retracement confluence, but also a prior swing high from the rally that ended at this level at noon EST on February 8 (remember to watch prior price highs as potential resistance levels, especially when they align with a Fibonacci retracement).

In the context of a rising uptrend, we can use the Fibonacci Retracement tool to find levels of expected support in order to initiate a retracement trade, buying into support and expecting the trend to continue to a higher price. Traders who locate simple Fibonacci retracements in price can identify more potential support levels than traders who do not, while traders who specifically locate Fibonacci confluence prices from multiple price levels can uncover hidden potential support levels that other traders miss.

THE MULTIPLE USES OF FIBONACCI TOOLS

Traders locate Fibonacci retracement prices not just for trade entries into prevailing uptrends or downtrends, but to find a reasonable price to locate a stop-loss order. Standard retracements in price should not retrace more than the 61.8 percent Fibonacci retracement price of a given swing, thus traders often locate reasonable stops underneath the 61.8 percent retracement price of a downswing in a prevailing uptrend, and above the 61.8 percent retracement of an upward swing in a prevailing downtrend. Thus, the Fibonacci retracement tool helps you identify places to enter a trade and locate a logical stop-loss order beyond a point where the market should not go.

Traders use Fibonacci to find the low of an expected bull or bear flag in this method, placing the stop beyond the 61.8 percent retracement. We will also see how Fibonacci prices align with general and specific retracement-style trade setups in Chapters 9 and 10, and also how to execute a trade with additional precision, accounting for conservative or aggressive tactics, in Chapter 8.

CHAPTER 7

Following the Life Cycle of a Price Move

A book on broad trading tactics in technical analysis cannot go far without mentioning the contributions of founding father Charles Dow and how his ideas paved the way for the charting methods we use today. In this chapter, we will compare the contributions of Charles Dow and Ralph Elliott as they relate to the life cycle of a stock's price move over time.

Ralph Elliott's writings build upon the foundation established by Charles Dow in discussing how stocks move from accumulation to distribution over time in more specific motions that he labeled as waves instead of swings. This chapter illustrates how to identify a stock in an accumulation phase, follow it through the mark-up in its realization phase, and lock-in your profits as the stock enters its final stage of distribution just before a mark-down phase occurs.

From 1890 to 1900, Charles Dow published his writings on stock market phenomena that would later form the foundation for technical analysis. We have already addressed some of Dow's work in Chapter 1 when we discussed the Trend Continuity Principle. Dow also believed that trends, once established, were more likely to continue than to reverse. In fact, Charles Dow separated the notion of trend into three separate trends: primary, secondary (or intermediate), and minor. To modern day traders, we often assess the primary trend of a stock by studying its monthly chart and use the weekly chart to determine the secondary or intermediate trend.

To Charles Dow and his contemporaries, the minor trend was of no importance because trading in the stock market had a completely different reality in 1900 than it did in 2000. Today, we would use both daily and intraday charts to define the short-term or minor trend of a stock. Mr. Dow did not have a computer to show him the charts of the stocks he wanted to analyze. Imagine a world not just without computers, but without stock charts themselves! Keeping a stock chart meant the trader had to write down the daily closing prices of the stocks and then draw individual charts laboriously by hand. How many traders today would keep up that discipline! When you read the works of Charles Dow, you should have a deeper appreciation for his insights, many of which still hold true today as the foundation for simple and complex trading strategies. For reference, what we know today as Dow Theory actually stems from the work of William Hamilton and Robert Rhea as they refined Dow's writings posthumously.

While you can research all of Dow's writings for deeper insights, this chapter addresses only one concept in Dow's teachings: that of the accumulation and distribution cycle in stocks.

THREE PHASES OF A LARGE-SCALE PRICE MOVE

Early market technicians focused on the larger picture on stock charts, concerned with identifying the balance of supply and demand between buyers and sellers. While the markets of today offer far superior opportunities for intraday traders, all traders can benefit from considering the larger cycles or phases that a stock transitions through from a move from the lows to the highs. Larger cycles can take years to form completely, and assessing the particular phase in which a stock trades greatly enhances your ability to position yourself and profit accordingly.

Charles Dow and early technicians defined three distinct phases of a bull market, and we still use these concepts today with advanced charting software packages that allow us to study price charts instantly. You can identify these phases best on a monthly or weekly chart in your favorite software charting program or web site. Also, it helps to think back to our discussion in Chapter 3 that simplified the market into buyers and sellers—bulls and bears—for visualizing these phases on higher timeframe price charts. Think of the market not in terms of indicators, but through the perspective of buyers and sellers as they interact over time, either willingly putting on positions in hopes of a future profit, willingly taking off positions to realize an actual profit, or being forced unwillingly out of a position to realize losses. In doing so, you will be able to understand the cycles of accumulation and distribution more accurately.

In addition to segmenting the market participants into buyers and sellers, you also need to visualize two separate classes of market participants. On one hand, we have the big money investors, also called smart money or the professionals. These funds or individuals are well-capitalized, experienced investors or traders who have been perfecting their craft for years and have developed time-tested strategies for long-term success in the market. They understand that strategy triumphs over individual psychology and emotion, and have actually developed methods to take advantage of crowd behavior or inefficiencies that arise from investors following their emotions as opposed to their strategies. In our discussion, visualize these participants as the smart money that profits over time from repeated psychological mistakes of newer or inexperienced traders with much smaller accounts.

On the opposite side of the big money investors, we have the small money investors, who you may also have heard called retail money or, less professionally, the dumb money investors. That is not to say that these investors are stupid, but that they are usually newer to the investment or trading environment and are more likely to fall victim to psychological or emotional traps that the professional traders exploit over time.

Examples include waiting on the sidelines during a steadily rising move in a stock and then buying at the top of the move just prior to a reversal in trend. Though perhaps their strategy told them they should have bought earlier, they doubted the chart signals and decided to buy only when the pain of not making money by participating in the upside action was too great for them to bear. Alternately, they may hold on to a losing position for weeks or months only to sell not when their strategies told them to sell earlier such as when price broke down through rising trendlines or moving averages, but when the emotional pain of losing money was too much to bear, which sometimes occurs ironically near the exact bottom of a price trend prior to an upside reversal.

Our discussion of accumulation and distribution cycles will help you understand how new traders consistently make the same mistakes when guided by emotion, and how professional traders exploit these investing errors by separating themselves from the crowd mentality through relying on time-tested price principles, strategies, and indicators.

First Phase: Accumulation

Let us begin our discussion on the life cycle of a price move at the end of a downward phase in the market, often called a bear market. Price has been falling as sellers have been dominant over buyers, and the price of the stock is treading continually to new 52-week lows. Recall from Chapter 3 that price alternates between periods of range expansion and range contraction. Let us assume that we are transitioning away from a range expansion sell-off phase into a range consolidation sideways phase in price.

If we segment the investing public into professionals and new traders in terms of psychology, we would notice that many traders would be psychologically unable to buy a position in a stock that remained in a persistent, multi-month downtrend. Some traders remained long during the persistent decline, hoping for an eventual reversal, and these traders remained stubbornly long with increasing losses and eventually capitulate by selling their shares when they can no longer tolerate the pain of financial loss. Over time, there will be far fewer traders who still hold shares long to liquidate.

On the other side of the transaction, professional traders with longer time horizons may decide to engage in a campaign of buying shares that the general public no longer feels they can hold. In simple terms, the accumulation stage occurs when the broader public sells shares unwillingly after a long down-move and professional traders buy these shares willingly that the majority of sellers liquidate. Shares transfer from the public (new traders) to professionals over a period of time.

The accumulation phase may last a long time, sometimes for a period of years. During an accumulation phase, expect to see lower volume and flat stock prices in a sideways consolidation move. Long-term investors and position traders want to identify phases of accumulation and establish positions that might last years.

Traders, however, want to avoid trading during this phase because they wish to engage in many transactions to capture the edge from short-term price movement. A trader seeks to play the edge in many positions over a year, rather than remain committed to a single position for a long duration of time. Traders seek to turn over their inventory (their trading capital) as a savvy store owner wishes to sell and replenish the stock of goods as many times as possible in a year. A stock in an accumulation phase will offer few opportunities for profit for most traders; instead, traders want to participate in the second phase of the life cycle: Realization.

Second Phase: Realization

It is impossible to assess how long an accumulation phase will last in a stock, and it is difficult to assess if professionals are actively accumulating shares over time or not. Remember, just because a stock is in a sideways range does not mean that large investors are buying shares. There is no easy way to distinguish whether the professionals are actively accumulating positions over time in a stock in a trading range environment or whether they have turned their attention elsewhere. If you buy a stock that is not in an accumulation phase, you may never see the stock transition into the second phase.

The realization phase occurs when price firmly breaks upward from a lengthy trading range after a downward move in price, usually in a clean breakout from the established trading range. Expect to see volume increase as price rallies upward from the established range as a positive feedback loop develops, which results from short sellers buying to cover their positions unwillingly with a loss as eager buyers willingly purchasing stock on the initial breakout and beyond.

To recognize the realization phase, observe a price breakout from a lengthy price range. The professional traders continue to buy shares over time, but eventually the price will begin to rise and the smarter investors or traders will begin to buy shares in a newly rising uptrend at the earliest stages possible.

Remember Martin Pring's definition of Technical Analysis as explained in Chapter 1: your goal is to recognize a trend reversal at the earliest stage possible and then ride that trend (trade in the direction of the trend) until the weight of the evidence has confirmed that the trend has reversed. Experienced traders will begin purchasing shares or trading breakouts, and as this occurs, a stock will begin to transition into the Realization Phase.

During the early realization phase, both the professional traders and experienced retail or non-professional traders buy shares, which pushes the price higher. As the price rises further, the stock enters a positive feedback loop where those who have been short the stock will be forced to buy to cover, as those who have no position in the stock will begin a campaign of buying shares.

Look for a steady, stable rise in prices that may take the form of a 45-degree or smaller angular price rise in an uptrend. Also, observe that the moving average structure remains bullish with price above the short-term average and the short-term average above the intermediate-term average. Observe momentum and volume rising along with the stable price ascension. As long as these conditions continue to persist, the stock remains in a realization phase and thus offers your best chances for profit as a trader, mainly through buying retracements to moving average or trendline support within the context of a developing uptrend.

Over time, more investors become aware of the steady rise in price and participate, either for short-term swing trades that form from retracements to the rising moving averages, trendlines, or Fibonacci retracement zones, or from price breakouts to new highs. Over time, as more individuals begin buying, the professionals will either cease buying shares or will start to sell shares they have purchased during the accumulation phase when the share price was much lower.

The realization phase begins with professionals buying shares, then intelligent retail (small) investors begin buying shares, which attracts more attention from the public as more traders begin buying shares over time to perpetuate the stable price rise. However as the price rises higher and more individuals participate, the professional traders have accumulated their desired amount of shares at lower prices and then cease buying. A professional trader who desires to acquire tens of thousands of shares will not do so in a single transaction, but through smaller purchases over many days, weeks, or even months. They will hold their shares in their accounts as the other traders continue to drive price higher in the context of a rising uptrend, and will begin selling their shares as the public eagerly continues buying shares. Notice the dynamic of the professional/amateur relationship: during accumulation, calm professionals buy shares over time from panicked amateur traders, then hold their shares as traders push price higher in an uptrend, and then eventually sell their shares calmly for a profit as the amateur traders rush in emotionally to purchase shares in a stock that seems to have no end to its rise.

Imagine a seesaw with professionals on one end and smaller, retail investors on the other end. At the start of the realization phase, professionals will be on the upper seat and retail investors will be on the lower seat in terms of activity. As the phase progresses, the seesaw eventually comes into balance as professionals reduce their activity and retail traders increase their activity. The end of the realization phase, and the start of the distribution phase, occurs when professionals completely stop purchasing shares and then begin selling shares to the eager and enthusiastic retail public, who now occupy the high seat on the seesaw. Eventually, realization gives way to distribution and the trend reverses down.

Third Phase: Distribution

The accumulation phase occurs when professionals buy shares over time and the retail public either sells shares or are not participating in a particular stock. In contrast the distribution phase begins when professionals sell the shares they purchased at lower levels to the crowd of eager and enthusiastic retail (small) investors and traders who only see the rising price and buy shares aggressively. The market does not create shares out of thin air; instead, if you think of investors in larger groups, when large groups of investors buy shares, there is another group of investors who are selling shares to them. Likewise, if a large group of investors sell shares, another group of investors buys these shares from them.

Unlike futures contracts or options, company shares are limited in supply, so shares are limited and must transition from buyers to sellers, and from sellers back to buyers over time. Though it may seem like a company has infinite shares for trading, they do not, and all shares must be owned by someone, be it company insiders, mutual funds, hedge funds, endowments, retirement accounts, speculative accounts, individual trading accounts, or other equity accounts.

During the distribution phase, one of two events can happen. The stable outcome occurs when price forms a lengthy trading range similar to that of the accumulation phase as a negative feedback, range consolidation phase occurs after a steep rise in price. The range occurs because the smaller number of professionals continues selling shares to the more numerous retail public, who continue buying shares. Keep in mind that professionals in the stock market tend to be fewer in number, but have considerably larger funds or accounts than the more numerous retail trading or investing public, which have much smaller accounts than full-time professional traders. You can often observe clean negative divergences and other nonconfirmations in volume with price during a steady turnover of shares. This transition either takes the form of a rectangle trading range or arc pattern on the chart that is called a Rounded Reversal. The main idea is that price gives clear warnings of an impending reversal ahead of the actual price reversal to a new downtrend.

The second, more volatile outcome occurs when a buying climax, or spike reversal occurs. Buyers become blinded by their emotion and the good news of the stock along with the rapidly rising prices that continue to push share prices to new highs in an almost vertical climb. Even professionals can be blindsided by a rapidly rising market. Eventually, like gravity, what goes up must come down. Principles of physics also apply to the stock market. Sometimes the fall in share prices can be much more violent than the rise.

This was the case for many technology stocks in 2000 and for the broader NASDAQ Index; a meteoric rise in price eventually gave way to a precipitous downtrend that wiped away the gains and more of those who purchased shares during the height of the rally. Individuals quit their day jobs to speculate on rising stock prices full-time; unfortunately, many were wiped out financially as they continued to buy falling shares in the context of the sudden bear market collapse they never saw coming. The nearly three-year NASDAQ collapse from a high of 5,100 to a low of 1,100 swept many inexperienced traders out of the market completely, taking their previously earned gains and more with them.

Whether the distribution phase ends with a stable turn-over of shares or a violent one, the life cycle of a stock reveals that price will eventually fall to retrace a portion of the gains that the stock achieved during the realization uptrend phase. Professionals will often sell stock short as the price falls, as will experienced small traders. Inexperienced and emotional retail traders and investors exist on the opposite end of the short-sale positions, and the damage comes to those individuals who are blinded by their hope, greed, and then fear. They will have purchased shares near the peak of the rally and sometimes will hold on to those shares for the entire downtrend until they can no longer endure the pain of loss, and will sell those shares at the bottom, when a new cycle of accumulation has begun.

VISUALIZING THE STAGES THROUGH CHARTS

Let us see these phases in an idealized chart and real-life examples. Figure 7.1 shows us the idealized line progression through the three stages. Accumulation contains a sideways action of negative feedback as professionals buy shares from the retail public who sell shares. It helps to conceptualize this in simplest terms. Eventually, price breaks above the upper horizontal resistance line as experienced retail traders begin to buy alongside the professional traders who continue buying shares.

Over time, retail (small) investors and traders buy shares for a long-term investment and execute trades for short-term profit, both of which drive the share price higher. Toward the later phases of the realization stage, professional investors stop buying shares, hold on to their established position as the price appreciates, and eventually begin selling shares ahead of the actual price peak. The retail public, on the other hand, increases their participation as the price continues to rise. Eventually, price will move into the final stage where the professional traders sell the shares, which they purchased at lower prices, to the mass public who only hear good news about the stock and see the rising prices on the charts. Shares transition from strong hands to weak hands during the distribution phase (from professionals selling to eager amateur traders) and then transition back from weak hands to strong hands (from distressed amateurs selling to professionals) during the accumulation phase, which will occur again after price falls in the later stages of distribution.

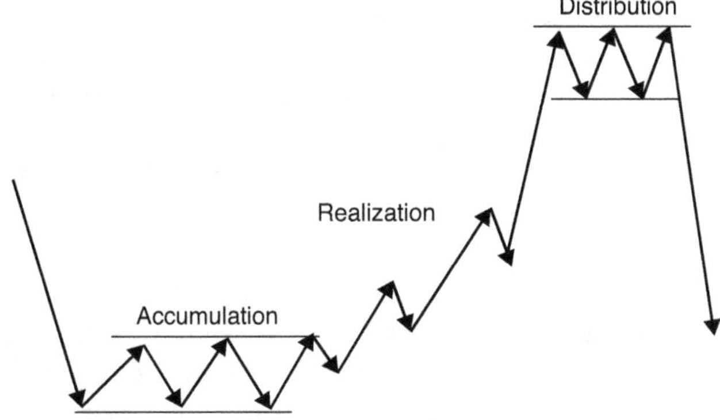

FIGURE 7.1 Idealized Chart of the Three Life Cycle Stages

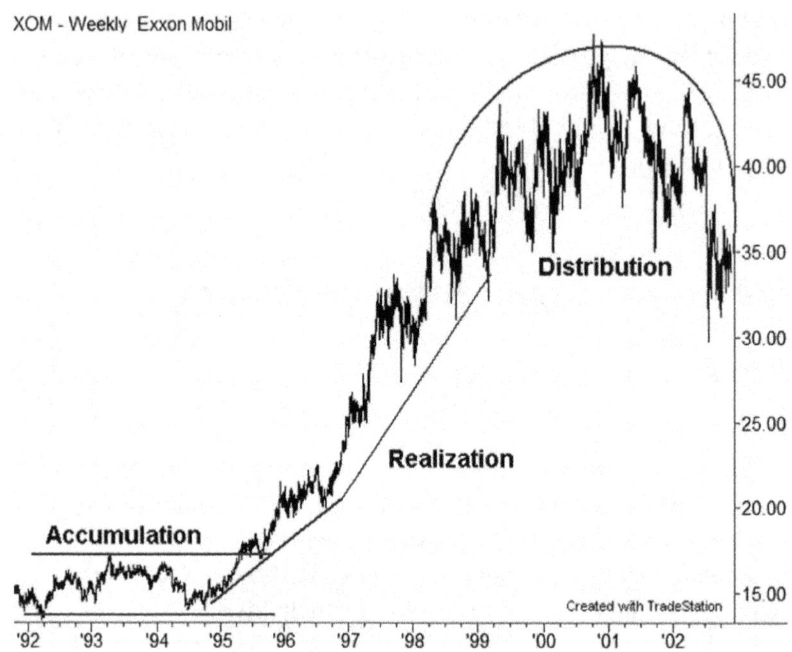

FIGURE 7.2 Real-world Example of the Three Phases as seen in Exxon-Mobil Weekly Chart

A Stable Progression Example: Exxon-Mobil

Figure 7.2 gives us a real-world example of this concept as we see Exxon-Mobil (XOM) break out in late 1995 after a multi-year trading range formed. Price travels up four years as we begin to see a rounded reversal or stable distribution phase that began in 1999/2000. Price then fell during the later stages of distribution that ended with a new phase of accumulation in 2002.

Beginning in 1991, we see a flat phase of negative feedback in the weekly chart of Exxon-Mobil. This rectangle pattern in price actually formed after an up-move in price, so technically we should label this a re-accumulation phase. Still, price broke to the upside above the upper resistance line at the $17.00-per-share level and embarked on a continuation move to the upside in a stable realization phase. Notice how I drew two trendlines during the realization phase to connect the respective price lows. You can often gauge the phase of realization by measuring the angle of ascent in price. Lower angles occur at the beginning of the phase while steeper angles occur at the later stage of realization, prior to the onset of distribution.

From 1996 to 1999, both professionals and smaller investors pushed the price of Exxon-Mobil higher to peak above $45.00 per share in 2000 as a clear arc pattern formed on the chart. Arc patterns represent stable distribution or transfer of shares from the professional investors to the more numerous retail public. During the distribution phase, which we can see began in late 1999 and early 2000, price stabilized between the $35.00-per-share and $45.00-per-share level. Instead of an arc, you could also draw a

FIGURE 7.3 Large-Scale Phase Transition in Exxon-Mobil (XOM)

rectangle pattern. The main idea is that buyers and sellers had established a trading range at the highs, and when you add in the dynamic of professional investors versus amateur investors and traders, you can visualize the transfer of shares from the professionals to the retail investors. Shares fell from the $45.00 peak to bottom at $30.00 in the two years of the selling phase of distribution.

Figure 7.3 picks up from here and shows the subsequent accumulation, realization, and then distribution phases that occurred throughout the decade of the 2000s.

The chart begins with the distribution phase from 1999 to 2002, which was an arc formation in price. Buyers and sellers stabilized price between $30.00 and $37.00 per share from mid-2002 to late 2003, at which time buyers pushed price upward through the horizontal resistance line at $37.00 per share in early 2004. Experienced speculators began to join the professionals in buying shares at the breakout in early 2004 as eventually more investors, driven more by emotions and less by experience perhaps, continued to buy price during the realization phase.

The Price Alternation Principle, introduced in Chapter 3, states that price alternates between states of range expansion (positive feedback) and range contraction (negative feedback). The sustained range breakout from early 2004 to early 2005 represented a classic range expansion positive feedback loop where buyers pushed price higher and short sellers also pushed price higher via their buying from covering their short positions.

Buyers and sellers met at the $60.00-per-share level throughout 2005 to establish a range contraction phase of negative feedback that gave rise to a clear horizontal trendline at the $65.00-per-share level as drawn along with a rising lower support line during this contraction phase. The important concept to know is that you must combine the Price Alternation Principle with the concepts of Accumulation and Distribution.

Be aware that price will not rise forever without small or even intermediate pullbacks or corrections during the realization phase. In other words, do not automatically assume that because price has entered a range contraction phase that the price has now entered a period of distribution. During such phases, it may be best to take profits on any long-term trend following positions while price bounces between the defined levels, and then wait to see if what you observe is truly a range contraction phase that marks distribution, or whether it marks a simple consolidation in the context of a rising, powerful uptrend that may be labeled a re-accumulation period.

Instead of attempting to outsmart the market by guessing in which direction price will break, stand aside or put your money to work in another stock that is showing a range breakout phase of positive feedback. Recall our discussion on triangle consolidation patterns in Chapter 5 and the benefit of waiting for an official breakout rather than trying to guess the direction of the break. In the event that the price breaks to the upside, you can always establish a new position in the direction of the breakout. Our goal is not to outsmart the market, but to manage risk and trade when the odds favor successful outcomes. Most traders find it extremely difficult to profit during a trading range environment and prefer the stability of a comfortably rising uptrend move of a stock during a realization phase.

Buyers and sellers formed a negative feedback loop or range compression environment between 2005 and mid-2006 that gave way in late 2006 to another range breakout and positive feedback loop to the upside that continued the Realization phase. Price eventually rallied above $90.00 per share and then formed another negative feedback, range consolidation phase with clear horizontal trendlines at the $80.00- and $95.00-per-share levels. Though this could have been another range compression phase that led to another new breakout phase to the upside, it did not. The period from 2007 to mid-2008 marked a clear distribution phase between professionals and amateurs that led eventually to a true distribution phase in the stock which took price 30 percent lower to the $60.00-per-share level in early 2010.

Figure 7.4 shows us the same Exxon-Mobil weekly chart as Figure 7.3 but adds the 3/10 MACD Momentum Oscillator to show that clear negative divergences often form during the price highs in the distribution phase.

In Figure 7.4 we see that the 3/10 MACD Momentum oscillator peaked in April 2000 with price trading at $42.00 per share. As price pushed its way to a new high in October 2000 at $47.70 per share, the oscillator registered a clear lower high, locking in a nonconfirmation of the price high with a negative divergence. During a clean transition phase that takes the form of a rounded arc instead of a spike, you will almost always observe a negative divergence with the 3/10 MACD Oscillator or other momentum oscillators including the Rate of Change and indicator named Momentum. Look for negative divergences to signal the onset of a likely distribution phase.

The same structure occurs in 2007, but this time we see a lengthy negative momentum divergence that began with the oscillator high in 2005. Look closely at the 3/10

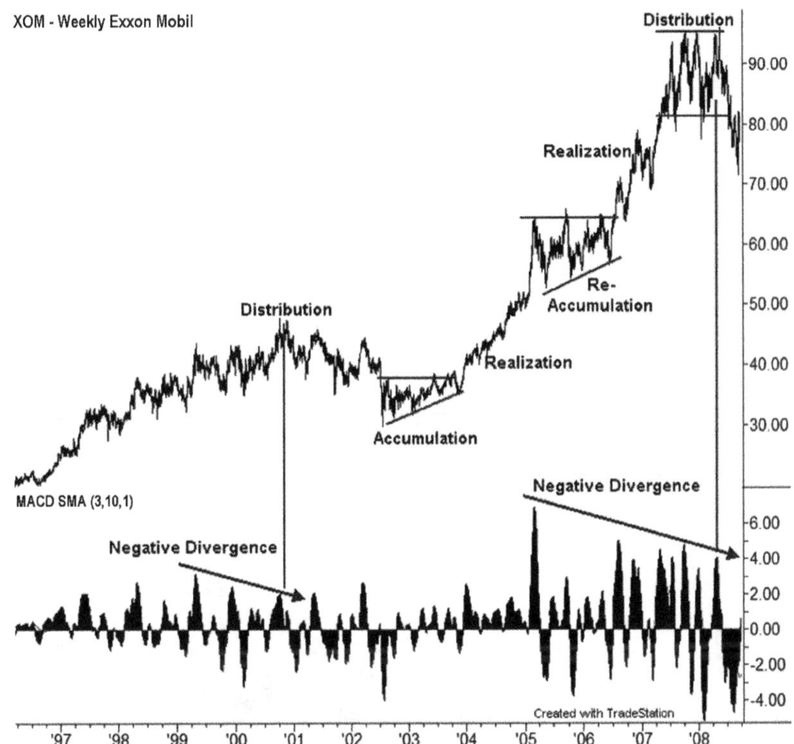

FIGURE 7.4 Large-Scale Stage Transition in Exxon-Mobil

MACD Oscillator throughout 2007 and into 2008 as you observe lower oscillator highs. Price peaked in May 2008 slightly above $96.00 per share, which was just higher than the two prior price peaks from 2007 at the $95.00 level. Notice the clear lower high in the oscillator. I drew vertical lines to reveal the absolute price highs in 2000 and 2008 as they corresponded with the momentum oscillator values.

As a rule, look for new price and momentum highs to highlight the likely transition from an accumulation phase into the realization phase, and look for momentum to confirm new price highs during the realization phase. Finally, look for lengthy or obvious negative momentum divergences to mark the final price highs during a likely distribution phase in price. Refer to Chapter 2 for full descriptions on how to use momentum oscillators along with price for confirmation and non-confirmation tactics.

A Violent Distribution Example: Potash Corporation of Saskatchewan

While Exxon-Mobil gave us an example of a stable transition through the three phases, high-volatile stock Potash Corporation of Saskatchewan (POT) provides an

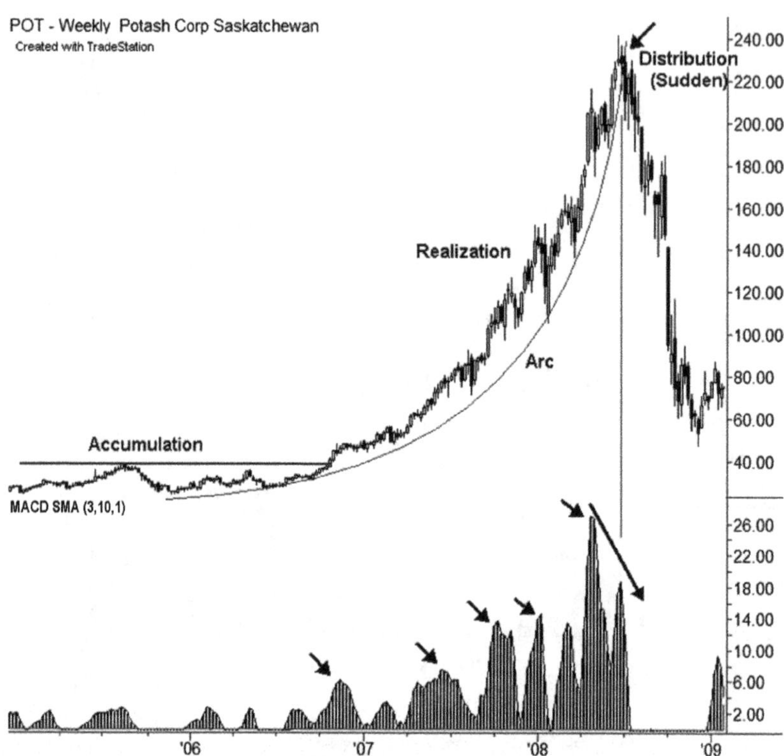

FIGURE 7.5 Stage Transition and Arc Pattern in Potash Saskatchewan Weekly

example of a V-spike or violent reversal as the stock transitioned from realization into sudden distribution.

The weekly progression through the three stages in the weekly chart of Potash-Saskatchewan shows the alternative progression to the distribution phase: a violent end. Potash Corp actually experienced a lengthier accumulation than shown in Figure 7.5 which begins in early 2005. The origin of the accumulation phase began in 1999 between $8.00 and $12.00 per share, and lasted until the re-accumulation phase seen here between 2005 and 2007 in the $25.00 to $35.00 two-year accumulation range phase.

Buyers pushed the price of Potash Corp above the $45.00 level in November 2006 to begin the two-year realization phase that began slowly and rallied to an exponential price peak above $240.00 per share in June 2008. Notice again the rising angles you can draw to connect the swing lows for the duration of the Realization phase. In fact, if you connect all lows as I have done in the chart, you can draw a clear rising arc trendline that occurs before the violent end to the uptrend. Notice during the early months of 2008 that the lower arc trendline turned vertical as the price trend also took a vertical shape to it. Professional traders know that such steep increases in price are unsustainable, and that the longer the vertical rally lasts, the more violent the sell-off phase will be.

Look closely at the absolute peak at $241.00 per share in June 2008 to note the shooting star weekly candle that formed the new all-time high in price. Look also at the 3/10 MACD Momentum oscillator to observe the clear negative momentum divergence that failed to confirm the new high in price. I drew a vertical line to connect the price peak to the final lower peak in the momentum oscillator. You cannot expect to find a clean negative momentum divergence on every single violent V-spike top formation as seen here, so do not be alarmed if you do not see a corresponding negative momentum divergence accompany a final price high after a near-vertical price rally.

On a related note about momentum, notice how the momentum oscillator formed higher indicator peaks as Potash Corp continued its uptrend to new highs through 2007. Recalling our discussion on the Momentum Principle in Chapter 2, new momentum highs and new price highs often lead to higher price highs yet to come after a retracement in price. Potash Corp shows this to be the case as the momentum oscillator on the weekly chart formed higher highs along with the corresponding new price highs. When you see this pattern, it indicates that the price remains in a steady rising Realization phase and that it is a generally safe, or at least low-risk, opportunity to buy pullbacks to rising short-term moving averages within the context of the developing uptrend.

Unlike Exxon-Mobil which transitioned into a stable distribution phase, Potash Corp transitioned almost immediately into a violent distribution phase without a meaningful sideways pause or consolidation period in price. Be aware that trading within the context of a vertical price move is like playing a child's game of musical chairs. When the music stops, everyone will be rushing for the nearest chair. However, when you extend the analogy to discuss participants in the market, realize that some participants will not hear the music stop (meaning the market has peaked), and will continue trading long well into the first sharp down-move of the sudden distribution phase.

From a chart standpoint, pay very close attention to stocks on higher timeframes that exhibit rising exponential arc formations similar to the chart of Potash Corp in Figure 7.5 When you see price break such a steeply rising trendline, it is almost always best to sell your position, take your profits, and move on to trade or invest in another stock that is in earlier stages of Realization. If you fail to understand this principle, you could be caught long stock in a price move from $240.00 to $60.00, as you see occurred in six-month's time from June to December 2008 in Potash Corp. You will do best as a trader to avoid attempts to capture the final part of a move, or sell as close as possible to the absolute high.

WYCKOFF'S ALTERNATE STAGE LABELS

Before discussing how Ralph Elliott built upon the early concepts from Dow and his contemporaries, it's worth noting the alternate terms for the accumulation/distribution cycle as explained by Richard D. Wyckoff, also in the early 1900s.

Wyckoff incorporated volume and sentiment into his explanation of the similar accumulation and distribution cycles he observed in his research. His contributions to technical analysis include the concept of the "Composite Man," and the Wyckoff Method, both of which focus on the deeper details of the larger accumulation/distribution cycles, supply/demand, and investor psychology.

This figure shows the two additional terms that Wyckoff uses to clarify the life cycle of a stock. The diagram is the same as Figure 7.1 only Wyckoff uses two different terms, as labeled.

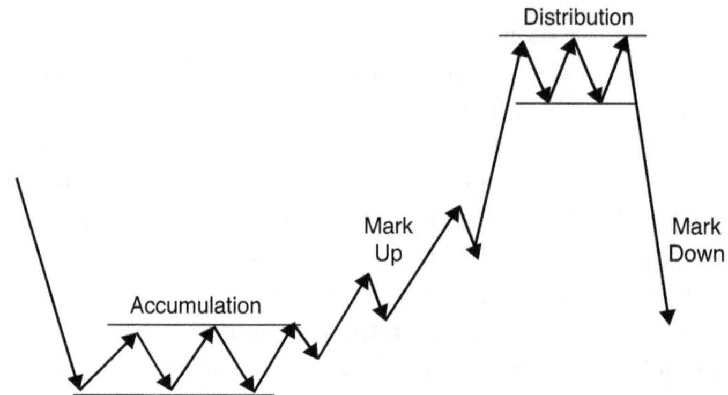

Idealized Progression through the Stages as Explained by Richard Wyckoff

While Wyckoff continues the use and same explanation for the accumulation and distribution phases as Charles Dow, Wyckoff first replaces the Realization term with the concept of Mark-up and then divides the distribution phase into an additional Mark-down phase to classify what happens when price falls sharply after a period of distribution. Just as one can characterize the Realization phase as both the professionals and amateurs buying stock, one can simplify the Mark-down phase as both the professionals selling or short-selling stock along with the broader public who is also selling stock. While the concepts are the same, Wyckoff adds an additional phase and reclassifies the Realization phase in his analysis.

For those who want to learn more about Wyckoff's methods, read Wyckoff's original works entitled *How I Trade in Stocks and Bonds,* or Wyckoff's *Stock Market Techniques.* Dr. Hank Pruden also published a book in 2007 entitled *The Top Three Skills of Top Trading* in which he summarized most of the Wyckoff Method for today's markets.

RALPH ELLIOTT'S WAVE THEORY

While it is impossible for one chapter in a book to address the Elliott Wave Principle adequately, I did want to highlight how Elliott's work complemented the larger life cycle concepts as explained by Charles Dow, Richard Wyckoff, and other early technicians.

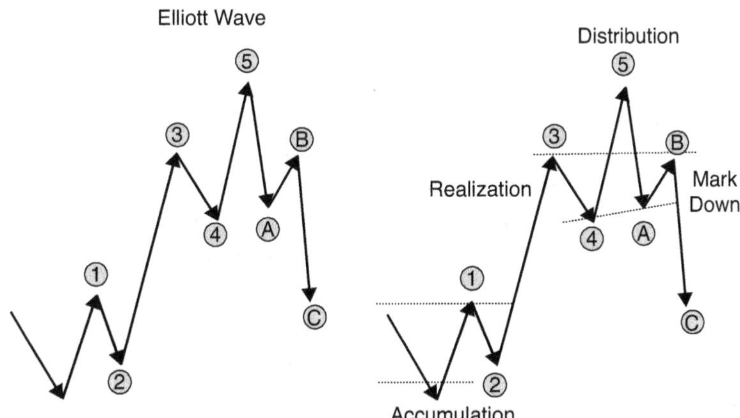

FIGURE 7.6 Elliott's Waves and Dow/Wyckoff's Stages Overlaid

For those interested in specific study and application of the Elliott Wave Principle, I recommend you begin your journey with the book traders consider the contemporary reference book for understanding Elliott's original work. A.J. Frost and Robert Prechter published *The Elliott Wave Principle* originally in 1978 and have updated the publication over the years. The book contains all of the rules, guidelines, and descriptions needed for a deeper understanding of the principle explained by Ralph Elliott's original work from the 1930s.

Where Charles Dow and others saw three stages, Ralph Elliott saw five waves to a bull market advance. Where Richard Wyckoff characterized a Mark-down phase after a peak in prices, Elliott saw a three-wave downward progression. Elliott's contributions added to the work of Dow, Hamilton, Rhea, Wyckoff, and other founding fathers of technical analysis.

Let us first see how Elliott conceptualized the life cycle of a stock and then compare his numbering scheme to the phrases of Dow and Wyckoff. Figure 7.6 begins with an ideal Elliott Wave full progression, and compares those numbers with the schema from Dow and Wyckoff.

Where Dow saw three stages, Elliott saw five. In simplest comparison, Elliott's Waves 1 and 2 represent Dow's Accumulation Stage, Wave 3 represents the Realization or Mark-up stage, and Waves 4 and 5 mark the start of the Distribution stage. When we add in Wyckoff's term of Mark-down to describe the sell-off phase after a distribution top has occurred, Elliott divided the Mark-down phase into three stages with letters A, B, and C instead of numbers to distinguish between the upward move and the corrective downward move. One can label the A Wave down as the ending phase of Dow's distribution phase and beginning of Wyckoff's Mark-down phase.

The main idea is that Elliott labeled the corrective waves or swings in price that divide the different phases, while Dow did not do so specifically. Charles Dow labeled smaller corrective swings against the rising upward primary trend as secondary reactions. Elliott classified these secondary reactions as corrective waves, numbered Wave 2 and 4, in the context of the three stage, or five-wave upward move that marked a standard bull market.

Like both Dow and Wyckoff, Ralph Elliott believed that the waves represented distinct stages that were best explained in terms of investor participation, expectations, and psychology. Similar to our discussion about the characteristics of the three different stages of accumulation, realization, and distribution, Elliott characterized common occurrences not just in these stages, but in the two corrective phases that temporarily interrupted the upward advance.

In general, the following discussion, adapted from Frost and Precter's *Elliott Wave Principle*, addresses how Elliott viewed the characterizations and expectations of each of the five waves of a bull market and three waves of a bear market on the larger scale.

Wave 1: The Beginning of Something New

Like the Accumulation/Distribution discussion earlier in the chapter, we begin our journey on the wave progression cycle after a lengthy sell-off or downward trend in the price of a stock or market. To outside observers, the first wave will be non-distinct from any of the other prior waves that have occurred in the context of the prevailing downtrend. Most participants will see it as another bear-market retracement and will either avoid buying shares or may even consider short-selling the perceived top of the wave into resistance. The public is bearish but the professionals may be buying shares in anticipation of a bottom in price, or during the beginning of a new accumulation phase.

However, if you look deeper inside the price components, you might see that what will later be described as a Wave 1 will have a possible new momentum high or an increase in breadth or market internals (if assessing a stock market index). This is also known as a Kick-off. Wave 1 might break upward through either the 20- or 50-period moving average in a sign of strength. Professionals often see these hidden bullish signals where amateur investors do not.

Wave 2: The Failed I-Told-You So Correction

If investors perceive what will later be Wave 1 as just another standard upward retracement within the context of a prevailing downtrend, then they will see what will later be labeled Wave 2 as any other downward swing within the context of the prevailing bear market. The sentiment still remains negative, bears continue holding short-sale positions, but professionals may be slowly accumulating shares in the context of a broadening trading range of the accumulation cycle.

Wave 2 is a down wave where the majority of participants expect the market to continue to a new low. However, second waves by definition do not make a new low. Instead, price forms a higher low above the prior low that began the first wave. This is confusing to many market participants as it occurs in real time, but most do not feel compelled to act yet. In this description, midway through the second wave, participants might declare "I told you we were still in a bear market" to those who believe the market has bottomed. However, their assessment will be short-lived, as second waves eventually give way to a pivotal third wave, which sets the stage for the Realization phase in a stock.

Wave 3: The Powerful Rally We All See

In Elliott Wave theory, the third wave is the most powerful, most dynamic wave. It makes sense why this occurs, because a market is now transitioning to new swing highs and evolving into a more powerful technical position that begins the Realization stage. Think back to Chapter 3 on the Price Alternation Principle to our discussion on Positive Feedback Loops. If indeed that the majority of market participants view Waves 1 and 2 as nothing more than movements in a continuing bear market, then when Wave 3 breaks above the prior resistance line of the peak of Wave 1, those traders who remain short will first start to buy back their borrowed shares, which drives the market higher. Aggressive traders see this new price breakout as a new buying opportunity in which to invest, and their buying also drives the market higher. The combination of bulls buying willingly and bears buying to cover unwillingly explains why Elliott observed the third wave to be the most powerful wave: it is the wave where we begin to see Positive Feedback Loops begin.

As price rises higher and higher beyond its prior resistance boundaries, more participants take notice and buy as price continues to rise. During the Realization phase, both professional and savvy retail traders purchase shares. Volume and momentum should confirm the new price highs and forecast higher price highs yet to come according to the momentum principle.

Despite the strength of the rally, many investors still doubt the price move and believe that it will end at any moment. It will take more than an initial breakout to compel them to buy shares. Remember that toward the later stages of a Realization phase, professionals cease buying, preferring to hold on to shares they have already accumulated. Eventually as price rises to their targets, they will start to sell shares to the eager public who are now aggressively buying shares. The fourth wave often interrupts the euphoria and often marks the beginning of a distribution phase ahead.

Wave 4: Profit Takers and Retracement Buyers

Wave 4 is a downward move in price that is often a stable, relatively mild correction that finds support at the daily or weekly short- or intermediate-term moving averages, or a popular Fibonacci retracement level. The selling pressure here comes from those who bought at much lower prices as they take their profits. Fourth waves often formally begin the transition of shares from the professionals who bought during the accumulation phase (characterized by Waves 1 and 2) to the broader retail public who have waited on the sideline until their greed forced them to buy shares of a stock that they believe will never reverse down. Aggressive short-term traders might decide to short sell shares here, perhaps believing that the market has moved too far and has already peaked.

These combined dynamics push the price lower, but because professionals are not yet aggressively selling and because there are traders waiting eagerly to buy comfortable pullbacks to support, Wave 4 finds support and begins a final push to new highs that mark the end of the upward move.

Wave 5: Distribution and Divergences

The emotional buying of a large number of retail investors, particularly as greed causes them to ignore developing weakness in a longstanding rally, pushes price to the final peak. Calm professionals sell (distribute) their shares to the eager and emotional public who buys the stock without fear of potential price declines. Wave 5 often reveals cracks in the price structure through negative momentum, breadth, or volume divergences. Experienced retail traders will immediately see these structural divergences, or nonconfirmations in price, and sell their shares to take whatever profit they have. Aggressive traders, including professionals, may decide to short sell shares as close to the top as they feel they can.

Fifth waves exhibit the battle between professional traders who use time-tested strategies and indicators to assess the signals from price and the life cycle of a stock and smaller, less experienced investors who are guided by emotion, specifically the fear of missing more of the continued rally. This fear of missing out, when combined with the greed of making money quickly, causes them to buy shares without observing the potential reversal signals or other dangers inherent on the chart.

Fifth waves often occur at the heart of the distribution phase between professionals and amateurs and eventually give way to a price breakdown that begins Wyckoff's Mark-down phase. Instead of labeling the Mark-down phase as waves 6, 7, and 8, Ralph Elliott chose instead to label this distinct sell-off phase with the letters A, B, and C to distinguish the two separate phases of the life cycle.

Wave A: Another Retracement to Buy or the Beginning of the End

The concepts of Accumulation and Distribution, as well as the life cycle of a stock, build upon the notion that professional investors consistently make money over time while amateur or retail investors consistently lose money to professionals over time. Notice the different actions professional and retail traders take during the accumulation phase or during Elliott's Waves 1 and 2. The first correction Wave has the same dynamics.

To the professionals, Wave A represents the beginning of a new bear market or a new Mark-down phase, so they have either exited their positions prior to the top or are doing so during the first wave down. Other professionals short sell shares in an attempt to establish a position as close to the top as possible. On the other hand, what are the vast majority of retail or amateur traders doing? For the most part, they are buying during this retracement wave down as they think it is just another opportunity to buy a retracement within the context of a lengthy rising uptrend that has no end in sight. If they just see the price on a standard line chart, then this retracement is no different to them than any of the prior retracements that resulted in higher price highs.

During Wave A, savvy traders often observe new momentum or breadth lows, or price breaking under long-term trendlines or important short- or intermediate-term moving averages. If you start to see a sudden down-move in price form after a clean negative divergence undercut the recent price high, you may be looking at Wave A beginning a new bear phase.

Wave B: The Phony Rally

B Waves can be enormously deceptive, even to experienced traders. Wave B forms after Wave A has taken price lower, usually after a clean negative divergence undercut the recent price high. Wave B might begin to form from under the 20- or 50-day moving averages. Again, conceptualize this in terms of professionals and amateurs. Professionals are positioned defensively during this phase and they are skeptical that this rally will carry price to a new high. Amateurs do not see the price chart damage (trendline or moving average breaks, new momentum lows) that occurred and thus fully expect that price will continue its merry way to a new high, and may be fully positioned long after buying what they believed was another typical retracement (which, in reality, was Wave A).

Just like the second wave is not another bear market swing that will take price to a new low, Wave B is not another bull market swing that will take price to a new high. However, here is where B Waves get tricky. While Wave 2 cannot form a new low in price under Wave 1, Wave B can form a new price high above Wave 5. This is one of the reasons why Elliott Wave is confusing to many people who study it for the first time.

Generally, Wave B does not form a new swing high but there are occasions where it does. In the event that Wave B does form a new high, the new price high is almost always undercut with negative breadth, volume, and momentum divergences. Thus, professional traders see the new price high but understand that the floor is likely to collapse in price in the next swing ahead. Amateurs will not see these blatant nonconfirmations and will continue buying shares eagerly during the false rally. Eventually, price will continue the Mark-down phase as the worst is yet to come.

Wave C: The Panic Phase

By the time the third wave, or swing, of the Distribution Phase, Mark-down phase, or Bear Market (whatever your definition of a down-trend in price) occurs, most professionals have completely sold their positions, are positioned short already, or will soon sell any remaining shares they own. C Waves can be similar to third waves in their dynamics, because at this time, a positive feedback loop develops that pushes price sharply to the downside. Those traders who bought long during the prior waves, including the B Wave, must now liquidate their shares as price triggers their stop-loss orders. In combination, Wave C often breaks sharply under the A Wave low, which triggers many aggressive traders to short sell shares, driving the price even lower. If Waves 4, 5, A, and B have formed a horizontal rectangle consolidation or negative feedback loop (price compression), then Wave C will often be the wave that breaks to the downside and triggers a breakout range expansion, positive feedback loop environment.

Amateur traders who bought shares at any time during Waves 4, 5, A, or B suffer potentially devastating losses as price falls sharply to the downside, and they often remain positioned long until the point where they can no longer bear the emotional pain of financial loss. Unfortunately, this point often occurs near the latter phases of Wave C, which ends the life cycle phase that Elliott defined and begins again with the dynamics of accumulation that sets the cycle in motion again for a Wave 1 yet to come, and thus the eventual birth of a new cycle.

THE THREE RULES OF ELLIOTT WAVE

Despite the complexities of Elliott's theory, the Elliott Wave principle lists only three rules that cannot be broken except in rare instances. In hindsight, identifying proper waves on a chart is simple, but in real-time, traders refer to the following three rules to guide both their primary and alternate assessments of waves in progress.

First, Wave 2 cannot retrace more than 100 percent of Wave 1. Stated differently, in a rising Wave 1, the corrective Wave 2 cannot trade under the low of Wave 1, and in the context of a falling Wave 1, Wave 2 cannot rally higher than the beginning high price of Wave 1. Traders often report difficulty in identifying Waves 1 and 2 as they develop, so this rule guides them in their real-time assessment. They must change their wave labels if their developing wave count violates the first rule.

Second, Wave 3 cannot be the shortest of the three impulse waves 1, 3, and 5. While Wave 3 cannot be the shortest wave in a proposed count, the rule does not necessitate that the third wave be the longest wave, which is most often the case. This rule comes into play when you label a very large wave as the first wave, and then a smaller middle wave as the third wave, and then believe price to be in a terminal fifth wave. When this situation happens, it is most likely that the price remains in a larger third wave that might be persisting longer than you think, which would cause you to label price in final fifth wave too early. Remember, look for divergences when you begin to label fifth waves.

Finally, Wave 4 cannot enter the price territory of Wave 2, or, stated differently, Wave 4 cannot end under the price high of Wave 1. This is also a cross-check on your real-time wave count that states that the third wave is usually the most dynamic. If you believe a third wave to have ended and you label price in a current fourth wave, then what you label as the fourth wave should not trade lower than the high of what you labeled as Wave 1, as Wave 2 begins at the high of Wave 1.

I suggest envisioning the character of waves as described above in terms of the characteristics to expect and the psychology of the traders involved, rather than getting bogged down in the tiny details of precise wave counting. Elliott Wave complements Charles Dow's work on trend, but what is most important is understanding the prevailing trend and then assessing the momentum structure that confirms or fails to confirm the trend. Elliott Wave is a formal method to achieve that same goal of assessing the trend direction and strength.

ELLIOTT WAVES EXAMPLE: RESEARCH IN MOTION

Let's take a real-world example to compare the progression of stages and waves. Research in Motion (RIMM) moves from accumulation through distribution on its weekly price chart from 2005 to 2009 in Figure 7.7.

Investors in Research in Motion held price within a two-year trading range from 2005 to early 2007 with an upper resistance line at $35.00 and a lower support line just above $20.00 per share. The two-year period marked an accumulation phase that gave way to the beginning of Realization with the October 2006 break above $35.00 per share.

Though the scale is small, notice the new price high and momentum high in the 3/10 MACD Oscillator that formed in the later part of 2006. This range breakout phase began the first wave, which marked a positive feedback loop until the sideways consolidation

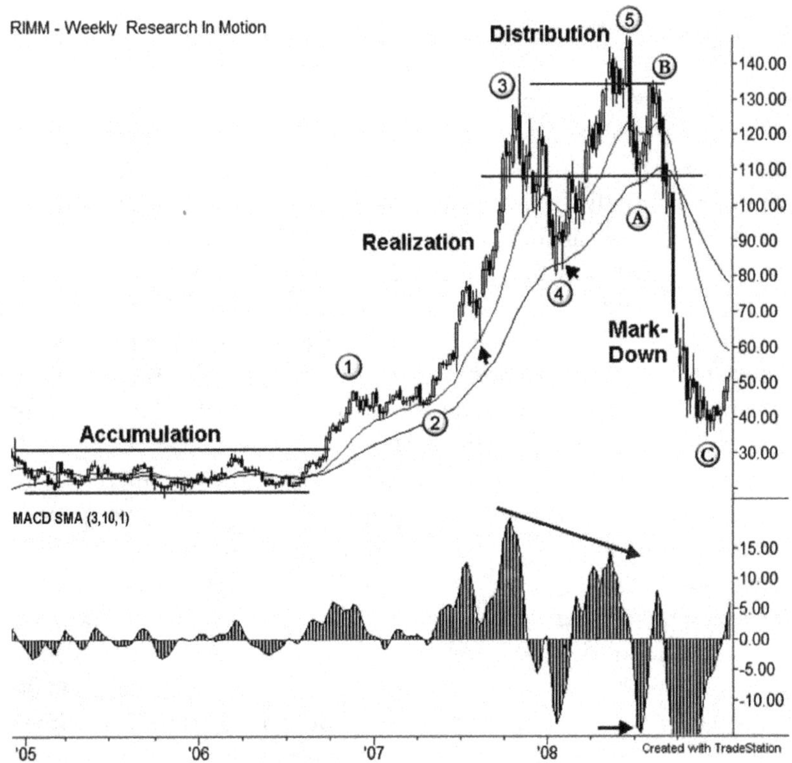

FIGURE 7.7 Elliott's Waves and Dow/Wyckoff's Stages Overlaid in Research in Motion

phase that marked Wave 2. Notice how price supported on the rising 20-week exponential moving average and then broke above the second accumulation phase, or negative feedback loop, in May 2007. The break to new price highs, which also formed another new momentum high, marked another confirmation of the Realization phase in progress and sparked the beginning of Elliott's third wave.

Third waves often mark the most powerful sustained move of a bull market, and Research in Motion's weekly chart highlights this concept. The realization phase continued with only a minor pause halfway through that took price back to the rising 20-week moving average. The third wave spanned from the $50.00 level to the peak at $130.00 in late 2007 in an almost vertical positive feedback loop that marked a powerful range expansion impulse to the upside. Traders took profits here and price fell back to the rising 50-week exponential moving average at the $85.00-per-share level. This relatively steep pullback was not the peak in the price move, but was only a Wave 4 pullback to rising moving average support that set the stage for the final distribution phase, or Elliott's fifth wave.

Price supported off the rising 50-week EMA in early 2008 as traders rushed to purchase shares. Professionals, who had purchased shares for a longer-term investment accumulated their positions at lower prices before the sharp price rise. These investors aimed to sell their shares to lock in their gains as eager amateur traders swooped in to purchase the shares that the professionals sold. Amateurs, driven mostly by emotion, whether fear of missing out on easy money or greed of making money very quickly, failed to see the negative divergence as price pushed to new highs beyond $130.00 to peak just shy of $150.00 per share in June 2008.

Pay close attention to the structure as price progresses down from the fifth wave to begin the first corrective wave lower. This is one of the main benefits of incorporating Elliott Wave into your analysis. Notice that price fell from $140.00 sharply lower to the $105.00 level to bounce solidly off the rising 50-week EMA at the point I labeled Wave A. Look closely at the new low that the 3/10 MACD Oscillator forms when price did not form a new price low under the early 2008 swing low labeled Wave 4. This pattern is called the Kick-off, and is a revealing signal that most traders miss; identifying it allows you to distinguish between a standard retracement swing in the context of an ongoing bull market (which should not form a Kick-off signal) and a potential first swing down in a new bear market that may be developing.

If the momentum oscillator breaks to a new indicator low beyond recent lows in the oscillator, but price does not break to a new price low beneath the prior swing low, then you have momentum sending you a potentially strong warning sign that the trend may be reversing. Again, the signal comes from the 3/10 MACD Oscillator or other momentum oscillator forming a new swing low in July 2008 that takes out the oscillator low formed in January 2008. Compare the oscillator lows to the price lows that formed them. The July 2008 price low bottomed above $100.00, while the January price low bottomed at the $80.00-per-share level. The momentum oscillator formed a new low while price did not. This Kick-off signal often warns of a turn in trend to mark an A wave down, which gives you an early warning signal of a potential trend reversal.

To anyone else, this downswing in price is just another higher low that bounces off a rising moving average, which is a classic buy signal. Amateur traders do aggressively buy here, which helps push the price higher in a false rally to create Wave B. Professionals observed the divergences that formed on the prior fifth wave impulse to new highs, and may also see the new oscillator Kick-off lows that characterized Wave A while amateurs will not see this warning signal. As such, when the buying that pushes price to a rally in Wave B ends, price will then transition to the final down move which can be as violent in terms of positive feedback and range breakout expansion as a rising third wave.

Whether you draw a rising trendline connecting the $60.00, $80.00, and $105.00 price lows, or draw a horizontal trendline at the $110.00 level, price breaks all trendlines as well as the rising 50-week EMA at the $110.00 level, which begins a violent positive feedback loop of selling, with bulls selling unwillingly to take stop losses and bears selling willingly to enter new short-sale positions. Either way, Wave C brings out panic selling from retail investors who purchased shares anywhere during the Distribution Stage or specifically from Waves 4, 5, A, or B.

If you combine the Elliott Wave notation and the distribution concept, you can visualize a trading range or distribution phase that occurred between the $110.00- and $135.00-per-share price level. Notice the particularly violent volatility in the form of a straight down move during Wave C or Wyckoff's Mark-down phase. During September 2008, price fell from a monthly high of $125.00 to a monthly low of $69.50, which was a 45 percent price drop in a single month. Traders or investors who held long during that month were shell-shocked and uncertain whether to lock in their losses or keep holding on in hopes that price would bounce so that they could recoup some of their sudden losses. Holding and hoping was the wrong decision: after the 45 percent one-month drop to $70.00, price fell another 50 percent to bottom three months later in December 2008 at $35.00 per share.

FINAL TIPS FOR APPLYING THE LIFE CYCLE IN REAL TIME

When doing your own analysis and trading, remember that it is far more important to understand the phases during the life cycle that a stock experiences rather than struggle with the precise wave count. If you have tried to apply Elliott Wave in any form other than hindsight, you will know that the real world does not always follow the textbook counts. Take the time to understand the psychology of the groups of investors or traders, specifically the thoughts of the professionals versus the amateurs as price moves from stage to stage. Understanding the insights from large-scale investor psychology will be far more important than perfect real-time labeling and the frustration traders experience when what they labeled as a fifth wave then springs new life on to a sixth, seventh, eighth, or even ninth wave.

Realize that you will probably miss real-time identification of a first and second wave as they form. To most people, waves 1 and 2 are indistinguishable from any typical bear market swing. The first clue for most people comes when price breaks to a new high above the peak of Wave 1—this is often the official Kick-off to the Realization phase and dynamic third wave.

Look beyond the price to volume, sentiment, breadth indicators (if assessing an index), and momentum oscillators. Look for new breadth, momentum, and volume highs to accompany what you believe to be third waves. Look to buy the pullback into support in what you believe is a fourth wave. Look for negative divergences in volume, momentum, and breadth to serve as nonconfirmation of price highs during what you believe to be a fifth wave.

Look for technical damage in the form of price penetrations under a key short- or intermediate-term average during a possible Wave A. Look to see if momentum forms a new low in a Kick-off signal when price does not form a new low on the chart; if so, you may be observing Wave A at the official start of a new Mark-down distribution phase. Look for Wave C to break through established trendlines, prior support areas, or moving averages and make sure momentum forms new lows along with price during this potentially violent final phase of distribution or the Mark-down phase.

We have now arrived at the end of the price principles and trading strategies that form the basis of specific trade setups. Using this as a departure point, we will now pivot to discuss how to incorporate all we have learned so far into specific setups. Our goal as traders is to recognize short-term, high-probability trading opportunities with low-risk entries.

Make sure you fully understand the principles of trend continuity, momentum's role, and the price alternation (range contraction and expansion). In your analysis, look for specific candle bars and price patterns to guide your analysis of the current price structure. Within the context of a trending move, draw Fibonacci grids over price swings to find hidden support or resistance levels that many traders miss. Finally, put all of your analysis into the broader picture of the life cycle of a price move on the larger frame from accumulation to distribution, and back again.

Armed with this knowledge of how to analyze price on a chart, you can now turn the page to the final section to learn how to execute specific tactics to take advantage of opportunities that exist within the developing price structure.

PART III

Execution and Trade Setups

CHAPTER 8

Edge, Expectancy, and Execution

So far, we have discussed trend, momentum, and volatility as the foundation price principles that define market movement. We then examined specific trading tools such as candlesticks, price patterns, and Fibonacci retracements to build upon the leading price principles of trend, momentum, and volatility. Moving averages assist in trend identification; unbound momentum oscillators reveal the momentum structure of the market as a confirmation of a price move or a nonconfirmation through divergences. For volatility, we assess the degree of price range compression or expansion directly on the charts, or through indicators such as Bollinger Bands, the ADX Indicator, or hand-drawn trendlines.

All of the information of a chart fits within the life cycle of a price move from accumulation through realization on to final distribution, and we can apply the appropriate strategy depending on our assessment of price's location in the broader cycle. No matter what timeframe you're using, understanding these principles and how to use the right chart tool at the right time will help you to locate the best opportunities for low-risk trades.

However, being able to recognize opportunities alone won't make you successful. You must have confidence to act on those opportunities and to focus on the big picture. Many traders fail to achieve long-term profits due to deficiencies in execution, risk management, money management, or emotional management.

Once you acquire the basic skills, you will find that long-term trading success requires balancing competing interests. Some of the factors you will have to balance as you develop your own trading plan and strategies are:

- How much money to risk (too much and you invite the risk of ruin, too little and you will not profit from your endeavors),
- How many markets or stocks to follow (too many and you miss opportunities, too little and you don't have enough opportunities)

- How to manage emotions (too much greed and you take risky bets that lead to large losses, but too much fear causes you to miss opportunities)
- When to enter a position (if you enter before a signal triggers, you will incur more losses but if you enter too late after a signal triggers, you will erode your risk/reward edge—inactivity is costly)
- When to exit a position (too early and you leave money on the table, or too late and you give back unrealized profits)
- How to balance bias with objectivity (if you are too biased that the market must rise or fall, you will miss conflicting evidence that suggests your bias is wrong)
- How much time you commit to trading (too much and you risk burnout and social isolation, too little and you miss critical information and opportunities)

Most of the decisions you make will be personal, tied directly to your personality, risk-tolerance, experience, age, account size, financial goals, and life experiences.

This chapter scratches the surface on some of the more important components of your trading plan. I would suggest you spend as much time seeking to answer these questions as you do learning about trade setups and management. It's one thing to know what to do, but it's an entirely separate thing to enter and exit trades in real time under conditions of uncertainty. Let's start our deeper journey by discussing why understanding edge is critical to every trader.

ALL ABOUT EDGE

Without an edge, you should not trade, but how do you define edge? In a probabilistic arena such as the markets with uncertain outcomes, an edge may be defined as a higher probability of one outcome occurring over another. Edge also represents an advantage over time. Education and experience give an advantage, or edge, to professional traders when compared to new or less-educated, less-experienced traders; this is the information and experience edge. There are actually many types of edge in the market, but for this discussion, we will focus on how to assess your mathematical accuracy edge and monetary edge, both in individual trades and over time as part of your broader trading strategy.

The Casino's Edge in Roulette

In the gambling arena, the casinos have the edge or advantage over the players in all games. One of the best examples to describe what an edge means is to consider a night at the roulette table, and how many gamblers misunderstand their odds of success. A typical roulette board contains 36 numbered spaces that are colored either red or black, and two green spaces numbered 0 and 00 (zero and double-zero). There are 18 red numbers and 18 black numbers and at first glance, it seems to the new gambler that there is an even 50/50 chance of a successful outcome if the gambler bets on a red number rather than a black number, because the number of red and black numbers is equal on the roulette wheel. This would be correct, except for the casino's addition of the two green zero and double-zero spaces.

Mathematically speaking, there are 38 squares on a roulette wheel in which the spinning ball can rest, and of those 18 are black and 18 are red. If we want to bet on a red number coming up, we need to find the probability of that outcome happening. To do so, we divide 18 (the number of red squares) by 38 (the total number of squares) and calculate that there is a 47.5 percent chance of success.

How did that happen? If there are an equal number of red and black squares, how is it that there is only a 47.5 percent chance of a red number coming up? The house edge is represented by the two green squares, which are neither red nor black, and occasionally the ball stops in one of these squares. In this event, no gambler who bet on red or black is paid—the house takes all the money of those who bet on either red or black. Because there are two green squares out of 38, there is a 5 percent chance that the ball will stop in one of the green squares.

Because players cannot bet on a green-color square coming up, they must limit their color bets to the 36 of 38 squares that contain a red or black color. So, if a player bets on the ball landing in a red square, the chance of success is actually 47.5 percent, but because the casino has the edge in terms of the green squares. The house has the opposite side of the bet, which is a 52.5 percent chance of achieving its goal of taking the player's money. Stated differently, the player wins only if the roulette wheel ends in a red square (47.5 percent chance), but the house keeps the entire bet if the wheel ends in a black square (47.5 percent chance, which is equal to the player) or a green square (5.0 percent chance, which represents the casino's advantage or edge).

We can speak in terms of outcomes on the next spin of the wheel, which gives the player a 47.5 percent chance of success if the bet is on either a red or black outcome, and in terms of expectancy, or edge over time. In other words, if the gambler bet red 100 times in a row in a single night, the gambler would lose slightly more money than the gambler expects to keep. Why? The gambler does not have the edge over the casino.

The pay-out from the casino on a correctly guessed color outcome is one to one, which means if you bet $100.00 on red and the ball ends in a red numbered square, then the casino would pay you $100.00. Each time you lose, you lose your initial bet of $100.00—it goes to the casino. If after 10 spins of the wheel, red came up five times and black came up five times, the player would have gained $500.00 but also lost $500.00, right back at the start. That's no good!

Let us now assume that the player bets on red 100 times in a row and the outcomes were exactly in line with the percentages from the odds and probabilities. Of the 100 times, 47 spins will come up red (win) 47 spins will come up black (loss) and five times will come up green (loss). We'll let the remaining spin be a loss. The gambler will have won 47 times, resulting in a gain of $4,700.00, but lost 53 times, losing $5,300.00. The gambler would end the night down $600.00, or stated differently, because the casino had the edge due to the two green squares, the casino would have profited $600.00 from the efforts of the gambler.

This is how you must approach edge in the market: you must have the edge or advantage in your favor over time. You increase your edge by locating, entering, managing, and then exiting high-probability trading opportunities, while controlling your risk on each trade. This chapter will teach you to assess the edge not just on individual trades, as the gambler did when betting on a single outcome of red on the casino wheel (47.5 percent), but over time as you take many, many trades each month, quarter, and year.

You are probably aware that trading on hot tips is not an effective long-term trading strategy. You must be able to do the work yourself, find opportunities, assess the probabilities, determine if an edge is present, and then execute the trade. Once in a trade, you must not let your emotions guide your decision to exit early, either if the trade ticks slightly against you but not yet to your stop-loss price, or ticks up to a profit but not yet to your expected target based on your analysis. Base your trading decisions on the facts from the charts as you understand them at the time. Monitor open positions for any unexpected developments that warrant an exit earlier than expected. Try to anticipate the outcomes as much as possible in advance.

Let's now take a moment to understand what edge means in the context of short-term trading strategies.

Are Markets Random or Predictable?

One of the most common questions you will be asked by the average person when you announce that you are a trader is the classic question "Markets are totally random—how then do you make money?" Do you know the answer to that question? Are markets totally random?

On one hand, the academic argument known as the Random Walk Theory states that markets are 100 percent random and that no individual or fund can consistently beat the market over time. In other words, it is impossible to gain an edge over the market because it is impossible to assess the odds of a purely random system. On the other hand, you have the argument that markets are totally predictable from advanced methods of discerning the future, and that charts, fundamentals, or quantitative strategies can indeed accurately predict the future, which allows those with the programs, tools, or techniques to achieve superior returns year over year.

The truth of the matter rests somewhere in the middle of these conflicting points of view. Markets do have repeating patterns and individuals or funds do consistently beat the market year over year, but it's not because these individuals have special insights into the future moves in the market. On the contrary, most successful short-term traders are masters of edge, probability, risk-management, and emotion. They often admit that they are uncertain of the next move in the market, but they know how they will be positioned if certain scenarios occur.

Think back to the roulette wheel example. While every single spin is totally random, the House has the edge by the configuration of the colored squares on the board, namely the two green squares. While an individual spin is random with fixed probabilities, the system and method of taking money steadily from the gambler each night is not random.

So it is in the market, and your goal is to assess the probability and trade with the larger picture of edge as it plays out on the chart.

For example, if a trader sees a price break through a key overhead resistance level after a consolidation period, that trader will buy shares as close to the breakout as possible and place a stop-loss order just under the resistance area. The trader is not completely certain as to whether the price will continue to rise in a range expansion breakout move as expected, but if price does continue to rally, then by the time the trader exits the position after price forms a new trading range at a higher level, the trader books a nice profit from the move. The trader appropriately managed the position such that the profitable exit was many multiples larger than the initial stop-loss price in the event the range breakout failed and price fell back under the overhead resistance level.

If we assume that the trader captured a $10.00 move but placed a stop-loss order $2.00 lower than the entry, then the profit was five times the risk in the position. If the trader takes 10 similar setups over the course of a year and half of these setups fail but half succeed, the trader would end the year with a nice profit, despite the fact that half of the trades failed. The five trades that succeeded generated a net $50.00 per share and then we would subtract the $10.00 per share from the five trades that failed, costing $2.00 each, which leaves the annual profit at a $40.00-per-share net gain. At no time was the trader certain that an individual trade would meet its upside target, or would stop with a loss. Instead, the trader knew that over time, the edge would lead to profits over time, assuming there was no deviation from the strategy.

This trader would still profit even if 70 percent of the trades taken that year failed with such a superior edge. How is that possible? The three successful trades gave a profit of $30.00 per share, but when we subtract the $14.00 from seven losing trades at $2.00 each, we arrive at a net profit for the year of $16.00 per share. In essence, a breakout strategy trader can fail to predict the future seven times out of 10, but still make money on the year.

This is the type of thinking you must adopt as a trader. Markets are neither totally random nor absolutely predictable, but if you use strategies based on foundation price principles and carefully assess your edge in each trade, then you have a much higher chance of success than if you do not.

Defining Edge

Most new traders focus on being right, or correctly forecasting the next swing in price and thus dedicate all their efforts to achieving winning trades. It is normal to want to be right, and is frustrating to analyze a particular trade setup and then lose money on a typical stop-loss order. It thus makes sense that traders are drawn to strategies or stock market courses which promise accuracy rates greater than 90 percent (some even promise zero losing trades).

If we think back to our analogy about the casino and the roulette wheel and our discussion on the red and black squares, the casino has the edge 52.5 percent of the time, which means that 47.5 percent of the time the casino will lose money to the gambler.

However, the edge will play out not necessarily on the next immediate spin of the wheel, but over the next 100, 1,000, and 10,000 spins of the wheel where money will flow over time from the gambler to the casino. This is the way you should develop your strategies and also cope with an individual losing trade.

When discussing the edge of a particular trade setup in the market, traders seek to maximize the two main types of edge: accuracy and monetary.

Accuracy Edge The accuracy edge refers to a greater than 50 percent chance of obtaining a winning outcome from a trade setup. In addition to assessing the probabilities of a winning trade, the accuracy edge describes the win rate or win percentage over a series of trades.

ACCURACY EDGE

Greater than 50 percent probability of obtaining a profitable outcome to a trade, which comes from time-tested price principles, setups, or strategies.

Traders use the 50 percent threshold as a baseline to assess their win rate, because a 50 percent accuracy rate indicates results that would be expected by picking entries and exits randomly. A win rate less than 50 percent indicates a negative edge while a win rate above 50 percent represents a positive edge. In the roulette wheel example, the House holds the accuracy edge over the gambler—52.5 percent to 47.5 percent.

In assessing the probability of success of any given trade, a trader must study the price chart, observe any key price in play, assess the volatility environment, measure the dominant trend, determine whether a price pattern exists, and weigh the balance of power between buyers and sellers. Through studying a particular price chart, traders assess the probability for the next likely swing in price and determine whether or not the odds favor participating in the anticipated move.

While new traders want a very high win rate, they soon discover that accuracy in forecasting the future price swings is not the only variable in trading success, nor is it even possible or necessary to know with absolute certainty where the market is heading next.

In fact, many professional traders post win rates less than 50 percent, which means they lose money on a larger number of trades than they win. How then can a trader make money with an accuracy rate less than 50 percent? They understand the importance of edge over time and how the accuracy edge is just one component in their trading plan.

Monetary Edge Professionals often argue that the more important edge is the monetary edge, which refers specifically to the reward-to-risk relationship in dollar or point terms of a setup. Because so many trading books stress that traders should refuse to take a trade setup that has less than a three-to-one reward-to-risk relationship, many traders demand a minimum of a three to one reward-to-risk relationship before they will commit money to a trade setup, even if the setup has a high probability of success. Other traders will not enter a position unless they can calculate a five-to-one reward-to-risk relationship between the profit target and the stop-loss prices. In the roulette example, neither the House nor the gambler claimed the monetary edge, as the risk was a fixed $1.00 to a potential reward of $1.00, or one-to-one reward to risk relationship.

If a trader seeks to profit $5.00 for every $1.00 at risk each time he puts on a trade, then the trader will make money over time due to the monetary edge as long as the accuracy rate remains above 20 percent. That means the trader can lose on eight trades and profit on two trades and still make money. Of course, the trader would make more money with a higher win rate, but this extreme example underscores the point. The eight trades that result in $1.00 stop-loss orders total a loss of $8.00, but the two $5.00 winning trades combine for a profit of $10.00. When you subtract the loss of $8.00 from the gain of $10.00, you find that the trader profited $2.00 from the 10 trades—this is the trader's mathematical advantage, or monetary edge, in trading performance.

Thus, traders calculate edge by combining the accuracy edge—their win rate—with the monetary edge—the reward-to-risk relationship. As you develop your strategies, seek strategies that favorably combine the accuracy and monetary edge into a duality of edge that tips the odds of success and profit in your favor. Know the tradeoffs that exist in certain strategies in terms of accuracy and monetary edge.

MONETARY EDGE

The reward-to-risk relationship in a trade; the profit target is larger than the risk in a trade as defined by a stop-loss price.

For example, most generic breakout trading strategies post lower win rates than other strategies, but also have higher reward-to-risk relationships. Long-term trend-following strategies often have a higher monetary edge at the expense of the accuracy edge, which is why new traders cannot endure the numerous losses trend following strategies generate in search of the small handful of trades that generate the majority of profits for a year.

Retracement trading strategies in the context of a dominant trend often have higher accuracy rates, but the smaller targets degrade the monetary edge. In terms of testing out different strategies, you will often find that there is an unfortunate tradeoff between the two types of edge, such that to obtain a larger monetary edge (larger profit target relative to the stop-loss price), one often sacrifices a proportion of the accuracy edge.

Sometimes higher accuracy strategies can be insidious to new traders because a string of small winning trades can lure the trader into a sense of invincibility, greed, and overconfidence. After five winning trades in a row, the trader will refuse to take a stop-loss price on the sixth trade, and that one trade will grow into a very large losing trade that erases the profits obtained on the prior five trades and more. Emotions override edge, and our emotions will always be part of discretionary trading plans.

Many mean reversion strategies fall in this category. Look back to Chapter 3 on the Price Alternation Principle, specifically when price remains within the boundaries of a horizontal resistance line and lower support line. Traders who enjoy playing positions between this range, for example, buying shares as price touches support and then selling those shares as price rises to touch overhead resistance, continue to make money as long as the price remains within the boundaries of this well-established range.

However, trading ranges cannot last forever, and when price breaks out of the trading range, a trader can become trapped on the wrong side of a suddenly violent and unexpected range breakout move. In this way, a trader obtains numerous small profits from small-target trades, but then loses those profits and more from a single loss by refusing to take a stop-loss price when the market breaks out of the trading range, or if price gaps strongly outside of the range unexpectedly. In that single event, the trader may suffer a large loss on a single trade, where the loss is greater than the smaller profits from the range-trading trades.

Beyond Accuracy and Monetary Edge

Before you put on a trade, quiz yourself on the specific edge in the trade. Do you know the expected probability for the trade? Is your trade based on a foundation price principle such as trend continuity (buying pullbacks to support in a rising uptrend), a momentum principle (buying after an impulse, or shorting after a lengthy negative momentum divergence), or a price alternation principle (buying a breakout up from a lengthy trading range)? How much confluence do you see in the trade? Do you observe a price rally that is extended beyond the rising 20-period moving average into the upper Bollinger Band that has formed a bearish engulfing candle as a negative momentum divergence formed? These questions help you assess the probability of a successful outcome for the trade setup you are about to take.

If you have determined that the odds favor a successful outcome for your trade, then your next goal is to assess the reward-to-risk relationship. Let's take the prior example of the overextended price swing into the upper Bollinger Band with a bearish engulfing candle on a negative momentum divergence. Generally, traders enter as price breaks under the low of the bearish engulfing candle and then place a stop above the candle high or the most recent swing high. From your entry, you assess where your expected price target exists, which is perhaps the rising 20-period moving average. This is a classic mean reversion trade to target a rising short-term average in the context of a prevailing uptrend.

If your price target is at least two times larger than your stop-loss, then you have assessed a setup that combines the accuracy (probability) and monetary (reward/risk) edge. You would want to take the setup and not concern yourself with the outcome of this individual trade, particularly if you are stopped out. Judge yourself by your ability to locate high-probability setups based on structure and then adhere to your price target and stop-loss price. Do not micromanage the trade or let your emotions affect your decision of the objective probabilities in the setup. If you only take discretionary setups that combine the accuracy and monetary edge, you will greatly enhance your chance for success as a developing trader.

Mark Douglas wrote about the importance of edge and probability in his classic text *Trading in the Zone*. In discussing trade outcomes and edge, Douglas compared trade outcomes to purely random events such as flipping a coin. If you bet money on a coin toss but the coin lands on tails when you bet heads, you completely understand that the outcome was random and you do not get upset with yourself. Contrast this with a trader who did his homework and just got stopped out of a trade. The trader then becomes frustrated, upset, or depressed due to the loss, because the trader felt that the next swing in the market could be perfectly predicted.

When the stop-loss execution indicates that the market was not predicted correctly, the trader feels defeated and personally assaulted by the market. Psychologically wounded, the trader is either more likely to skip the next high-probability, low-risk trade setup and thus miss opportunity, or engage in revenge trading and jump into the next quasi-setup seen, which usually is a low-probability, high-risk setup. Whatever psychological error the trader is prone to make, what fails is the understanding that ability had nothing to do with the outcome of a single trade.

What began as a high-probability setup that resulted in a random loss devolves into a downward spiral of revenge trading and missed opportunities. If you lose money on a well-researched high-probability, low-risk opportunity, view it as just a roll of the dice, flip of the coin, spin of the wheel, or deal of the cards. Do not let the experience derail you from finding similar setups in the near future. Trading is a game of probabilities, not certainties.

While you must assess the accuracy and monetary edge of each trade setup you take, you should also assess your performance over time in terms of your larger accuracy and monetary edge. Specifically, calculate your weekly or monthly win rate and large scale reward-to-risk ratio. This type of discussion takes you into the world of expectancy, which further explains the importance of the duality of edge in developing your trading strategy.

EDGING OUT YOUR EXPECTANCY

Simply stated, the expectancy formula combines your accuracy edge and monetary edge over time and then calculates your expectancy per trade of your strategy or performance. The expectancy formula is a formal representation of the importance of both your win rate and your reward-to-risk relationship. In an ideal world, both factors would be as high as possible, but expectancy reminds us that the interaction of these two components is more important than either in isolation.

To calculate your personal trading expectancy, you need to have a track record of at least 30 closed positions, though more is preferred. Using Excel or any trading journal program, find your average winning trade and then your average losing trade both in dollar terms. These figures should be readily available from the distribution of trades. Then, calculate your percentage of winning and losing trades. These are the four components you will need to assess your expectancy for your trading performance.

First, multiply your average winning trade by your percentage of winning trades. Then, multiply your average losing trade by your percentage of losing trades. Subtract the losing trades number from your winning trades number to arrive at your expectancy per trade.

EXPECTANCY

To calculate the expectancy of your strategy, you must calculate your average winning trade, average losing trade, and your win rate as a trader. With these variables, insert the information into the following formula:

(Average Win \$ × Percentage of Winning Trades)
− (Average Loss \$ × Percentage of Losing Trades)

For example, a retracement-style swing trader named Joe calculated that his average winning trade was \$500.00 and he had a win rate of 60 percent. He then found that his average losing trade was \$300.00 and of course he had a loss rate of 40 percent. He calculated that \$500.00 times 0.60 was \$300.00 and that \$300.00 times 0.40 was \$120.00. He then subtracted \$120.00 from \$300.00 to arrive at a final number of \$180.00, which was his expectancy. Using these statistics, he can expect to make \$180.00 on every trade. That of course doesn't mean he makes exactly \$180.00 per trade, but that the components of accuracy and monetary edge combine to produce the \$180.00 positive expectancy figure per trade. Notice that Joe possesses a duality of accuracy and monetary edge, which is the best situation.

Think of this example another way. Out of 10 trades, six of which were winners and four of which were losers, Joe made \$3,000.00 from his winning trades (\$500.00 × 6) and lost a total of \$1,200.00 (\$300.00 × 4) from his losing trades. If we subtract his losses of \$1,200.00 from his profits of \$3,000.00, we arrive at \$1,800.00. In this example, Joe took 10 trades, so if we divide \$1,800.00 by the number of trades he took, we arrive at his expectancy per trade of \$180.00, as calculated above.

Expectancy literally tells you how much money you can expect to make on each of your trades, if you continue to take similar setups and opportunities as you did with your prior trades. If a particular trade deviates too far from your normal distribution, it will affect your expectancy calculation accordingly.

Let's take a look at an expectancy calculation from breakout trader Jane, who only maintains a monetary edge instead of an accuracy edge because she focuses specifically on breakout trading strategies, where her winning trades are much larger than her losing trades, but as a trade-off, she has a larger number of losing trades due to false breakouts.

Over the last month, Jane's average winning trade was \$5,000.00, but she maintained a win rate of only 30 percent. Her average losing trade was small, only \$500.00, and her loss rate was high at 70 percent. Jane calculated her expectancy per trade as \$1,150.00 through the following calculation:

$$\$5{,}000.00 \times 0.30 = \$1{,}500 \text{ and } \$500.00 \times 0.70 = \$350.00.$$
$$\$1{,}500.00 - \$350.00 = \$1{,}150.00$$

Though Jane had a much smaller accuracy rate than Joe, she had a much larger expectancy per trade. Jane could psychologically tolerate a string of losing trades because she was confident that, over time, her strategies would produce a small number of large winners if she kept taking the trade setups she knew had a larger-than-normal chance of breaking out into a range expansion mode.

Let's look at one more hypothetical example, but this time let's view a trader with a negative expectancy.

Reversal-style, new trader Jim loves to string together a series of small winning trades, but because he is accustomed to winning so frequently, he often stubbornly holds on to a position that goes against him, which subjects him to infrequent but very large losing trades. This behavior typically results in one larger-than-normal average losing trade in relation to his smaller, more-frequent winning trades each month. Over the course of a month, Jim calculated his average winning trade to be $500.00 with an enviable win rate of 85 percent. However, Jim's average losing trade was $5,000.00.

Using these figures, Jim calculated his expectancy per trade to be –$325.00 as seen below:

$$\$500.00 \times 0.85 = \$425.00 \text{ and } \$5{,}000.00 \times 0.15 = \$750.00.$$

$$\text{Then } \$425.00 - \$750.00 = -\$325.00$$

Jim's calculation showed that he could expect to lose $325.00 per trade. Jim was puzzled—last month, he traded 60 times and only nine of those trades were losers. However, three of those nine trades were big losers: $10,000.00 each! Those trades caused his average losing trade to spike to $5,000.00. Despite winning almost nine times out of every 10 trades, Jim still lost money for the month and if he keeps trading that way, he could lose his entire account over time! Jim is trading an anti-edge or counter-edge strategy that, despite his win rate, bleeds his account value month by month.

Calculate your expectancy at the end of each month to make changes as needed. Specifically examine the largest losing trade per month and ask yourself if that outcome was a result of random probabilities in the market (perhaps an unexpected overnight gap) or the result of your emotions degrading your edge. Perhaps you held on to a losing trade longer than anticipated or you purchased more shares than you should have (also called doubling down). Eliminating large losing trades as much as possible will have a very positive effect on your monthly expectancy calculations.

When discussing the larger picture of your strategy's overall edge, you must incorporate two other factors into your calculation: transaction costs and trading frequency.

Minimizing Costs from Commissions and Slippage

Trading is not free; each time you execute a trade, you must pay your broker a commission. Also, each time you enter and exit a trade, you will pay a hidden cost called slippage. Slippage occurs when you wish to execute a trade at a quoted price on your screen but learn that you were filled on your trade at a price higher or lower than where you wished. In most cases, slippage per trade will be minimal, but there are certain factors that lead to increased slippage costs on your executions.

First, the larger the number of shares you trade, the larger your slippage will be. It is easier for a stock to absorb a 500 share order than it is for a 5,000 share order. As your account grows, you may not be able to avoid this situation, but larger block orders suffer more price slippage than smaller ones. Instead of putting on a 5,000 share position all at once for a swing trade that will last at least a week or more, try breaking down the order into ten 500 share lots executed over the course of a day (or two days).

Second, the less liquid the stock you select, the larger your slippage will be. If you trade small capitalization stocks with low volume per day, expect to experience more slippage than if you trade large capitalization stocks that trade millions of shares per day. As such, you may be able to purchase a 5,000 share order with no problem in Microsoft (MSFT) which generally trades over 50 million shares per day. However, trying to purchase the same 5,000 share position in a less liquid stock that trades 500,000 shares per day will almost certainly result in higher slippage.

Third, the larger the volatility is, the larger the slippage will be. If a stock is in a calm trading range, you will be more likely to be filled with less slippage than if you try to trade a stock that is in a volatile range expansion move. During volatile times, prices move quickly which results in higher slippage for entry. In general, the summer months are less volatile than the winter months due to seasonal tendencies. Stocks also undergo their own range contraction and expansion cycles as described in Chapter 3.

Finally, if you are an intraday or swing trader executing positions during the day, the time of day affects your expected slippage. Each day, stock prices are more active and thus volatile in the opening session and closing session. For this reason, many swing traders avoid executing positions within the first 15 or 30 minutes after the day's open and within 15 to 30 minutes before the day's close. Though volume will be higher during this time, volatility will also be higher, and the closer you trade to the open and close, the higher your slippage will be.

Steps to Minimize Slippage and Commission To minimize slippage, traders can take the following steps:

1. Trade smaller share size if possible; break down large orders into smaller ones.
2. Trade only liquid stocks—the higher the liquidity, the lower the slippage
3. Trade during less volatile times if you can help it
4. Avoid executing swing trading positions in the first 15 minutes or last 15 minutes of the day.

In addition to reducing slippage per transaction, you also want to reduce commissions as much as possible. In today's world of online trading accounts with commissions under $10.00 per trade, you should have your own online account and not trade through a full-service broker who charges high commissions per trade. Some online brokers offer per-share pricing which may be as low as $0.01 per share, or $1.00 per 100 shares.

If you trade less than 1,000 shares at a time, this will be more advantageous to you than other online brokers who advertise fixed prices of around $10.00 for an unlimited share size. You will save 50 percent in commissions if you consistently trade 500 shares with a fixed price of $0.01 per share ($5.00 per trade) than you will by trading 500 shares with a fixed commission of $10.00 per trade. However, you will benefit more from the fixed $10.00-per-trade plan if you trade 5,000 shares at a time than you would with a fixed $0.01-per-share plan, which would be $50.00 per trade in commissions. Remember, you pay a commission both on your entry and your exit! You'll also experience slippage on both your entry and your exit. Very small improvements in either slippage or commission result in big changes at the end of the year, depending on how actively you trade.

Trade Frequency That brings us to our next point regarding edge: trade frequency. The number of trades you take in a week or month affects your edge and overall performance as a trader. Some strategies require more active trading than others, and some traders' personalities are geared for more active trading tactics than others. As a discretionary trader, you are not a computer and should not trade like one. If you do not have an edge in a trade, do not take it. You have advantages a computer does not, and that comes from the ability to create a narrative regarding the supply/demand relationship between buyers and sellers as well as the integration of structure, patterns, and indicators into specific high-probability, low-risk trading setups.

If you are beginning your trading journey, you probably do not want to quit your full-time job until you have a proven track record of success. This means that you will most likely focus on the higher timeframes and practice swing trading strategies on highly liquid stocks or ETFs. If you focus your analysis and trade setups on the higher timeframes of the daily and weekly charts, then you will aim for larger price targets and hold your trades longer than an individual who uses the intraday charts to take advantage of more frequent trading opportunities.

There are caveats to the number of positions you take. First, if you are a swing trader and put on too many trades at once, you will spread your account too thin for each position and miss critical information that you would see if you focused only on a handful of trades at a time. Most traders have a limited attention span in terms of the number of open positions they can manage without sacrificing quality. The same is true for investors building a multi-stock portfolio—keeping track of too many stocks at once often invites trouble.

In addition, by managing a smaller number of open positions, you learn lessons for improvement on future trades that you miss if you manage dozens of open positions at once. You should perform end-of-trade analysis on each position to learn what went right, what went wrong, if you committed any unforced errors during the position, and how you could have improved your performance so you can continue to grow as a trader.

However, you must have a larger edge if you trade fewer positions. For example, if you swing trade three positions per month, you will trade 24 positions in a year. If you find that your accuracy edge is close to 55 percent and your reward-to-risk relationship is one-and-a-half to one for each trade, then you experience a very low dual edge. It would be better to deploy that smaller edge more frequently through day trades to make more money from the reduced edge. However, if you found that your accuracy rate was closer to 75 percent and your reward-to-risk relationship was three to one, you could afford the luxury of fewer trades per month and year.

Of course, if you are an intraday trader, you should be keenly aware of the vital need to reduce slippage and commissions as much as possible. Let us assume that you trade five times per day for 250 days of the year. That results in 1,250 trades over the course of the trading year. Let us also assume that your round-trip commission fee per trade is \$20.00, and you find that you slip \$5.00 round-trip per trade. 1,250 trades multiplied by \$20.00 in commissions results in \$25,000.00.

When we add the slippage of 1,250 trades multiplied by \$5.00 per round-trip trade, we have a hidden cost of \$6,250.00. Slippage is a hidden cost because your broker will never tell you how much you slipped in executions per trade; you might be completely unaware that your execution tactics are bleeding edge in the form of slippage unless you look very closely and understand the factors that contribute to increased slippage. While you do not specifically pay slippage like you pay commissions, you need to reduce slippage per trade as much as possible. Think of slippage costs as money you could have retained in your account if slippage was not an issue.

If you are new to trading, you probably cannot overcome the commissions it takes to trade 1,250 times per year, as the \$25,000.00 commission fee represents 50 percent of a \$50,000.00 account or 25 percent of a \$100,000.00 account. On a \$50,000 account, a trader would need to generate a 50 percent annual return to overcome commissions, not including taxes. It is more feasible to generate a 25 percent annual return on a \$100,000.00 account than a 50 percent return on a \$50,000.00 account. If a trader cuts the commission cost in half by switching brokers, then the money saved in commissions is a direct addition to the trader's account.

As a rule, newer traders execute far fewer trades than professionals and also pay higher commissions. No matter your trading experience, you will do well to reduce both commissions and slippage as much as possible. It will ultimately be up to you to balance your trading frequency with the size of your edge, and reduce commissions and slippage as much as possible.

Planning Your Position Size

Traders often read about position-sizing tactics but spend little time incorporating them into their future trades. Professional traders use rigid position-sizing models while most new or amateur traders decide how many shares to purchase depending on less stringent factors.

Your position-sizing model does not have to be complex, but you do need to know how to determine the number of shares you purchase or short-sell in advance of every position you take. Like most aspects in trading, there is a distinct balancing act when determining your position size: if your position size is consistently too small, you will not profit sufficiently from your endeavors whereas if your size is consistently too large, you invite the risk of ruin and could lose half or your entire trading account on a consecutive series of losing trades.

If your size is too small and you are too risk-averse in your position-sizing strategy, your winning trades will not generate enough large profits and may not allow you to continue trading because your profits do not cover your expenses in terms of data feed, operating expenses, software, research, commissions, and other costs associated with operating a trading business. Keep in mind that each trade you take will result in slippage and commissions, as well as taxes you must pay on your profitable trades, all of which reduce your income when focusing on the big picture.

On the other hand, if you consistently use a position-sizing strategy that results in taking too much risk for your account size, particularly for smaller accounts, then you invite the risk of ruin which means that a series of consecutive losses, or even one major unexpected loss, can deplete your trading account where recovery back to breakeven would either be impossible to achieve, or would take years to accomplish.

New traders make the mathematical error of assuming if they lose 50 percent of their account, then they can just as easily put on larger positions and eventually generate a 50 percent gain to cover the ground they lost. Mathematically, that is not possible. A loss of 50 percent of capital actually requires a gain of 100 percent on remaining funds to return to the capital high-water mark of the account. To make the math simple, assume a trader begins the year with a $100,000.00 account. By mid-year, the account decreased to $50,000.00, which is of course a 50 percent account value decline. To return the account back to the original $50,000.00, the trader must achieve a rate of return of 100 percent on the remaining $50,000.00 to see that account climb back to $100,000.00, where the trader began the year. While that is not impossible, it is certainly a low probability outcome that the trader will be able to achieve this. Had the trader not used such an aggressive position-sizing strategy in the beginning, the account would not have decreased by 50 percent.

The position-sizing question answers the question of "how much" variable in your trading plan, specifically how many shares do I trade, or how many contracts to purchase on my next trade. Investors and traders will approach this question differently, as investors will diversify risk across many positions, while traders may hold open one to five positions at a time. In addition, traders will be more likely to take on larger position sizes, even trading on margin, due to their decreased holding period and speculative activities than investors.

Fixed-Share Size and Fixed-Dollar Amount Strategies In his book *Trade Your Way to Financial Freedom*, Dr. Van Tharp describes four distinct strategies for how a trader can select a position size that is appropriate. This section discusses three of those strategies.

Many new traders gravitate toward fixed-dollar or fixed-share size strategies, which are extremely easy to calculate and require no advanced mathematics. These strategies include selecting the same number of shares or dollar amount for each trade, relative to the size of the account. For example, a trader might decide to purchase 100, 500, or 1,000 shares at a time for each position.

Fixed-Share Size Strategy Assume temporarily that a particular day trader only trades one vehicle, be it a particular stock, ETF, or futures contract. In this case, the trader can decide to adopt a fixed share size strategy, which equalizes every tick in price. For example, for every 1,000 shares purchased, a move of 10 cents results in a profit or loss to the account of $100.00, just as a $1.00 move in the stock results in a profit or loss of $1,000.00. The size of the trader's account will determine how many shares can be purchased, and whether or not the trader decides to trade on margin to meet the predetermined fixed number of shares or contracts.

The strategy of fixed share size or contract position-sizing will result in a variable dollar amount of shares purchased. If a trader decides to trade 1,000 shares per position, the trader would need at least a $50,000.00 account to trade a stock worth $50.00 per share, or a $75,000.00 account to trade a stock worth $75.00 per share. While that is more appropriate for day trading, swing traders may not find this strategy appealing, as they will want to have more positions open at a time, and thus purchase more positions using the limited capital in their account than a strict day trader would, who could use the entire account on one or two trades in an aggressive position-sizing strategy.

This type of strategy is more common with futures day traders or very short-term futures swing traders holding positions less than a week. Fixed contract traders may decide to trade one contract per every $20,000.00 or $40,000.00 in their account, and they determine the dollar-value threshold to allow them to purchase one contract. If their account size is $100,000.00 and they determine that they will trade one contract per every $20,000.00 in their account, then they can purchase five contracts per trade. A trader who decided to purchase one contract per every $50,000.00 in the account—a conservative strategy with futures—would be able to buy two contracts per $100,000.00 in the account.

As the account grows, the trader would thus be able to purchase more contracts per trade, and if the account declines, the trader would reduce position size accordingly. Futures contracts are highly leveraged vehicles, and if you use a smaller threshold such as $15,000.00 to trade one contract, that would result in a much more aggressive position-sizing strategy than a similar trader who decides on a more conservative strategy of trading one contract per $50,000.00 in account value (which might be too conservative a strategy). Again, you must balance risk with reward.

Fixed-Dollar Strategy The alternate strategy would be to allocate a fixed-dollar amount per each trade, which would result in a variable number of shares or contracts to purchase. Assuming a trader decides to purchase no more than $50,000.00 for each position, this would result in a share size purchase of 1,000 shares for a $50.00 stock, 2,000 shares for a $25.00 stock, and 5,000 shares for a $5.00 stock. Fixed-dollar strategies appeal to stock- and ETF-specific swing traders because they can equalize the dollars at risk in a number of open positions.

Traders refer to this type of fixed dollar amount strategy as a fixed unit size strategy, because they can visualize each trade as one unit of the account. If you put on five positions at a time, each position is equally divided from the amount in the trading account, regardless of the number of shares or contracts you purchase. It can be easier to track positions, particularly as a swing trader, because you can instantly know which positions are profitable, which are currently losing, and which are nearing the stop-loss threshold for a trade exit.

For example, if you trade in $50,000.00 fixed dollar account positions for each trade and determine that you will sell any individual position that declines 10 percent against your entry, you will thus exit trades that show a loss greater than $5,000.00. If you determine that you will sell all swing trades that exceed a 5 percent position loss, then you would sell positions that show a $2,500.00 loss. You may also use a total account equity stop-loss for each position, which might be a 2 percent risk rule. For example, in an account that is $100,000.00 and you have two open positions at $50,000.00 each, you would stop out of a trade that declines more than 2 percent of your account value, or $2,000.00.

Percent Risked or R-Value Strategy As your account grows over time, or if you begin with a large account, you will be able to employ more sophisticated position-sizing strategies. Some traders bypass fixed share size or fixed dollar amount (unit) strategies to adopt the popular Percent Risked models, which focus on the risk of each individual trade as the determining question to answer how many shares to purchase for the next trade. Because this strategy results in variable outcomes for each trade, it requires more math but often results in favorable outcomes and better performance over time when compared to the simpler fixed-dollar or fixed-share size strategies.

The Percent Risk strategy begins with asking how far away your stop-loss price is from your entry to determine how many shares or contracts to purchase. In this way, your position size is controlled by a factor of the quantified risk, in terms of distance from entry to stop-loss price, of your potential trade opportunity. For example, if you have an account size of $100,000.00 and determine that you will not risk more than 2 percent of your account on any one position, then you can afford to risk $2,000.00 on the next trade. Let us also assume that you wish to purchase a stock that trades at $30.00 per share and that you determine that there is chart support above $25.00 per share to play for an upper price target to $40.00 per share, so you wish to place your stop at $25.00, which is $5.00 away from your entry. Notice how you placed your stop according to the chart here. Now, we need to know how many shares it would take for that $5.00 stop-loss move to result in an account value loss of $2,000.00, which is your 2 percent rule. Dividing $2,000.00 by $5.00 per share results in 400 shares, thus, you will be able to purchase 400 shares of the stock because a $5.00 move against your position of 400 shares down to your stop-loss price will result in a $2,000.00 account-value loss, which is your predetermined threshold.

But wait, we're not finished yet. You then need to assess how this will affect your account. If you purchase 400 shares of a $30.00 stock, the total dollar value will be $12,000.00, or 12 percent of your entire account value. You will need to determine how much of your account capital, in terms of a percentage, to allocate to each position. If you choose to limit no position to larger than 33 percent of your account (allowing you to have three open positions at a time), then you would certainly be able to take this particular trade, which would use 12 percent of your total account value.

Let's see what the position size would be on the same position, but with a smaller stop-loss. Let us assume the same $100,000.00 account size and 2 percent threshold rule for an acceptable loss. This time, you determine that you wish to locate your stop at $27.50 per share instead of your original stop-loss price at $25.00 per share. Thus, your stop-loss stock risk is $2.50. How many shares can you purchase?

First, ask how many shares would it take at $2.50 per share to achieve a $2,000.00 account loss. Divide $2,000.00 by $2.50 to learn that you can purchase 800 shares this time. Now, let's see if the 800 share size position allows you to execute this trade, assuming you will not allow a single position to be larger than one-third of your account (33.3 percent). Multiply 800 shares that you plan to purchase by the current price per share at $30.00 to arrive at $24,000.00. The dollar amount of $24,000.00, which is 24 percent of your account is within your allowable 33 percent threshold, so you certainly can take this trade. Notice how the closer stop resulted in a larger position size in terms of both the number of shares you purchased and the dollar amount of the position, which is of course a different strategy than the prior fixed-share size or fixed-dollar amount strategies.

Let's look at this example one more time and assume that you determine that the stop-loss should only be $1.00 beneath your entry price at $30.00, resulting in a very low-risk position. How many shares can you purchase where a $1.00 move against your position results in a $2,000.00 equity account loss? That's right—2,000 shares. Now, we determine if a 2,000 share size position meets our rule that no trade can occupy larger than 33 percent of our account. We multiply 2,000 shares by the purchase price of $30.00 per share to arrive at $60,000.00 for the position, which is almost double our allowable dollar amount for this position. Unfortunately, we would have to reject this trade setup and move to a more appropriate opportunity, either with a lower-priced stock or one with a larger dollar-value-per-share risk. As you might guess, this model is not appropriate for conservative traders who wish to place their stops extremely close to their entry price.

This model tends to be more effective in terms of using the charts to determine logical places to locate stop-losses as opposed to exiting when price has moved a fixed dollar amount against you, which may actually be just above a key support point in the market at which the price finds support, turns higher, and rallies up to your target. If you chose to locate your stop based on the chart, you would have held on to this trade and achieved profit, as opposed to using a strategy with fixed dollar stop-loss prices that focuses more on your account value than the logic of the charts in terms of placing stops.

The advantage of the strategy allows for appropriate position sizing based on the unique risk in the trade setup you are about to take, but the disadvantage comes in the reality that you must reject certain trades that do not meet your dollar-per-position threshold. Unfortunately, the trades that you reject will most frequently be those with very tight stops, and if you decide to use a very large stop-loss, you may result in a position size that requires you to buy 100 shares or fewer, which would most often not make expected profit from the position worth the time in the trade.

Traders refer to this strategy as the R-Value position-sizing strategy (a term coined by Dr. Tharp), because you can then quantify each trade by its value at risk, which will always be 2 percent of your account, or whatever value you chose, be it 1 percent, 3 percent, or greater. Over a series of 10 trades, if you used the same tactic on each setup, all trades will thus risk 2 percent of your account. Van Tharp suggests labeling your risk by the letter R and then quantifying your profit in terms of R. If you risked 2 percent on a given position and then profited 10 percent on the trade, your 10 percent gain was five times larger than your 2 percent risk, and thus you have a winning trade with an R-Multiple of five.

In doing this, you can assess the long-term edge or expectancy of your trading performance in terms of profit multiples of risk or R-Multiples. You can also quantify your risk in fixed dollar terms instead of fixed percentage terms if you decide to adopt a fixed dollar amount stop-loss strategy. If you are interested in learning more about this type of position-sizing method, study Van Tharp's section on position sizing in his *Trade Your Way to Financial Freedom*.

THREE POPULAR POSITION-SIZING METHODS

Fixed-Share Size

Traders purchase the same number of shares or contracts in every position depending on the size of the account. For example, a trader might buy one futures contract or trade 1,000 shares for every $50,000.00 in the account. As the account grows, so does the position size. Fixed-size strategies work best for day traders who trade the same stock, ETF, or contract exclusively.

Fixed-Dollar Size

Also called Fixed-Unit Size, this strategy allocates the same fixed amount of capital—a unit—for every trade. A trader might allocate $30,000.00 for every position regardless of the price of the stock, ETF, or futures contract. This is best for swing traders who want to hold numerous open positions and diversify risk across multiple opportunities over time, while keeping positions equal in dollar terms.

Percent Risked

Traders determine their share size as a function of the risk in the position as determined by the distance from the trade entry to the stop-loss price. A trader allocates a different number of shares and dollar amount for each position depending on the fixed percentage, usually 1 percent to 4 percent, in relation to the overall affect on the entire portfolio. This strategy is appropriate for swing and day traders alike, but unfortunately causes them to reject good opportunities, usually the ones with tighter stops which result in a very large position size that is too large for a given account. While day traders may be able to allocate 50 percent or even 100 percent of the account for an individual trade, swing traders cannot.

Depending on your experience, risk-tolerance, and timeframe, certain strategies are more appropriate than others. Any strategy is better than randomly or emotionally sizing your position, which effectively is no position-sizing strategy at all. Professional traders often remark that long-term success in the market is a factor of the edge in your strategy and position-sizing tactic you use consistently, which is a balance of taking on too much risk or not enough in each position.

TRADE EXECUTION TACTICS

So far, we've discussed edge and how that applies to your trading. However, to maximize your edge in trading, or to have any chance of making money at all, you must put your analysis into action in the most efficient way possible, and that's where trade execution tactics come into the picture. You put your advantage, or edge, into action through recognizing opportunities, and then execute a position to participate in the expected price move and then exit the market either at your expected target or at your predetermined stop-loss price. Trade execution tactics help you maximize your entry into a position, and exit from an open position as efficiently as possible, while minimizing slippage and unforced errors as much as possible.

While specific patterns such as bull flags or head and shoulders offer specific places to enter a position, other setups do not. It's up to you to determine the price you enter, price you locate your stop, and price at which you exit your position either with a loss or a gain. In addition to answering the question of *where* to execute, you need to answer the question *how* to execute. This section will cut through the confusion and address the importance of trade execution tactics.

Common Types of Orders

The two most common order types you will use as a discretionary trader include market orders and limit orders. No matter what online trading platform you use to execute your trades, you can send your order to buy or sell shares as a market order or a limit order, usually with the click of a button. At the time of entry, you also should place a stop-loss order which will predetermine your risk in a position if the market does not behave the way you expect.

Stop-losses prevent normal, small losses from becoming abnormal, very large losses. Too many large losses not only erode your edge over time, but they can destroy a positive expectancy that you work so hard to achieve. To enter and exit trades, you will need to use the most appropriate type of order for the specific situation and volatility environment of the market at the time of your trade opportunity.

Market Orders A market order sends your order immediately to the electronic routing network to have your order filled as soon as possible, and as close as possible to the last price quoted. With a market order, your order is often filled within seconds of you clicking the buy or sell button from your platform. The benefit lies from the speed of execution, however this speed usually comes with an associated cost. The price you pay in achieving a fast execution result in a higher rate of slippage, which adds up over time. Market orders are filled at the best available price when the exchange receives the order, and if the market is illiquid or moving very quickly in a range expansion breakout intraday, you may find that your fill is at a much higher price than you expected.

For example, let's assume you want to enter a breakout trade from a particular stock that broke above resistance at $50.10 per share. You enter your number of shares and click on the market order option to send your order to the market as it begins to break above $50.10. Immediately, your system notifies you that your order has been filled for $50.20 per share. You check your screen to see that the price now trades at $50.18. While the price traded at $50.10 when you sent your order, you were actually filled 10 cents higher, which represents 10 cents per share of slippage. Remember the factors that affect slippage: they include the number of shares you are executing, the volatility of the market, the liquidity of the stock, and the time of day you are executing your trade. If you execute your trade with a market order to buy 5,000 shares of a low-priced stock in the first five minutes of the day in a stock that trades 100,000 shares per day, you can expect much larger slippage than if you entered a market order during the third hour of the trading day to buy 500 shares of a higher priced stock that trades 10,000,000 shares per day. Keep these factors in mind when you develop your trading plan. Slippage is the hidden cost of executing trades, and the more you can minimize its effects, the better you will be at the end of the year.

You may be thinking that market orders are the worst type of orders to use. While market orders do have their drawbacks, they do have significant benefits that you miss if you abandon these types of orders completely. Though you can expect to pay in terms of slippage to buy a stock intraday in a volatile range-breakout, you do get your trade filled if you execute into a rapidly rising market. If you are playing for a range breakout target of $1.00 or more intraday, a slippage cost of 5 cents is a negligible part of the total expected move. Because the market is moving so quickly toward the breakout target, you want to participate in this move, and if you attempt to minimize your slippage as much as possible, you will find you have missed the trade entirely. Thus, in order to save 5 cents of slippage on the trade, you let 95 cents pass you by; instead of losing money, you lost opportunity. Sometimes the hidden costs of trading, such as watching an opportunity pass you by, can be worse than the losing trades that actually cost money. While slippage certainly is bad, saving a few pennies per share is not worth missing entire price moves that you saw develop.

Limit Orders In contrast to market orders, limit orders allow you to specify a price at which you are willing to be filled but no higher (or lower if you are short-selling). Traders use limit orders to minimize slippage as much as possible, and once some traders begin using limit orders, they never use a market order again.

To execute a trade with a limit order, type in the price of the stock at which you wish to be filled and then send the order through your broker. The electronic exchange will fill your order as soon as possible at a price that is equal to or better than your limit price. You may wait seconds or even minutes for your order to be filled, and if the market is moving rapidly in a volatile environment, you may not be filled at all. In such cases, you can decide to cancel your open order and then resend a new order at a higher limit price in the hopes that it will be filled. Traders can repeat this process until they receive a confirmation that their order has been filled at the price they specified for entry. Sometimes this is at a price far beyond the initial order to enter, especially in the case of a range breakout.

Swing traders who study daily and weekly charts benefit from limit orders because they can perform their analysis overnight and then specify a price at which they wish to execute a trade. This is especially helpful if they have a full-time job or otherwise cannot monitor each price tick intraday. If the market trades to that price during the day, their order will be filled and they will be in a position that may last weeks or months depending on their time horizon. Day traders also benefit from limit orders because they can control the price of execution to minimize slippage as much as possible.

While it may seem that limit orders are superior to market orders, keep in mind the factors that affect slippage affect the ability for your order to be filled. Let us revisit our earlier example of a price breaking intraday above a known resistance level at $50.10 per share. Our first trader entered a market order and was filled immediately at $50.20. Our second trader did not want to pay more than $50.15 to enter the position, so he executed a position with a limit order to buy 1,000 shares at $50.15 or better. After a few minutes go by, he notices that not only has he not received notification of a trade fill, but the stock is now trading above $50.20 and rallying sharply to the upside as he expected. Within moments, the stock is now trading at $50.30. Immediately, he rushes to cancel his first order and place another limit order to buy 1,000 shares at $50.30 or better. However, he finds the same outcome, with no notification of a fill and the stock rallying even higher to trade above $50.40.

The trader is left now with two options: either pay the price and execute the same position with a market order as the stock rallies higher to the target of $51.00 per share intraday, or stand aside and miss this opportunity completely because the stock has now broken higher halfway to the target, and the reward-to-risk relationship severely deteriorated. Defeated, our trader decides to pass and watch the stock rally to $51.00 without him. In his attempt to save $50.00 to $100.00 of slippage (5 or 10 cents), he left up to $900.00 on the table in a missed opportunity. While losses show up in our trading accounts where we can see them clearly, missed opportunities like this do not.

Thus, all things being equal, traders do well to use limit orders to execute the majority of their trades with the exception of trading range breakout impulse moves to play breakout trading strategies. A trader should minimize slippage costs as much as possible, but not to the extent that clear opportunities for profit are missed because of an overzealousness to reduce slippage. Decide in advance and clarify in your trading plan the circumstances and specific trade setups where you will use limit orders or market orders for entry, and be sure to understand the tradeoffs of the decision.

Stop-Loss Orders While no trader enjoys taking a stop-loss, stops are necessary to protect capital and exit positions where the edge in a trade has deteriorated. Not only do stops preserve capital, but they allow you to preserve your expectancy in terms of your accuracy and monetary edge. If you let too many losing positions grow from small losses into large losses, you deteriorate your monetary edge in your expectancy calculation by increasing the size of your average losing trade.

You cannot let your emotions or psychological need to be right overrule the necessity to exit a trade that has fallen to trade at the stop-loss price you set when you entered the position. Exiting a position at a predetermined stop-loss price frees up your capital to be able to execute a new position with a more favorable opportunity in the near future.

You also must minimize slippage as much as possible when exiting a position with a loss. The same discussion applies for minimizing slippage with trade exits as it does with trade entries: market orders allow you to exit a position immediately though at a cost of higher slippage, while a limit order allows you to fix your price of execution but at the potential of the order not filling.

If you are a purely discretionary trader, the emotions you feel when exiting a losing position are different from those you feel either when entering a fresh new position or exiting a position with a win. Depending on your personality, you will either feel the need to widen your stop-loss price in order to give your position more room to breathe, and perhaps recover to a win, or will you will feel the need to exit your position as soon as possible, perhaps even before the market touches the price of your stop-loss order. Both scenarios have their advantages and disadvantages.

In general, if you give a trade a wider stop, it will have the potential to trade lower and then recover back to the profitable side, resulting in a win. However, if you tend to exit trades before the price reaches your predetermined stop, you may find that you exit positions early that fall pennies lower and then reverse back to the profit zone without you in the position. In such cases, your decision to end the trade early resulted in a loss, decreasing your accuracy rate, but had you obeyed your predetermined stop and not exited early, you would have experienced a winning trade.

The opposite is also true. If you find yourself unwilling to take losses appropriately and thus widen your stop-loss as the price approaches it, you will find that you will more frequently suffer larger losing trades than had you exited when the market touched your predetermined stop-loss price. How you solve this dilemma depends on your individual personality, strategy, and experience as a trader.

However you decide to take a stop, it is preferable to place your stops as market orders instead of limit orders with few exceptions. You should place stops just beyond confluence support or resistance prices where price touching your stop would result in a clearly failed trade and shift in the expected supply/demand relationship.

Let us assume that you are buying shares because you observe price to be in a rising uptrend and the most recent swing retraced back to the rising 20-day moving average, which happened to form a confluence with the 38.2 percent Fibonacci retracement that you drew from the recent swing higher. You bought because price formed a hammer candle in a sudden bounce higher from the 20-period average. In this example, you would want to place the stop a safe distance under the rising 20 period average, and perhaps even under the 50 percent Fibonacci retracement.

In the event that price broke under the rising 20-period moving average and then lower through the 50 percent Fibonacci retracement, then you would assume that price was forming a reversal swing lower instead of forming a retracement swing that would support off the 20 average and continue on to make a new swing high. You will allow the price to trade slightly under the 20-period average without exiting your trade, but you determine that if sellers push price under the 50 percent Fibonacci line, or especially under the 61.8 percent line, then the probabilities of a successful trade have greatly diminished. In this way, you place stops based on what you expect price to do, or not do, in terms of price principles, patterns, and setups.

In terms of executing your stop-losses, you would prefer market orders in most cases because if you just entered a losing trade, there is a good chance other traders have entered the same position you did and have located stop-loss orders near the same price levels you have. As a result, a positive feedback loop can develop when the market moves to hit this pocket of stop-loss orders. If you used a limit order to minimize your slippage, you might not get filled if price moves sharply against you, and might be forced to send two or three orders to exit your position, which would result in a worse situation than had you used a market order initially to exit. Instead of a trader missing a breakout opportunity by not getting filled due to using limit orders, you would be losing actual money continuously by not getting filled.

This is especially true if you are expecting price to remain within the confines of a trading range, and then the price unexpectedly breaks down through the trading range in a range expansion move at the same time you just entered a long position to play an expected bounce. You want to exit your position as soon as possible, accepting your slippage, and not accepting further larger losses in the event that price continues its breakout to the downside. Remember, the beginning of most breakout moves occurs when one side of the market is trapped and forced to cover their positions, which is combined with the other side entering new positions in expectation of a breakout to continue. You do not want to be caught in such an environment and unable to get filled on a stop-loss order.

Degrees of Risk

Deciding where to enter a trade will be determined by your experience, personality, and goals as a trader. Some traders are inherently risk-averse while others are inherently risk seeking. You will find that risk-seeking traders often exhibit risk-seeking behaviors in other facets of their lives, just as risk-averse traders will exhibit risk-averse behaviors in their lives. Trading ultimately is a private performance art that requires the balancing of many factors, with execution tactics being one of many variables to balance.

While most trading books or courses tell you to enter here and exit there, traders will be unable to execute those strategies over time if the strategies do not align with their personalities or experience levels. A trader with a conservative risk tolerance will be unable long term to execute aggressive-style trading strategies consistently, just as an aggressive trader will be unable to execute defensive, risk-averse trading strategies. The mismatch between trader personality and strategy results in frustration and unnecessary losses, and may be the reason for an early end to an otherwise promising trading career.

Conservative Traders Conservative traders tend to be risk averse and prefer strategies that are low impact that allow for more time to contemplate a trade, and execution tactics that allow for the processing of as much information as possible. These traders tend to prefer low-volatility stocks or environments, incorporate smaller stops and moderate targets into their strategies, and focus more on maximizing their accuracy edge—being right in a series of trades—than their monetary edge.

In his 1932 course *Technical Analysis and Stock Market Profits*, early technician Richard Schabacker described the benefits and caveats of being a conservative market speculator:

> *The conservative student will err on the side of his nature. He may, for that reason, be more successful in the long run. But... he must guard against over-conservatism, against over-caution, against too much doubt and timidity. The chief stumbling block for this type is hesitation. He reasons out a perfectly clear and correct case for a certain type of direct and definite action, then he weighs the opposite possibilities too carefully, and decides to wait.*
>
> *The market movement gets away from him. His judgment was correct, but the longer he procrastinates, the more hesitant he becomes, the more psychologically uncertain, and the less likely to profit from his correct analysis. The result of such procrastination... is the tendency finally to force himself to rush in [to a trade] without the usual careful analysis and sound sense, at a time when the movement... is just about over with or is about to reverse itself.*

Schabacker reminds us that conservative traders have their place in the market and may be more likely to experience long-term success, as their risk-averse nature allows them to remain capitalized to endure the early learning curve in their career. In addition, their tendency toward deeper analysis will better enable them to locate high probability/low-risk opportunities, provided they can act decisively once they have found these opportunities.

Conservative traders must adopt strategies that align with their personalities and conduct their evening analysis accordingly. These traders must not fall victim to the over-analysis trap, or paralysis by analysis. A conservative trader will assess the odds, wait for the moment when the price chart indicates a high probability setup, but then must act on that setup with minimal hesitation or doubt. This is a balancing act that will remain with the trader throughout the entire career: too much analysis leads to hesitation, but not enough analysis leads to impulsiveness.

In terms of execution tactics, conservative traders prefer to enter their trades after price rallies upward from a support zone, often breaking above the high of a reversal candle or short-term trendline in price. Instead of executing a trade as price tests a confluence support price exactly, a conservative trader demands to see some sort of rally upward, particularly in the form of a reversal candle, before committing capital to the position.

When compared to aggressive traders, conservative traders tend to take fewer trades and have a higher accuracy edge or win ratio than their more aggressive counterparts. This greater accuracy edge often comes at the expense of their monetary edge because they will be entering at a price further away from their stop-loss order, which is under the confluence support zone, and closer to their target, which slightly degrades edge by increasing the average losing trade and decreasing the size of the average winning trade. Aggressive traders need less price proof before entering a position, and thus have a superior monetary edge, but often at the expense of their accuracy edge.

Aggressive Traders In contrast to conservative traders, aggressive traders focus more on the components of edge than of accuracy, and need less information to execute a trade. Aggressive traders may spend less time on analysis and trade more frequently than conservative traders. In general, more professional traders tend to be aggressive than conservative, as the game of speculation tends to attract more risk-seeking personalities to the arena. All games of speculation, from poker to trading, involve risks of loss that not all people can tolerate psychologically. Risk-seeking personalities gravitate to risk-seeking professions and activities, and trading stocks is no exception.

While a conservative trader waits to see proof of a price inflection upward off of a confluence support zone, an aggressive trader would buy shares as close as possible to the confluence support price before a candle reversal signal forms. They may even start to establish a position prior to price trading exactly at the support zone, which may include a rising trendline, moving average, prior price support line, or Fibonacci retracement.

By entering as close as possible to the confluence support price, aggressive traders can place tighter stops in the event that price breaks downward through the expected support zone. This allows them to have a higher reward-to-risk ratio, or monetary edge, because their stop-loss prices will be closer to the price where they will exit a failed trade, which is often under a confluence support zone, or above a confluence resistance zone if short selling. By executing a trade before price begins to rally upward toward the higher price target, an aggressive trader also has more ground to cover as price moves to the target. Because of these two factors, aggressive traders tend to have smaller average losing trades and larger average winning trades than conservative traders.

But before you rush out to adopt aggressive trading strategies, understand that the higher monetary edge often comes at a price: because an aggressive trader takes positions in advance of price bouncing higher from a support zone, the trader will be

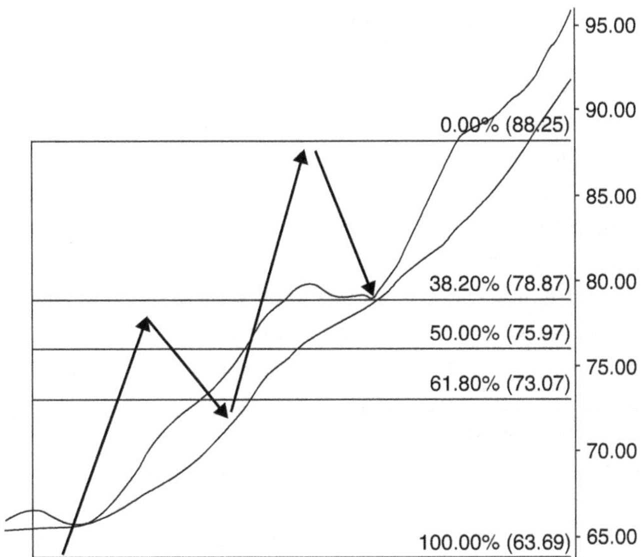

FIGURE 8.1 How Conservative and Aggressive Traders Approach a Retracement Trade into Confluence Support

forced to stop out of more positions than conservative counterparts who waited for confirmation, and thus will have a lower accuracy rate as a result. It is not uncommon for aggressive traders to report win rates close to 50 percent or lower, though they profit over time due to the frequency of their trades and the increased monetary edge.

Conservative versus Aggressive Tactics Let's visualize the example I have been describing when discussing conservative versus aggressive trade execution tactics. Figure 8.1 gives us an idealized example of how conservative and aggressive traders approach an identical setup.

In Figure 8.1, we see price as represented by arrows in a prevailing uptrend and rallying above the 20- and 50-period simple moving averages. This logic is the same for any time period you find a trade setup. An aggressive and conservative trader see the same setup and wish to buy shares in anticipation of a continuation of the uptrend and a rally off the confluence support at the $80.00-per-share level.

An aggressive trader would execute a position where the arrow ends, as price traded at the $78.87 level which reflects an exact confluence of three variables: the 20-period moving average, the 50-period moving average, and the 38.2 percent Fibonacci retracement as drawn. Our aggressive trader then decided to place a stop just under the 50 percent Fibonacci Retracement at $75.97 to allow the market to fall slightly and potentially support on the 50 percent retracement if by chance buyers do not support price at the $75.00-per-share level. Our aggressive trader targets a minimum of a continuation of the uptrend to target the prior high at the $88.00 level, but intends to hold on to exit above

$90.00 per share. To keep the analogy simple, we will assume that both our aggressive and conservative trader will exit if price rallies to $90.00 per share.

While a conservative trader sees the identical setup and believes the same logic that the $79.00 area is a triple-confluence support zone to move up off support in the context of an uptrend, the conservative trader wants to be sure that sellers do not push price through the support, which would result in a frustrating losing trade. Instead, the conservative trader will enter only if price breaks above a short-term rising trendline that began from the $88.00 level on the recent downswing to $80.00 per share. In addition, the conservative trader would feel more confident in the entry if price formed some sort of reversal candle, perhaps a bullish engulfing, doji, spinning top, or hammer candle for confirmation. The conservative tarder would certainly get long with a break above the high of the reversal candle and a break above the trendline.

Assume that the preferred reversal candle formed, and price broke the declining short-term trendline at $81.00 per share. Our conservative trader is now long at $81.00 and plays for an upside target of $90.00 per share, and has two decisions on whether to locate the stop-loss order in the event that price does begin to fall back under $80.00 per share. If very conservative, the trader will prefer the peace of mind that very tight stops can give, which means that very little will be lost in the trade. If this is the case, then the conservative trader will place the stop just under the moving average confluence and 38.2 percent retracement at the $78.87 level—perhaps at $78.80 (though you should rarely place stops at round numbers like that). Placing the stop here does not offer protection if the stock returns to test this level and then rallies higher—in that case, the trader will be stopped out with a loss and sidelined in the event that the market rallied as expected.

The trader knows that the stop should be placed under the 50 percent Fibonacci Retracement, but doing so would severely degrade the reward-to-risk ratio to the point where the trade would not meet the criterion that each trade must have a strict two-to-one reward-to-risk ratio. If the trade is entered at $81.00, a stop at $76.00 per share with a target of $90.00 per share results in a reward-to-risk ratio of $9.00 to $5.00. This makes the ratio one point eight to one, which is just shy of the two-to-one rule. The trader can still take the trade, but doing so would violate the trading plan. However, by choosing to use the tighter stop price at $78.00 per share, the trader then achieves a reward-to-risk ratio of $9.00 to $3.00, which is a three-to-one ratio. Our conservative trader decides to use a tighter stop.

Let us do the math for the aggressive trader. Our aggressive trader entered exactly on the test of support at $79.00 per share, and placed the stop a safe distance beneath the entry, under a level that price should not trade if this is a typical retracement swing. If sellers break under the 20 and 50 moving average as well as the 50 percent Fibonacci average, then odds are the price is experiencing a reversal down instead of an expected retracement. The trader would not want to hold long under $76.00 per share, so that is where the stop is logically and safely placed. Entering at $79.00 and placing a stop at $76.00 while still targeting $90.00 per share gives a reward-to-risk relationship of $11.00 to $3.00, which is a three-point-six-to-one reward-to-risk ratio, which is almost four to one on a simple retracement trade setup with a reasonable and logical stop.

By entering exactly at the price retracement to confluence support, our aggressive trader plays for a $90.00 target with a three-point-six-to-one monetary edge, but is not certain price will hold there. Just like in poker, each trade is like betting on a hand in which you perceive the odds to be in your favor, but you are uncertain of the outcome until all players reveal their cards. Finding high-probability setups as described above is similar to betting when the odds favor a positive outcome in poker, or passing on a trade or hand in poker (folding) when odds do not. Unlike in poker, you are not required to pay an ante each time you analyze your probabilities in a potential trade setup. You decide when the odds favor a successful outcome and you manage the trade either to the price target or fold with a stop-loss execution if the odds shift while you are engaged in a trade.

The descriptions of conservative and aggressive traders above assume the best qualities of these strategies and personalities. Schabacker hinted at the downside of conservative personalities as well as aggressive strategies. While conservative traders are more likely to analyze a setup more deeply before entering, preferring to wait for proof before committing capital to a trade, these same beneficial qualities can also be their downfall. If a trader demands absolute perfection in a setup before entering, that trader may never enter a position at all! There is no such thing as perfection in a setup.

Ideal versus Real World Setups Authors and educators select ideal examples or descriptions when they explain setups and strategies to you. That is not a criticism, but a reality of trader education—educators present the best setups as examples for you, but those setups rarely form with the same clarity while you assess the probabilities of a setup forming before your eyes in real time. As a result, traders who demand perfection defeat themselves when real-world events do not conform exactly to the expectations they learned from the textbooks.

On the other hand, conservative traders may seek out too much information and overlay too many indicators on their charts, and thus miss simple, high-probability setups because their conflicting indicators obscure the pure signals from price. What is a trader supposed to do when a stochastic says buy, reversal candle says sell, MACD says be flat, moving averages reveal an uptrend, and the low ADX reveals a trading range? This is part of the reason aggressive traders take more trades than conservative traders. However, there is a downside to over-aggression just as there is a downside to over-conservatism.

Aggressive traders often enjoy the thrill of trading and enjoy exhilarating events in their personal life. It is no surprise then that they are more prone to overtrading, trading without an edge, trading for no reason other than entertainment, and risking too much money in their positions. An aggressive trader who does not take the time to assess the probabilities may leap into a trade blindly as a market simply tests a standard trendline. There may not be enough chart evidence to expect the trendline to hold, and if it doesn't, the trader just suffered an unnecessary losing trade. The trader may also put on a larger position-size than is recommended for the trading account, and thus lose money very quickly in a string of bad trades.

All of your trades should have a reason for entry. Think back to the first three chapters of the book that explained three foundation price principles. Memorize these principles deeply and ask yourself on which price principle you base the current trade you take. Is the price retracing off support in the context of an uptrend? Are you buying the first pullback from a new momentum high? Where is price in terms of the alternation principle—range or expansion?

Breakout strategies gain their edge from the price alternation principles; retracement strategies base their edge in the trend continuity and momentum principles. Reversal trades utilize the divergences and overextended trends for their edge. Know why you are expecting one outcome over another, and build your confidence from these principles.

Aggressive traders should always pause to question the reason behind their next trade, while conservative traders should not pause too long to find reasons to put on their next trade. Most traders fall on a continuum between over-conservatism and over-aggression and can change tactics as they gain more experience in the markets. However, traders do best to unite their own unique personalities with the strategies and opportunities they select in their trading endeavors.

Now that we have covered foundation principles, explained how to recognize opportunities, and defined ways to maximize edge via efficient trade execution tactics, let's combine everything we've learned as we discuss basic types of trade setups, and then move into the culmination of our work by identifying specific setups we can take as price gives us the opportunities to do so.

CHAPTER 9

Four Basic Trade Setups

This chapter presents four basic trades setups that you can use as templates when creating your own trades. Allow your creativity to guide your analysis or depend more on the quantifiable mathematics of the trade: the possibilities are numerous. These specific setups work for any market, stock, or timeframe. Before we address the basic setups, we must start with a discussion on the four components present in any trade you will ever take.

COMMON COMPONENTS OF EVERY TRADE

Any trade you take has a broader context, and no trade exists in isolation. Though it may seem simple to non-traders, the act of entering and exiting a particular trade is actually much more difficult than clicking a mouse button two times. To a non-musician, playing the trumpet may seem easy, as the instrument only has three keys to press. There is a huge difference between blowing air into an instrument while pressing one of the three keys and a professional trumpet player who masterfully combines rhythm, tone, dynamics, and other elements of music as represented by pressing the three keys at the right time in the right combination to the right rhythm. Professional traders perform a similar incorporation of many factors at once to produce profits instead of music.

Entering and exiting trades is actually very simple, but doing it masterfully may take as long as it takes for a musician to progress from a beginner to a professional. Trading is a performance discipline not very different from the mastery of a musical instrument, sport, or vocation. Books such as Dr. Brett Steenbarger's *Enhancing Trader Performance* (John Wiley & Sons, 2006) and Daniel Coyle's *The Talent Code* (Bantam, 2009) are excellent resources for learning how to cultivate skills and talents. You must first recognize an opportunity that gives you an edge, or else the trade is not worth the risk.

Then you must put on the trade, manage it properly, and eventually exit your position, hopefully for a profit.

Before we discuss specific trade setups further, let us address the four common components of every trade: recognizing the opportunity, entering the trade, managing the trade, and exiting the trade. Each element has individual parts you can study and master to make yourself a better trader as you develop your expertise.

Opportunity Recognition

There are hundreds of books and thousands of seminars that tell you how to spot opportunities in the market, using new technology, indicators, and methods. Finding opportunities is actually not that difficult for most traders. Traders report that execution (entry) and then management is difficult, sometimes because they locate too many opportunities and are unsure exactly which one to take. Paralyzed by indecision, a trader might not put on a trade at all. Before you put on a trade, you must make sure you know why your trade has an edge and why the opportunity is a good one.

Experience helps, but this phase is where your education comes into the picture. Most traders must learn the basics of opportunity recognition before placing trades, and often they write detailed rules for what constitutes an opportunity and what does not. In your trading plan, you should include a section that includes what specific conditions must occur before you commit your capital to a trade opportunity. For example, if you trade a breakout strategy, label specifically what must occur on the chart first before you deem it worthy to execute a trade.

The opportunity recognition phase consists of research, daily charting, knowledge of trade setups, and price principles, along with an assessment of the pertinent chart features such as trend structure, volatility environment, key support or resistance levels to watch, any developing price patterns, or any number of factors appearing in technical analysis. Because traders will discover different opportunities in the same chart, it is important to have a set of rules that guide your behavior. After all, if you cannot recognize an opportunity on the chart, you should not execute a trade. Boredom is not a reason to put on a trade! It is also not a sufficient reason to enter a trade because of a suggestion from a person on television, Twitter, or the Internet. By doing your own research and finding specific opportunities, you will have the confidence to enter a position and then manage it with confidence to completion.

Trade Entry

After finding an opportunity, you face a go-or-no-go decision, wherein you enter as price reaches your expected price and meets your conditions for trade entry, or you do not. As discretionary traders, it is easy to let doubt destroy an edge and keep us sidelined when we observe that the odds favor putting on a trade as opposed to not doing so. But again, unless you work for a trading firm, no one can force you to enter or exit a trade, which gives you unique freedom that can be either a blessing or a curse.

Other traders, eager for the thrill of the action, leap into a trade before specific criteria are met, and thus jump the gun just to feel excited. There is a balance between waiting for confirmation, which can lead to missed opportunities, and jumping the gun, which can lead to a quick unprofitable stop-loss execution. In his *Trading in the Zone*, Mark Douglas expressed trade entry by describing that the market offers endless possibilities, but you must be the one to determine when the trade starts and when it ends. You choose when to participate by putting on a position, and then you later choose to exit either when price achieves your target, or when the pain of holding a losing position is too great for you to endure if you let the price run beyond your stop-loss order.

Once price meets your specific criteria for entry, you can enter using the specific trade execution tactics described in Chapter 8, which includes placing a market or limit order depending on the type of trade. In addition, you must decide whether to use aggressive tactics, which favor edge over accuracy, or conservative execution tactics which favor price making a confirmed move in your expected direction before executing a position. Conservative tactics often result in a higher probability of a successful trade outcome, but at the expense of edge as the stop will be further away from entry and price will be closer to your target when compared to the execution of an aggressive trader on the same setup. Again, the decision of conservative or aggressive entry tactic rests with you alone, and you should match the decision with your personality, be it one of risk-aversion or risk-seeking.

For most traders, it is preferable to place a stop-loss order as soon as possible after executing an entry into a trade. While some traders prefer to use mental stops, which have the advantage of your position surviving sudden price moves that dissipate as soon as they happen, most new traders do well to use hard (actual) stops because it not only creates discipline, but prevents them from playing the game of hope and hold when a position turns against them. A professional trader will exit immediately when price hits the predetermined stop, which was placed logically, while a new trader—convinced that the next trade will be a surefire winner—may be prone to letting price run beyond the predetermined stop-loss. The new trader justifies holding on to a losing position until he or she can no longer emotionally stand the pain of financial loss, and thus exits at a much larger loss than expected. Such unexpected large losses often result in feelings of personal failure, which increases doubt, fear, and hesitation. Trading is a game of probabilities rather than certainties, and stop-loss orders help keep the results within the parameters of predetermined risk-reward parameters and edge.

In addition to assessing where to locate our stop-loss price and also potential target, we then must assess how many shares or contracts to put on in the position. As described in Chapter 8, this decision may be fixed, as in purchasing 500 or 1,000 shares or one or two contracts on every position, or may be part of a more sophisticated formula such as using the risk in a trade to determine position size. For example, if I decide I can risk no more than $2,000.00 on my next trade and I determine that my stop-loss price in a swing trade from the daily chart is $2.00 lower than my entry, then I can purchase 1,000 shares of the stock to trade. If my stop was $1.00 lower than entry, I could purchase 2,000 shares, provided my account was large enough for me to do so. Your trading plan includes your decision for your position-sizing parameters on each position you take, and you must determine this formula or value in advance of executing your trade.

Trade Management

Most traders spend far more time planning their entry than they do planning their exit. Like Mark Douglas wrote, we determine when to enter our trades, and we do so out of a clear mind without the pressure or stress of having a position in the market. Having a trade on may cause us to fall victim to ownership bias, which states that we value something we own more than something we do not own. Also, we can analyze more clearly when we do not have a position on as opposed to when we do, because if we are long shares of a stock, we may miss or ignore bearish chart signals that hint that we should exit early. Studies show that when presented with conflicting chart information, traders who have a position on tend to value information that confirms their position and expected outcome (bullish information if long, for example) and discount or ignore information that contradicts their position (bearish information such as negative divergences or reversal candles).

The time between trade entry and trade exit is the trade management phase, which can make or break you as a trader. Just as you determine when exactly to enter a new position, you determine when to exit it, unless you are losing money in a leveraged position and your broker forces a margin call on you, demanding either you add additional funds to your account or liquidate your position. In this sense, only you can determine when to enter, but there are conditions, such as remaining stubbornly in a mounting losing trade, where outside forces can force you to exit your trade unwillingly.

Managing Open Positions The determining factor of your ultimate trade outcome is how you manage the open position. A trade reflects a temporary position when the odds favor one outcome occurring over another, which often derives from an opening in the structure of price that allows for a low-risk opportunity. Stated in simpler terms, a retracement trade in the context of an uptrend bets that price will stabilize at support then rise higher off of that support level. If price breaks under support, then the trader will need to close the position because the price did not achieve the desired outcome. With similar logic, traders expect a price breakout to continue once price breaks free from a lengthy trading range, but if the breakout does not materialize, then a trader will need to take a stop-loss execution in the event that price returns back inside the trading range.

You cannot control what happens to price between your trade entry and your trade exit; you can only monitor what happens and avoid the emotional biases that befall many traders. You control when you enter, how many shares or contracts to purchase, and when you exit. Everything else is out of your control and is determined by buying and selling pressure of market participants in an environment of probabilities, not certainties. That is why it is important to locate your stop-loss orders at an area that would disconfirm your market thesis, such as a break under confluence support in an uptrend, or a break to new highs after you shorted shares expecting the market to reverse lower.

After you put on a trade based on a high probability setup, one of two outcomes will occur: either the price will fulfill your expectation and touch your target, allowing for a profit, or price will move the opposite way than you expected and touch your stop-loss price, at which time you probably should exit your position to prevent a small loss from turning larger. While these are the two standard outcomes of trade management, these are not the only outcomes. A trader who went long could see price trade slightly below the entry but above the stop, which could scare the trader into exiting the entire position early. This is how emotions destroy a positive expectancy. Alternatively, a trader who purchased shares in a breakout move places a stop $2.00 lower and envisions a price move at least $10.00 higher in a trade, but decides to exit the position when a single shooting star candle appears when there is a $3.00 profit from the trade, which is $7.00 lower than the target. Again, fear of losing the open profit actually cost in the position because the market rose to and above the initial target.

While it's been said "You cannot go broke by taking a profit" and while that might be technically true, a trader who employs breakout or reversal strategies often needs to manage the position for very large targets in order to overcome the numerous smaller losses the strategy generates. Each trade we take costs us in slippage and commissions, so we need to overcome not just the losses from the losing trades, but the slippage and commissions from every single trade we take. If we leave too much money on the table, which is the term used for when a trader exits a trade too early, then we will not capture the monetary edge from our activities and will not make as much money as we anticipate.

Alternately, a trader may see price rally up to the initial target but then decide that the price will continue higher. The trader mismanages the trade and remains in the position after price hit the initial profit target. While this can work sometimes, other times it will lead to situations where price begins to fall from the target and the trader decides not to exit, thinking price will return to the initial high. However, if price never returns to that swing, then the paper profits will evaporate and then the trader holds on to the position until it devolves into a loss, despite the fact that the price hit the overhead target exactly as expected. Greed, in this case, prevented the trader from selling when the price structure suggested it, and thus the trader lost not only unrealized paper profits, but real money when the position was exited later than anticipated with a loss. The common theme is that the trader failed to manage the trade appropriately by basing entry or exit decisions on emotion, rather than objective evidence from the charts.

Traders should not exit a position early for emotional reasons, but rather maintain a concrete set of rules for when to exit a position early should the need arise. Specifically, conditions may change while the trader is in a trade, but before the price reaches the upside target. A common example is when a trader plays a retracement trade off support in the context of a rising uptrend and sets a stop under the support, as well as a price target above the most recent swing high in the uptrend. However, as price rallies upward off confluence support as expected, it finds unexpected resistance at the prior price swing high. At the same time, the chart may be showing a distinct negative momentum divergence at the retest of the prior price high, along with a reversal candle or a double-top price pattern formation. What is a trader to do? This is where management is key.

We do not know the exact outcome of any trade; all we can do is monitor the probabilities as they develop while we are in a position. In this case, the failure to break through overhead price resistance from the prior high, in conjunction with a negative momentum divergence and reversal candle, is most likely evidence that the price will reverse lower soon. Seeing that evidence objectively, a trader should take profits before price reaches the desired upside target because the evidence of further upside potential deteriorated due to the bearish chart evidence. A trader who firmly believes price will continue to the upside target beyond the prior price high may decide to sell half of the position and keep the reminder open in the event that price does overcome the divergence and resistance and continues to the target. Doing so could also be good management, because the trader was not blinded by greed or certainty that price was required to hit the target, such that the trader ignores chart evidence to the contrary. Selling half the position into a bearish chart development may also be considered good trade management. While price did not reach the official target, the trader was open to information that disconfirmed the bullish bias and exited when the chart evidence shifted against the position, saving what profits there were and exiting when the odds turned against the position.

Trade Management of Specific Types of Trades In terms of trade management, when trading fade trades, look for unexpected bearish weakness if playing long from a bounce off support to target the upper horizontal resistance line in the context of a sideways trading range. Unexpected weakness may indicate price may fall shy of the full upside target. For fade trades in particular, trade management is key because fade trades are counter-trend in the context of a prevailing trend, and subject to an eventual strong range breakout in the context of a sideways consolidation.

For retracements, look for price to find unexpected resistance, negative divergences, or reversal candles at prior highs in the context of a rising trend, or alternately, unexpected support, positive divergences, or bullish reversal candles in the context of a short-sell in the context of a prevailing downtrend.

If you are playing for a very large target in the context of either a trend reversal or breakout trade, you may choose to trail a stop in your position either beyond the 50 period or other intermediate term moving average or beyond recent swing highs in the context of a down move or beneath recently formed swing lows in the context of an uptrend. Look for multi-swing divergences to signal a potential reversal of trend, and be willing to hold through the counter-trend swings or waves that form in the context of a new up or down trend, so that you can capture a larger profit over time rather than just swing to swing as in fade or retracement strategies.

If you are day trading, you have much less time to make decisions and must rely in part on reflex and a focus on the developing price structure, though swing traders on the daily chart have extra time to assess the current structure of open positions in the evening, to determine whether the technical structure requires adjusting your position mid-course.

Trade Exit

The final component to any trade is the exit, which results either in a profit or a loss to the trader. The trade exit is a factor of the initial opportunity, type of trade setup, and discretionary management while the trade remains open. The ideal exit results in a profit from the price moving in the expected direction, with the trader managing the position appropriately and exiting at the predetermined price target indicated by the original opportunity. Not all trades produce profits of course, and it is important to assess the reasons for a losing trade.

Trading is a numbers game of probabilities, risk management, and opportunity maximization; you control when you enter and exit a trade, but not what happens to price between that time. After taking a loss, it is important to distinguish between the reason for that outcome, namely to discern if the loss was due to random probability that is out of your control (meaning you did the right thing), or if your emotions or other discretionary errors resulted either in an unnecessary loss, or a larger than expected loss (meaning you did something incorrect that needs adjusting in the future).

If the loss resulted from poor trade management, such as holding on to a profitable trade so long after an exit signal developed that it turned into a loss, or exiting a trade the moment you saw a frightening single bar or candle against your position that did not touch your predetermined stop-loss price, then your emotions were a factor in the loss.

If you develop a consistent pattern of allowing emotions to dictate when you exit a trade, particularly when fear forces you to sell either ahead of the predetermined stop-loss price or expected price target, then you create unforced trading errors that erode both your accuracy and monetary edge, and possibly end your trading career early.

In assessing your trading performance, note the specific reason for a trade exit. Clarify if a loss resulted from normal market action or from an emotional mistake on your part. Eliminate emotional mistakes, or unforced trading errors, as much as possible. If you fail to detect destructive patterns early, then they become destructive habits that will be much more difficult to break later. Answering this simple question after a trading loss helps you understand what went wrong and if there was anything you did to cause the loss; if so, you can strive not to repeat the same mistake.

On the same thought, if price behaved in the opposite direction than the chart indicated, then it was the result of random probability and a shift in the supply/demand relationship. In this event, you must not blame yourself for a loss that occurred as a result of an unexpected price move. Most likely, if you observed a very high probability trade setup, then other traders observed it as well and took a very similar trade that you did, and are stopping-out right there with you. Other traders may decide to fight the unexpected price action, which could result in a very large loss if a positive feedback loop develops quickly. In fact, there are some advanced trading techniques and setups that take advantage of this exact situation where very obvious trade setups fail.

Never seek 100 percent trading accuracy as your goal—it is unachievable. Traders who use fade strategies or retracement strategies can expect to have an accuracy rate greater than 50 percent, while traders who employ reversal or breakout strategies can expect to have an accuracy rate close to or less than 50 percent. In real terms, a 50 percent accuracy rate means five trades out of every 10 are winners, or 50 trades out of every 100 are winners; by the same token, the remaining trades are losers, but if traders manage them correctly, the losers are smaller than the winning trades.

Conservative and Aggressive Exits For both profit targets and stop-loss orders, you must decide between conservative or aggressive tactics, as similar logic applies to entries as exits. Review Chapter 8 for a deeper discussion on these types of tactics for trade entries. A conservative trader might exit the whole position exactly at the expected price target, or might exit the whole position exactly at the predetermined stop-loss price. However, an aggressive trader might monitor price closer and determine that odds favor a move through the expected price target, perhaps if momentum and volume increase as price travels quickly toward a price target. If so, the aggressive trader might keep at least half the position open beyond the expected target, but only because the chart evidence suggested bullish strength. An aggressive trader might decide to sell half the position at the target and then hold on to see if price can continue to move through the expected target, and sell only on a confirmed sell-signal from a long trade, perhaps when a negative divergence develops, or price breaks a rising trendline or breaks under the low of a reversal candle. In this sense, aggressive traders will monitor conditions as they exist at the time of exit to determine whether or not new information suggests that holding on to the trade would be better than exiting the whole position.

In contrast, a conservative trader might sell the entire position as price touches the expected target and then move on to the next trade immediately, booking profits and feeling satisfied. In some cases, a conservative trader might decide to sell the whole position early when price approaches, but not officially touches, the expected target.

In the same thought process, a conservative trader might exit a full position in the event price touches the predetermined stop-loss price and then the trader will move on to the next position. An aggressive trader might decide to evaluate conditions as they exist closely at the time price touches the stop-loss price to see if price may be forming a stop-gun or rinse and wash situation wherein it would be best to hold the full or partial position to see if this situation resolves in a continuation in the original direction of the trade as expected. Markets are so sophisticated today that if a trade setup is too obvious, price can often try to throw-off the weak traders who have extremely tight stop-loss orders in what is called a stop-gun or rinse and wash situation.

For example, in a retracement setup, price may fall to an expected support zone, which triggers traders to buy and then place stops under the support zone. In the event the market continues falling through support, it may start taking out these stop-loss orders of those traders who use a very tight stop-loss price and then stabilize and rise in the original expected direction upward to the price target, leaving aggressive traders who had wider stop-loss orders, or held through this phase, in their original positions to profit from the move. In this sense, trades can be envisioned as holding on to a bucking bull, where only the strong survive and the weak ones get thrown off the bucking bull.

TABLE 9.1 Common Components of Any Trade

Component of any Trade	Sub-components
Opportunity Recognition	Price principles Trend structure Price pattern Volatility structure
Trade Entry	Specific price Conservative or aggressive Amount of confluence Initial stop-loss order Position size
Trade Management	Confirmation or non-confirmation New price data
Trade Exit	Specific price Conservative or aggressive Stop-loss order or target Hold beyond target

Conservative traders demand as much price information as possible before executing a trade, and then exit a trade as quickly as possible or on the first sign of trouble, both of which lessens their actual time in a trade. Aggressive traders might enter a trade earlier, perhaps as price touches support, and then hold on to that trade as long as possible, demanding that price reveal negative divergences or some sort of confirmed sell-signal develop before exiting. Aggressive traders thus hold through the random wiggles that occur as prices moves forward in time from price to price.

That's not to say you must employ conservative or aggressive tactics at both entries and exits; you might prefer to take a more conservative approach to your trade entries and a more aggressive approach to your trade exits, or vice versa. Again, the decision is completely up to you, but do monitor your choices to see what works best for your unique personality, risk-tolerance level, and experience.

Table 9.1 summarizes this entire discussion into a neat grid you can use as a quick reference for planning your trades.

Though not mentioned specifically in the components, asses the performance of your trades with regard to entry, management, and exit in your trade journal. Go beyond labeling the essentials such as stock symbol, number of shares purchased, entry price, initial stop price, exit price, and so on. Discretionary trading is a performance discipline where a great deal of individual success comes from personal performance, specifically in finding opportunities and managing them properly, balancing the pull of emotions with the objective evidence in the price chart. Make comments as needed in respect to how you entered, how well you managed, and why you exited, paying specific attention to any unforced mental errors you created which resulted in any unexpected losses.

Without further delay, let us put all this information into practice and examine just some of the basic trade setups you can employ right now on any timeframe in any market!

HOW TO CLASSIFY TRADE SETUPS

When you look at a chart for the first time, you may see endless possibilities and opportunities to make money; on the other hand, you may see the price chart as a series of random wiggles that mean nothing to you. Hopefully, after progressing through this book, you see more opportunity than randomness, but if not, you will develop your skills with time. Like any performance discipline, the more you practice, the better you will become at your skills.

The young piano student sits down at the keyboard for the first lesson and sees nothing but white and black keys. Over time, the student will not only learn the names of these keys, but how to form chords, melodies, and songs from them. The skills required and the study hours necessary to play piano do not materialize overnight; rather, students develop the skills over time through continuous practice and learning. It is no different in learning how to play the market effectively.

With practice, you will be able to see bull flags, head and shoulders patterns, divergences, bullish engulfing candles, range breakouts, new momentum lows, and many other chart components that you never knew existed. You will then progress from learning the names of these components to the next phase of incorporating them within the context of a broader trading strategy and day-to-day game plan. Like the piano student who first learns the names of the keys, terms used in rhythm, dynamics (when to play softly or when to play loudly), and all sorts of musical notation required to be able to convert knowledge into the skill of playing sheet music, you will begin learning trading terms and then progress to finding opportunities for key turning points in the price structure as you learn to read the rhythm of price swings.

Trade setups guide your analysis into concrete opportunities of favorable outcomes for a price move in one direction instead of the other. The logic of trade setups is to find a point where price has hit a wall and cannot stand against the wall forever. The price either must inflect and bounce back from that wall, or break through the wall as price travels through the destroyed wall. Such is the logic of retracement and breakout trades: either price will find support and rally higher in an uptrend, or it will break through support and fall to a lower level. When price is in an established trading range, either price will hold at the prior upper horizontal resistance line and travel lower, or it will break upward through the resistance line in a breakout mode of positive feedback. Your trade is a calculated bet that price will do one thing and not the other; either that price will support at an expected price level and then rally higher as you expect, or it will break through the support line and stop you out with a smaller loss than the profit you would have achieved had price rallied upward off support as you assessed.

With that logic in mind, there are two distinct camps of trading opportunities: Mean reversion strategies and mean departure strategies. Within those, there are four specific types of trade setups from which to build more complex strategies, though you need not stray beyond the basic concepts of these setups. As we will soon see, the four basic trade setups include breakouts, retracements, reversals, and fades.

MEAN REVERSION STRATEGIES

If we think of price behavior as a distribution, price is either moving toward or away from the average price over time, also called the mean. You may view the mean as any of the moving averages we have discussed, as price is either moving toward or away from its respective short and intermediate term moving averages. Thus, if price moved a reasonable distance away from its short-term average to the upside, then odds favor a downward move in price to return back to the mean or average price. Once price has moved back to the average price, odds then may favor a rally within the context of a continuing uptrend to take price higher from the average price in a range expansion move.

The first two setups we will discuss build on the concept that price, once stretched away from its average, will return to the average as the next likely immediate move in price structure. The easiest way to describe this class of setups is to use the term Fade Trades, where our trade opportunity is to take the opposite action of what has just happened in price. We thus fade rallies in price away from the mean by short-selling them, and then fade declines in price away from the mean by buying oversold conditions in expectation that price will rally back to the mean. Such fade trading strategies tend to work best within the context of a range consolidation, negative feedback move during the accumulation phase when price establishes clear trading range boundaries. As you might suspect, mean reversion strategies perform the worst during periods of a market in a range breakout mode (positive feedback loop) after price has broken out of a known trading range.

Fade Trades

Fade Trades are often simple setups that capitalize on overbought and oversold conditions in price within an established trading range. The goal of a fade trade is to find the point at which price is stretched too far above or beneath the average price and must snap back like a rubber band. Alternately, we expect a past resistance or support level to hold price again as it tests this level and rises up off of it.

It is important to underscore the two separate types of fade trade logic: first, within the context of a stable rising uptrend, we want to find areas where price has rallied up too far above the mean and is likely to fall back down toward the rising moving average rather than continue to rally in a further overbought condition. Second, fade trades take advantage of clear support and resistance levels during a range contraction phase in price, as we short sell a move that rallies up to the upper resistance line and then buy moves that decline to test the lower support line. Figure 9.1 illustrates these two concepts.

The left side of the figure shows price in the context of a stable uptrend or downtrend, where the setup is to fade the rally in an uptrend or buy the downswing in a downtrend. In the context of a trend, the short-term moving average, usually the 20-period

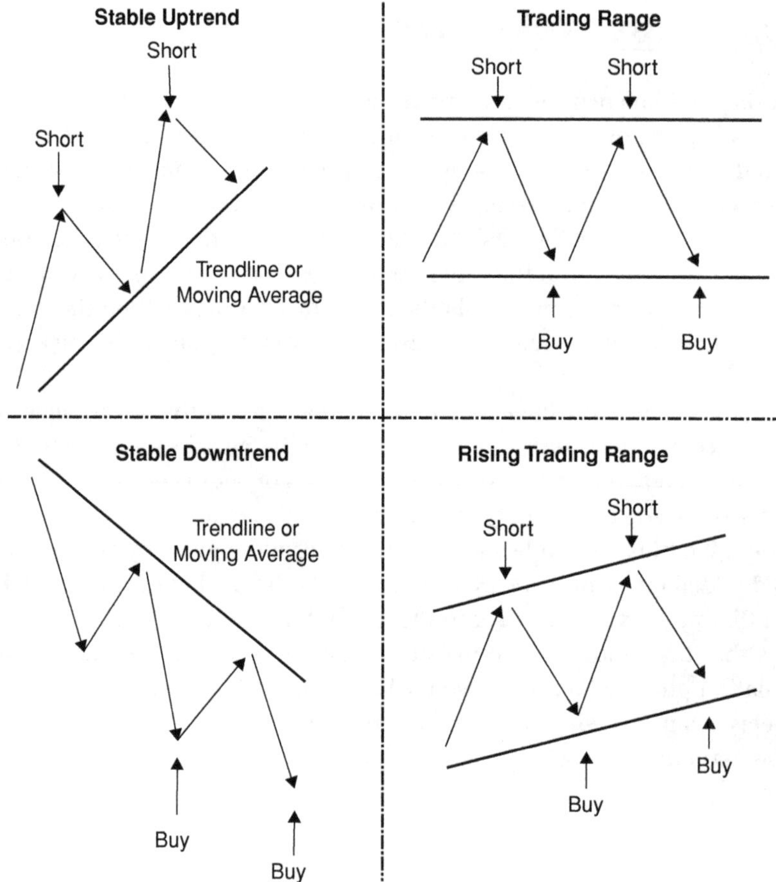

FIGURE 9.1 Fade Trades in the Context of a Trend or Trading Range

exponential average, represents the visual average price to serve as a reference. In addition to stable moving averages, traders can use rising or falling hand-drawn trendlines to substitute for the average or mean price from which to define price as stretched from the mean.

These fade trades within the context of an established trend are more risky than their fade trade counterparts when price is within the context of an established trading range, because shorting price in the context of an uptrend or buying price in the context of a downtrend fights the established trend in place by the very nature of the setup. While it is certainly possible to profit from mean reversion retracements within the context of a trend, this strategy is recommended only for advanced or experienced traders, as new traders should never fade or trade against an established trend.

In terms of probability, once a trend is established in the market, odds favor that the trend will continue rather than reverse. Also, within the context of an uptrend, price rallies in the direction of the primary trend will by definition be larger and last longer than retracements against the prevailing trend, which makes your profit potential and time in the trade much smaller. As a result, you must be extremely precise with these types of opportunities, and more times than not, you will find it best to pass on these opportunities and wait for the market to return to the average or trendline so you can establish a retracement trade with higher probabilities of success.

While fading established trends is not a recommended strategy, fading price moves within the context of an established trading range is a good strategy for active traders who are aware of the risks in such opportunities. In Chapter 3 we discussed the Price Alternation Principle and how it determines the structure not just of the recent action, but the expectations of the future move in price. While price is in the context of a trading range consolidation environment, we look to hand-drawn trendlines to define the upper resistance line and the lower support line for reference.

Quite simply, a trader looks to buy shares as price returns to test the lower support line and places a stop just beneath that support line and plays for an upper price target at the higher resistance price. If price rallies to the upper resistance price, the trader will then take profits on the long position and then might decide to sell shares short in an expectation that price will return to test the lower support line again and the range will continue. If so, then the trader profits from the setup and the established trading range.

The risk in the setup stems from the second half of the Price Alternation Principle, which states that price alternates between periods of range expansion and range contraction. Eventually, price will break out of the boundaries, either with an upside break or a downside break. In the event that the trader established a short-sale position at the upper resistance line and price gaps higher above the line and begins to rally, the trader must close the position quickly or suffer potentially devastating losses by being caught short in a rapidly expanding breakout move where other traders are purchasing shares in expectation of further highs in a breakout mode. Alternately, a trader who purchased shares as price tested the lower support line only to see price break sharply under the support zone will be caught in a position that loses money rapidly as price breaks in a range expansion mode to the downside.

You can see the logic behind these trading range fades on the two right-hand images of Figure 9.1. A trading range environment need not always be horizontal; instead, a trading range may take the form of a gently sloping range higher or lower. If so, then you will need to reference the angled trendlines as both the expected entries and targets in the price structure.

Bollinger Bands and Fade Trades To increase the odds of a successful fade trade, look for price to be at the upper or lower Bollinger Band. The lines of the Bollinger Bands represent two standard deviations from the mean or the 20-period moving average, which gives you an instant glimpse into where price rests in terms of its standard deviation. Many trading strategies take advantage of short-selling price at the upper Bollinger Band or buying price at the lower Bollinger Band.

In addition to using Bollinger Bands for reference points of overbought or oversold levels, look for price to form a basic reversal candle at either the upper or lower

Bollinger Band or prior trendline. Specifically, look for engulfing candles, doji candles, spinning tops, bullish hammers, or bearish shooting stars. You will enhance the probabilities of a successful fade trade if you can first identify a reversal candle at the upper or lower Bollinger Band extremes before entering your position. You may also choose to wait until price breaks under the low of the reversal candle before putting on your position.

While you do have a reference price for an overhead resistance level in the context of a trading range, you do not have this reference in the context of a steady rising trend where price has rallied higher from the moving average or rising trendline. You will need to rely on Bollinger Bands and reversal candles to have the confidence that odds favor a move back down to return to the mean or moving average as opposed to continuing the rally higher in a perpetual range breakout that would stop you out if you tried to short the uptrend.

Divergences and Fade Trades Finally, look for any type of clear divergence on any fade trade you consider entering. For example, if price rallies to a higher high but you find that the 3/10 MACD momentum oscillator, Rate of Change, volume, breadth, or other momentum oscillator formed a lower high than the indicator achieved on the prior rally, then you increase the odds of a successful fade trade. Refer to the discussion on momentum divergences from Chapter 2 for more details.

In summary, be sure to distinguish first whether a trend exists or not. The odds of a successful fade trade increase when fading a move within the context of a range contraction environment with clear boundaries than when fading a rally in the context of a price uptrend. In either case, you can increase your odds of a successful trade outcome by demanding that price be at the upper or lower Bollinger Band before entering, demanding that a reversal candle form at or near the Bollinger Band extreme, or observing some sort of divergence as price extends beyond the mean.

While the best scenario would be a price move up into a known resistance area that happens to coincide with price forming a reversal candle at the upper Bollinger Band as a negative momentum divergence forms, you cannot demand absolute perfection in fade trade setups. The more chart evidence you can put in your favor, the better the odds of a successful outcome will be. Despite overwhelming evidence you still need to place your stop appropriately and honor your pre-established stop-loss price in the event that the market continues its rally in the context of an established uptrend despite divergences, or breaks out suddenly from an established trading range and moves into a range expansion mode that leaves you with sudden losses.

Mean Reversion in Johnson and Johnson Figure 9.2 shows us JNJ's 30-minute chart in the context of a prevailing downtrend on the timeframe, as evidenced by the series of lower lows and lower highs, as well as the negative moving average orientation (the 20 EMA is steadily under the 50 EMA). We also see the default Bollinger Bands indicator and the 3/10 MACD Momentum Oscillator.

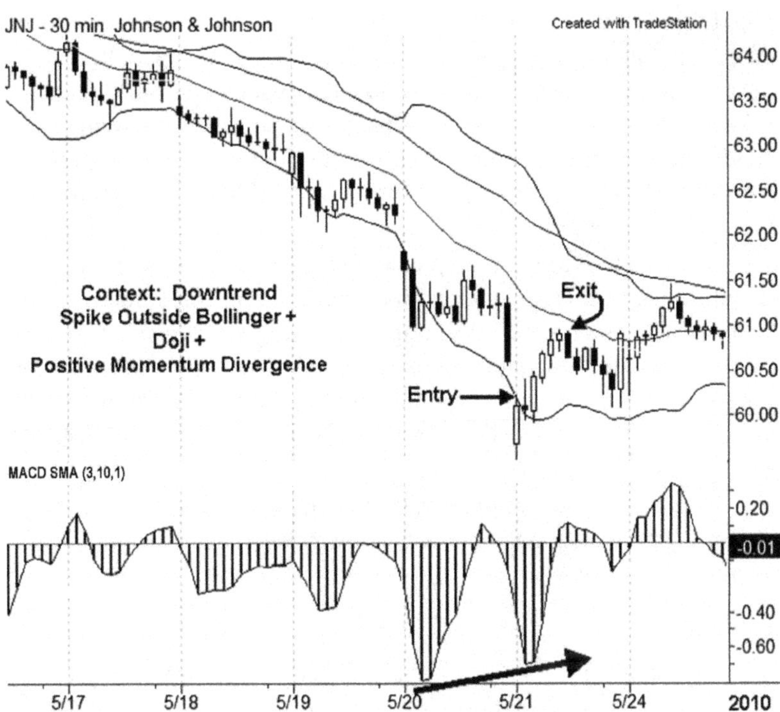

FIGURE 9.2 A Quick Fade Trade Opportunity in Johnson and Johnson on the 30-minute Chart in late May 2010

The fade trade comes from an extension $1.50 downward from the 20 period moving average at the $61.00-per-share level on the gap down on May 21, 2010, to the $59.50 area. Price formed a bullish bar on the first 30 minutes then formed a doji candle that closed just above $60.00 per share by the first hour. An aggressive trader would enter once the doji formed and price rallied above the close of the doji at $60.10. The trader would place the stop either just under $60.00 per share, or under the opening low of $59.50 and play for an upper price target back to the $61.00 level which was the declining short-term 20-period exponential average on the session.

A conservative trader might have demanded that price break above the high of the doji at the $60.50 area before entering, which would increase the odds of a successful trade, but decrease the distance to the target at $61.00 and increase the logical price at which to locate a stop, under $60.00. Thus, a conservative trader would risk 50 cents to profit 50 cents, which does not enhance the monetary or reward-to-risk edge, while an aggressive trader would enter near $60.00, place a stop 10 to 20 cents under $60.00 per share, and play for an upper target of $61.00 per share, giving both an accuracy edge (odds favor but do not guarantee a mean reversion swing in price back to the 20 EMA at $61.00 because of the positive divergence, doji reversal candle, and lower Bollinger Band indicator) and the monetary edge (the trader risks 10 to 20 cents to play for an upside target 90 to 80 cents higher).

Price rallied upward in a mean reversion play with four successive up bars in the morning of May 21 to fall just shy of the overhead target at $61.00 per share. Price formed a spinning top and then a bearish engulfing candle to trigger an earlier than expected exit. Keep in mind that a fade trade targets a return to the short-term moving average only, and not beyond. The opportunity plays upon the action/reaction cycle in the context of a prevailing trend, where the 20 period EMA becomes a reference point for traders to establish new short-sale positions in the context of the prevailing downtrend.

Such strategies give rise to mean expansion strategies such as retracements, which aim to short sell rallies into EMA or trendline resistance in the context of downtrends or buy downward retracements into the support of rising moving averages or trendlines in the context of prevailing uptrends. As you can see from this example, retracement trading strategies in the context of a trending environment are not only simpler strategies than fade strategies, which require absolute precision in entry and exit, retracement strategies are often more profitable as well.

Before we discuss the more popular retracement strategies, let us now discuss the reversal trade setup, which also falls under the mean reversion heading.

Reversal Trades

As you progress through different stages as a trader, you will likely gravitate toward certain strategies over others. Reversal strategies often appeal to new traders who want to be heroes by buying at the exact bottom and then selling at the exact top, but it only takes a series of failed reversal trades to teach these new traders that alternate, more profitable strategies exist with less risk and better outcomes. Like a child who burns a hand on the stove and learns never to touch a hot stove again, many new traders attempt reversal strategies with high hopes of quick riches, only to find the outcome to be a much larger-than-expected loss, or a series of frustrating small losses as the trader incorrectly shorts a rising trend or buys consistently into a perpetually falling trend.

Reversal trading strategies can be described as catching a falling knife, or at least attempting to do so. If you visualize that statement, you will see that there is certainly more risk in trying to catch a falling knife than in stepping out of its way. After all, why not wait until the knife has hit the floor and then bounced off the floor before picking it up? As you progress as a trader, you will likely want to avoid these high-risk, high-reward strategies that appeal to the risk-seeking traders in the market. However, it is important to understand these strategies and when playing for a reversal in a trend is appropriate, and when it is not.

Let us return to the same 30-min intraday chart of Johnson and Johnson in Figure 9.2 and expand the chart to see the larger picture of the prevailing intraday downtrend. Let us also assume that we want to employ a basic reversal strategy of trying to call a bottom in the stock by buying new lows that touch the lower Bollinger Band.

Keep in mind that reversal strategies differ from fade strategies, in that reversal strategies seek to play not just a return to the mean, but a pure reversal in the prevailing trend and thus achieve a larger target. While buying the absolute low can be very

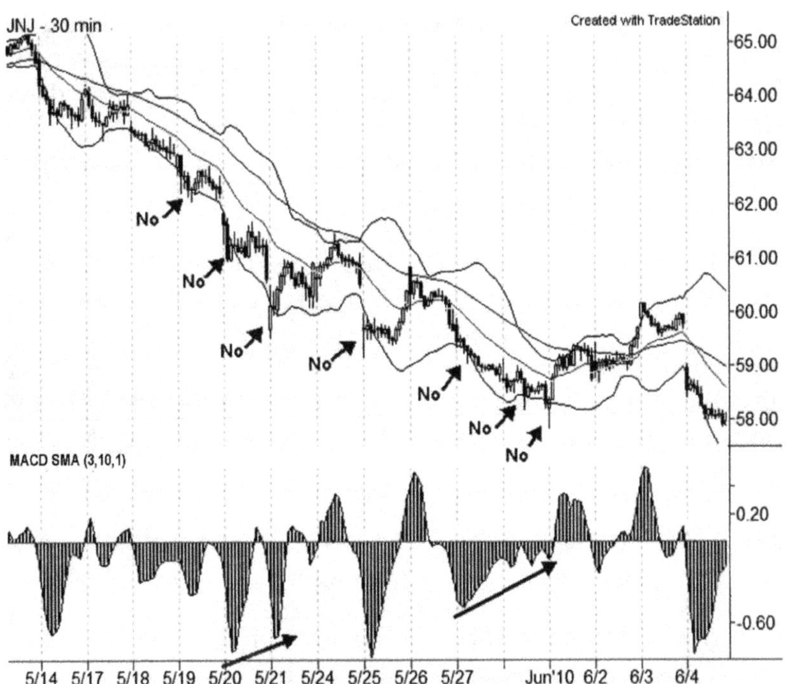

FIGURE 9.3 Failed Reversal Trades in Johnson and Johnson 30-minute Intraday Downtrend

lucrative to a trader, Figure 9.3 shows us why the strategy is not for new traders, as they attempt to buy new lows hoping for a reversal in trend.

In Figure 9.3, we see the larger picture of Johnson and Johnson's prevailing intraday downtrend in which we captured a very small profit earlier from a Fade Trade mean reversion setup on May 21, 2010. Assuming a trader bets on a reversal occurring each time price hits a new low and touches the lower Bollinger Band, we see the fruitless outcome of his trades in the chart.

Every single time price hit a new low, price rallied but then fell within days to a new price low, stopping out our eager trader with a new loss. Undeterred, the trader continued buying new price lows, but Johnson and Johnson never seemed to reverse. After a series of seven consecutive painful losses, our trader gave up the search for a bottom in JNJ, the account much smaller from the effort.

If you desire to trade reversal strategies, you need a lot of patience, a focus on the edge and probabilities (and not on your losses), fortitude, and sometimes luck. However, you can avoid a lot of frustration by trading alternate strategies such as breakout or retracement trades.

Reversal strategies build on the friction between the two major principles that trends established, have greater odds of reversing than of continuing, and the momentum principle in regard to lengthy momentum divergences that often precede trend reversals. We know that trends cannot persist forever, and they must reverse at some point just as price must eventually break out of an established trading range. However, entering at the exact low or high of a move requires a great deal of advanced charting skills, experience, and patience. Most professionals avoid trying to buy the exact high or low, and new traders benefit from avoiding this as well.

While you will certainly do best to avoid attempts to find the absolute low or high of a move, you can do well to incorporate reversal strategies into your trading plan if you think of reversals in a slightly different light. Let us return to Martin Pring's definition of technical analysis as the art of identifying a trend reversal at the earliest stages and then riding that trend until the weight of the evidence proves it has reversed. This is the definition you should adopt when trading reversal strategies: employ the weight of the evidence criterion before trying to bet your capital on a trend reversal. This means that you will never (or at least very, very rarely) enter at the absolute high or low of the move, sacrificing instead to play a reversal strategy once certain pre-determined chart conditions occur.

The Sequence of Events that Precedes Trend Reversals Watch first for a multi-swing divergence to form. Multi-swing divergences, as opposed to single-swing divergences, increase the odds of a trend reversal. Trends often slow down before they fully reverse, just as a freight train must slow down and stop before reversing course. Also, look for lengthy divergences to form on multiple timeframes, from the weekly chart down to the intraday charts. Momentum is a leading indicator of price, and momentum divergences often signal trend reversals as likely outcomes. In the absence of lengthy divergences, odds tend to default to favor trend continuity.

Second, watch for structure to change in the short-term and intermediate-term moving averages. If you are watching a daily chart, watch for the 20-day EMA to cross under the 50-day EMA. That's certainly not enough evidence to expect a trend reversal, but all trend reversals will have this structure occur before reversing. Look also for price to cross under the 200-day simple moving average. Some investors will declare price to be in a downtrend once price crosses under this key average. The bearish cross under the 200-day average will occur after a sustained down-move in price, but it is part of the criterion for establishing the weight of the evidence.

Third, look for price to make lower lows, lower highs, and break key support areas on the charts of multiple timeframes. Recall our discussion in Chapter 1 on the Trend Continuity Principle that up-trends are a series of higher price swing highs and higher price swing lows, just as downtrends are a series of lower price swing lows and lower price swing highs. That is the purest definition of a price trend possible. When price begins to break these progressions of higher highs and higher lows, look for a potential reversal in trend as a likely outcome. You can never declare an uptrend reversed from an objective price standpoint unless price has formed a lower low, lower high, then swung down to take out the support of the prior low. Alternately, price can first form a lower high then swing down to take out the support from a prior price low. Either way, price must reverse course and progress through this series of observable lower lows and lower highs to change course. Many traders use this definition as a trend reversal, and will wait to establish a new position in the direction of the potential newly forming trend only after this sequence has formed; you will do well to adopt this strategy.

Finally, in addition to monitoring momentum divergences, moving average structure, and price highs/lows, you can look for a Kickoff in the momentum oscillator, volume, or breadth to increase the odds further of a trend reversal. Kickoffs occur when a momentum oscillator, breadth, or volume forms a clear higher high on a price swing up after price has been in a sustained downtrend, but price is a far distance away from forming a higher high. You can often see this Kickoff occur at the same time price crosses above the 20- or 50-period EMA or breaks above a key long-term trendline.

Envision the Kickoff as the initial sign of strength (momentum burst) that sends the price surging higher in a new uptrend, or falling lower in a new downtrend. In physics terms, think of the Kickoff as the force that overcomes the inertia of an object either at rest (trading range) or in motion (established trend). When you throw a ball into the air, the ball has the most acceleration the moment it leaves your hand. Acceleration declines as the ball continues to rise, but eventually the ball will stop rising (negative divergences) and then fall back to earth. Think of this as the life cycle of a stock (Chapter 7) that begins with a sharp supply/demand imbalance that awakens price from a lengthy Accumulation phase into the Realization phase.

These four components put the odds strongly in your favor when you place a trade that assumes that price has reversed from one trend to the next. In this way, you wait until the weight of the evidence suggests strongly that the trend is reversed. Such signals can only occur after price has moved upward from the absolute low, or downward from the absolute high. What you surrender in potential profit is the much higher probability of a successful reversal trade setup as opposed to a trader who shorts all new highs or buys all new lows expecting a reversal. Just remember that it is better to pick up a fallen knife off the floor than it is to try and catch a falling one.

Trend Reversal Example in the U.S. Dollar Figure 9.4 shows these steps taking place on a daily chart of the Bullish U.S. Dollar Index ETF (UUP).

Where do you officially call the persistent downtrend in the Bullish U.S. Dollar Index ETF fund reversed from bull to bear? Can you identify the exact price at which the fund reverses its trend? If you can, then that is your buy point for a trend reversal trade and no sooner. Hint, the price is not the November 2009 of $22.00 per share.

Let's start with the left side of the chart and work our way forward, keeping in mind the four steps I described earlier. We see price in a persistent downtrend since the chart began in early 2009 with the PowerShares U.S. Dollar Index ETF at the $26.00-per-share level. Price continued its series of lower lows and lower highs, along with a bearish EMA orientation (the 20-day EMA remained under the 50 EMA) until the positive crossover just before 2010 began.

As we will see when we discuss retracement trades, the best strategy was to short all pullbacks to the 20 or 50 EMA within the context of this persistent downtrend. There were a limited number of fade trades when price became overextended to the downside

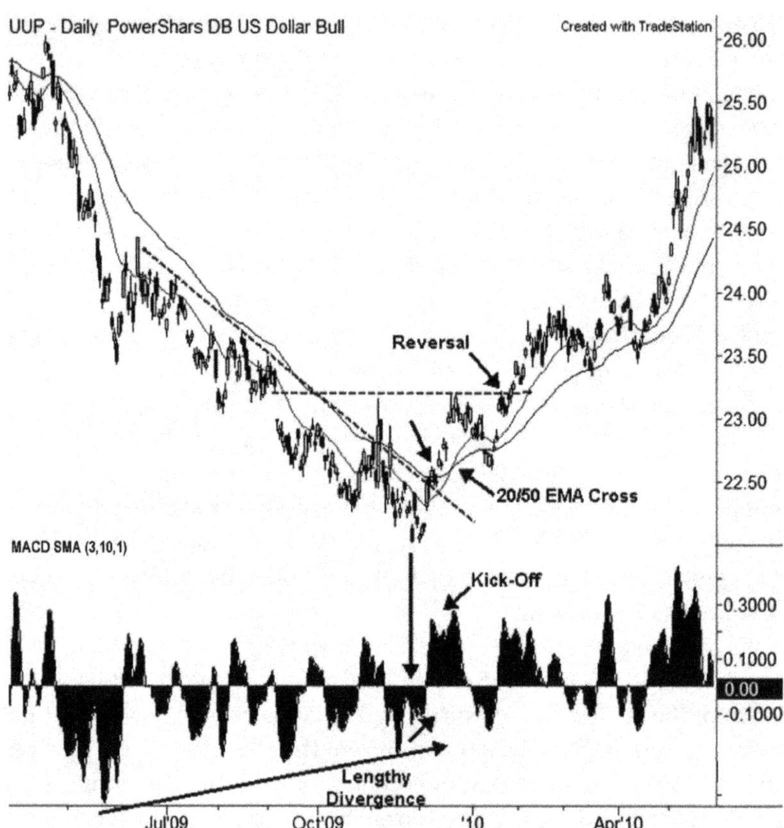

FIGURE 9.4 Trend Reversal Progression in Bullish U.S. Dollar ETF Daily Chart in late 2009

from the falling 20 EMA, but those opportunities required precise entries and exits, and went against the prevailing downtrend.

Let's assume you are a risky trader who loves reversal strategies. Notice that a lengthy positive momentum divergence formed in the 3/10 MACD Oscillator, starting with the move off the oscillator low in May 2009. Divergences do not require a trend to reverse, nor do they tell you when to enter a reversal trade; rather, they only tell you that odds are decreasing for a continuation of the downtrend and are increasing for an eventual reversal. We need additional chart evidence to inform us when it is safe to make a reversal play, and until then, it is unsafe to do so.

Nothing changed in the structure of lower lows, lower highs, and the bearish EMA structure until a sudden pop took price above the 20 EMA, 50 EMA, and declining trendline on the swing up in November 2009. That pop-up in price undoubtedly lured some aggressive buyers off the sidelines to bet on a trend reversal in the Dollar Index, which failed next month when price made a new low and these eager traders took their stop-loss executions accordingly, with a stern reminder of the danger and risk of trading reversals, even if price breaks above a trendline on positive divergences.

Look closely at the massive multi-month divergence that culminated with the absolute price low of $22.00 per share in November 2009. Again, divergences do not guarantee reversals, nor do they signal when it is safe to enter, but generally, the larger the divergence, the larger the eventual reversal you can expect when price does reverse.

In December 2009, price gapped higher, breaking again through the declining trendline as well as the 20- and 50-day EMAs at the $22.50-per-share level. Look very closely at the 3/10 MACD Momentum Oscillator in December 2009. The oscillator forms a new indicator high of 0.30 which is a high not seen since April 2009, at the same time the ETF traded at the $25.50 level. This is a powerful technical signal that most traders miss or don't know how to identify. It is called a Kickoff and is the first true sign of momentum or strength that signals the odds shifting strongly to favor a reversal in trend as opposed to a continuation of the trend.

In terms of identifying trend reversals in price on any timeframe, use the 3/10 MACD or other momentum oscillator to find lengthy divergences and then to locate a Kickoff signal in the oscillator when price begins to rally off the lengthy divergence. A higher high in the oscillator when price is not forming a higher high is most likely a Kickoff signal of a momentum burst, and potential new birth of an uptrend.

Like divergences, Kickoff signals do not tell you when it is safe to enter, only that conditions now strongly favor a reversal in trend. Aggressive traders will buy the immediate pullback in price after a Kickoff signal occurs and place a stop under the most recent price low in anticipation of a true trend reversal. This is generally the safest spot in the price structure to position yourself for a trend reversal.

The alternate safe spot to position for a reversal, which appeals to conservative traders, is to wait for price to complete the official reversal by forming a series of higher highs and lows, and taking out a key resistance level. The break above the most recent initial higher high in price is true reversal where it is safest to establish a long-term position or swing reversal trade. This is the type of signal you must identify when trading reversals: stay on the sideline until the weight of the evidence, in terms of price structure, moving average orientation, momentum divergences, and momentum Kickoffs, favor that the trend has reversed and signaled you a safe entry into the newly developed trend.

I labeled this spot on the chart in January 2010 when price breaks above the horizontal resistance line at $23.20 per share. This is not only the safest spot on the chart to position yourself for a reversal trade, but it is the location that officially confirms that the trend has reversed using the weight of the evidence model. Once a trend has reversed, the new trend stays in effect until we have a similar multi-step trend reversal, or price falls sharply to resume the larger downtrend, which is a lower probability, but certainly possible outcome.

In trading, we cannot know the future with certainty, but can only assess the probabilities as they exist at the time we analyze the price structure and trade opportunities in that structure. Ensuring that price meets these criterion before entering a reversal trade will enhance the odds in your favor that over time, you will trade more successful reversals than other traders who merely find a bottom and buy. Hopefully, you're no longer one of those traders!

MEAN DEPARTURE STRATEGIES

If fade and reversal trades depend on price returning to the mean, specifically a swing higher in an uptrend returning back to the rising moving average, or a long-term uptrend trend reversing and falling lower to a lower average price, then mean departure strategies depend on price trading at or near the average price and then moving away from that average price. Instead of expecting price to return to the mean, we expect it to depart from it as the next likely swing in price.

Our final two types of trade setups build upon this concept of mean departure, and best fit within the context of a market in range expansion mode breaking out of an established trading range, or rising in the context of a prevailing uptrend. Specifically, we can label these types of trades classic breakout trades, with which you are no doubt familiar now, and retracement trades. Let's examine them both.

Breakout Trades

By now, we have discussed breakout trades in detail, especially during the Price Alternation Principle in Chapter 3. Breakout trades take advantage of the Price Alternation Principle as the structure breaks free from an established trading range or negative feedback loop environment into a new range expansion phase of positive feedback.

A trader using range breakout trading strategies seeks to enter a position as close as possible to a confirmed breakout from an established trading range or price pattern such as a triangle or rectangle. Refer to Chapter 5 for the types of price patterns that allow for specific breakout trading strategies, namely the rectangle and three different triangle patterns. Shorting the breakdown from the neckline of a head and shoulders pattern is also a type of breakout trading strategy.

The risk that breakout traders face comes from the potential for bull and bear traps, which occur when price breaks out of an established boundary and then immediately returns inside the boundary, trapping the aggressive traders who established positions as soon as the break occurred. Thus, if you employ breakout strategies, you will need to determine whether to use an aggressive strategy that aims to establish a position as soon as a breakout occurs, or a more conservative strategy that demands that price hold the breakout for at least two bars, penetrate the boundary by at least 2 percent (or some other predetermined percentage), or be confirmed by some other concept in technical analysis such as a corresponding volume or momentum surge.

While no potential breakout setup is guaranteed to produce the desired positive feedback loop of range expansion expected, traders can assess the broader structure and look for confirmation from specific indicators. A corresponding increase in volume during a suspected breakout setup increases the odds of a successful trade outcome. If you see a volume spike on the breakout, you can enter a position with greater confidence than if you did not see a respective increase in volume. In fact, sudden price breaks from an established trading range that occur on average or less-than-average volume have a higher probability of being a false break, so be sure to monitor volume in relation to the recent past figures when deciding whether or not to trade a breakout setup.

In addition to volume, a trader would also want to see a corresponding spike in a momentum oscillator to confirm a potential breakout trade. Often, this momentum impulse will come in the form of a price gap or powerful impulse bar such as a marabozu or other large candle. Look for a sign of impulse in the form of immediate range expansion as price breaks free of an established trading range. On the other hand, if you see price break free from a trading range on an intraday penetration that forms a long upper shadow, this indicates a lack of impulse and may result in a trap.

Bollinger Band Squeeze Plays If you use Bollinger Bands on your charts, look for a noticeable compression or narrowing of the bands as price forms an extended consolidation. Then, wait for price to break and close at least one bar outside either the upper or lower Bollinger Band. If this setup occurs, you can interpret this not only as a sign of impulse, in that price closed two standard deviations away from the compressed mean, but you can take it as a trade entry signal. When using Bollinger Bands, traders refer to this specific setup as the Bollinger Band Squeeze when the bands have noticeably narrowed in range and then price breaks strongly outside of the compressed bands. Many trend-following strategies demand that price close outside Bollinger Bands, Keltner Channels, or Donchian Channels before establishing a trade that is designed to capture the expected range expansion phase in price that originates from a break beyond these indicator extremes.

Figure 9.5 shows two examples of simple price breakouts from compressed Bollinger Bands, known as the Bollinger Band Squeeze Setup, on the daily chart of Ford Motor Company (F) in 2009.

For this setup, the first condition to observe is a visual compression in the Bollinger Bands that corresponds with a range consolidation phase in price that you can identify without the assistance of indicators. You may also want to confirm that the Average Directional Index (ADX Indicator) is under 20, but that also is not necessary. A trader enters a position when price breaks outside the Bollinger Band extreme and closes above the band, particularly with a large single bar or a price gap.

The breakout in March 2009 formed range expansion bars and broke above the horizontal trendline high at the $2.00-per-share level and led to a rally above $6.00 per share by May. The second example shows price breaking not only clear horizontal trendlines at the $6.50- and $5.00-per-share level, but gapping strongly above this level in July 2009 on a sign of impulse. Aggressive traders seek to buy shares immediately on a sharp range breakout, while conservative traders might wait to see if price closes for two bars outside the break in order to avoid the potential of a bull or bear trap.

Holding on for the Ride To capture the edge in this type of strategy, a trader would want to hold the position as long as possible until noticeable momentum or volume divergences occurred, or some other known sell signal developed on the price chart. Remember, you are trying to capture the edge from a positive feedback loop that gives rise

FIGURE 9.5 Bollinger Band Compressions and Price Breakouts in Ford Daily 2009

to a lengthy range expansion in price. Traders often place stops conservatively under the low of the initial breakout bar, or more aggressively under the most recent swing low in price prior to an upside break, or above the most recent swing high price in a downside break.

When determining when to enter a breakout trade, the best indication of a potential break comes from simple hand-drawn trendlines from prior price highs and lows, specifically when these trendlines compress into a triangle pattern formation. While not all traders use advanced technical indicators, all traders monitor price highs and lows, and when price clearly breaks an established price trendline, traders take notice and adjust positions accordingly, whether that means putting on a new position willingly or taking off an old position unwillingly to limit losses. Either way, breakouts from established trendlines often serve as self-fulfilling prophecies that create positive feedback loops that give the edge inherent in such strategies.

In terms of edge, most breakout strategies have superior monetary edges over other strategies because of the much larger expected price gains of the winning trades to the smaller losing trades. However, to achieve this superior monetary edge, breakout strategies often suffer a reduced accuracy edge that may not reach over 50 percent, which means that half or more of the attempted trades will result in a loss from a bull or bear trap developing, instead of the desired breakout. Thus, the average breakout strategy is lower in the accuracy edge but higher in the monetary or reward-to-risk edge than many other strategies.

Professional traders do not mind sacrificing accuracy for profits over time, but many new traders find such strategies difficult to trade because a string of consecutive losses can occur and frustrate inexperienced traders. Keep this in mind when trading these types of strategies.

Retracement Trades

Retracement trading strategies take advantage of two foundation price principles, namely the Trend Continuity principle and Momentum principle in terms of new momentum highs forecasting higher price highs likely yet to come. By combining two principles when locating a trading opportunity, you increase your odds of a successful trade outcome, and thus most well-planned retracement-specific trading strategies have higher accuracy rates than other strategies, but a moderate monetary edge when compared to breakout or trend reversal strategies. Retracement trades are often shorter in duration than breakout or reversal trades, but the increase in frequency can make up for this seeming disadvantage.

Retracement trades require the presence of a prevailing trend, whether up or down, and specifically bet on the trend in place continuing. The setups from retracement strategies come from pullbacks to key support levels, such as prior price support levels, or more commonly moving average support or Fibonacci Retracement prices. Figure 9.6 shows us basic retracement strategies of buying shares when price in an established uptrend retraces back to a rising short- or intermediate-term moving average.

Apple (AAPL) hit a major price low in January 2009 at $80.00 during a period of accumulation and range compression with price boundaries between $80.00 and $100.00 per share. Figure 9.6 shows the Realization stage in the stock, though price continued its uptrend to the $300.00-per-share level in October 2010, though neither the low nor the high appear on this chart. The main purpose of the daily chart of Apple is to show the numerous simple retracement trade opportunities that occurred while price traveled from the initial breakout above $100.00 in April 2009 higher in a steady, stable uptrend, as seen in the chart.

The basic idea of a retracement trade is to purchase shares as price retraces downward in a normal profit taking swing to the support area either of a rising short- or intermediate-term moving average, a trendline, a Fibonacci Retracement price, or some other known price support level. Each opportunity grants a buy setup to purchase shares on a downswing within the context of a rising primary uptrend. I drew arrows on six specific simple retracements to the rising 20- or 50-day exponential moving average, though pay special attention to the three retracements back to the rising 20 EMA at the $160.00- and $180.00-per-share level.

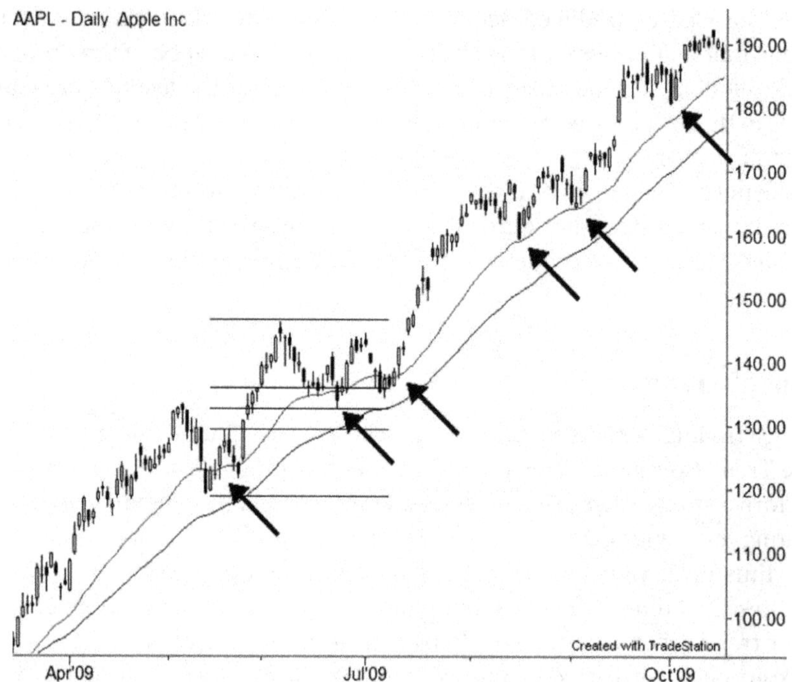

FIGURE 9.6 Basic Retracement Trades in an Uptrend—Apple Daily (AAPL) 2009

I also drew a standard Fibonacci Retracement grid that stretched from the May 2009 swing low of $120.00 per share to the June high under $150.00 per share. The respective 38.2 percent, 50 percent, and 61.8 percent retracements intersected the rising 20- and 50-day moving averages as shown, forming a support confluence and two trade entry opportunities as price retraced to the $135.00 level at this time.

The Simplicity of Retracements While retracement trades need only be as simple as price and a rising moving average, you can enhance your odds of a successful trade outcome by buying shares only after a reversal candle, such as a hammer, doji, bullish engulfing, or spinning top forms at the support of a trendline, moving average, or Fibonacci retracement. You can know in advance exactly what price to purchase shares, whether you are a conservative or aggressive trader. A conservative trader would demand proof that price began its rally upward off support, or downward from resistance before putting on a trade.

Specifically, the trader would wait to buy shares only after price rises above the specific high of a known reversal candle. The aggressive trader, more focused on the larger concept of edge and less specifically on the accuracy edge, as described in Chapter 8, would buy shares the moment price touched the rising trendline, moving average, or Fibonacci retracement price. By establishing a position at the likely support price, a trader will establish a more favorable reward-to-risk relationship in terms of establishing a reasonable stop-loss position and a larger potential profit target.

Though there is no guarantee price will support as expected, in the event that it does, the aggressive trader will have established a more favorable position than the conservative trader who waited for proof in the form of an upward move off of support before participating in the move. Remember, you must determine if you are more suited for conservative or aggressive execution tactics, and understand the compromise in each strategy.

Combining Elements for Successful Trades So far, we have incorporated moving averages, trendlines, Fibonacci retracements, and candles into the retracement opportunities. If you prefer to increase the odds of a successful trade outcome, you can incorporate the momentum principle into the setup by observing a new momentum high form on the most recent swing to a new price high. According to the momentum principle, new momentum highs often precede new price highs yet to come after a retracement.

Once you observe a new price high that forms on a corresponding new momentum high, if you buy shares after a retracement forms into an expected support area, you are wisely combining the two foundation price principles into a single trade setup, which increases the odds of a successful outcome. To identify new momentum highs, compare the most recent price swing with an unbounded momentum oscillator such as the 3/10 MACD Oscillator, Rate of Change, or Momentum indicator. By identifying confluences of separate methods, you will increase the odds of a successful trade outcome and increase your edge over time.

Beyond momentum, you can incorporate volume into your analysis. Like momentum, volume is a confirming indicator and can be used in a similar fashion. In the context of a rising uptrend, you want to see volume rise during the up-swings in price and either consolidate or decrease slightly during the retracements in price. If you begin to see volume rise as price rallies upward from a confluence support price, then you are observing a confirmation that suggests, like momentum, that higher prices are yet to come because buyers are eagerly supporting price and demand is overcoming the supply from the sellers.

If you are monitoring a major market index like the Dow Jones, S&P 500, or the NASDAQ, you can also look at breadth indicators such as the McClellan Oscillator, number of advancing stocks minus declining stocks (called breadth), net new highs, or other forms of market internals in a similar method to volume. You want to see market internals rise and confirm new price highs in a prevailing uptrend instead of forming divergences with price. If price forms a new swing high and a key market internal confirms the new high by forming its own new relative indicator high, then that also suggests that higher index prices are yet to come and that it is safe to establish retracement trades in the direction of the prevailing trend.

The same is true in the context of a downtrend and new price lows confirmed by new breadth or market internal lows, which suggests that lower index price lows are yet to come, and you should take retracements up into declining moving averages as opportunities to short sell index ETFs or purchased inverse ETFs if that is your dominant strategy.

In terms of price patterns, bull and bear flags are perfect retracement trade setups. Refer to Chapter 5 for more information on the specifics of these popular price patterns. The initial impulse that creates a new price and momentum high serves as a catalyst to expect potential higher price highs yet to come, and the expected retracement back to either a moving average, trendline, or Fibonacci retracement price serves as the specific entry for your trade execution. The retracement down to support in the context of a bull flag is called the flag portion, while the initial impulse up is called the pole. Your trade target is an exact measured move or equal swing of the pole, which is then added to the low of the flag as price tests and bounces upward off the expected support zone.

Again, aggressive traders would purchase shares as price tested the expected support zone while a conservative trader would purchase shares after price broke to the upside above the declining flag trendline, or broke a high off a classic reversal candle that formed off support. A trader would place a stop-loss order under the moving average support, trendline, or 61.8 percent Fibonacci retracement to play for a much larger, specific price pattern projection target.

Bull Flag Retracement Example: Visa Inc. (V) Figure 9.7 shows an intraday bull flag retracement trade setup on the 15-minute chart of Visa Inc (V), complete with new momentum highs and a confluence support buy opportunity at the rising 50-period exponential moving average and 50 percent Fibonacci retracement.

In Figure 9.7 we see the intraday chart of Visa during early June 2010 as price forms a classic bull flag example. Bull flags are inherently retracement style trade set-ups that build upon an initial impulse that leads to a second impulse high after an initial retracement. Your opportunity is to trade the retracement into expected support to take advantage of the momentum concept as a leading indicator on price.

Price forms a sharp impulse swing higher during June 9, 2010, peaking mid-day at the $75.50 level. Notice that the 3/10 MACD Momentum Oscillator actually registered two new momentum highs during this time, which served as a confirmation of the recent price swing highs and suggested that higher price highs were yet to come after an immediate retracement. The retracement, in the form of stable profit-taking, occurred into the close of the session as price moved lower to test the rising support of both the 50-period EMA and the 50 percent Fibonacci Retracement price as drawn at the $73.50 level. For aggressive traders, this was the entry opportunity for a specific bull flag trade setup, or a more generic retracement trade opportunity.

While the aggressive trader established a position on the test of confluence support, a conservative trader would have demanded to see a bullish candle or the break of the declining trendline at the $74.00-per-share level before executing a position, and thus went home without a position on the close of the session. Visa gapped strongly overnight, gapping through the $74.00 level where the conservative trader anticipated executing a trade; this sometimes happens and is a consequence of waiting for confirmation before establishing a trade.

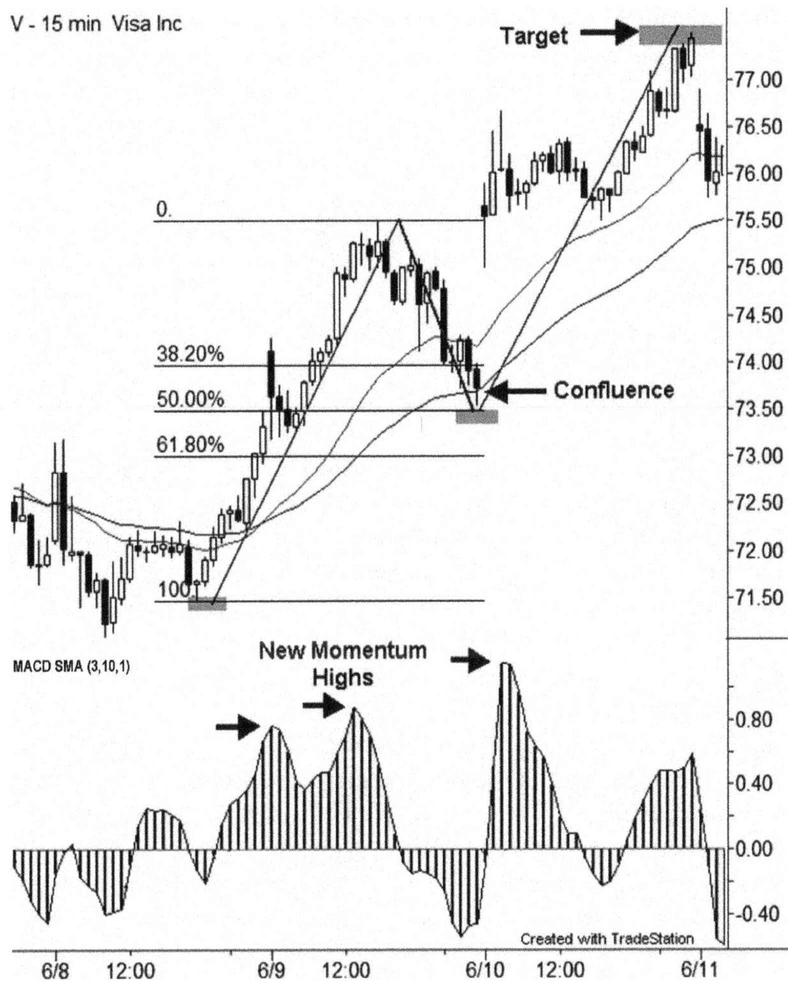

FIGURE 9.7 Bull Flag Retracement Trade Setup with Confluence Support in Visa 15-minute Chart—June 2010

In terms of stop-loss and target, the aggressive trader purchased shares before the close on July 9 at the $73.50 level and placed a stop under both the 50-period EMA and 61.8 percent lower Fibonacci retracement at $73.00, which was also round-number support. Thus, the risk in the position totaled roughly 50 cents. How does a trader set a price target for a bull flag? It's easier than you might expect. Measure the vertical distance from the immediate swing low price of the pole to the high of the pole, which is where I drew the Fibonacci retracement.

This will often be the case when drawing a Fibonacci retracement grid from an impulse—the grid will be the distance from the pole low to the high. In this case, the measurement from $71.50 to $75.50 was $4.00 per share. Taking that figure, we then add $4.00 per share to the bottom of the flag, or the retracement swing into support. Because we established a position at the expected confluence support at $73.50, this is then the bottom of the flag. In the event that the price breaks through the confluence support and under $73.00 per share, then it is no longer a bull flag retracement setup and we want to be out of the position to limit further losses. When we add $4.00 to our entry at the flag low at $73.50, we arrive at an upside target of $77.50 per share.

From a reward-to-risk standpoint, this opportunity gives us a 50-cent risk to play for a $4.00 upside target, or an eight-to-one reward-to-risk opportunity. Such outsized reward-to-risk opportunities are only available to the aggressive trader who is willing to purchase shares as close to the expected confluence support level, which he can discern in advance. In contrast, a conservative trader who hoped to enter as price crossed above the declining trendline at the $74.00-per-share level, if given the opportunity, would also locate a stop under $73.00 per share and thus risk $1.00 in the position to play for a $3.50 upside target.

Notice how waiting for proof, or more specifically a higher probability of a successful outcome, cost the conservative trader in terms of the reward-to-risk relationship. Instead of a 50-cent risk and $4.00 reward potential that the aggressive trader enjoys, with a lower probability of a successful outcome, the conservative trader degrades the monetary edge to a $1.00 risk for a $3.50 reward. The difference in an additional 50-cent risk and decreased 50-cent target degrades the overall edge from the eight-to-one relationship enjoyed by the aggressive trader to a three-and-a-half-to-one reward-to-risk ratio obtained by the conservative trader.

This is not to make a criticism of the conservative trader, because the break above $74.00 per share officially triggers the bull flag setup and increases the odds of a move higher to the target that an aggressive trader cannot realize when price simply tests the rising confluence support at $73.50.

For all trades that you take, you will have to balance the accuracy edge with the monetary edge, which usually means the longer you wait for additional favorable chart evidence to develop, increasing the odds of a successful outcome, you decrease your reward-to-risk ratio or monetary edge. This bull flag trade setup helps explain that concept. You should think of all trades in terms of an interaction of accuracy and monetary edge, and how that plays out over time within the context of your broader goals and trading strategy, which you develop in advance of the setups you take as a trader.

WHERE TRADES FIT IN THE LIFE CYCLE

Think back to Chapter 7 on the accumulation/distribution cycles and Elliott Wave Principle, and incorporate that into the broader perspective of the trend continuity principle, momentum principle, and price alternation principle. Using the life cycle of a price move as a background, we can thus highlight where these four basic setups apply best, as seen in Figure 9.8.

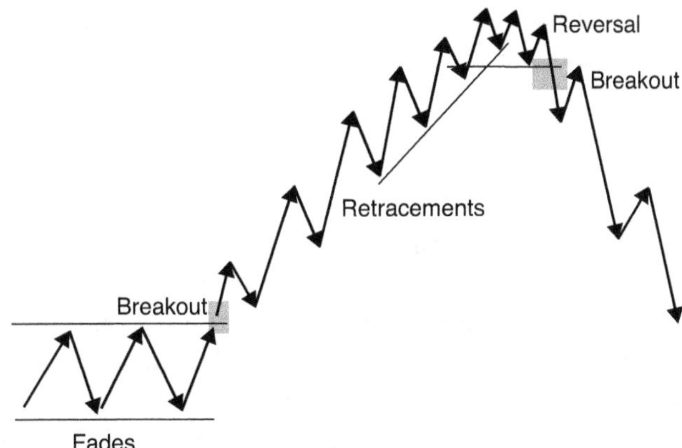

FIGURE 9.8 Categories of Trade Setups within the Life Cycle of a Price Move

Let us take this same figure and overlay the accumulation/distribution cycle. The range contraction phase at the left side reflects the Accumulation phase, while the move up out of the breakout highlights the Realization phase, and the final consolidation at the highs prior to a downside reversal labels the Distribution phase. If we overlay Elliott Wave characteristics, Waves 1 and 2 occur during the Accumulation Phase, waves 3 and 4 occur during the Realization phase, and the final 5th wave and transition into the ABC Corrective phase occur during the Distribution phase at the highs.

Adding Wyckoff's terms to the structure, Realization is also known as Mark-up, and the downward move in price after the Distribution phase is the Mark-down additional phase. Eventually price will move so low as to attract buying from the professionals and thus create a new Accumulation phase, and the cycle will repeat.

With that information as a guide, let us now overlay our four categories of trade setups to the structure. During the accumulation phase, the best strategies to use include fade setups, which take advantage of fading strength and weakness by purchasing shares when price tests the lower horizontal support trendline of the range and then selling, then perhaps short-selling, shares as price returns to the upper horizontal resistance line. As long as price remains in a Negative Feedback Loop (see Chapter 3) of a consolidation phase, then fade strategies will work best.

Fade Trades in Accumulation

Fade trades work best by using the Bollinger Band indicators along with hand-drawn price trendlines as price boundaries that the market should not break. Thus, you would enter a fade trade as price tests a support or resistance level, place a stop outside the boundary where you expect price to inflect up or down, and then play for a target of the opposite Bollinger Band or trendline. Oscillators such as the Stochastic or RSI can be helpful in assessing overbought or oversold levels, but often price levels work better than oscillators, particularly in allowing you to identify a price level to enter, place your stop, and then target for a profit. Due to the price consolidation, moving averages are useless in assessing support or resistance, as price moves up and down through the averages as if they were not even there.

Breakout Trades out of the Range

As the life cycle informs us, price cannot remain bound within the confines of a trading range forever. According to the Price Alternation Principle (Chapter 3), price will break out one way or the other from the consolidation into a range expansion impulse phase, which gives rise to Breakout trading strategies. Though price may give false breakouts, called traps, price will eventually eject to a positive feedback loop above the upper boundary, which often begins with an initial buy impulse from the bulls that leads to a sudden short-covering phase of bears buying back shares to cover their short positions. A similar positive feedback loop begins when bears push price down through the lower support trendline in an impulse that forces buyers to liquidate (sell) their positions and take their stop-loss executions, further extending the downside breakout in price.

Traders who employ breakout strategies enter positions as soon as they believe price has officially penetrated the support or resistance boundary, and thus will experience a potentially strong positive feedback loop that will carry price up to a higher level or down to a lower level in a sustained range breakout expansion mode. To the extent that price remains in the impulse trend breakout, these breakout traders will profit from the expected move.

Retracement Trades in Realization

Price does not move straight up or straight down during its range expansion phase, nor does any trend in price travel straight up or straight down. Instead, price moves in action and reaction cycles that form waves or swings on the chart as price travels through time up or down in a steady trend. These steady swings in price in the context of a market in a trend mode give rise to retracement strategies, which is where most traders find it easiest to profit from trading.

The highest probability, lowest risk trades come from buying pullbacks to support, such as a trendline, moving average, or Fibonacci retracement price (or confluence Fibonacci level) in the context of a rising uptrend, or short selling pullbacks higher to a resistance level in the context of a confirmed downtrend in price.

Retracement traders seek to buy shares as price retraces to a known support level, with aggressive traders buying shares immediately as price trades at the support level while conservative traders demand that price form a reversal candle or show some official sign of rising off of the expected support level before buying shares. Traders place stops under the expected support level and play for a minimum target of the retest of the prior swing high in the context of an uptrend, or for a push higher beyond the prior swing high when some other sell signal, such as a divergence, short-term trendline break, or break under a reversal candle occurs. Retracement traders want to buy the first pullback in price to support after a new price and momentum high form, as the momentum principle states that new price highs are expected after an initial pullback when both price and momentum form new swing highs together.

Fade Trades in a Prevailing Trend

Though not as high probability due to the positioning against the established trend, some traders seek to use fade strategies in the context of rising uptrends by short-selling shares as price reaches an overextended condition away from the 20-period moving average or other average or rising trendline. Fade traders take advantage of the mean reversion principle, which states that the more price stretches above or beneath the 20-period (or other short-term) moving average, the greater the odds are for a snap-back move to that average price. Thus, fade traders want to short overextended swings higher that pop outside the upper Bollinger Band particularly as a reversal candle such as a shooting star forms, or buy overextended swings to the downside also as price trades outside the lower Bollinger Band with a reversal candle such as a hammer.

Fade traders who trade in the context of overbought or oversold levels in the context of a trend wish to enter a position when price begins traveling back toward the mean, perhaps on the break of a short-term trendline or price break under the high or low of a reversal candle that forms with a momentum divergence. They will place stops just above the most recent swing high in an uptrend or just beneath the most recent swing low in a downtrend to play for a mean reversion swing, most likely to the 20-period moving average.

Fade traders must understand their positioning is for a very short-term scalp play only—trying to capture a quick swing in price—and should use tight stops. They must be prepared to exit ahead of the full target in the event that the trend reasserts itself, or else they could face very large losses by fighting the trend. Of all the common trading strategies, this type of counter-trend mean reversion fading strategy can be the most difficult for new traders to profit consistently over time, as they may have a string of numerous very small winners but be exposed to one or more large losing trades that overcome the small string of profits from prior trades.

Reversals in Distribution

In this example, price broke out from a range consolidation phase into a range expansion trend mode, but we return to the price alternation principle to note that after an expansion phase, price alternates back into a range contraction phase. While it is difficult to assess correctly whether a range consolidation phase is a simple pause in the context of a rising uptrend or the beginning of a distribution phase that will mark the end of a trend, eventually the price trend will reverse, as no stock or market can rise forever. It is a fact of the market that all markets must reverse eventually, and price almost always gives clear signals in advance of a trend reversal to those experienced traders who can pinpoint the reversal evidence.

The easiest objective evidence comes from multi-swing momentum divergences after a lengthy price move, particularly one which you can identify the accumulation phase and lengthy realization phase, or if you are proficient with Elliott Wave, a series of five waves on the price chart, where the expected fifth wave forms on obvious negative momentum or volume divergences. In this sort of environment, a trader employs a reversal strategy, though if the price forms a distribution trading range, fade traders may benefit from trading from the extremes of the range just as explained in the initial accumulation phase.

Use Martin Pring's weight of the evidence model before betting on a trend to reverse. Such chart signs of evidence that an uptrend is ending include a lengthy or multi-swing negative divergence in momentum or volume, or in market internals such as breadth if you are analyzing a stock market index such as the S&P 500. Though divergences never guarantee trend reversals, they are clues that the odds of a reversal are increasing, particularly to the extent that price continues rising in the context of an ever-increasing negative divergence.

Next, look for price to break under the 20- and then 50-period exponential moving average. In the context of an uptrend, price should support on these averages, as that is the logic of retracement trading strategies. However, if price breaks under the 50-period EMA and remains under it, eventually these moving averages will cross bearishly, which is your signal from the moving average method as described in Chapter 1 that a trend is perhaps in the final phases and could be reversing.

Look also for price to break under the 200-day simple moving average on a daily chart. Be on guard for a Kickoff, which would be a sudden down thrust in the momentum oscillator or breadth (in a stock market index). If price makes a simple downswing but the momentum oscillator makes a distinct new momentum low, this is a Kickoff and early signal that the trend is likely reversing.

Finally, watch for price to make a lower low, swing up to a lower high, and then close under the recent lower low for the official trend reversal, and highest probability to put on a reversal trade to play for a larger target at the most likely spot that a trend officially has reversed.

Reversal traders enter short at the exact spot of a trend reversal, or aggressively put on a reversal position at a break of an established rising trendline after observing multi-swing negative momentum divergences. Either way, they will place a stop-loss order either above the most recent swing high, or trail a stop above the 50-period moving average. Like break-out trades, reversal trades have a very large target that usually includes price completing the process of an upside trend reversal after being in a confirmed downtrend.

Within the context of the Mark-down or down trend in price, traders employ the same type of retracement strategies they do as in an uptrend. They would sell shares short as price rallies to the underside of a falling trendline, falling 20- or 50-period moving average, or Fibonacci retracement price (see Chapter 6). Fade traders also would buy shares on overextended swings beyond the falling 20 period moving average to play a mean-reversion play back to the average.

TRADING CONFIDENTLY

Much of your success as a trader comes from learning the basics of price movement, learning to recognize the price structure which clues you in to future expectations along with which indicators to use, and learning what tactics to apply given this knowledge from your analysis. However, knowing what to do is not enough; you must develop the confidence to implement the decisions you make from your analysis in real-time. I strongly suggest learning from the insights of trading psychologists, which will give you the confidence and mental edge, as well as the motivation for peak performance.

You develop confidence through applying the principles you learn and building your experience day by day. You also develop confidence when you understand exactly what it is you are doing when you put on a trade, in terms of the larger picture. This is why I hope you took the time to understand the foundation principles in Chapters 1 through 3 and then understood the methods of candle charts, price patterns, Fibonacci, and the life cycle move. Once you have this as your foundation, you will be much more prepared to understand the probabilities of the next likely move in price, the context in which that move appears, and how exactly to take advantage of it. Not every trade will be a winner, but over time, the edge will carry you forward.

It is with this background that the next chapter—the final chapter—presents some specific trade setups. I encourage you to create your own setups using this chapter as a guide and use your creativity in recognizing opportunities from price behavior in the context of the trend continuity principle, momentum principle, and price alternation principle. Remember that the most important factor is to get the main idea correct, and then build specific rules around the main idea (such as "trends are more likely to continue than reverse"). When you take ownership of the trade setup, you increase your confidence and enjoyment of the process, and bring it to life. You will find that, as a trader, motivation is key. Find the unique balance between your skills and talents, the market principles, trade setups, and the many methods, vehicles, and timeframes available to you as a trader.

CHAPTER 10

Specific Trade Setups for Today's Markets

This chapter describes some of the specific trade setups I have developed for use in my trading. All traders gravitate toward certain setups over others, so it is useful to build a toolbox of specific trades from which to pull depending on the market conditions that exist at the time. You might even improve on these setups or develop your own variations. It is best to use the work and insights of others as a foundation upon which to build your own personal methods. In so doing, you will progress beyond simple pattern recognition to full integration, which will make you an even better, more confident trader. Each specific trade setup will be discussed and then accompanied by rules and examples for maximizing your trading performance with that particular trade. Let's start with the Cradle Trade.

THE CRADLE TRADE

I have always used moving averages on my price charts, from the first day I viewed a price chart. Moving averages are so helpful in revealing structure, trend, and potential trading opportunities on pullbacks to the averages. It is no surprise then that one of the first trade setups I developed for myself was the Cradle Trade.

Specifically, the Cradle Trade requires the 20- and 50-period exponential moving averages on any timeframe. The Bullish Cradle forms when the 20-period EMA crosses above the 50 EMA, and I label the exact spot of the crossover as the "Cradle." Similarly, the Bearish Cradle forms when the 20-period EMA crosses under the 50 EMA.

Technically, this trade is a retracement style setup, but it incorporates elements from reversal trades. Specifically, it is the point where it would most likely be safest from a trend reversal standpoint to play a reversal trade, while giving you a very tight stop in the event that price fails to complete a true reversal. Most reversal trades require wide stops, while most retracement trades allow for tight stops. The Cradle Trade combines elements of the weight of the evidence model for reversal trades with the known moving average support or resistance area of a retracement trade.

Being a reversal-style trade, we want to see a market ideally forming lengthy, multi-swing momentum divergences ahead of an expected price reversal. Remember that the 20/50 EMA crossover is an early precursor to a trend reversal, but that does not mean you can put on a trade just because the moving averages crossed. The Cradle Trade Setup forms when price breaks the moving averages, the moving averages then cross, and then price moves into the Cradle Crossover and ideally forms a reversal candle at the crossover of the moving averages. Let us see an ideal setup with Parker-Hannifin (PH) in Figure 10.1 before we discuss the logic of entry and exit.

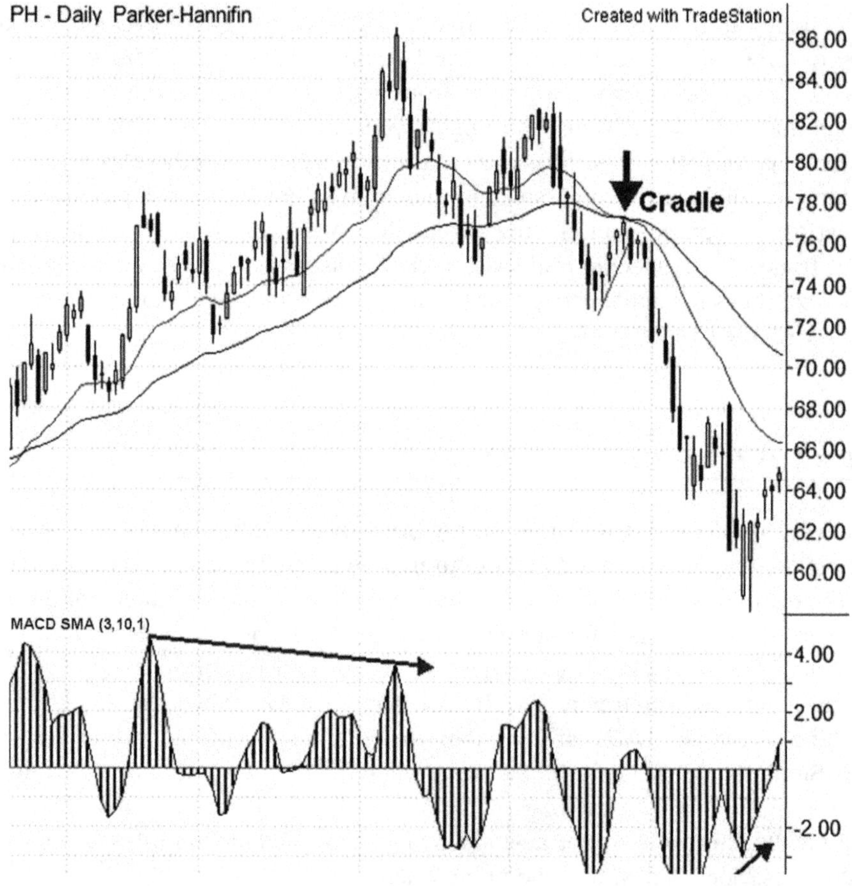

FIGURE 10.1 The Cradle Trade Setup in Parker-Hannifin

From the end of 2007 to the beginning of 2008, Parker-Hannifin's stock pushed to new highs at the $86.00-per-share level after an up-trending move in the stock, but the negative momentum divergence served as a nonconfirmation for the recent price high. Immediately, price swung lower, breaking under both the 20- and 50-period EMAs on the daily chart above, as the custom 3, 10 MACD Momentum Oscillator forged a new chart low when price was not making a new low—creating a Kickoff signal.

After a quick rally to $82.00, price broke under the rising 20- and 50-day EMAs again, but this time those averages crossed at the $77.00 level officially on December 24, 2007. Notice also that price formed a lower low after a lower swing high in the process, casting doubt on the further prospects of the uptrend continuing. So far, we have discussed changes in structure and conditions such as momentum divergences and price's relation to the respective moving averages. But how do you profit from the structural change?

That is where the Cradle Trade comes in, combining the weight of the evidence model for trend reversals with the precision of a confluence overhead resistance area from retracement trading strategies. Price rallied immediately up to the 20/50 EMA crossover, the Cradle, on December 26, forming a hanging man candle after a small doji. The hanging man candle tested the 20/50 EMA confluence exactly at $77.16, giving aggressive traders an immediate entry, executing their short-sale position as close to $77.00 as possible.

Traders would place a stop-loss order slightly above $78.00 per share, or even $80.00 to protect the position, but at least above $78.00, which gives price roughly $1.00 to trade intraday slightly above the EMA crossover. A conservative trader would wait to see if price proved it was more likely to reverse lower at the overhead confluence resistance, and would enter short only on a price break under the lower short-term rising trendline as drawn, or under the hanging man candle intraday low at $75.75. The conservative trader would still locate a stop above $78.00 to be safe, and it would be illogical to locate a stop anywhere under the 20/50 EMA Cradle at $77.00 per share.

Both traders would play for a potential trend reversal, or large target move to test either a higher timeframe prior swing low (such as on the weekly chart), or instead would continue holding a short-sale position until the price formed positive divergences or broke a declining trendline. The Cradle Trade allows you to play for a theoretically unlimited, large price target if the trend truly reverses, while combining the benefit of a precise stop which other reversal trades lack. Most reversal trades require much wider stops than would be granted by a confluence of the 20/50 EMA.

The exit for the Cradle is a countervailing price buy signal, or higher timeframe prior low as you determine to be a reasonable target. Cradle trades require active trade management by monitoring for bullish chart evidence to develop. In the absence of any bullish developments, such as positive divergences, bullish trendline, or EMA breaks, or major reversal candles forming off of a positive divergence, a trader will remain holding a short position to profit from the expected down-trend continuation move.

With an entry as close to $77.00 as possible and a stop placed above $78.00 or as high as $80.00 to ensure safety, where might a trader play for a reasonable target? Though we do not see it in Figure 10.1, Parker-Hannifin had a major price support line at the

$60.00-per-share level, which would be your initial target. As price fell as expected from the Cradle Crossover, we could set a target at $60.00 per share, and we would monitor what chart formations developed in the event price fell to that level over time.

On January 24, 2009, one month after entry, price officially tested our potential downside target at $60.00 per share. A conservative trader might have exited immediately as soon as price tested $60.00, perhaps from a resting order for a price target at that level. If so, the trader profited roughly $17.00, with a stop sized from $1.00 to $3.00, depending on entry. An aggressive trader would examine the price structure closely to see if it was worth holding short and playing for an even larger downside target yet to come.

As price tested the $60.00 level, which was established as prior price support, we can observe a clean positive momentum divergence in the 3/10 Oscillator as a powerful marabozu (strong bullish) candle formed, and on January 23, 2009, a clean bullish hammer candle formed with a long lower shadow that bounced higher from $60.00 per share. An aggressive trader would see the positive divergence and bullish candles off of expected support, and would exit the position on a close above the high of the candle at $62.50, which occurred on January 25 at the gap candle that opened at $63.75. By waiting to see if price was going to break support at the expected support at $60.00 per share, the aggressive trader exited late at $63.75, but that is still lower from the initial entry short at $77.00 per share.

Rules for a Bearish Cradle Trade

The rules for the Bearish Cradle Trade are as follows:

1. Observe a lengthy rising trend in place that shows negative momentum divergences, preferably multi-swing divergences.
2. Observe price breaking under both the 20- and 50-period EMAs (or similar moving averages that you use).
3. Observe the 20- and 50-period EMAs crossing bearishly, which is labeled the Cradle.
4. Observe price retracing back into, or as close as possible to, the 20/50 EMA crossover, and see if any reversal candle forms.
5. Sell short as close as possible to the EMA crossover if aggressive, or wait for price to break under a candle low under the Cradle to execute a position.
6. Place a stop-loss order above the EMA crossover, but never directly at the EMA crossover. Allow the price room to run slightly through the Cradle so you are not stopped out prematurely. Re-enter if you are stopped out but price falls back under the Cradle if you desire.
7. Play for a large price target in a trend reversal style trade that either continues your position until price signals a classic buy signal when positive divergences form or price breaks a falling trendline or 20-period EMA. You may also trail a stop slightly

above the 20-period EMA. Look for the higher timeframe to see if there are any obvious downside support targets and monitor price action closely at these levels.

8. Exit the position either when price tests a higher timeframe support zone, or when price forms a clear buy signal from positive divergences, a trendline break, or a move above the 20-period EMA.

Figure 10.2 represents an idealized Bearish Cradle Trade setup on any timeframe.

In Figure 10.2, we see price in an uptrend ending its move on a negative momentum divergence with an initial price break under the 20/50-period EMAs. Then, the next swing higher takes price into the official crossover of the 20- and 50-period moving average, setting up your trade entry with a stop above the EMA crossover and a reversal-style large downside price target. In this case, price continued lower to end its move and break back above the falling 20-period EMA on the right side of the chart after a distinct positive momentum divergence, which was a buy signal that signaled an exit to the cradle trade and potential new reversal in trend.

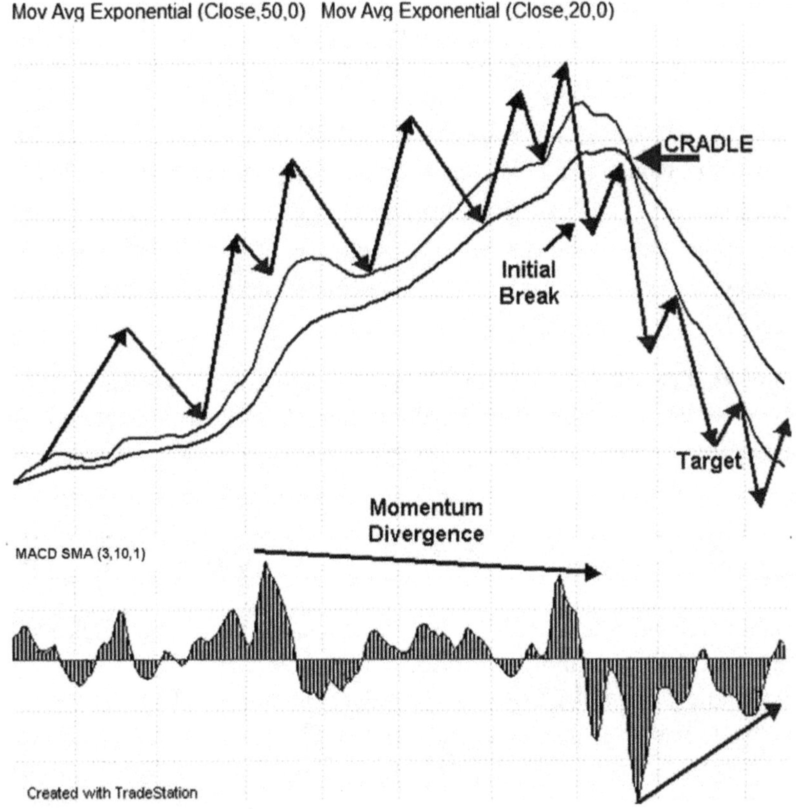

FIGURE 10.2 The Idealized Cradle Trade Setup

Rules for a Bullish Cradle Trade

The logic is the same as a Bearish Cradle trade, only you are trading long after a downward trend in price breaks in an expected trend reversal to the upside.

1. Observe a lengthy downtrend in place that shows positive momentum divergences, preferably multi-swing divergences.
2. Observe price breaking above both the 20- and 50-period EMAs (or similar moving averages that you use).
3. Observe the 20- and 50-period EMAs crossing bullishly.
4. Observe price retracing back into, or as close as possible, to the 20/50 EMA crossover, and see if any reversal candle forms.
5. Buy as close as possible to the EMA crossover if aggressive, or wait for price to break above a candle high above the Cradle Crossover to execute a position.
6. Place a stop-loss beneath the EMA crossover, but never directly at the EMA crossover. Allow the price room to run slightly through the Cradle so you are not stopped out prematurely. Re-enter if you are stopped out but price rises back above the Cradle if you desire.
7. Play for a large price target in a trend reversal style trade that either continues your position until price signals a classic sell or sell-short signal when negative divergences form or price breaks a rising trendline or 20-period EMA. You may also trail a stop slightly beneath the 20-period EMA. Look for the higher timeframe to see if there are any obvious upside resistance targets, and monitor price action closely at these levels.
8. Exit the position either when price tests a higher timeframe resistance zone, or when price forms a clear sell or sell-short signal from negative divergences, a trendline break, or a move beneath the 20-period EMA.

Remember that Cradle trades form on all timeframes, from the one-minute chart to the monthly chart so you can incorporate this setup into your trading arsenal no matter what market or timeframe you trade.

THE IMPULSE BUY AND IMPULSE SELL TRADE

The impulse buy trade builds specifically on the concept that momentum precedes price, which is the momentum principle as described in Chapter 2. Specifically, new momentum highs along with new price highs often precede new price highs likely yet to come after an initial pullback. While this is a concept, we can build a set of specific rules around the principle in order to generate a labeled trade setup. This is the Impulse Buy trade not just because of the catchy name, but also because it describes the concept exactly.

The initial supply/demand imbalance creates an impulse swing in price, and we wish to buy after the impulse in price retraces to the rising 20-period EMA for a specific setup to capitalize on the long-standing price momentum principle. In the context of a prevailing trend, the Impulse Buy setup also builds its edge from the Trend Continuity principle, which states that trends are more likely to continue than to reverse.

Though it is not required, Impulse Buy trades often produce better results in the context of a prevailing uptrend, but sometimes price impulses can arise from a trading range environment on the initial breakout. As such, the impulse buy trade builds upon the momentum principle and can sometimes build also from the price alternation principle and breakout strategies.

While a pure price breakout requires a trader to enter as soon as price breaks free of a trading range, the Impulse Buy setup demands that price retrace to a key support level before entering a position to take advantage of a precise entry into a market that likely will resolve again with a second impulse or price swing to the upside off of the expected support zone, thus producing a profit.

Impulse buy trades are very similar to bull flag price patterns, and it can be stated that virtually all bull flags are Impulse Buy trade setups, but not all Impulse Buy setups are bull flags. Impulse buys that set up from range breakouts are not bull flags, though most Impulse Buys that trigger in the context of a rising uptrend are bull flag price patterns with similar expectations.

To set up an Impulse Buy trade, you must first observe an initial powerful swing in price, or the initial impulse. This impulse swing in price must be confirmed by a new corresponding high in the momentum oscillator, such as the 3/10 MACD oscillator, Rate of Change, or other unbound momentum oscillator that is not an overbought or oversold oscillator such as the stochastic or RSI. After the initial impulse occurs, look for price to retrace back to the rising 20-period EMA specifically.

You can also draw a Fibonacci retracement grid on the most recent impulse in price to expect support at the 38.2 percent or 50 percent Fibonacci retracement, and can locate your stop under the 61.8 percent Fibonacci retracement or under the rising 20- or 50-period EMA, depending on your risk tolerance for tight or wide stops.

There are actually two targets for the Impulse Buy, also depending on your tolerance for risk. The immediate, specific price target from the Impulse Buy is a simple retest of the most recent price high at the top of the impulse. A trader would exit immediately upon price touching the most recent swing high regardless of other factors.

While that is the simple exit that conservative traders seek to target, other traders may seek to play for a larger target situated just beyond the recent swing high. Namely, an aggressive trader might decide to exit an Impulse Buy trade only after price trades above the upper Bollinger Band, forms a reversal candle, or breaks a short-term rising trendline. In other words, an aggressive trader would employ more active trade management and thus play for a larger, less specific target than a conservative trader who seeks to exit

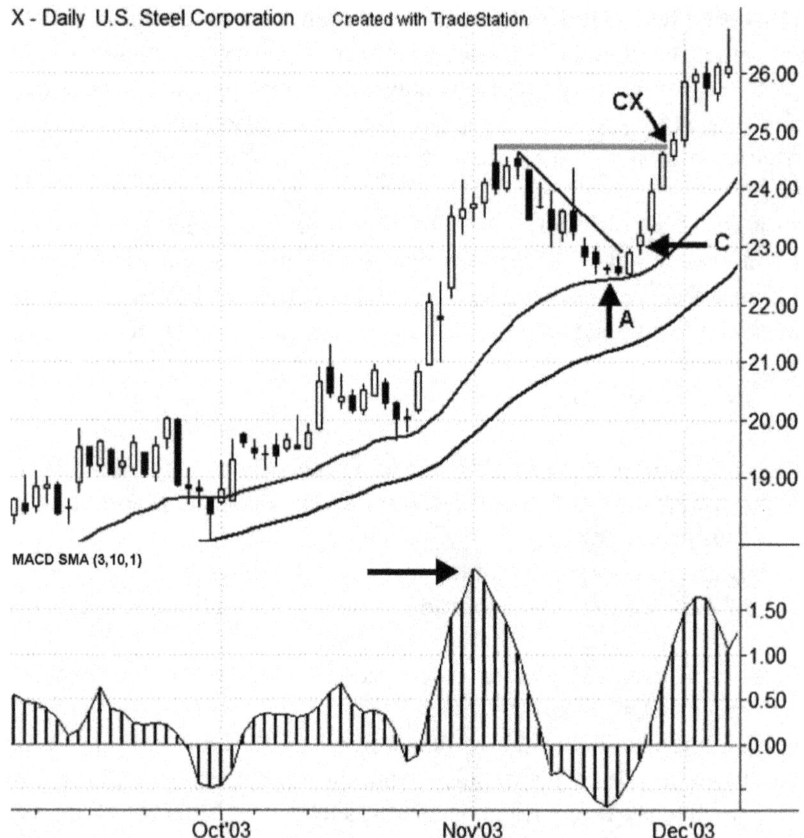

FIGURE 10.3 Impulse Buy Setup in U.S. Steel Daily—2003

only on a retest of the prior high. Figure 10.3 reveals an ideal example of the Impulse Buy setup in U.S. Steel (X) in 2003.

From the April 2003 price low, U.S. Steel remained in a stable uptrend in its daily chart, which meant that any pullback to the rising 20- or 50-period EMA, particularly if a reversal candle formed at the level such as was the case in late September and October 2003, was a classic though generic retracement buy setup.

However, the sharp impulse higher in late October and the respective pullback retracement to the rising 20-period EMA in mid-November triggered the official Impulse Buy entry, which could also be labeled a Bull Flag with similar parameters. Notice the strong up-swing in price that was confirmed with a clean push to new highs in the 3/10 MACD Oscillator—this is the initial condition that triggers an Impulse Buy setup.

A trader looks to buy shares when price retraces to the rising 20-period EMA, particularly if price forms a reversal candle or breaks a short-term descending trendline.

The trader would place a stop tightly under the 20 EMA, though preferably in most cases under the rising 50-period EMA in the context of a rising uptrend.

Though I did not draw a Fibonacci retracement grid, the respective Fibonacci retracement prices from the $20.00 per share low of the impulse to the $25.00 high of the impulse rest at $22.83 for the 38.2 percent retracement, $22.24 for the 50 percent retracement, and $21.64 for the 61.8 percent retracement. In this example, the best price to locate a stop for this trade with an entry at $22.50 would be either directly under the 61.8 percent retracement at $21.64 or under the rising 50-period EMA just under $21.00 per share, which would place your stop safely under the 61.8 percent Fibonacci retracement, rising 50-day EMA, and round number price value of $21.00, all of which converge as expected support prices, though you would not want to continue holding long on a price break under $21.00 per share.

In terms of entry, notice how price retraced in an ABC three-wave corrective fashion to the rising 20-period EMA support level. As price retraced to the 20-period EMA, two doji candles formed at the support of the rising moving average. An aggressive trader would enter as close as possible to the rising 20 EMA, and that entry is labeled on the chart with the letter A at $22.50 per share.

A conservative trader would demand that price rise upward off the 20 EMA and break the high of the doji candles at $22.75, or break above the short-term falling trendline at $23.00. The conservative entry is labeled on the chart with the letter C. Price officially broke and closed above both the doji candle high and the falling trendline on November 24, 2003 at $23.20.

A conservative trader would play only for a retest of the prior swing high from early November at $24.75 and may set a market or limit order to sell if price reached that prior high. However, an aggressive trader would likely hold through the potential resistance in order to capture the full edge possible from the trade setup.

Recall the momentum principle: it states that a new high is likely yet to come in price after a new momentum and price high, not just a retest of a prior high. However, there are instances where price will form a double-top and fail to overcome the resistance of the prior price high, thus a conservative trader would be wise to exit there. An aggressive trader would monitor the price structure as it approached the high, and hold on for a slightly larger target if price closed above resistance, as was the case in U.S. Steel.

Look carefully after price rose above the $25.00 level in early December to note a negative momentum divergence along with spinning top candles and a shooting star that closed just above $26.00 per share. These chart developments are objective warning signs that price may be heading lower soon in a standard downward retracement, at which time fade traders may be preparing to enter a short-sale position to play for a quick retest of the rising 20-day EMA at $24.00 per share.

For reference, U.S. Steel continued higher after the end of the chart, and an aggressive trader would have benefitted from that unexpected windfall profit, as price did not break or close under the lows of the spinning top candles or shooting star candle, nor the rising trendline that began at the $23.00-per-share level that continued to $26.00. Remember, an aggressive trader desires to stay in a position for as long as possible, and will exit when conditions and price structure dictate an exit, often in the form not just of negative divergences or reversal candles, but a confirmed price break under a reversal candle low or rising trendline.

The Impulse Sell trade is identical to the Impulse Buy trade, only the setup requires a downward impulse in price, either from a downward break from a trading range or shorting the retracement up after a downward impulse in the context of a confirmed downtrend.

Rules for the Impulse Buy Trade

An Impulse Buy seeks to capitalize on buying the initial pullback after price forms a new price and momentum high after a sudden impulse swing in price. While the most common place to expect support is the rising 20-period EMA, a trader can look to buy shares into a rising trendline or other confluence support level.

1. Observe a clear impulse in price, which often consists of a string of powerful candles in a row. Make sure the momentum oscillator also registers a new indicator high along with the recent price impulse high, that can either originate from the break outside a trading range or within the context of a confirmed or new uptrend.
2. Observe that price retraces downward to the rising 20-period EMA or other expected support zone. You may also draw a Fibonacci Retracement grid from the impulse low to the impulse high to obtain the retracement grid to fine-tune expected support. An impulse that originates from a trading range may retrace to find support at the prior horizontal resistance price, as prior resistance may become future support. For added confirmation, look for the retracement phase to form an ABC corrective pattern.
3. An aggressive trader buys shares as soon as price touches the 20-period EMA or alternate expected support price, while a conservative trader buys shares only after price breaks above the high of a reversal candle or falling trendline that connects the highs of the retracement period.
4. Traders place stops tightly under the 20-period EMA or more appropriately under the 50-period EMA in an uptrend, or under the prior support zone after a break from a trading range. Traders may also draw a Fibonacci retracement grid to place a stop under the 61.8 percent retracement.
5. A conservative trader would target the most recent swing high only, exiting automatically at that price, while an aggressive trader would expect price to make a new swing high beyond that possible resistance level, and would sell if negative divergences formed and price broke under a rising trendline or the low of a bearish reversal candle.

Rules for the Impulse Sell Trade

There is no structural difference between an Impulse Buy setup or an Impulse Sell setup. As a general rule, prices tend to fall faster than they rise, so at times, a trader will need to act more quickly or monitor positions more closely with an Impulse Sell trade, as price may hit or exceed a downside sooner than expected when compared with an Impulse Buy trade.

1. Observe a clear impulse in price, which often consists of a string of powerful candles in a row. Make sure the momentum oscillator also registers a new indicator low along with the recent price impulse low that can either originate from the break down from a trading range or within the context of a confirmed or new downtrend.
2. Observe that price retraces higher to the falling 20-period EMA or other expected resistance zone. You may also draw a Fibonacci Retracement grid from the impulse high to the impulse low to obtain the retracement grid to fine-tune expected resistance. An impulse that originates from a trading range may retrace to find resistance at the prior horizontal support price, as prior support may become future resistance. For added confirmation, look for the retracement phase to form an ABC corrective pattern.
3. An aggressive trader sells shares short as soon as price touches the 20-period EMA or alternate expected resistance price, while a conservative trader sells shares short only after price breaks beneath the low of a reversal candle or rising trendline that connects the lows of the retracement period.
4. Traders place stops tightly above the 20-period EMA or more appropriately above the 50-period EMA in a downtrend, or above the prior resistance zone after a break from a trading range. Traders may also draw a Fibonacci retracement grid to place a stop above the 61.8 percent retracement.
5. A conservative trader would target the most recent swing low only, exiting automatically at that price, while an aggressive trader would expect price to make a new swing low under that possible resistance level, and would buy to cover the short if positive divergences formed and price broke above a rising trendline or the low of a bearish reversal candle.

USING MULTIPLE TIMEFRAMES TO ENTER AN IMPULSE BUY TRADE

Traders who identify setups off the daily chart can benefit from precise execution into a trade setup by studying the lower timeframe structure. In Figure 10.3, we had an Impulse Buy setup as price tested the rising 20-day EMA at $22.50 per share after a clear impulse higher and retracement into support. An aggressive trader would buy shares as soon as price touched the 20-day EMA at $22.50 and hold to the target.

However, traders can take an extra step to gain perspective and assess the internal probabilities of success by studying the intraday timeframe price structure. This insight allows a trader to enter at a much more precise entry price while increasing confidence in a successful trade outcome, as well as a more appropriate level to locate a stop-loss order.

Let us take the exact same parameters as in Figure 10.3, but then examine the structure of the 30-minute intraday chart at the time of trade entry at \$22.50 per share on November 20, 2003. This is Step-Inside Analysis, and Figure 10.4 walks us inside the Impulse Buy setup to a much more precise level.

Figure 10.4 reveals the intraday structure through the duration of the Impulse Buy trade from the daily chart of U.S. Steel. As a reference, the 20-day EMA at time of trade entry was \$22.51, as labeled with a horizontal line on the intraday chart. You can draw higher timeframe reference points, such as moving averages or Fibonacci retracement prices, on to your intraday charts to see how price reacts intraday to these levels.

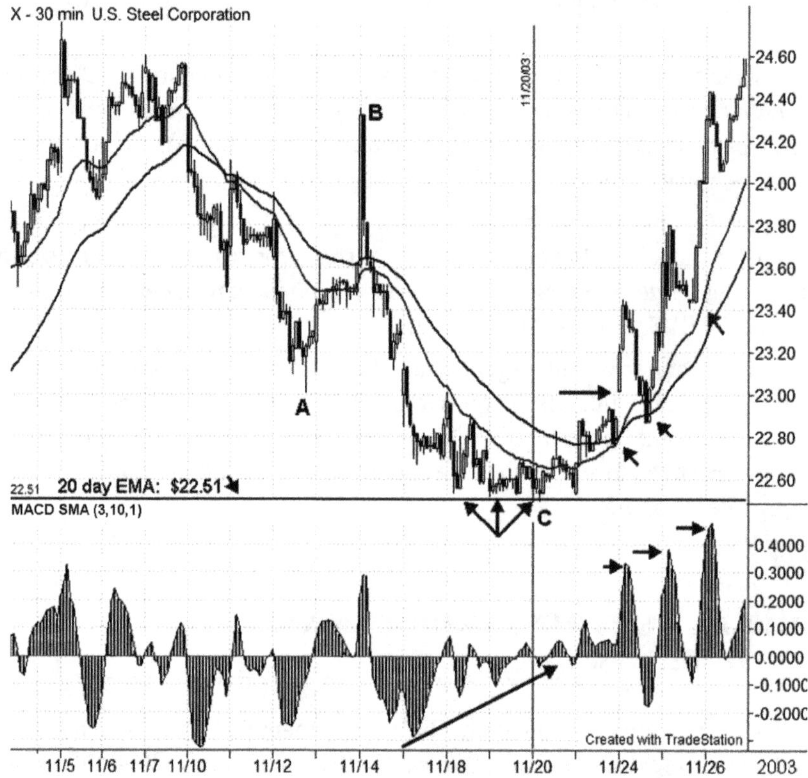

FIGURE 10.4 "Step-Inside Analysis" in the Impulse Buy Entry in U.S. Steel: 30-minute chart—November 2003

In this example, the move in early November is the impulse high, and the move lower from November 10 to 20 is the retracement phase prior to the buy signal in the Impulse Buy at the 20-day EMA at $22.50. Look closely to see the ABC Elliott Wave correction, as labeled with the A Wave lower that ended on November 12; B Wave higher that ended on November 14, and final C Wave lower that ended on November 20.

The structure not just of the retracement swing becomes clearer, but also the lengthy multi-swing positive momentum divergences and Rounded Reversal Price Pattern (also called a Saucer) that ended with the horizontal support line at $22.50, which was the rising 20-day EMA. This is an excellent lesson in how to identify structure on the lower timeframe that corresponds with an expected support level from a higher timeframe (daily chart). Seeing the multi-swing positive momentum divergence form intraday at the daily expected support from the 20-period EMA gives you added confidence as a trader that you are doing the right thing by purchasing shares at the $22.50 level in expectation for a trend reversal on the 30-minute chart to correspond with a move higher as you expect on the daily chart.

Notice how conservative traders can pinpoint their exact entry by studying intraday price and momentum structure in the context of the daily chart expectation. A trader who was hesitant about purchasing shares aggressively at $22.50 could demand that the intraday price structure turn bullish, or specifically, reverse officially into an uptrend on the intraday frame before entering.

Let us walk through the official steps as described in Chapters 1 and 9 in terms of an official trend reversal. First, look for a multi-swing positive momentum divergence, which we can see was clearly the case from November 19 forward; as price made new lows and supported at the $22.50 level, the momentum oscillator clearly formed a series of higher lows. Then, early on the morning of November 21, price broke above both the 20- and 50-period EMAs for the first time since the B wave sudden break. Price remained above the 20- and 50-period EMAs as these averages crossed bullishly into the close of November 21.

Recall earlier from our discussion about the Cradle Trade setup: the sudden retracement into the close on November 21 at the bullish crossover of the 20 and 50 EMA set up the Bullish Cradle Trade officially at $22.80 per share. On the morning of November 24, price surged higher in a gap and impulse higher to the $23.40 level. Look very closely at the 3/10 MACD Momentum oscillator to recognize this new oscillator high, exceeding that of November 14, as a Kickoff, which signals a likely reversal in trend.

Look even closer to see that the pullback to the 20- and 50-period EMA toward the end of the session on November 24 was a tiny Impulse Buy trade setup. Yes, there can be smaller Impulse Buy setups on the intraday frames within the context of a daily chart Impulse Buy—this is described as the fractal component of the market. Bull flags can trigger setups for intraday traders during the Measured Move portion of a daily chart Bull Flag, which is in essence what we have in this example of U.S. Steel.

On November 25, price officially completed a full intraday trend reversal after forming a lengthy positive momentum divergence, breaking above the 20/50 EMA levels, witnessing a bullish cross of the 20/50 EMAs, forming a Kickoff signal in momentum, and forming a higher price high at $23.40, higher price low at $22.90, then taking out the prior price high at $23.40 on November 25. Notice that each subsequent new price high and new momentum high from November 24 forward generated a new and successful Impulse Buy trade setup on each pullback to the 20- or 50-period EMA.

As price retested the visual chart high from the prior impulse at $24.60, a conservative trader would exit the position established at the $23.00 level, locking in a quick profit and end to the daily chart Impulse Buy trade. However, as we see on both the daily chart at this time and the 30-minute intraday chart, odds favored a continuation move through the overhead resistance, meaning an aggressive trader could have held shares through the prior price high at $23.00. The trader would then monitor both the daily and intraday chart closely for any sign of reversal, which would emerge first in the intraday chart in the form of a negative divergence, confirmed trendline break, or EMA trend reversal. We see none of these structures forming, and in fact end the chart on November 26 with price rising rapidly in a powerful confirmed trend impulse after forming a recent new momentum high, which favors even higher prices yet to come.

MORE ABOUT MULTI-TIMEFRAME ANALYSIS

All of the principles and trade setups I have discussed in this book are applicable to traders of all markets on all timeframes. The wise traders, however, will take the time to do the extra analysis on multiple timeframes to combine these principles and setups.

Traders can practice this by predicting what will happen for the next likely swing in price on the daily chart and then play out that prediction or thesis with precise execution tactics on the intraday timeframes. In other words, if a trader observes an Impulse Buy setting up on the daily chart, he can then drop to monitor the intraday chart, such as the 60-minute, 30-minute, or 15-minute chart to assess what the structure reveals to him, specifically in terms of trend continuity versus reversal, momentum divergences present, or any established trading ranges or intraday support or resistance levels to watch.

Furthermore, most traders are better off adopting a strict method of interpreting multiple timeframes rather than trying to analyze all timeframes at once. If you are undisciplined in your multi-timeframe analysis, you will find that the weekly chart is setting up a sell-signal while the daily chart shows price at a support zone, but the intraday charts reveal their own conflicting or confusing signals. Analyzing all timeframes for a single trade is like having too many indicators on the chart at once; you get so much information, but most of it conflicts and confuses you to the point where you take no position at all.

Specialize the core of your analysis on one timeframe, perhaps the daily chart, and then the moment you see a trade setup or suspected opportunity, drop down either to the

60-minute (hourly) chart or the 30-minute chart to study afresh the structure that appears before you on the intraday chart. Remember the context and your thought process from your analysis on the intraday chart and note confirmations or conflicting signals. Take trades when the two timeframes align and signal a safe pathway forward for price, and be risk averse when the timeframes conflict.

At times in your analysis, look at key levels to watch on the timeframe higher than your core frame, which might be the weekly chart if you focus on the daily chart. Do not do in-depth analysis on the higher timeframe, but only note key price levels, trend structure, and any insights from momentum you may derive.

You can think of your chosen timeframe as your home base upon which you do most of your chart work, and then your lower timeframe as seen with a magnifying glass where you study closely and then execute your positions. This is similar to a jeweler who first examines the characteristics of a diamond by holding in the hand, but then executes precise cuts on the diamond only through a specialized magnifying glass. Your higher timeframe can be like climbing a mountain to see what is going on around you, so that you can see the broader perspective you miss just by looking at the environment from your back yard.

Traders who specialize on the daily chart can climb to see the higher perspective of the weekly or monthly chart, but only as a guidepost for long-term trend and volatility structure. You want to be aware specifically if your daily chart calls for an immediate buy signal that looks clear on the daily chart, but has a confluence resistance area overhead perhaps from the 20-week moving average and a prior price high from two years ago, neither of which you will be able to see on the daily chart.

You might want to pause in entering your trade to make sure that buyers can clear above the higher timeframe resistance before you put on a bullish trade. The buyers may not be able to overcome the sellers from the higher timeframe structure, and thus you would endure a losing trade that you could have prevented had you taken at least a quick look at key levels to watch on the higher timeframe.

Day traders might specialize on the five-minute chart and use the one-minute chart specifically for execution, in terms of entering a trade setup observed on the five-minute chart only when price breaks a trendline on the one-minute chart, or drop to the one-minute chart to see momentum divergences clearly that might not be so evident on the five-minute structure. Intraday traders will always need to know of key levels to watch and structure from the daily chart, particularly if price is about to test a major daily moving average or other well-known support or resistance price.

It's smart to gain experience with the principles and concepts that appear on one timeframe before incorporating your findings into higher or lower timeframes. Remember, the principles, setups, and strategies work on all timeframes, so it is just a matter of learning the principles and then applying them for enhanced execution of your trades. This will allow you to find the lower and higher timeframes for any hidden levels of support or resistance you would have missed if you had only analyzed your chosen timeframe.

CONCLUDING THOUGHTS

The Impulse Buy, Impulse Sell, and the Cradle Trades are only some of the many trade setups you can discover and incorporate into your own personalized trading plan. When creating your own trade setups, be sure you base them firmly on at least one of the three guiding price principles defined in Chapters 1 through 3. From there, you can enhance your setup with the strategies and techniques described in Chapters 4 through 7, specifically in regard to candlesticks, price patterns (more numerous than this book can define), Fibonacci principles (that extend beyond simple retracements), and Elliott Wave concepts (that appear on all timeframes).

If you can combine more than one price principle, you will increase your chance of a successful trade outcome. Notice how the Cradle Trade incorporates elements from the Momentum Principle and Trend Continuity Principle, namely in momentum divergences and weight of the evidence in assessing a trend reversal. The Cradle Trade also incorporates the positive elements of precise stop-losses from general retracement strategies with the larger target provided by trend reversal strategies.

Similarly, the Impulse Buy incorporates both the Momentum and Trend Continuity Principle as an enhanced Retracement trading strategy. These two specific setups go beyond the basic definitions of retracement, reversal, or breakout trades, and add parameters that must trigger before entering a position. As you develop your experience as a trader, you will create your own setups from your past trading performance and observations.

Treat each day as a learning experience. While we often learn more from our losing trades, be sure to reinforce what you did right for your winning trades. Do more of what works for you personally, and less of what does not; do not try to be a type of trader that you are not.

Seek strategies that align with your talents, skills, and market opportunities, as explained by Dr. Brett Steenbarger in his essential reading for new traders entitled *Enhancing Trader Performance* and his more specific book on coaching entitled *The Daily Trading Coach*. Read and re-read *Trading in the Zone* by Mark Douglas, as he teaches how to think in terms of probabilities along with how important it is to perceive the market not as a scary entity, but as an object of endless possibilities. Knowing setups is only one part of the journey; incorporating them within a framework of your own unique personality, talents, and skills is the next step.

Learn something new from all of your trades, especially the losing ones. Learn what went wrong and if the loss was a result of standard probability in a good setup (the loss was not your fault), or if your emotions degraded the edge of the opportunity (the loss was your fault).

I hope that I have broadened your awareness to foundation price principles and given you a solid boost in your education as a trader. I hope also that you accept the challenge to think critically about why you take the trades you do and why they have edge.

Use your new knowledge to base your decisions more on the chart structure as you understand it and less from your emotions, though that is much more difficult than it seems. Seek to sustain the initial excitement and motivation that you have or had as a new trader; if you feel as though you are losing motivation as a trader, return to the feeling of wonder you had when you first began and recall the thrill of your first profitable trade.

Keep moving forward, keep focused on the larger concepts beyond your next trade, and keep up your motivation that will carry you through your learning curve and the bumpy patches along the road. Every step brings you closer to your goal, and every day is a new day to achieve your lifelong goal of becoming the most successful trader you can possibly be.

About the Author

Corey Rosenbloom, CMT, founded the trading education site www.afraidtotrade.com, where he offers a variety of services and market analysis. A Chartered Market Technician, Rosenbloom speaks regularly at industry trading conferences. His work appears on a number of other trading web sites, such as www.greenfaucet.com, traderkingdom.com, moneyshow.com, www.dailymarkets.com, www.wallstreetcheat.com, www.bestwaytoinvest.com, and others. His strategies have also appeared in Dr. Brett Steenbarger's book *The Daily Trading Coach.* Rosenbloom earned a masters degree in political science and a bachelor's degree in psychology from the University of Alabama in Huntsville.

Bibliography

Appel, Gerald. *Technical Analysis: Power Tools for Active Investors.* Upper Saddle River, NJ: Financial Times Prentice Hall, 2005.

Aronson, David. *Evidence-Based Technical Analysis.* Hoboken, NJ: John Wiley & Sons, 2006.

Achelis, Steven. *Technical Analysis from A to Z.* New York, NY: McGraw-Hill, 2001.

Bensignor, Rick, editor. *New Thinking in Technical Analysis: Trading Models from the Masters.* New York, NY: Bloomberg Press, 2000.

Bellafiore, Michael. "Old-School Lessons for Mastering Today's Markets," *SFO Magazine* (June 2010) 26–35.

Bellafiore, Michael. *One Good Trade: Inside the Highly Competitive World of Proprietary Trading.* New York, NY: John Wiley & Sons: 2010.

Bellafiore, Michael. "Traders Ask: What is the Proper Exit on a Swing Trade," SMB Training Blog. May 29, 2010. <http://www.smbtraining.com/blog/traders-ask-what-is-the-proper-exit-on-a-swing-trade>

Bollinger, John. *Bollinger on Bollinger Bands.* New York, NY: McGraw-Hill, 2002.

Boroden, Carolyn. *Fibonacci Trading: How to Master the Time and Price Advantage.* New York, NY: McGraw-Hill, 2008.

Boucher, Mark. *The Hedge Fund Edge.* New York, NY: John Wiley & Sons, 1999.

Brown, Constance. "The Derivative Oscillator: a New Approach to an Old Problem," *Journal of Technical Analysis* (Winter-Spring 1994) 45–61.

Brown, Constance. *Technical Analysis for the Trading Professional.* New York, NY: McGraw-Hill, 1999.

Brown, Constance. *Fibonacci Analysis.* New York, NY: Bloomberg Press, 2008.

Brooks, Al. *Reading Price Charts Bar by Bar: The Technical Analysis of Price Action for the Serious Trader.* New York, NY: John Wiley and Sons: 2009.

Bulkowski, Thomas. *Encyclopedia of Candlestick Charts.* Hoboken, NJ: John Wiley & Sons, 2008.

Bulkowski, Thomas. *Encyclopedia of Chart Patterns*, 2nd ed. Hoboken, NJ: John Wiley & Sons, 2005.

Bulkowski, Thomas. *Trading Classic Chart Patterns.* New York: John Wiley & Sons, 2002.

Carter, John. *Mastering the Trade.* New York: McGraw-Hill, 2005.

Chande, Tushar. *Beyond Technical Analysis.* New York, NY: John Wiley & Sons, 2001.

Colby, Robert. *The Encyclopedia of Technical Market Indicators*. New York, NY: McGraw-Hill, 2003.

Connors, Laurence and Linda Bradford Raschke. *Street Smarts*. Los Angeles: M. Gordon Publishing, 1996.

Connors, Laurence and Conor Sen. *How Markets Really Work: A Quantitative Guide to Stock Market Behavior*. Sherman Oaks, CA: Trading Markets Publishing Group, 2004.

Coppola, Al. *The Step-by-Step Guide to Profitable Pattern Trading*. Greenville, SC: Trader's Press, 2007.

Covel, Michael. *Trend Following: How Great Traders Make Millions in Up or Down Markets*. Upper Saddle River, NJ: Financial Times Prentice Hall, 2004.

Dalton, James F., Robert B. Dalton, and Eric T. Jones. *Markets in Profile: Profiting from the Auction Process*. Hoboken, NJ: John Wiley & Sons, 2007.

Davis, Ned. *Being Right or Making Money*. Venice, FL: Ned Davis Research, 2000.

De Bondt, W.F.M. "Betting on Trends: Intuitive Forecasts of Financial Risk and Return," *International Journal of Forecasting* (1993) 9, 355–371.

Derman, Emanual. *My Life as a Quant: Reflections on Physics and Finance*. Hoboken, NJ: John Wiley & Sons, 2007.

Desmond, Paul. "Identifying Bear Market Bottoms and New Bull Markets," *Journal of Technical Analysis* (2002) 57, 38–42.

Detry, P.J., and Philippe Gregoire. "Other Evidences of the Predictive Power of Technical Analysis: The Moving Averages Rules on European Indexes" European Finance Management Association: 2001 Lugano Meetings. Available at Social Science Research Network: http://ssrn.com/abstract=269802.

Dewey, Edward. *Cycles: The Mysterious Forces that Trigger Events*. New York: Hawthorn Books, 1971.

Douglas, Mark. *Trading in the Zone*. New York: New York Institute of Finance, 2000.

Douglas, Mark. *The Disciplined Trader: Developing Winning Attitudes*. New York: New York Institute of Finance, 1990.

Dunlap, Richard. *The Golden Ratio and Fibonacci Numbers*. Singapore: World Scientific, 1997.

Edwards, Robert, and John Magee. *Technical Analysis of Stock Trends*, 8th ed., 2003. 1948 edition revised by W.H.C. Bassetti, Boca Raton, FL: St. Lucie Press.

Ehlers, John. "MESA Adaptive Moving Averages," *Technical Analysis of Stocks and Commodities* (September 2001) 19:9, 30–35.

Elder, Alexander. *Come into My Trading Room*. New York, NY: John Wiley & Sons, 1993.

Elder, Alexander. *Entries and Exits: Visits to 16 Trading Rooms*. New York, NY: John Wiley & Sons, 2006.

Elder, Alexander. *Trading for a Living*. New York, NY: John Wiley & Sons, 2002.

Fama, Eugene. "The Behavior of Stock-Market Prices," *The Journal of Business* (1965). University of Chicago, 38, 1.

Fisher, Mark. *The Logical Trader*. New York, NY: John Wiley & Sons, 2002.

Forman, John. *The Essentials of Trading: From the Basics to Building a Winning Strategy.* Hoboken, NJ: John Wiley & Sons, 2006.

Fosback, Norman. *Stock Market Logic: A Sophisticated Approach to Profits on Wall Street.* Chicago, IL: Dearborn Financial Publishing, 1976 (1993 edition).

Frost, A.J., and Robert Prechter. *Elliott Wave Principle: Key to Market Behavior*, 20th Anniversary Edition. Gainsville, GA: New Classics Library, 2000.

Gehm, Ralph. *Quantitative Trading and Money Management.* New York, NY: John Wiley & Sons, 1983.

Grant, Kenneth. *Trading Risk: Enhanced Profitability through Risk Control.* Hoboken, NJ: John Wiley & Sons, 2004.

Granville, Joseph. *A New Strategy of Daily Stock Market Timing for Maximum Profit.* Englewood Cliffs, NJ: Prentice-Hall, 1976.

Grimes, Adam. "Technical Analysis: A Little Background and History." SMB Training Blog. May 5, 2010. <http://www.smbtraining.com/blog/technical-analysis-a-little-background-and-history>

Gujral, Ashwani. "ADX: The Key to Market Trends," *Futures Magazine* (May 2005) 34–36.

Hamilton, William. *The Stock Market Barometer: A Study of its Forecast Value Based on Charles H. Dow's Theory of the Price Movement*, reprint of the 1922 edition. New York, NY: John Wiley & Sons, 1998.

Harris, Michael. *Short-Term Trading with Price Patterns.* Greenville, NC: Traders Press, Inc, 2000.

Hayes, Timothy. "Momentum Leads Price: A Universal Concept with Global Applications," *Journal of Technical Analysis* (Winter-Spring 2004) 19–24.

Horowitz, Andrew. *The Disciplined Investor: Essential Strategies for Success.* Weston, FL: HF Factor Publishing, 2008.

Hutson, Jack. *Charting the Stock Market: The Wyckoff Method.* Seattle, WA: Technical Analysis, Inc., 1986.

Ilinski, Kirill. *Physics of Finance: Gauge Modelling in Non-Equilibrium Pricing.* New York, NY: John Wiley & Sons, 2001.

Kamich, Bruce. *How Technical Analysis Works.* New York, NY: New York Institute of Finance, 2003.

Kaufman, Perry. *New Trading Systems and Methods*, 4th ed. Hoboken, NJ: John Wiley & Sons, 2005.

Kirkpatrick II, Charles, and Julie Dahlquist. *Technical Analysis: The Complete Resource for Financial Market Technicians.* New Jersey: FT Press, 2006.

Knapp, Volker. "The RSI Trend System," *Active Trader Magazine* (August 2004). 5:8, 64–65.

Kurczek, Dion, "Basic Pullback Buyer," *Active Trader Magazine* (March 2003) 4:3, 9.

Kurczek, Dion, "Two-bar Breakout System," *Active Trader Magazine* (November 2003) 4:11, 56.

Landry, David. *Dave Landry's 10 Best Swing Trading Patterns and Strategies.* Los Angeles, CA: M. Gordon Publishing Group, 2003.

Lane, George C. "Lane's Stochastics: The Ultimate Oscillator," *Journal of Technical Analysis* (May 1985) 37–42.

Lind, Douglas, William Marchal, and Samuel Wathen. *Basic Statistics for Business and Economics*. New York, NY: McGraw Hill, 2002.

Link, Marcel. *High Probability Trading*. New York, NY: McGraw-Hill, 2003.

Livio, Mario. *The Golden Ratio: The Story of Phi, the World's Most Astonishing Number*. New York: Broadway Books, 2002.

Lo, Andrew, and A. Craig MacKinlay. "Stock Market Prices do not Follow Random Walks: Evidence from a Simple Specification Test," *Review of Financial Studies* (1998) 1, 41–66.

Lo, Andrew. *A Non-Random Walk Down Wall Street*, Princeton, NJ: Princeton University Press, 1999.

Lo, Andrew, Harry Mamaysky, and Jiang Wang. "Foundations of Technical Analysis: Computational Algorithms, Statistical Inference, and Empirical implementation," *Journal of Finance* (2000) 55, 4.

Lucas, R. "The Usefulness of Historical Data in Selecting Parameters for Technical Trading Systems," *Journal of Futures Markets* (1989) 9, 55–65.

Mackay, Charles. *Extraordinary Popular Delusions and the Madness of Crowds*. Petersfield, Hampshire, UK: Harriman House, 2003.

Mandelbrot, Benoit. "The Variation of Certain Speculative Prices," *Journal of Business* (1963) 36, 394–419.

Merrill, Arthur. "Advance-Decline Divergences as an Oscillator," *Stocks and Commodities Magazine* (September 1988) 6:9, 354–355.

Miner, Robert. *High Probability Trading Strategies*. Hoboken, NJ: John Wiley & Sons, 2008.

Murphy, John. *Intermarket Technical Analysis*. New York, NY: John Wiley & Sons, 1991.

Murphy, John. *Technical Analysis of the Financial Markets*. New York, NY: New York Institute of Finance, 1999.

Nassar, David, and William Lupien. *Market Evaluation and Analysis for Swing Trading: Timeless Methods and Strategies for an Ever-Changing Market*. New York, NY: McGraw-Hill, 2004.

Nassar, David. *Rules of the Trade: Indispensable Insights for Active Trading*. New York, NY: McGraw-Hill, 2001.

Neely, Glenn. *Mastering Elliott Wave*. Brightwaters, NY: Windsor Books, 1990.

Nison, Steve. *Japanese Candlestick Charting Techniques*, 2nd ed. New York: New York Institute of Finance, 2001.

Osler, Carol. "Identifying Noise Traders: the Head and Shoulders Pattern in U.S. Equities," Federal Reserve Bank of New York (1998).

Painter, William. "On Balance Open Interest Indicator," *Journal of Technical Analysis*, Fall-Winter 1995, 48–56.

Pesavento, Larry. *Trade What You See: How To Profit from Pattern Recognition*. New York, NY: John Wiley & Sons, 2007.

Pesavento, Larry and Steven Shapiro. *Fibonacci Ratios With Pattern Recognition*. Greensville, SC: Traders Press, 1997.

Plummer, Tony. *The Psychology of Technical Analysis*. Chicago, IL: Probus Publishing Company, 1989.

Poser, Steven. *Applying Elliott Wave Theory Profitably*. New York, NY: John Wiley & Sons, 2003.

Pring, Martin. *Martin Pring on Market Momentum*. Homewood, IL: Irwin Professional Publishing, 1993.

Pring, Martin. *Pring on Price Patterns: The Definitive Guide to Price Pattern Analysis and Interpretation*. New York, NY: McGraw-Hill, 2004.

Pring, Martin. *Technical Analysis Explained*, 4th ed. New York, NY: McGraw-Hill, 2002.

Pruden, Hank. *The Three Skills of Top Trading: Behavioral Systems Building, Pattern Recognition, and Mental State Management*. New York, NY: John Wiley & Sons, 2007.

Rhea, Robert. *The Dow Theory: An Explanation of its Development and an Attempt to Define its Usefulness as an Aid to Speculation*, reprint of 1932 Barron's Publishing edition Burlington, VT: Fraser Publishing, 1993.

Raschke, Linda B. "Capturing Trend Days." *TradersLog*. Website: www.traderslog.com/capturing trend-days.htm. Accessed November 1, 2010.

Raschke, Linda B. "Classic Technical Trading: Become a Technical Purist," *International Traders Expo* presentation, Ft. Lauderdale, FL: June 10, 2006.

Raschke, Linda B. "Swing Trading and Underlying Principles of Technical Analysis." Quoted in Bensignor, Rick, editor. *New Thinking in Technical Analysis: Trading Models from the Masters*. New York, NY: Bloomberg Press, 2000.

Raschke, Linda B. "Tape Reading." *Traderslog*. www.traderslog.com/tape-reading/. July 29, 2009.

Rotella, Robert. *The Elements of Successful Trading*. New York, NY: New York Institute of Finance, 1992.

Schwager, Jack. *Getting Started in Technical Analysis*. New York, NY: John Wiley & Sons, 1999.

Schwager, Jack. *Market Wizards: Interviews with Top Traders*. New York: New York Institute of Finance, 1989.

Schwager, Jack. *The Market Wizards: Conversations with America's Top Traders*. New York, NY: John Wiley & Sons, 1995.

Schwager, Jack. *Technical Analysis*. New York, NY: John Wiley & Sons, 1996.

Schabacker, Robert. *Stock Market Theory and Practice*. New York, NY: B.C. Forbes Publishing, 1930.

Schabacker, Robert. *Technical Analysis of Stock Market Profits*. New York, NY: Puttman Publishing, 1932.

Shannon, Brian. *Technical Analysis Using Multiple Timeframes*. Centennial, CO: LifeVest Publishing, 2008.

Shaw, Alan. *Technical Analysis*, reprinted by the Market Technicians Association from the *Financial Analysts Handbook*, Homewood, IL: Dow Jones-Irwin, 1988.

Shefrin, M., and M. Statman. "The Disposition to Sell Winners Too Early and Ride Losers Too Long: Theory and Evidence," *Journal of Finance* (1985) 40, 777–790.

Shiller, Robert J. *Irrational Exuberance*. New York, NY: Broadway Books, 2000.

Shiller, Robert. *Irrational Exuberance*, 2nd ed. New York, NY: Broadway Books, 2001.

Shleifer, A. *Inefficient Markets: An Introduction to Behavioral Finance.* New York, NY: Oxford University Press, 2000.

Steenbarger, Brett. *The Psychology of Trading: Tools and Techniques for Minding the Markets.* Hoboken, NJ: John Wiley & Sons, 2003.

Steenbarger, Brett. *Enhancing Trader Performance: Proven Strategies from the Cutting Edge of Trader Psychology.* Hoboken, NJ: John Wiley & Sons, 2007.

Steenbarger, Brett. *The Daily Trading Coach: 101 Lessons for Becoming Your own Trading Psychologist.* Hoboken, NJ: John Wiley & Sons, 2007.

Steenbarger, Brett. "Market Context: The Importance of Non-Confirmations," TraderFeed Blog, July 24, 2009. <http://traderfeed.blogspot.com/2009/07/market-context-importance-of-non.html>

Taleb, Nassim N. *The Black Swan.* New York, NY: Random House, 2007.

Tharp, Van K. *Trade Your Way to Financial Freedom.* New York, NY: McGraw-Hill, 2006.

Toma, Michael. *Trading with Confluence: A Risk-Based Approach to Trading Equity Index Futures.* Denver, CO: Outskirts Press, 2010.

Wilder, J. Welles Jr. *New Concepts in Technical Trading Systems.* Greensboro, SC: Trend Research, 1978.

Williams, Larry. *Long-Term Secrets to Short-Term Trading.* New York, NY: John Wiley & Sons, 1999.

Wyckoff, Richard D. *Studies in Tape Reading.* New York, NY: Traders Press, 1910. Reprinted in 1982 by Fraser Publishing, Burlington, VT.

Wyckoff, Richard D. *Stock Market Technique, 2 vols.* New York, NY: Traders Press, 1933. Reprinted in 1984 by Fraser Publishing, Burlington, VT.

Yoder, Bo. *Optimize Your Trading Edge.* New York, NY: McGraw-Hill, 2008.

Zweig, Martin. *Martin Zweig's Winning on Wall Street,* 4th ed. New York, NY: Warner Books, 1997.

Index

R

S

T